Basic Statistics Using Excel and MegaStat

The McGraw-Hill/Irwin Series Operations and Decision Sciences

BUSINESS STATISTICS

Aczel and Sounderpandian
Complete Business Statistics
Sixth Edition

ALEKS Corporation
ALEKS for Business Statistics
First Edition

Alwan
Statistical Process Analysis
First Edition

Bowerman and O'Connell
Business Statistics in Practice
Fourth Edition

Bowerman, O'Connell, and Orris
Essentials of Business Statistics
First Edition

Bryant and Smith
Practical Data Analysis: Case Studies in Business Statistics
Volumes I, II, and III*

Cooper and Schindler
Business Research Methods
Ninth Edition

Delurgio
Forecasting Principles and Applications
First Edition

Doane
LearningStats CD Rom
First Edition, 1.2

Doane, Mathieson, and Tracy
Visual Statistics
Second Edition, 2.0

Gitlow, Oppenheim, Oppenheim, and Levine
Quality Management
Third Edition

Kutner, Nachtsheim, Neter, and Li
Applied Linear Statistical Models
Fifth Edition

Kutner, Nachtsheim, and Neter
Applied Linear Regression Models
Fourth Edition

Lind, Marchal, and Wathen
Basic Statistics for Business and Economics
Fifth Edition

Lind, Marchal, and Wathen
Statistical Techniques in Business and Economics
Twelfth Edition

Merchant, Goffinet, and Koehler
Basic Statistics Using Excel for Office XP
Third Edition

Olson and Shi
Introduction to Business Data Mining
First Edition

Orris
Basic Statistics Using Excel and MegaStat
First Edition

Sahai and Khurshid
Pocket Dictionary of Statistics
First Edition

Siegel
Practical Business Statistics
Fifth Edition

Wilson, Keating, and John Galt Solutions, Inc.
Business Forecasting
Fifth Edition

Zagorsky
Business Information
First Edition

QUANTITATIVE METHODS AND MANAGEMENT SCIENCE

Bodily, Carraway, Frey, and Pfeifer
Quantitative Business Analysis: Text and Cases
First Edition

Bonini, Hausman, and Bierman
Quantitative Analysis for Business Decisions
Ninth Edition

Hesse
Managerial Spreadsheet Modeling and Analysis
First Edition

Hillier and Hillier
Introduction to Management Science
Second Edition

*Available only through McGraw-Hill's PRIMIS Online Assets Library.

Basic Statistics Using Excel and MegaStat

J. B. Orris, Ph.D.

Butler University

McGraw-Hill
Irwin

Boston   Burr Ridge, IL   Dubuque, IA   Madison, WI   New York   San Francisco   St. Louis
Bangkok   Bogotá   Caracas   Kuala Lumpur   Lisbon   London   Madrid   Mexico City
Milan   Montreal   New Delhi   Santiago   Seoul   Singapore   Sydney   Taipei   Toronto

BASIC STATISTICS USING EXCEL AND MEGASTAT
Published by McGraw-Hill/Irwin, a business unit of The McGraw-Hill Companies, Inc.,
1221 Avenue of the Americas, New York, NY, 10020. Copyright © 2007 by The McGraw-Hill
Companies, Inc. All rights reserved. No part of this publication may be reproduced or distributed
in any form or by any means, or stored in a database or retrieval system, without the prior
written consent of The McGraw-Hill Companies, Inc., including, but not limited to, in any
network or other electronic storage or transmission, or broadcast for distance learning.

Some ancillaries, including electronic and print components, may not be available to customers
outside the United States.

This book is printed on acid-free paper.

1 2 3 4 5 6 7 8 9 0 QPD/QPD 0 9 8 7 6

ISBN-13: 978-0-07-352141-1
ISBN-10: 0-07-352141-8

Editorial director: *Stewart Mattson*
Executive editor: *Richard T. Hercher, Jr.*
Developmental editor: *Cynthia Douglas*
Senior marketing manager: *Douglas Reiner*
Senior media producer: *Victor Chiu*
Project manager: *Kristin Bradley*
Lead production supervisor: *Michael R. McCormick*
Senior designer: *Mary E. Kazak / Jillian Lindner*
Lead media project manager: *Cathy L. Tepper*
Cover design: *Jillian Lindner*
Typeface: *10/12 New Century*
Compositor: *Interactive Composition Corporation*
Printer: *Quebecor World Dubuque Inc.*

Library of Congress Cataloging-in-Publication Data

Orris, J.B.
    Basic statistics using Excel and MegaStat / J.B. Orris.
       p. cm. — (The McGraw-Hill/Irwin series operations and decision sciences)
    Includes a student CD with tutorials, worksheets, and exercises to supplement
the text.
    Includes index.
    ISBN-13: 978-0-07-352141-1 (alk. paper)
    ISBN-10: 0-07-352141-8 (alk. paper)
    1. Microsoft Excel (Computer file). 2. MegaStat. 3. Mathematical statistics—Data
processing. I. Title. II. Series.
QA276.45.M53 O77 2007
519.50285'536—dc22

                                    2006041949

www.mhhe.com

About the Author

James Burdeane "Deane" Orris

J.B. Orris is a professor of management science at Butler University in Indianapolis, Indiana. He received his Ph.D. from the University of Illinois in 1971, and in the late 1970s with the advent of personal computers, he combined his interest in statistics and computers to write one of the first personal computer statistics packages—MICROSTAT. Over the past 20 years, MICROSTAT has evolved into MegaStat, which is an Excel add-in statistics program. In 1999 he wrote an Excel book (*Essentials: Excel 2000 Advanced*) and has done work in neural networks, spreadsheet simulation, and statistical analysis for many research projects. He has taught statistics and computer courses in the College of Business Administration of Butler University since 1971. He is a member of the American Statistical Association and is past president of the Central Indiana Chapter. In his spare time, Professor Orris enjoys reading, working out, and working in his woodworking shop.

To my children, Amy and Bradley, and to my grandson Charlie.

Preface

I wrote *Basic Statistics Using Excel and MegaStat* to be as concise as possible while covering all chapters needed in a one-semester—and many two-semester—course. The target audience is undergraduates, but I also use it for my pre-MBA course at Butler University. Although it is a relatively short book, it was not designed to be an "easy" book. It covers the real thing, but tries to avoid getting overly theoretical or mathematical.

Hierarchical Approach: Concepts and Modules

Rather than taking a traditional, strictly linear approach to the subject matter—which can make it difficult to separate the conceptual material from the details—this book takes a hierarchical approach with two levels, as illustrated in the graphic below.

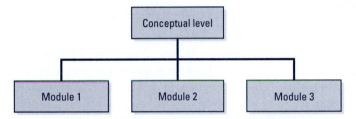

The first, conceptual level contains the main chapter sections and focuses on a discussion and integration of the topics. This discussion contains references to the second level—Modules that contain "how to do it" topics, support material, and topics that might be considered optional. Students can get the big picture without being distracted by detail, and when they want to study or review a specific topic it is easily found and clearly delineated.

Contained within the conceptual level are Learning Activities and references to the many Excel worksheets created to illustrate the topics, as well as to the Tutorials created to demonstrate concepts within the chapter.

Learning Activities

Most statistics texts have numerous problems and exercises at the end of each chapter. While the student CD does contain more than 350 problems presented in Excel spreadsheets, the main learning tool of every chapter is the Learning Activities.

The Learning Activities focus on learning how to learn—they were written in response to a question I was asked by a very serious student: "What should I do to learn this material?" Each Learning Activity is targeted to a different, specific concept and when appropriate directs the student to an Excel worksheet they can use to work through, explore, and understand that concept. The Learning Activities are boxed elements within the chapter text, and are numbered for easy reference.

MegaStat and Excel

This book was intended to be modern in that it avoids computational methods and equations and emphasizes computer use. It is my belief that Excel is a wonderful learning tool, as a sort of super-calculator. By freeing students of computational drudgery, they can then focus on trying different calculations to see how things work.

The book includes the Excel add-in *MegaStat*. However, it is not a book about MegaStat or Excel. The focus is always on learning statistics—MegaStat is just one tool for doing so. For example, most of the Learning Activities have students work through computations and concepts manually and then verify with MegaStat.

It is assumed that students have access to a computer and have basic computer and Excel skills; however, they need not be Excel experts to do the activities in this book. Students will undoubtedly expand and reinforce their Excel skills but in this course their focus should always be on the important statistics concepts. The text avoids detailed MegaStat instruction but frequently discusses MegaStat output, and it does occasionally mention features or issues related to MegaStat.

Tutorials

The CD that accompanies the text has several "screencam tutorials." In these screen movies, I work through various computer activities with a recorded voice overlay. These screencam tutorials include a MegaStat setup walk-through, an introduction to MegaStat, two Excel "primers," and 14 tutorials on various statistics topics. The tutorials are referenced by an icon at the point in the text where they are relevant, and they are listed in Appendix E.

Worksheets

Excel files created expressly for this text are housed in worksheets on the Student CD. Within the text, these are referenced as worksheets.

Exercises

For additional practice and assessment, Exercises for each chapter are presented in Excel files on the Student CD. These are intended to serve in place of traditional End-of-Chapter problems. A tabular listing of the chapter Exercises is presented at the end of each chapter.

Acknowledgments

I'd like to extend special thanks to the Butler University students who, for three semesters, used the pre-publication version of this text in class and provided me with valuable feedback.

Equally important to the development of this book was the feedback I got from our reviewers:

Jafar Alavi
East Tennessee State University

Djeto Assane
University of Nevada–Las Vegas

Scott Bailey
Troy University

Yu-Chi Chang
University of Notre Dame

Gordon Dahl
University of Rochester

Emin M. Dinlersoz
University of Houston

Fiseha Eshete
Bowie State University

Ellen Fuller
Arizona State University

J. Morgan Jones
University of North Carolina–Chapel Hill

Paul Judd
Drake University

Mark G. Kean
Boston University

B.M. Golam Kibira
Florida International University

Mary Ruth J. McRae
Appalachian State University

Abdel-Aziz M. Mohamed
California State University–Northridge

Suleyman Ozmucur
University of Pennsylvania

Bonnie Schroeder
Ohio State University

Dang T. Tran
California State University–Los Angeles

I'd also like to thank my book team at McGraw-Hill/Irwin, who were so helpful in moving the book through the publication process: Brent Gordon and Stewart Mattson, Editorial Directors; Dick Hercher, Executive Editor; Cynthia Douglas, Developmental Editor; Kristin Bradley, Project Manager; Douglas Reiner, Senior Marketing Manager; Mary Kazak, Senior Designer; Angela Cimarolli, Marketing Coordinator; Victor Chiu, Media Technology Producer; Cathy Tepper, Media Project Manager; Sesha Bolisetty, Production Supervisor.

Brief Contents

About the Author   v
Preface   vii
Acknowledgments   ix

Chapter 1   Introduction   1
Chapter 2   Descriptive Statistics   11
Chapter 3   Frequency Distributions   33
Chapter 4   Probability Concepts   53
Chapter 5   Discrete Probability Distributions   65
Chapter 6   Normal Distribution   81
Chapter 7   Sampling and Sampling Distributions   95
Chapter 8   Confidence Intervals   109
Chapter 9   Hypothesis Testing Concepts   123
Chapter 10   Hypothesis Testing Applications   135
Chapter 11   Analysis of Variance   169
Chapter 12   Linear Regression Analysis   203
Chapter 13   Multiple Regression   231
Chapter 14   Chi-Square Applications   249
Chapter 15   Time-Series Analysis   269
Chapter 16   Summary and Integration   295

APPENDICES

A   Excel Statistical Functions   299
B   Hypothesis Test Summaries   303
C   Glossary and Key Equations   311
D   Tables   325
E   Tutorial List   331

INDEX   333

Contents

About the Author   v

Preface   vii

Acknowledgments   ix

Chapter 1
Introduction   1

1.1   Definitions and Types of Data   2
  Statistics   2
  Data versus Information   2
  Data (Qualitative and Quantitative)   2
  Cross-Sectional versus Time-Series Data   3
  Variables   3
  Discrete versus Continuous Variables   4
  Levels of Measurement   4
  Identifying Data   5
  Sample versus Population   5
  Statistical Tools   6
1.2   Using This Book   6
  Tutorials   7
  Computer Skills   7
  Learning Activities   8
  Notation and Conventions   8
1.3   Summary   9
  Concepts   9

Chapter 2
Descriptive Statistics   11

2.1   Measures of Central Tendency   12
  Mode   12
  Median and Quartiles   14
  Arithmetic Mean   15
  Outliers   17
2.2   Measures of Variation   18
  *Range, Mean Deviation, and Mean
    Absolute Deviation   19*
  Variance and Standard Deviation   20
  *Definitional Form for Variance and
    Standard Deviation   21*
2.3   Sample MegaStat Output   24
2.4   Other Descriptive Measures   26
  Boxplot   26
  Scatterplot   28
  Stem and Leaf Plot   29

2.5   Summary   30
  Conceptual   30
  Applied   31
2.6   Exercises   31

Chapter 3
Frequency Distributions   33

3.1   Qualitative Frequency Distribution and
  Histogram   34
  How to Lie with Statistics   36
3.2   Quantitative Frequency Distribution
  and Histogram   38
  *How to Determine Interval Width and
    Setup Intervals   38*
  *Output Example Including a Frequency
    Polygon and Ogive   41*
3.3   Summary   43
  Conceptual   43
  Applied   43
3.4   Exercises   44
  Modules for Frequency
  Distributions   44
  3.A   Custom Intervals   44
  3.B   Capping the Top Interval   46
  3.C   Estimating the Median and Quartiles
    from a Frequency Distribution   48
    Interpolated Median   48
    *Estimating the Median
      from an Ogive   50*

Chapter 4
Probability Concepts   53

4.1   Introduction   54
4.2   Probability Terms and
  Definitions   54
  Assessing Probability   55
4.3   Probability Concepts   56
  Statistical Independence   58
4.4   Summary   60
  Conceptual   60
  Applied   60
4.5   Exercises   60

Modules for Probability Concepts   61
4.A   Probability versus Odds   61
4.B   Counting Rules   62
   *Fundamental Rule of
      Multiplication   62*
   *Special Case of the Fundamental
      Rule   62*
   Factorial   63
   Permutations   63
   Combinations   63

Chapter 5
**Discrete Probability
Distributions   65**

5.1   Discrete Probability Distributions
      and Expected Value   66
   *Three Discrete Probability
      Distributions   67*
5.2   Binomial Distribution   68
   *When Would You Use the Binomial
      Distribution?   69*
   *Assumptions of the Binomial
      Distribution   70*
5.3   Using the Computer Output for the
      Binomial Distribution   71
   Probability for Exact Value   72
   *Probability for Less Than
      (Cumulative Probability)   72*
   Probability for Greater Than   72
   Probability for Range of Values   72
5.4   Hypergeometric Distribution   73
   *When Would You Use the Hypergeometric
      Distribution?   74*
   *Assumptions of the Hypergeometric
      Distribution   74*
5.5   Poisson Distribution   75
   *When Would You Use the Poisson
      Distribution?   75*
   *Assumptions of the Poisson
      Distribution   75*
5.6   Summary   77
   Conceptual   77
   Applied   77
5.7   Exercises   77
   Module for Discrete Probability
   Distributions   78
   5.A   Discrete Distribution Simulation   78

Chapter 6
Normal Distribution   81

6.1   Normal Distribution   82
   z-Values   83
   *Determining Normal Distribution
      Probabilities   83*
   *Determining Values Corresponding to a
      Given Probability   84*
   An Important Assumption   85
   Benchmark z-Values   86
   Empirical Rule   88
   *Why Is the Normal Curve
      Important?   88*
   *Relationship between the Normal and
      Binomial Distributions   89*
6.2   Summary   90
   Conceptual   90
   Applied   90
6.3   Exercises   90
   Module for Normal Distribution   91
   6.A   How to Determine Probabilities for a
      Normal Distribution   91
      Using Tables   91
      Using Excel Functions   92
      Using MegaStat   93

Chapter 7
**Sampling and Sampling
Distributions   95**

7.1   Sampling Concepts   96
7.2   Sampling Distributions   98
   Proportions   100
7.3   Summary   101
   Conceptual   101
   Applied   102
7.4   Exercises   102
   Modules for Sampling and Sampling
   Distributions   103
   7.A   Generating Random
      Numbers   103
      *Random Numbers with
         MegaStat   103*
      Randomizing Data   103
   7.B   Central Limit Theorem
      Simulation   106
   7.C   A Proportion Is a Mean   107

Chapter 8
Confidence Intervals   109

8.1   Confidence Intervals   110
  Confidence Interval: Mean   110
  Confidence Interval: Proportion   113
8.2   Sample Size Estimation   114
  Sample Size: Mean   114
  Sample Size: Proportion   115
  Relationship between Sample Size
  Estimation and Confidence
  Intervals   116
8.3   Summary   117
  Conceptual   117
  Applied   118
8.4   Exercises   118
  Modules for Confidence Intervals   118
  8.A   Equations for Confidence Intervals and
    Sample Size   118
    Confidence Interval   119
    Sample Size   119
  8.B   Confidence Interval Simulation   120

Chapter 9
Hypothesis Testing Concepts   123

9.1   Introduction to Hypothesis
    Testing   124
9.2   Steps of Hypothesis Testing   124
  Step 1: Specify the Null Hypothesis and
    the Alternative Hypothesis   125
  Step 2: What Level of Significance?   125
  Step 3: Which Test and Test Statistic?   127
  Step 4: State the Decision Rule   127
  Step 5: Use the Sample Data to Calculate
    the Test Statistic   129
  Step 6: Use the Test Statistic to Make a
    Decision   129
  Step 7: Interpret the Decision in the
    Context of the Original Question   130
  Hypothesis Testing as a Sampling
    Process   132
9.3   Summary   132
9.4   Exercises   133
  Module for Hypothesis Testing
  Concepts   133
  9.A   Hypothesis Testing Simulation   133

Chapter 10
Hypothesis Testing Applications   135

10.1   Introduction   136
10.2   Mean versus Hypothesized
    Value (Test #1)   136
  Example of Mean versus Hypothesized   137
10.3   Compare Two Independent
    Groups (Test #2)   140
  Example of Comparing Two Independent
    Groups   142
10.4   Paired Observations (Test #3)   146
  Example of Paired Observations   147
10.5   Proportion versus Hypothesized
    Value (Test #4)   151
  Example of Proportion versus
    Hypothesized Value   151
10.6   Compare Two Independent
    Proportions (Test #5)   154
  Example of Comparing Two Independent
    Proportions   155
10.7   Tests for Variance   158
10.8   Confidence Intervals Revisited   158
  Relationship between Confidence
    Intervals and Hypothesis Testing   159
10.9   Summary   160
  Conceptual   160
  Know When and How to Use These Tests   161
10.10   Exercises   161
  Modules for Hypothesis Testing
  Applications   161
  10.A   The t-Distribution   161
    t-Table   162
    Excel t-Functions   163
    MegaStat t-Distribution   164
  10.B   Issues Related to Paired
    Observations   164
  10.C   Proportion versus Hypothesized Value
    Using the Binomial Distribution   167

Chapter 11
Analysis of Variance   169

11.1   One-Factor ANOVA (Test #6)   170
  Example of One-Factor ANOVA   171
11.2   Randomized Blocks ANOVA (Test #7)   176
  Example of Randomized Blocks
    ANOVA   177

11.3 ANOVA Compared to t-Tests   181
11.4 Two-Factor ANOVA (Test #8)   181
11.5 Summary   182
    Conceptual   182
    Applied   182
11.6 Exercises   183
    Modules for Analysis of Variance   183
    11.A Partitioning the Sum of Squares   183
    11.B Worksheet Showing Partitioning   184
    11.C Using the F-Distribution   186
        F-Table   186
        Excel F-Functions   187
        MegaStat F-Distribution   188
    11.D ANOVA Simulation   188
    11.E Post Hoc Analysis   190
    11.F ANOVA versus t-Tests   194
        Independent Groups   194
        Paired Data   194
        Mean versus Hypothesized   194
    11.G Randomized Blocks Compared to One-Factor ANOVA   198
    11.H Example of Two-Factor ANOVA Showing Interaction   201
        Hypothesis Testing Steps   201

Chapter 12
Linear Regression Analysis   203

12.1 Introduction to Linear Regression   204
12.2 Scatterplot   205
12.3 Regression Line   206
12.4 Measuring Strength of Relationship   207
12.5 Regression Computer Output   210
    r^2 and the Correlation Coefficient (r)   211
    Standard Error of Estimate   211
    ANOVA Table (Test #9)   212
    Slope and Intercept   212
    t-Test for Slope (Test #10)   212
    t-Test for Intercept   212
    Confidence Interval for Slope and Intercept   212
12.6 Making Predictions with Regression   213
    Confidence Intervals for Prediction   213
12.7 Other Issues Related to Regression   215
    Assumptions of Regression   215
    Correlation Does Not Imply Causation   215
    Extrapolation   216

    Outliers   216
    Using Regression to Test Group Means   217
12.8 Summary   218
    Conceptual   218
    Applied   218
12.9 Exercises   218
    Modules for Linear Regression   219
    12.A Partitioning the Sum of Squares   219
    12.B Examples of Hypothesis Tests for Regression   220
        ANOVA Test   220
        t-Test for Slope   221
    12.C Equations for the Confidence Intervals for Prediction   222
        A Closer Look   222
    12.D Regression Diagnostics   223
        Leverage   223
        Residual Diagnostics   224
        Influential Values   225
    12.E Indicator Variables   228

Chapter 13
Multiple Regression   231

13.1 Introduction to Multiple Regression   232
    Equations   233
    Graphical Representation   233
    Correlation Matrix as a Prelude to Multiple Regression   233
13.2 Interpreting Multiple Regression Computer Output   235
    Correlation Matrix   235
    R^2 and Multiple R   235
    Adjusted R^2 236
    Overall ANOVA (Test #9) and Test for Each Slope (Test #10)   237
    Standardized Coefficients   238
    Variance Inflation Factors   238
    Prediction   239
    Analysis of Residuals: Looking for Outliers   240
    Model Building and Stepwise Selection   240
13.3 Summary   244
    Conceptual   244
    Applied   245
13.4 Exercises   245

Modules for Multiple Regression   246
13.A   What Is the Multiple Correlation, R?   246
13.B   Exploring Standardized Regression Coefficients   247

Chapter 14
Chi-Square Applications   249

14.1   Nonparametric Methods and Chi-Square Tests   250
14.2   Contingency Table: Chi-Square Test of Independence (Test #11)   250
   Example of Contingency Table Test of Independence   252
   Comparing Multiple Proportions   255
   Crosstabulation   256
   Other Contingency Table Options   257
14.3   Goodness of Fit Test (Test #12)   257
   Introduction and Uniform Distribution Goodness of Fit Test   257
   Example of a Goodness of Fit Test   258
   Other Goodness of Fit Tests   259
14.4   Summary   260
   Conceptual   260
   Applied   260
14.5   Exercises   260
   Modules for Chi-Square Applications   261
   14.A   Using the Chi-Square Distribution   261
      Chi-Square Table   261
      Excel Chi-Square Functions   261
      MegaStat Chi-Square Distribution   262
   14.B   Contingency Table Options   262
      Phi   263
      Cramer's V   263
      Coefficient of Contingency   263
      Fisher's Exact Test   263

14.C   Dice Toss Goodness of Fit Simulation   263
14.D   Normal Curve Goodness of Fit   263
   Hypothesis Testing Steps   266
   An Alternative Normal Curve Goodness of Fit Test   267

Chapter 15
Time-Series Analysis   269

15.1   Introduction to Time Series and Forecasting   270
   Basic Model   270
15.2   Linear Trend   270
15.3   Polynomial Trend   272
15.4   Exponential Trend   278
15.5   Which Trendline Is Best?   283
15.6   Moving Averages   283
15.7   Deseasonalization   285
15.8   Summary   290
   Conceptual   290
   Applied   290
15.9   Exercises   291
   Module for Time-Series Analysis   291
   15.A   Durbin-Watson Statistic   291

Chapter 16
Summary and Integration   295

16.1   A Brief Review   296
16.2   Putting It Together   297

Appendices

A   Excel Statistical Functions   299
B   Hypothesis Test Summaries   303
C   Glossary and Key Equations   311
D   Tables   325
E   Tutorial List   331

Index   333

Basic Statistics
Using Excel
and MegaStat

CHAPTER ONE

Introduction

1.1 Definitions and Types of Data (p. 2)

1.2 Using This Book (p. 6)

Summary (p. 9)

1.1   Definitions and Types of Data

The purpose of this book is to introduce basic statistical concepts to help the reader understand data and make decisions by using data. The focus is on choosing the appropriate type of analysis and understanding the results. Statistical analysis should be thought of as commonsense problem-solving techniques, not the rigid application of mathematical equations.

Learning any topic depends on learning precise definitions of the words used in that discipline. Let's get started with some definitions.

Statistics

What is statistics? Or since *statistics* ends with an "s," should it be, What *are* statistics? Actually, both can be correct. There are three definitions of statistics:

- **Statistics** can be synonymous with data or summarized data. For example, one can talk about baseball statistics, sales statistics, Labor Department statistics, and so on. It has been suggested that the root word in *statistics* is *state*—"state-istics," that is, data about the state.
- A specific technical definition of a **statistic** is a value calculated from a sample. For example, if one calculated the **average** age of a sample of college students, that value would be a statistic.
- When you see ***statistics*** in the title of a textbook, it is not referring specifically to data or calculated values; it is referring to the things one learns in a statistics course. In this sense statistics are tools and concepts that are used to analyze data and make decisions from data.

So which is the correct definition? All three are correct, but the last definition is the most common one, especially in the context of a statistics course.

Data versus Information

People often confuse the terms *data* and *information* and use them synonymously. **Data,** however, is raw material, and information is data put to use in a meaningful way. One way to convert data into information is through statistical analysis. Throughout this book we explore many ways of getting information from data.

In the early chapters we get information from data by summarizing the data, and in the process we develop the tools and concepts that are used for decision making in the later chapters (hypothesis testing and regression analysis).

Data (Qualitative and Quantitative)

One common element in the definitions given below is the word *data*.

data $\equiv$ recorded symbols that represent things or events.[1] Although data is a plural term, it is often used incorrectly in the singular sense. The correct singular term is **dataset.**

datum $\equiv$ singular of data

---

[1] "$\equiv$" reads "by definition."

There are two types of data, **qualitative** and **quantitative.**

> *Qualitative* data ≡ data that identify or classify. Some terms commonly associated with qualitative data are *text, words, names, labels, identification, categorical,* and *nominal.* Examples of qualitative data include your address, the type of car you drive, your political preference, and your Social Security number.

> *Quantitative* data ≡ numbers that measure something. Examples of quantitative data are age, weight, height, distance, and examination scores.

Although quantitative data are always numbers, not all numbers are quantitative. Examples of numbers that are qualitative include telephone numbers, ZIP codes, highway numbers, Social Security numbers, credit card numbers, and numbers on sports uniforms, among many others. Although these numbers may contain information, they do not measure anything and are thus qualitative, not quantitative. A common statistical mistake is to treat numeric qualitative data as if it were quantitative.

Statistical analysis always works with quantitative data. Does this mean that it is impossible to analyze qualitative data? No; we analyze qualitative data by converting it to quantitative data. How do we do that? By counting. For example, if you ask a sample of people how they will vote, each vote is qualitative data, but if you say that 44 out of 82 people will vote for a particular candidate, you have quantitative data. Frequencies and percentages are quantitative because they measure how many occurrences there are in a sample. When we analyze qualitative data, we really are analyzing the quantitative values we get from counting the qualitative data.

Cross-Sectional versus Time-Series Data

Another distinction that can be applied to data is the timing. If all the data in a sample are collected at more or less the same point in time, the data are said to be **cross-sectional.** This is the most common type of data.

If the data are collected at specific points over time (e.g., monthly or quarterly), they are **time-series data.** Quite often the goal of time-series data is to extend the data into the future. That process is discussed in Chapter 15.

Variables

Another term that is used frequently in statistics is ***variable.*** The mathematical definition of a variable is "a symbol for an unspecified quantity." For example, the letter "X" is a commonly used mathematical variable, but in a more general sense the word *variable* refers to the underlying entity that is being represented with data. If we have data that are dollar amounts, we say that the underlying variable that is being measured is value. When one is doing data analysis, the term *variable* refers to a column of numbers (often in an Excel worksheet), usually with a label at the top. For example, when we study scatterplots, we refer to the variables for the horizontal and vertical axes (Exhibit 2-11), and the MegaStat dialog box has you select the cells containing the data for the variables.

Discrete versus Continuous Variables

Discrete variables are specific, countable outcomes or events. Qualitative data are always discrete by definition, but quantitative data also can be discrete. The integers used in counting are the primary example; however, a variable does not have to be an integer to be discrete. For example, if you placed a bet for $2.73 and could win $10.45, you would have a discrete variable because there are two discrete outcomes—win and lose—even though the associated values are not integers.

A **continuous variable** is one where you have an infinite number of points along a scale and could do more and more precise measurement with more precise instrumentation. Time, distance, and weight are classic examples. People sometimes refer to continuous *data,* but whenever a data value gets recorded, it is always a particular value. The value 8.4859845 inches is a precise measurement, but it is discretely different from 8.4859846 inches. If people say they have continuous data, what they really mean is that they have data that represent specific measurements of a continuous variable. In other words, the distinction between discrete and continuous data refers to the underlying variable being measured, not to the data.

Levels of Measurement

Another concept that relates to data is levels of measurement: **nominal, ordinal, interval,** and **ratio:**

Nominal. Refers to qualitative data. There is no measurement unless you are referring to numbers you get by counting the different qualitative outcomes.

Ordinal. Refers to sequencing or ranking. For example, a market researcher asks you to rank five similar products from "like best" to "like least." Are ordinal data quantitative? If you assign a number, say, 5, to the product one likes best and assign 1 to the product one likes least, this roughly measures how much a person likes the product, but it is a very imprecise measurement. All we can say is that a higher number means a person likes the product more, but we can't say how much or even how much more than another product. For example, the person may not really like the product he or she rated best and might really like the product rated at the top and hate the others, but we cannot discern that from the rankings.

Interval. Refers to data with constant units but no absolute zero. Temperature is the classic example. Ten degrees is the same anywhere on the scale, but 80 degrees is not twice as hot as 40 degrees. Another example would be standardized examinations such as SAT scores; 100 points presumably means the same anywhere along the scale, but we cannot say that a person with a score twice as high is twice as smart.

Ratio. Here we have constant units *and* an absolute zero. Ratio data are the best data and the most common. How do you know if you have ratio data? Ask this question: Does a number twice as big mean you have twice as much? If the answer is yes, you have ratio data. For example, measures of time, weight, and distance are all ratio data.

PRACTICE IDENTIFYING TYPES OF DATA

- Open **RealEstateData.xls!Data**. Examine the data.
- Open **RealEstateData.xls!Variable_Description**. Examine the variables.
- For each variable, look at the data and determine if it is
  - ◦ Qualitative or quantitative
    If it is quantitative, is it
  - ◦ Discrete or continuous?
  - ◦ Ordinal interval or ratio?

Solution

A sequential counter variable is qualitative even though it could be thought of as measuring a position in the data; for example, house 40 is twice as far down as house 20.

Price, LotSize, SqrFt, Distance

These are quantitative, continuous, and ratio.

Bedrooms, Bathrooms

These are quantitative, discrete, and ratio.

Pool? Basement?

These are qualitative variables. 0 means no, and 1 means yes sometimes 0–1 variables are called indicator variables, binary variables, or dummy variables.

Rating

This is a seven-point scale of a person's rating of how nice a house is after that person looks at it. Although this sort of data is treated as ratio, it may be just ordinal. For it to be ratio, a rating of 6 always would have to be twice as good as a rating of 3.

SubDiv

Even though there are numbers, they are just labels. The data are qualitative.

Identifying Data

Whenever you see data, ask yourself the following questions:

1. Does this data measure something (quantitative) or does it identify something (qualitative)?
2. If it is quantitative data, is it ratio data? Does a number twice as big mean you have twice as much?

Sample versus Population

In a general sense a **population** is the entire universe of objects we are studying, but since statistics works with data, we really are thinking about data associated with the physical objects. For example, if we are considering a population of college students, we really are considering the population of data associated with the students that we are interested in studying, such as their grade point average (GPA), income, and age.

A **sample** is a subset of a population. Why take a *sample?* If we are interested in a population, why not just do a census, that is, look at every item in the population? Chapter 7 discusses this in more detail, but it is obvious that most populations are too large to allow a census. For example, even the federal government, with all its resources, cannot do a completely accurate census of the U.S. population.

One of our goals in using statistics is to estimate values of a population on the basis of a sample. For example, if we want to know the true average value of a population, that value is a **parameter.** In most cases we will never know the value of the parameter because we cannot assess the entire population, but that does not mean the value does not exist. At any instant in time the population parameter has a value; we just do not know what that value is. If we take a sample from a population and calculate the average of the sample, that value is called a *statistic* (the second of the three definitions of statistics). It would be logical to say that the value of the statistic is a reasonable estimate of the population parameter. However, if we keep taking samples, we will get different values of the statistic for each one, but there is only one true population parameter. We will come back to this issue in Chapter 7 after we have introduced more precise terms and concepts in the earlier chapters.

Statistical Tools

We have seen that statistics refers to the procedures we can use (i.e., tools) to analyze data, in other words extract information from the data. What are these tools? Basically they are the Table of Contents. The book is grouped into the following topics:

- Descriptive Statistics (Chapters 2–3)
    These are tools that help us summarize large amounts of data and give us the foundation for the later chapters.
- Probability and Probability Distributions (Chapters 4–6)
    Probability is the mathematical foundation of statistical analysis.
- Estimation (Chapters 7–8)
    Here is where we tackle the issue of estimating population parameters based on sample statistics. These chapters also give the foundation for inferential statistics.
- Inferential Statistics

The remainder of the book develops the tools of hypothesis testing which allows us to make inferences, i.e., decisions, based on data.

- Differences between groups (Chapters 9–11)
- Relationships within groups (Chapters 12–15)
    ◦ Regression analysis for quantitative data
    ◦ Chi-square contingency table for qualitative data

1.2 Using This Book

Traditional books are arranged in a linear manner: One starts at page 1 and reads through the book. Such books tend to be cluttered, and it is difficult to separate the conceptual material from the detail material. As illustrated in the next page, this book takes a hierarchical approach with two levels.

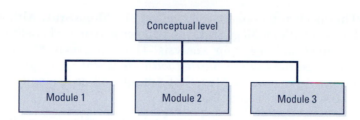

The conceptual level that contains the main chapter sections features a discussion and integration of the topics, and this discussion contains references to modules that contain "how to do it" topics, support material, and topics that might be considered optional. This way you can get the big picture without being distracted by detail; when you want to study or review a specific topic, it is easily found and clearly delineated. If you are using this text for a course, your instructor probably will give you guidance on which modules are critical and which are less important or can be skipped. Chapter sections are identified with numbers—Section 2.1, Section 2.2—and modules are identified with letters—Module 2.A, Module 2.B. When you initially encounter a reference to a module, it is a good idea to take a quick look at that module and then go back and study it in more detail after you have finished the section.

This book has many references to Excel workbooks that give demonstrations and have a hands-on approach. It is *highly recommended* that you open the workbooks, look at the cell formulas, replicate the output, and then experiment with changing the data or doing different analyses. To get the full benefit of the text, it is critically important to at least look at, and preferably work with, the referenced Excel files. The workbooks are not protected, and you are encouraged to work with them. It is recommended that you copy them from the CD to your computer. You can always use the CD to reload the original.

Tutorials

The CD that accompanies the text has several "screencam" tutorials. These tutorials work through various computer activities while recording a voice overlay. The tutorials obviously will work better if your computer can play the sound track; however, they are of some value even without sound. The tutorials are referenced by an icon at the point in the text where they are relevant. There is a list of tutorials in Appendix E.

Computer Skills

It is assumed that you have access to a computer and have basic computer and Excel skills; however, you do not have to be an Excel expert to do the activities in this book. The computer is a great learning tool, but this is a statistics book, not an Excel training book. You undoubtedly will expand and reinforce your Excel skills, but your focus should always be on statistics.

EXCEL TUTORIALS 1 & 2

There are two screencam tutorials on the CD that should get you up to speed with Excel even if you have little or no prior experience with it. Even if you consider your Excel skills pretty good, it is a good idea to look at the tutorial.

This book integrates the Excel add-in **MegaStat.** Although the book could be used without MegaStat, you will get maximum benefit if you have MegaStat installed and use it for analysis. The text avoids detailed MegaStat instructions (see the *Getting Started with MegaStat* user's guide and Tutorial 1) but frequently discusses MegaStat output and occasionally mentions features or issues related to MegaStat.

TUTORIAL 1

Although MegaStat can do analyses efficiently, in most instances it is a useful learning technique to do calculations with a calculator or using Excel as a calculator. At this stage in your statistics education the goal is not efficient calculation but to see how and why things work. Performing an analysis with a calculator and/or basic Excel functions and then verifying the result with MegaStat and/or Excel's statistical functions is a learning technique that is recommended and demonstrated throughout this book.

Learning Activities

Most statistics books have numerous problems and exercises at the end of each chapter. This book takes a different approach by having Learning Activities that are targeted at specific concepts. To get the full benefit from this book and really learn statistics, you need to do the Learning Activities. Learning Activities are shown in boxes that are placed where they are relevant.

There are some exercises at the end of most of the chapters for additional practice and assessment.

Notation and Conventions

- Excel workbooks (sometimes also called spreadsheets) are referenced in the text with a specific font style, for example, **RealEstateData.xls.** If you are instructed to go to a particular *worksheet* within the workbook, it will look like this: **RealEstateData.xls!Data** to refer to the worksheet called "Data."
- Excel functions are referenced in all-capital letters followed by parentheses, such as AVERAGE(); the capital letters are not required by Excel. If the parentheses are empty, it means that the function has no input values (sometimes called arguments or parameters) or that values are not of interest in the display context. Appendix A provides a summary of the most frequently used Excel statistical functions.
- Equation numbers are shown with square brackets [ ]. Equations are numbered only if they are referenced in the text or might be referenced by an instructor.
- Menu levels: If you are to navigate through menu levels for Excel or MegaStat, the | symbol is used. For example, Excel | Tools | Add-ins refers to the menu levels that would get you to the Add-in dialog box in Excel; MegaStat | Hypothesis Tests | Paired Observations would get you to a particular section of MegaStat.
- Test summaries: In the table of contents and throughout the text you will see numbers Test #1 through Test #12. These numbers refer to the 12 main hypothesis tests that are described in the text (starting in Chapter 10) and summarized in Appendix B.

- Calculations: When sample calculations are shown in the text and the same values also are shown on the computer output, the sample calculations are shown to match the computer output. If you use a calculator to replicate the calculations (a good idea), you may not get exactly the answer displayed because the computer uses the full 15-digit accuracy and the displayed values are rounded. However, the answers should match very closely and be a little off only at the last decimal places.

  If you use a calculator to do calculations on raw data, you may get a slightly different answer than that given by MegaStat or Excel because the computer uses all 15 digits of accuracy and does not round intermediate results. You also may get slightly different results if you use the memory register on your calculator instead of rounding and reentering the values, but again, the result should be very close.

  If the learning activities say to calculate something with a calculator and you do not have a calculator, you can use Excel as a calculator; in other words, use the basic Excel functions that also would be available with a calculator. The Excel SUM() function is considered a calculator function. However, if you will need to do calculator calculations on an examination, it is a good idea to practice with the calculator you will be using.

- Scientific notation: Excel and MegaStat use scientific notation for very large and very small numbers. For example, if you see the number 6.43E-07, the number that follows the E is the number of places you would move the decimal to the left (negative) or right (positive) if you wanted to write the number in standard form. Thus, 6.43E-07 would be 0.000000643.

- Spreadsheets, workbooks, worksheets: *Spreadsheet* is a general term for a file consisting of cells that can contain numbers, text, and formulas. The most common spreadsheet program is Excel; however, Excel calls spreadsheets workbooks, and each workbook consists of one or more worksheets that are selected by tabs at the bottom of the screen. This book uses the Excel terms *workbook* and *worksheet*. The term *spreadsheet* is ambiguous since it can refer to a workbook or a worksheet within a workbook.

Summary

The study of any discipline starts with learning the vocabulary, and that was the purpose of this chapter. We saw that statistics is the body of knowledge and the tools and techniques used to extract information from data.

Data are the raw material of statistics, and it either identifies something (qualitative data) or measures something (quantitative data). Always explicitly identify what type of data you have before you do an analysis.

The chapter ended with a section that explained some details of using this book. We all tend to skip over such material; however, you will find use of the book easier and more effective if you read through it.

Concepts

- Qualitative versus quantitative data
- Discrete versus continuous variables
- Levels of measurement

CHAPTER TWO

Descriptive Statistics

2.1 Measures of Central Tendency (p. 12)

2.2 Measures of Variation (p. 18)

2.3 Sample MegaStat Output (p. 24)

2.4 Other Descriptive Measures (p. 26)

Summary (p. 30)

Exercises (p. 31)

In this chapter and Chapter 3 we look at descriptive statistics: the tools used for summarizing data. This is a very important topic because it often is necessary to make sense of a large set of data and because the methods and concepts used for descriptive statistics also provide the tools we will use in later chapters for making decisions with data.

Take a look at **RealEstateData.xls!Data.**[1] This dataset contains data for 124 homes for sale in a particular real estate market. If you were a realtor and an out-of-state client asked you a question such as "What is the average price of homes for sale in your city?" or "What is a typical lot size?" or asked about some other characteristic, could you look at the 124 numbers in any of the variables and give the client a precise and concise answer? You might have some sense of the data, but you could not give an exact answer.

In this chapter we look at particular tools for summarizing data. First we examine measures of central tendency that are used in an attempt to find one number that best represents the data. Then we look at measures of variation that give us information about the dispersion of the data.

We also will look at some graphical means of summarizing data, and in Chapter 3 we will continue this theme by looking at frequency distributions and histograms.

We can summarize data from a population or a sample. The definitions of *population* and *sample* are dealt with more carefully in Chapter 7, but essentially a population is all possible values and a sample is a subset of a population. Since we rarely can access an entire population, our actual calculations usually involve samples.

2.1   Measures of Central Tendency

Measures of central tendency are the methods we use to summarize data by trying to find one number that best represents all the numbers in a sample or population. There are three primary measures of central tendency: the mode, the median, and the mean.

Mode

The **mode** is the most frequently occurring number; intuitively, it makes sense to consider it the most representative number. However, the mode can have problems. If you have a continuous variable, it is possible for every number to be unique, and thus there would be no mode; this is the case with the Price variable in **RealEstateData.xls!Data.**

In the SqrFt variable the value 2156 occurs twice and every other value is unique, and so technically 2156 would be the mode. However, it hardly makes sense to say that 2156 is the most representative value just because it occurs twice. Thus, a sample may have no distinct mode.

You also could have a situation in which two or more values occur the same number of times and thus there are multiple modes. The Excel MODE() function does not detect multiple modes. If you think the mode is an appropriate measure of central tendency for your data, you should examine the data

---

[1] This font style is used for a workbook or worksheet reference. It refers to the "data" worksheet in the workbook RealEstateData.xls.

CALCULATING THE MODE (1)   Learning Activity **2.1–1**

- Open **Price.xls!Data_sorted.** This worksheet contains the Price variable sorted ascending.
- Determine the mode by looking at the data and using the Excel MODE() function.
- Since all the values are unique, there is no mode and thus the Excel function displays #N/A. You probably noticed that it was not that easy to determine visually that all the numbers were different or if any were the same. If the numbers had more digits, it would be even harder, and it would be almost impossible if the numbers were not sorted.

The **Mode_solution** worksheet shows an Excel technique for quickly checking if all the numbers are unique. Column D subtracts from each number the one above it. For example, cell D4 contains =C4-C3. Look at the cell formulas in column D. This approach will work only if the values are sorted.

If any adjacent numbers are the same, column D will contain a zero, and it is easy to scan for zeros. You also could use the Excel MIN function on column D (or the status bar MIN) to see if the smallest value is zero. If the data has a distinct mode, there will be a large block of zeros.

CALCULATING THE MODE (2)   Learning Activity **2.1–2**

- Open **Bedrooms.xls!Data sorted.** This worksheet contains the Bedrooms variable sorted ascending.
- Determine the mode by looking at the data and using the Excel MODE() function.
- As shown in the **Mode_solution** worksheet, there are 44 three-bedroom homes, and so 3 is the mode; however, there are 40 four-bedroom homes, and so 3 is not a distinct mode.
- *Excel note:* Since there are only a few unique values, it is not necessary to subtract adjacent pairs of numbers as in the previous Learning Activity. Excel has a handy way to count cells (or do other basic operations on selected cells). Exhibit 2-1 shows how to count the number of cells containing 5's quickly. Select the cells, right-click the status bar, and select the operation you want, which is Count for this example. Replicate Exhibit 2-1 and then try counting other values. You will find that you do not have to select the Count option in subsequent selections; it will be on the status bar whenever you select a range of cells. You need to right-click only when you want to perform another operation.

EXHIBIT 2-1   Using Excel's status bar to count cells.

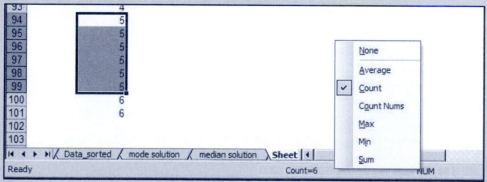

visually to see if the mode is distinct or, better yet, run a frequency distribution and histogram (see Chapter 3). The mode should be visually distinct, and you can look for multiple modes.

The mode most often is used for qualitative data such as the SubDiv variable; it rarely is used for quantitative data.

Median and Quartiles

The **median** is the middle number of a set of data. To find the median, you first sort the numbers from low to high. If you have an odd number of data values, there will be one middle value. For example, if you have 31 sorted data values, the median will be the 16th value; there would be 15 numbers above and 15 numbers below that value. If you have an even number of numbers, the median is the average of the middle two numbers. In **RealEstateData.xls!Data** the middle two numbers (the 62nd and 63rd numbers) of the sorted Price variable are 346.2 and 347.4, and so the median will be the average: $(346.2 + 347.4)/2 = 346.8$) although any number between the middle two numbers could be considered the median since half the numbers would be below and half would be above it.

The median sometimes is called the 50th percentile since 50% of the numbers fall below it and 50% fall above it. We also can calculate the 25th and 75th percentiles as descriptive measures. Sometimes the 25th percentile is referred to as Q1 and the 75th percentile as Q3. Using this terminology, the median would be Q2. Since **Q1, Q2,** and **Q3** split the data into four sections, they are called **quartiles.**

Section 2.4 shows how the median and quartiles are combined into a graphical display known as a **boxplot.**

CALCULATING THE MEDIAN (1)   Learning Activity **2.1–3**

- Open **Price.xls!Data_sorted**. This worksheet contains the Price variable sorted ascending.
- Find the median by taking the mean of the middle two numbers.
- Find the median by using Excel's MEDIAN( ) function.
- Find the median by using MegaStat | Descriptive Statistics. Check Median in addition to the default options.
- Confirm your answers by looking at **Price.xls!Median_solution**.

CALCULATING THE MEDIAN (2)   Learning Activity **2.1–4**

- Open **Bedrooms.xls!Data_sorted**. This worksheet contains the Bedrooms variable sorted ascending.
- Find the median by taking the mean of the middle two numbers.
- Find the median by using Excel's MEDIAN() function.
- Find the median by using MegaStat | Descriptive Statistics. Check Median in addition to the default options.
- Confirm your answers by looking at **Bedrooms.xls!Median_solution**.

CALCULATING QUARTILES

- Open **Quartiles.xls!Data.** This worksheet contains the first four variables of the RealEstateData file (Price, LotSize, SqrFt, and Bedrooms). At the top of the file is the median and quartile output from MegaStat.
- Use MegaStat | Descriptive Statistics to verify the calculations at the top of the sheet.
- Verify a few of the quartiles by using Excel's QUARTILE( ) function.
- Sort the Price variable (ascending) and verify that the first quartile is between the 31st and 32nd values (i.e., one-fourth of the values are below) and that the third quartile is between the 93rd and 94th values.
- Repeat the previous step for LotSize, SqrFt, and Bedrooms.
- Why are the median and quartiles not a very good descriptive measure for bedrooms?
  - *Answer:* Since there are many discrete occurrences of each number of bedrooms, there is no distinct division between the quartiles.
- *Technical note:* Although quartiles seem like a simple concept, there are actually several ways quartiles can be interpolated when there is not a specific value corresponding to the quartile (as in the above data). **Quartile_calculation.xls** shows the method used by Excel.

The median is a reasonable descriptive measure, but it rarely is used in a detailed statistical analysis since the arithmetic mean has better mathematical properties.

Arithmetic Mean

Although the mode and the median are sometimes useful for descriptive purposes, the most commonly used measure of central tendency is the **arithmetic mean,** commonly known as the **average.** However, the word *average* should be avoided in a statistical context; although it usually means the sum of the numbers divided by the number of numbers, in a very general sense it may refer to any measure of central tendency. In a statistical context you should use the word ***mean*** instead of *average* or, more formally, use *arithmetic mean*.

The equation for the sample arithmetic mean is

$$\overline{X} = \frac{\sum X_i}{n} \qquad \text{[2.1]}$$

This is the first occurrence in this book of the dreaded sigma, Σ. Try not to succumb to sigmaphobia. Sigma notation is just shorthand for the word *sum;* it means to add some numbers, in this case the numbers in a sample in which n is the sample size. The subscript "i" on the X refers to any particular value in the sample. The bar over X is the convention for the mean of the variable. A more formal statement of the sample mean is

$$\overline{X} = \frac{\sum_{i=1}^{n} X_i}{n} = \frac{X_1 + X_2 + X_3 + \cdots X_n}{n} \qquad \text{[2.2]}$$

The values above and below the sigma are the starting and ending values, and so the equation says to sum the values of X_i for i starting at 1 and ending at n. This text uses the simpler notation in Equation [2.1] since it generally is assumed that you are summing the entire sample.

INTRODUCTORY PRACTICE WITH THE ARITHMETIC MEAN

Learning Activity **2.1–6**

- Open **Mean1.xls.**
- Calculate the mean by using a calculator.
- Calculate the mean by using Excel's SUM() and COUNT() functions.
- Calculate the mean by using Excel's AVERAGE() function.
- Calculate the mean by using MegaStat | Descriptive Statistics.

You should get the same answer using all these methods. (Check **Mean1.xls!Solution1.**)

The equation could have been written as mean $= \dfrac{\text{SUM}(X)}{n}$. Whenever you see a capital sigma, associate it with the Excel function SUM().

If you want to refer to the mean of an entire population, you just change the notation. Greek letters are used for population values, sometimes called population parameters. In this case μ (mu) (lowercase Greek) refers to the population mean. The capital letter N is used to represent the population size; thus, the equation for the population mean is

$$\text{Population mean} = \mu = \frac{\sum X_i}{N} \qquad \text{[2.3]}$$

As we discuss in more detail in Section 7.1, we rarely have access to all the items in a population, but the population mean exists even though we rarely can calculate it.

Here is an example for the sample mean. The file **Mean1.xls** contains the following sample: 4, 4, 6, 2, 5, 9, 5, 7, 5, 2, 14, 7, 14, 7, 7, 2, 9, 8. What is the mean using Equation [2.2]?

$$\overline{X} = \frac{4+4+6+2+5+9+5+7+5+2+14+7+14+7+7+2+9+8}{18}$$

$$= \frac{117}{18} = 6.5 \qquad \text{[2.4]}$$

Graphical Representation of the Mean

If we let each number be a block of wood and stack the blocks as shown in Exhibit 2-2, the balance point is at 6.5; that is the mean of the numbers

EXHIBIT 2-2
The mean as the balance point (center of gravity).

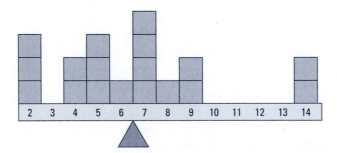

EXHIBIT 2-3 The sum of deviations is always zero.	X	X – M
	4	–2.5
	4	–2.5
	6	–0.5
	2	–4.5
	5	–1.5
	9	2.5
	5	–1.5
	7	0.5
	5	–1.5
	2	–4.5
	14	7.5
	7	0.5
	14	7.5
	7	0.5
	7	0.5
	2	–4.5
	9	2.5
	8	1.5
	6.5 Mean	0

EXHIBIT 2-4 The influence of an outlier.	X	X – M
	4	–15.5
	4	–15.5
	6	–13.5
	2	–17.5
	5	–14.5
	9	–10.5
	5	–14.5
	7	–12.5
	5	–14.5
	2	–17.5
	14	–5.5
	7	–12.5
	248	228.5
	7	–12.5
	7	–12.5
	2	–17.5
	9	–10.5
	8	–11.5
	Mean = 19.50	0 Sum

(assuming that the bar does not affect the balance). This is true no matter what data we use: The mean is always the balance point, sometimes called the center of gravity.

To see how this works mathematically, we subtract the mean from each number to see how far away each number is from the mean, as shown in Exhibit 2-3. The distances below and above the mean (the negative and positive values) always cancel, making the sum zero.

Outliers

An **outlier** is a number that is not close to the other numbers in a sample. For example, what would happen if the second 14 in Exhibit 2-3 was changed to 248? Clearly, it would be an outlier since it is not close to the other values. The mean of the sample changes from 6.5 to 19.5 is shown in Exhibit 2-4.

Imagine taking one of the 14 blocks in Exhibit 2-2 and moving it far to the right to 248. To make the bar balance, the balance point also would have to move to the right to 19.5. Exhibit 2-4 shows that the sum of the deviations is still zero, and thus the bar balances. However, the mean could be considered a poor descriptive measure since it is not near any of the data values.

Usually outliers are identified visually, but how does a computer identify an outlier? Here is a frequently used definition of an outlier[2]:

Let: Q1 = 25th percentile
Q3 = 75th percentile
H = Q3 – Q1 (the interquartile range)

[2]Source: http://www.itl.nist.gov/div898/handbook/prc/section1/prc16.htm.

EXPLORING HOW OUTLIERS AFFECT THE MEAN AND THE MEDIAN

Learning Activity **2.1–7**

- Open **Dataset1.xls!Data.**
- Use MegaStat | Descriptive Statistics.
  - Specify A3:B27 as the input range.
  - In addition to the default options, select **Definitional form** and "Median and Quartiles."

The mean for the second group is higher than most of the values but is far lower than the outlier. Thus, even though it is the "center of gravity" for the data, it is not representative of any of the values.

The median, however, is the same for both groups. When the data are skewed or contain an outlier, the median is a better descriptive measure.

The definitional form output for the first group shows four shaded values that contribute more than 10% to the **SSX**, but there are no obvious outliers. The definitional form for the second group, however, shows the outlier contributing more than 95% of the SSX.

MORE PRACTICE WITH THE MEAN AND STUDYING THE EFFECT OF AN OUTLIER

Learning Activity **2.1–8**

- Open **Mean2.xls!Data.** This file shows the annual income of 20 students in an MBA course. Note that one student makes far more than the other students do.
- Calculate the mean by using Excel's AVERAGE() function.
- Note that the mean of 51480 is larger than the value for 19 of the 20 students but is far lower than the outlier. In this case the mean is not representative of any of the numbers. (See **Solution1.**)
- Delete the outlier and calculate the mean of the remaining numbers. (See **Solution2.**)

An *outlier* is defined as any value less than $Q1 - 1.5*H$ or greater than $Q3 + 1.5*H$. An *extreme outlier* is defined as any value less than $Q1 - 3.0*H$ or greater than $Q3 + 3.0*H$.

2.2   Measures of Variation

In addition to a measure of central tendency we need a measure of variation or dispersion. In other words, are all the numbers in a sample or population fairly close to each other or are they spread out? Why is a measure of variation needed? Because if we are using a sample to estimate a population value, we will have a more precise measure if the values in the sample are close to each other.

Variation.xls and Exhibit 2-5 show two samples that have the same mean, but the right variable obviously has more variation than does the left variable. We can use these data to illustrate the measures of variation in this chapter.

Variation	
Low	**High**
97	155
99	22
101	160
99	6
102	52
97	198
104	86
99	121
104	86
98	114
100	100
	Mean

EXHIBIT 2-5
Comparison of variables with low and high variation.

Although measures of variation are useful descriptively, they are also important because they give us the tools we will need in later chapters to make decisions from data.

Range, Mean Deviation, and Mean Absolute Deviation

One simple measure of variation is the **range** that is the distance between the largest number and the smallest number. Although the range is a simple concept, it is limited by the fact that it uses only two data values: the largest and smallest values in the sample.

If you want a measure that reflects all the data, you can measure the mean distance of the numbers from the mean. In other words, calculate the **deviations** from the mean $(X - \overline{X})$ for every data value and then take the mean of the deviations. However, as Exhibit 2-3 shows, this does not work because the sum of the deviations is always zero and thus the **mean deviation** is always zero. This is actually a consequence of the center of gravity property of the mean that is discussed in Section 2.1: The negative deviations always cancel the positive deviations. You can avoid having the values always sum to zero by

STUDY THE RANGE AND SEE THAT THE RANGE CAN BE A MISLEADING MEASURE OF VARIATION

Learning Activity **2.2–1**

- Open **Range1.xls!Data.** Note that most of the values in variable X1 are pretty close to 300 whereas variable X2 has much more variability.
  - Calculate the minimum, maximum, and range of both variables by using Excel's MIN() and MAX() functions and then calculating max – min to get the range.
- Note that the range is the same for both variables because they both have the same min and max. This shows that the range can be a misleading measure of variation because it looks only at two data values: the largest and the smallest.
- Verify your results by using MegaStat | Descriptive Statistics. In addition to the default options, check the Median and BoxPlot options. Compare the MegaStat output with the output in the previous step. Look for Min, Max, and Range. The other output values will be studied later. We also will study BoxPlots later (Section 2.4), but you should be able to see how they relate to the range.

CALCULATE DEVIATIONS FROM THE MEAN AND OBSERVE THAT THEY SUM TO ZERO

Learning Activity **2.2–2**

- Open **Mean1.xls!Data.**
- Put formulas in cells C2:C19 to subtract the mean from each data value. For example, the first cell (C2) would contain =B2−M. *Note:* M is the name that already was assigned to cell B22. (See **Mean1.xls!Solution2.**)
- Sum the deviations and note that the sum is zero.
- Change some of the data values and note that the sum is always zero.
- Place the original data values in the cells and save the file.

SHOW THAT VARIATION CAN BE MEASURED WITH ABSOLUTE DEVIATIONS

Learning Activity **2.2–3**

- Open **Mean1.xls!Data** after completing Learning Activity 2.2–4.
- Add formulas in cells D2:D19 to calculate the absolute value of the deviations in column C. For example, cell D2 would contain =ABS(C2).
- In cell D20, calculate the mean of the absolute values. The result is the mean absolute deviation. (See **Mean1.xls!Solution MAD.**)

ignoring the minus signs, that is, by taking the absolute value of the deviations and calculating the **mean absolute deviation (MAD)**. Although the MAD makes sense as a descriptive measure, it is not used often in statistical analysis because it is hard to treat mathematically.

Variance and Standard Deviation

The concept of a mean deviation from the mean makes sense, but instead of using the absolute value to avoid the negative deviations from canceling the positive deviations, statisticians square the deviations. The reason squaring is used instead of absolute value is that it is more amenable to algebraic manipulation (we will see an example of this in Module 11.A). The primary component of measuring variation is the sum of the squared deviations. If we calculate the mean squared deviation, we have one of the main measures of variation, which is known as the **variance:**

$$\text{Population variance} = \sigma^2 = \frac{\sum(X_i - \mu)^2}{N} \qquad \textbf{[2.5]}$$

(Note that σ (sigma) is used; it is a lowercase Greek s.)

To change this to a sample variance, we would use s^2 instead of σ^2, change μ to $\overline{X}$, and change the population size N to the sample size, lowercase n:

$$\text{Sample variance} = s^2 = \frac{\sum(X_i - \overline{X})^2}{n - 1} \qquad \textbf{[2.6]}$$

Note that there is one other difference. Instead of dividing by n, we divide by n − 1. Why do we divide by n − 1 instead of just calculating the mean squared deviation? Since we are using the sample variance to estimate the population variance, it can be shown that the estimate is better (i.e., unbiased) when we divide by n − 1 rather than by n. The way "it can be shown" is beyond the scope of this book, so just accept it or plan to take an upper-level mathematical statistics course to see the proof.

Since we typically do not have access to an entire population, the sample variance is the one we work with most of the time. Since the variance is defined by the sum of the squared deviations, this equation sometimes is called the definitional equation. Working out the answer by finding the deviations, squaring, and then summing them is called the definitional method or **definitional**

form. Since the equation for sample variance—Equation [2.6]—is very important, let's focus on it here:

- The real measure of variation is the numerator, the sum of the squared deviations, which often is referred to as **SSX** (sum of the squared deviations for the variable X).

$$SSX = \sum (X_i - \overline{X})^2 \qquad \textbf{[2.7]}$$

- The denominator $(n - 1)$ also is known as the **degrees of freedom,** abbreviated **df**. Thus, a shorthand version of the sample variance is

$$s^2 = \frac{SSX}{df} \qquad \textbf{[2.8]}$$

- If all the numbers in the sample were the same, SSX and thus the variance would be zero, meaning no variation.
- We saw above that the mean is sensitive to outliers, and so is the variance; it is even more sensitive because the deviations are squared.

Since the variance is made up of squared values, it makes sense to take the square root of it to scale it back to the original units. This quantity is called a **standard deviation** (often abbreviated as: **s, stdev, s.d., or sd**).

$$\text{Population standard deviation} = \sigma = \sqrt{\sigma^2} \qquad \textbf{[2.9]}$$

$$\text{Sample standard deviation} = s = \sqrt{s^2} \qquad \textbf{[2.10]}$$

The variance (and SSX) often is used for further statistical analysis, and the standard deviation is a descriptive measure. Just what does a standard deviation measure? If someone says he or she has data with a standard deviation of 23.4, what does that tell us? Is that a lot of variation or a small amount? A larger number means more variation, but a standard deviation is usually meaningful only as a comparison value. However, when you work through Learning Activity 2.2–8, you will see that the standard deviation can have a geometric interpretation.

Definitional Form for Variance and Standard Deviation

The variance is defined in Equation [2.6] as the sum of the squared deviations divided by $(n - 1)$, and the standard deviation is the square root of the variance. Excel and MegaStat can calculate these values easily, and that is what typically is done. However, if you want to learn how these measures of variation work or want to study your data carefully, you could use the full definitional form. This is done by actually calculating each deviation, squaring the deviations, and then summing the squared deviations to get SSX, which then is used to calculate the variance and the standard deviation.

Exhibit 2-6 (**DefnForm.xls**) shows the definitional form for the center of gravity data from Section 2.1.

TUTORIAL 1

You also may check the Definitional form box on MegaStat's Descriptive Statistics options. The output is shown in Exhibit 2-7. Note that MegaStat adds another column that calculates the percentage each data value contributes to SSX and shades values that contribute more than 10%. In examining the output, we see that the two 14's account for over half of the SSX, and so they may be considered outliers.

TUTORIAL 2

EXHIBIT 2-6
Definitional form for variance and standard deviation.

X	X – M	$(X - M)^2$
4	−2.5	6.25
4	−2.5	6.25
6	−0.5	0.25
2	−4.5	20.25
5	−1.5	2.25
9	2.5	6.25
5	−1.5	2.25
7	0.5	0.25
5	−1.5	2.25
2	−4.5	20.25
14	7.5	56.25
7	0.5	0.25
14	7.5	56.25
7	0.5	0.25
7	0.5	0.25
2	−4.5	20.25
9	2.5	6.25
8	1.5	2.25

Mean = 6.50   0 Sum   208.500 SSX

12.265 variance, s^2

n = 18   3.502 standard deviation, s

EXHIBIT 2-7
MegaStat's definitional form output.

Descriptive statistics

Definitional form for: X

i	X	X – Mean	$(X - Mean)^2$	% of SSX
1	4	−2.50	6.25	3.00
2	4	−2.50	6.25	3.00
3	6	−0.50	0.25	0.12
4	2	−4.50	20.25	9.71
5	5	−1.50	2.25	1.08
6	9	2.50	6.25	3.00
7	5	−1.50	2.25	1.08
8	7	0.50	0.25	0.12
9	5	−1.50	2.25	1.08
10	2	−4.50	20.25	9.71
11	14	7.50	56.25	26.98
12	7	0.50	0.25	0.12
13	14	7.50	56.25	26.98
14	7	0.50	0.25	0.12
15	7	0.50	0.25	0.12
16	2	−4.50	20.25	9.71
17	9	2.50	6.25	3.00
18	8	1.50	2.25	1.08

6.50 Mean   0.00 Sum   208.500 deviation sum of squares (SSX)

12.265 sample variance

3.502 sample standard deviation

(shaded rows represent more than 10% of SSX)

STUDY THE VARIANCE AND STANDARD DEVIATION BY USING THE DEFINITIONAL FORM
Learning Activity 2.2–4

Note: This Learning Activity and the next one are similar to Tutorial 2. Even if you have looked at Tutorial 2 and feel you understand it, there is still value in doing the definitional form from scratch.

- Open **Stdev1.xls!Data.** This file has the same data as **Mean1.xls.**
- In the shaded areas in columns C and D, enter Excel formulas to calculate the deviations $(X - M)$ and the deviations squared $(X - M)^2$.
- Sum column C to verify that the deviations sum to zero.
- Sum column D. This is the sum of squared deviations, SSX.
- Divide SSX by $n - 1$ to get the sample variance.
- Take the square root of the variance to get the sample standard deviation.

This is called the definitional form since the variance is based on the sum of the squared deviations.

CALCULATE MEASURES OF VARIATION BY USING EXCEL FORMULAS AND MEGASTAT
Learning Activity 2.2–5

- Open **Stdev2.xls!Data.** This file starts with the solution of **Stdev1.xls.**
  - In cells F21:F23 use the functions DEVSQ(), VAR(), and STDEV() to calculate the SSX, variance, and standard deviation, respectively. You should get the same answers as those in cells D21:D23.
- Use MegaStat | Descriptive Statistics to calculate the same values. Check the Definition form option and the "Sum, Sum of squares, SSX" option.
- Compare the MegaStat output with your output.

FURTHER EXPLORATION OF THE DEFINITIONAL FORM
Learning Activity 2.2–6

- Open **Stdev2.xls!MegaStat_Output.** This file contains the MegaStat output of the data from **Stdev2.xls.**
- Note the column labeled "% of SSX." This column calculates every squared deviation divided by SSX to see how much each data value contributes to the variation. Values that contribute more than 10% are shaded. We see that the two 14's together contribute more than half of the SSX; therefore, they could be considered outliers.
- Go to the **Solution1** worksheet. Replicate the "% of SSX" values in column E and verify that your percentages sum to 100%. See **Solution2.**
  - *Excel note:* The **Solution2A** page uses D21 as an absolute cell reference to refer to the SSX cell. Try naming cell D21 "SSX" and create the formulas using that name. Named cells are easier to use than absolute cell references, and the resulting formulas are easier to read (**Solution2A**).

EXPLORING HOW DIFFERENT DATA AFFECT THE MEASURES OF VARIATION   Learning Activity 2.2–7

- Open **Stdev3.xls!Data.** In columns F through J there are data values that represent different degrees of variation, and columns I and J show outliers.
- Copy/Paste cells F2:F19 into cells B2:B19. Since the copied cells have no variation, the SSX, variance, and standard deviation are all 0.
- Do the same thing with the data in columns G through J and note the effect on the SSX, variance, and standard deviation.
- Run MegaStat | Descriptive statistics.
  - Specify F1:K19 as the input range.
  - In addition to the default options, select Definitional form.
  - Examine the output and see how the measures differ for each of the variables.

GRAPHICAL INTERPRETATION OF THE STANDARD DEVIATION   Learning Activity 2.2–8

- Open **GraphicSD.xls!Data.** Note that columns A to C show SSX calculated by using the definitional form for six numbers. This example assumes that the numbers are a population.
  - Since SSX is made up of squared deviations, we can think of each squared deviation as a measure of area, that is, a square. The squared deviations are shown as squares that are the same color as the data values.
- Read the text boxes at the bottom from left to right.
- The end result is that the standard deviation is the size of each square when the squared deviations are averaged across all the data values. This shows that the "standard" in a standard deviation is a standard in the sense of typical or average.

Technical notes:

1. This is not a live display; that is, if you change the data values, the numbers will recalculate but the graphics will not change (maybe in the next edition).
2. The hidden columns B:M contain the calculations for the sizes of the squares and rectangles. Look at them only if you are curious. If you do look, note cell F10. Click the plus sign + above column N to show the hidden columns.

The example treated the data as a population to emphasize that a standard deviation is like an "average" deviation. To make it correspond to a sample version, the right-hand square would have been divided into five equal parts.

2.3   Sample MegaStat Output

Exhibit 2-8 and Exhibit 2-9 are outputs from the Descriptive Statistics option for the **variation.xls** file and the first three variables in the **RealEstate-Data.xls!Data** worksheet. In addition to the default options, it shows the output for the median and SSX. Remember that you can do what you want with the output. MegaStat attempts to make it look nice in terms of the number of decimal places and the column widths, but feel free to customize it. For example, you may want to see SSX but have no interest in the sum and the raw sum

EXHIBIT 2-8
MegaStat Descriptive Statistics output for variation.xls.

Descriptive statistics		
	Low	*High*
count	10	10
mean	100.00	100.00
sample standard deviation	2.62	61.90
sample variance	6.89	3,831.33
minimum	97	6
maximum	104	198
range	7	192
sum	1,000.00	1,000.00
sum of squares	100,062.00	134,482.00
deviation sum of squares (SSX)	62.00	34,482.00
mean absolute deviation (MAD)	2.20	49.60
1st quartile	98.25	60.50
median	99.00	100.00
3rd quartile	101.75	146.50
interquartile range	3.50	86.00
mode	99.00	86.00
low extremes	0	0
low outliers	0	0
high outliers	0	0
high extremes	0	0

EXHIBIT 2-9
MegaStat Descriptive Statistics output for RealEstateData .xls.

Descriptive statistics			
	Price	*LotSize*	*SqrFt*
count	124	124	124
mean	347.403	0.7284	3,154.53
sample standard deviation	74.129	0.4100	666.28
sample variance	5,495.071	0.1681	443,922.76
minimum	192.9	0.26	2080
maximum	511	2.18	4756
range	318.1	1.92	2676
sum	43,078.000	90.3200	391,162.00
sum of squares	15,641,329.880	86.4642	1,288,535,646.00
deviation sum of squares (SSX)	675,893.719	20.6763	54,602,498.87
1st quartile	288.975	0.4475	2,614.75
median	346.800	0.6050	3,132.50
3rd quartile	405.900	0.8475	3,636.75
interquartile range	116.925	0.4000	1,022.00
mode	#N/A	0.3000	2,156.00
low extremes	0	0	0
low outliers	0	0	0
high outliers	0	9	0
high extremes	0	2	0

of squares, and so you can delete those rows. Also remember that any part of the output can be copy/pasted into other applications.

Note how the measures of variation (sample standard deviation, sample variance, range, SSX, MAD, and interquartile range) are all larger for the high variable.

PRACTICE WITH DESCRIPTIVE STATISTICS (1)

Learning Activity **2.3–1**

- Open **Variation.xls!Data.**
- Use MegaStat | Descriptive Statistics to replicate Exhibit 2-8.
  - Specify B3:C13 as the input range.
  - In addition to the default options, select Median . . . and SSX.
- Note how the outputs are different for the two variables; in particular, the measures of variation are larger for the High variable.
- Replicate as many of the values as possible by using a calculator or using Excel as a calculator.
- Replicate as many of the values as possible by using Excel functions.
  - The worksheet has tabs for the solutions. Your output probably will not be formatted the same way, but the numbers should match.
- Open **RealEstateData.xls!Data.**
- Use MegaStat | Descriptive Statistics to replicate Exhibit 2-9.
  - Specify the Price, LotSize, and SqrFt variables (B2:D126) as the input range.
  - In addition to the default options, select Median and SSX.

PRACTICE WITH DESCRIPTIVE STATISTICS (2)

Learning Activity **2.3–2**

- Open **Income1.xls!Data.**
- Use MegaStat | Descriptive Statistics.
  - Specify the Income variable (B1:B95) as the input range. These data are the annual incomes for 94 families in a particular apartment complex.
  - In addition to the default options, select Median and Boxplot.
- What does the output tell you about the data? (See **Solution_descriptive.**)
- If you want more practice, do the manual calculations and Excel functions as in Learning Activity 2.3–1.

2.4 Other Descriptive Measures

The mean and the standard deviation are the primary ways of describing data by using a measure of central tendency and variation. However, the MegaStat Descriptive Statistics menu also has other items that sometimes are used for summarizing data.

Boxplot

A **boxplot** is a graphical means of summarizing data. Exhibit 2-10 shows a boxplot for the LotSize variable of **RealEstateData.xls.** Sometimes a boxplot is called a box and whisker plot. The ends of the box represent the first and

EXHIBIT 2-10
MegaStat
boxplot.

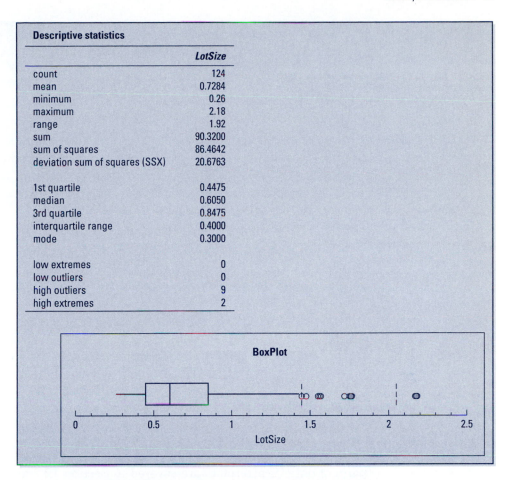

Descriptive statistics

	LotSize
count	124
mean	0.7284
minimum	0.26
maximum	2.18
range	1.92
sum	90.3200
sum of squares	86.4642
deviation sum of squares (SSX)	20.6763
1st quartile	0.4475
median	0.6050
3rd quartile	0.8475
interquartile range	0.4000
mode	0.3000
low extremes	0
low outliers	0
high outliers	9
high extremes	2

BoxPlot

LotSize

INTRODUCTION TO BOXPLOTS
Learning Activity **2.4–1**

- Open **RealEstateData.xls!Data.**
- Use MegaStat I Descriptive Statistics to replicate Exhibit 2-10.
  - Specify C2:C126 as the input range, the LotSize variable.
  - Select the options Median and Boxplot.
- Compare the output to Exhibit 2-10. Note how both show the data skewed to the right.

third quartiles, Q1 and Q3, and the line in the middle of the box is the median. The lines going to the left and right out of the box (the whiskers) show the maximum and minimum values, excluding any outliers. If there are outliers[3] or extreme outliers, the boundaries for those values are shown by vertical dashed lines called fences. The outliers are shown by markers on the boxplot. In this example, there are nine high outliers and two high extreme outliers. Since there are no low outliers, the lower fences are not shown.

[3]See Section 2.1 for a definition and discussion of outliers.

PRACTICE WITH BOXPLOTS   Learning Activity **2.4–2**

- Open **Variation.xls!Data.**
- Use MegaStat I Descriptive Statistics to replicate Exhibit 2-8 and also include the boxplot output.
  - ○ Specify B3:C13 as the input range.
  - ○ In addition to the default options, select Median . . . and BoxPlot.
- For the two boxplots to be comparable, they need to have the same scaling. Do this for each boxplot:
  - ○ Right-click the axis I select Format Axis from the menu I select Scale tab I type 0 for minimum and 200 for maximum.
- Open **Stdev3.xls!Data.**
- Run MegaStat I Descriptive statistics.
  - ○ Specify F1:K19 as the input range.
  - ○ In addition to the default options, select Median . . . and Boxplot.
  - ○ For each variable, compare the boxplot output with the definitional form output in the **Solution_1 worksheet.**

The fact that the right-hand part of the box is wider, the right-hand whisker is longer, and there are high outliers indicates that the data are skewed to the right; this will be confirmed by the frequency distribution discussed in Chapter 3 (Exhibit 3-7). If the distribution were symmetrical, the boxplot also would be symmetrical.

Scatterplot

A **scatterplot** is a way of looking at how two variables are related by plotting pairs of data. Scatterplots are covered in Section 12.2 as a preliminary to regression analysis, but they could be considered a descriptive statistics topic since a scatterplot shows (i.e., describes) the relationship of two variables.

Exhibit 2-11 shows a MegaStat scatterplot of the SqrFt and Price variables from the **RealEstateData.xls** dataset. As you would expect, larger houses tend to have higher prices.

EXHIBIT 2-11
Scatterplot showing the relationship between house size and price.

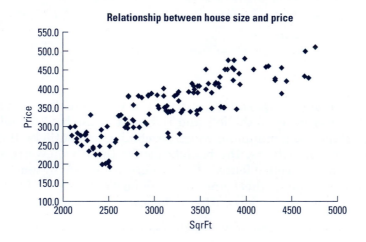

INTRODUCTION TO SCATTERPLOTS   Learning Activity **2.4–3**

- Open **RealEstateData.xls!Data.**
- Use MegaStat | Correlation/Regression | Scatterplot to replicate Exhibit 2-11. Use the SqrFt variable as the horizontal axis and the Price variable as the vertical axis. Uncheck the "Plot linear regression line" box. Put a title in the title box.
- Redo the previous step, checking the "Plot linear regression line" as a preview to Chapter 12. Don't worry about the details but see if you can get the gist of what we will be studying in Chapter 12.

PRACTICE WITH SCATTERPLOTS   Learning Activity **2.4–4**

- Open **RealEstateData.xls!Data.**
- Use MegaStat | Correlation/Regression | Scatterplot to look at some other scatterplots and see if the relationship is what you would expect. For example, do larger lot sizes have larger houses?

Stem and Leaf Plot

A stem and leaf plot describes data by counting the number of occurrences of different values. Exhibit 2-12 shows a MegaStat stem and leaf plot of the Price data in the **RealEstateData.xls** dataset.

Since the house prices are in thousands of dollars, the "stem" represents the major digit in the price. In other words, the stem of 1 represents houses in the $100,000 range, the stem of 2 represents houses in the $200,000 range, and so forth. A "leaf" is displayed for each occurrence of the next digit. For example, the use of the two 9 leaves for the 1 stem means there are houses priced 19x and 19x where x could be any digit.

EXHIBIT 2-12   MegaStat stem and leaf plot.

Descriptive statistics

	Price
count	124

Stem and Leaf plot for Price
stem unit = 100
leaf unit = 10

Frequency	Stem	Leaf
2	1	9 9
36	2	0 0 0 2 2 2 3 3 4 4 4 4 4 5 5 6 6 6 7 7 7 7 7 7 8 8 8 8 9 9 9 9 9 9
53	3	0 0 0 0 1 1 2 2 2 3 3 3 3 3 3 3 3 4 4 4 4 4 4 4 4 5 5 5 5 5 5 6 7 7 8 8 8 8 8 8 8 8 8 8 8 8 9 9 9 9 9 9
31	4	0 0 0 0 0 1 1 1 1 1 1 1 2 2 2 2 3 3 3 5 5 5 5 5 5 5 5 6 7 7 8
2	5	0 1
124		

INTRODUCTION TO STEM AND LEAF PLOTS

Learning Activity **2.4–5**

- Open **RealEstateData.xls!Data.**
- Use MegaStat | Descriptive Statistics to replicate the stem and leaf plot in Exhibit 2-12.
- Find the data values corresponding to the first two and last two leaves.
- Rerun the stem and leaf plot, checking the "Split stem" box. What does it do? Why would you use it?

Counting the number of occurrences of data is an important way to summarize data, and the stem and leaf plot is a method for doing this without a computer. However, with MegaStat it is preferable to do a frequency distribution. Chapter 3 is devoted to frequency distributions.

The remaining items on MegaStat's Descriptive Statistics menu are covered as they are encountered in later chapters.

Summary

In this chapter we started creating our statistical tool kit. Being able to summarize data descriptively is a primary means of extracting information from data. Summarizing data is useful, but it also provides the foundation for the decision-making techniques we will discuss in later chapters.

We also looked at graphical ways to summarize data. A boxplot is graphical representation of the median and quartiles using a box and whiskers, a scatterplot shows the relationship between two variables, and a stem and leaf plot is a quick way to look at the frequency of occurrence of data values—a rough version of a frequency distribution. Frequency distributions and histograms are the most important graphical representations of data; so important that they get their own chapter: Chapter 3.

Conceptual

- Measures of central tendency give one number that best describes the data:
  - Mode: the most frequently occurring value.
  - Median: the halfway point.
  - Mean: the "average." The sample mean is the most frequently used measure of central tendency.

$$\text{Sample mean} = \overline{X} = \frac{\sum (X_i)}{n} \qquad \textbf{Equation [2.1]}$$

- Measures of variation indicate whether the data values are close to each other or spread out. The most frequently used are the sample variance and sample standard deviation based on the sum of the squared deviations (SSX):

$$\text{Sample variance} = s^2 = \frac{\sum (X_i - \overline{X})^2}{n - 1} \qquad \textbf{Equation [2.6]}$$

$$\text{Sample standard deviation} = s = \sqrt{s^2} \qquad \textbf{Equation [2.10]}$$

Applied

- Be able to calculate a mean and a standard deviation by using the definitional form.
- Be able to interpret boxplots, scatterplots, and stem and leaf plots.

Exercises

The exercises and data are found in **Ch_02_ Descriptive_Statistics.xls** in the exercises folder of the CD.

No.	Content
1	Mode
2	Mode
3	Median
4	Median
5	Mean and stdev—defn method
6	Mean and stdev—defn method. Create your own data.
7	Compare two variables with range and boxplot
8	Compare two variables with range and boxplot
9	Use RealEstateData to review descriptive statistics

CHAPTER THREE

Frequency Distributions

3.1 Qualitative Frequency Distribution and Histogram (p. 34)

3.2 Quantitative Frequency Distribution and Histogram (p. 38)

Summary (p. 43)

Exercises (p. 44)

Modules for Chapter Three

3.A Custom Intervals: for situations in which intervals of equal width do not work well (p. 44)

3.B Capping the Top Interval: an option for certain types of data (p. 46)

3.C Estimating the Median and Quartiles from a Frequency Distribution (p. 48)

In this chapter we look at another tool for summarizing data: frequency distributions that show the "shape" of the data. A **frequency distribution** counts the number of occurrences of different data values and indicates the frequency of each; thus, it is called a frequency distribution. There are frequency distributions for qualitative data and quantitative data.

3.1   Qualitative Frequency Distribution and Histogram

If you wanted to count qualitative data, you would do a qualitative frequency distribution by counting the number of occurrences of each value. You also could do a qualitative frequency distribution if you wanted to count a small number of quantitative outcomes, for example, numbers of bedrooms or bathrooms. A frequency distribution usually is accompanied by a graphical representation called a **histogram.**

Exhibit 3-1 shows a qualitative frequency distribution for the number of houses in each subdivision in **RealEstateData.xls!Data.** How does MegaStat know which values to count? It uses a "specification range," that is, a range of cells that specify the values to be counted. See the *Getting Started with MegaStat* user's guide for details and an example.

Note 1: The output is labeled with the subdivision names because those names were included in the specification range.

Note 2: The space between the bars on the histogram indicates that this is a qualitative variable. Remember that all MegaStat charts can be

EXHIBIT 3-1
Qualitative frequency distribution and histogram.

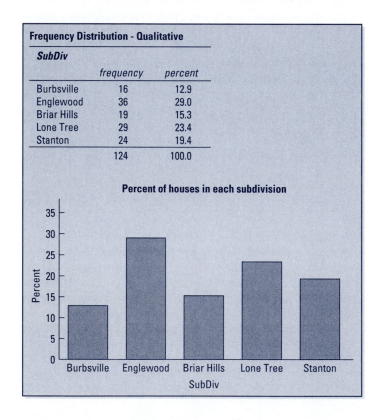

Frequency Distribution - Qualitative

SubDiv

	frequency	percent
Burbsville	16	12.9
Englewood	36	29.0
Briar Hills	19	15.3
Lone Tree	29	23.4
Stanton	24	19.4
	124	100.0

INTRODUCTION TO QUALITATIVE FREQUENCY DISTRIBUTIONS

Learning Activity **3.1–1**

- Open **RealEstateData.xls!Data.**
- Use MegaStat | Frequency Distributions | Qualitative to replicate Exhibit 3-1.
  ○ Specify K2:K126 as the input range.
  ○ Specify N5:O9 as the specification range.
- Change the title to "Percent of Houses in Each Subdivision."
- Practice modifying the chart. For example, right-click one of the histogram bars, | Format data series | Fill Effects, and select something creative.
- Rerun using N19:Q20 as the specification range. This counts subdivisions 2, 4, and 5 on the east side of town and subdivisions 1 and 3 on the west side.

PRACTICE WITH QUALITATIVE FREQUENCY DISTRIBUTIONS (1)

Learning Activity **3.1–2**

- Open **Region.xls!Data.** The State variable shows the location of the sales offices for a company.
- Use MegaStat | Frequency Distributions | Qualitative to count how many offices are in each state.
  ○ Specify B3:B220 as the input range.
  ○ Specify E5:E13 as the specification range.
- The left-hand column can contain a label for the row, but in this case the state names are self-identifying.
- *Further practice:* Type the full state name to the left of the abbreviation and rerun with those cells included in the specification range.
- Now assume the company wants to count how many offices are in each *region*. To do this, the specification range is set up as shown in cells E18:I20. Note that the left-hand cell has the name for the region; every state listed in the row is counted in the same region.
- Rerun using this specification range. Try "Repeat Last Option" on the MegaStat menu and then select E18:I20 as the specification range.

formatted to change any features, such as the color of the bars and the spacing of the bars.

Note 3: A descriptive title has been added. If you are going to include the output in any report, you should change the generic title "histogram" to something more meaningful. Someone should be able to look at a histogram and make sense of it without having you there to explain it.

TUTORIAL 3

What does this output tell us that we did not know before? If you were on the phone with a prospective client, you could say, "We have a good representation of houses in all the townships, but Englewood contains about a third of all of our listings." You most likely could not have made that statement just by looking at the raw data.

PRACTICE WITH QUALITATIVE FREQUENCY DISTRIBUTIONS (2)

Learning Activity **3.1–3**

- Open **Poll1.xls!Data.** A campus newspaper took a sample of 133 students. One of the questions asked was academic status: freshman, sophomore, junior, senior, MBA, Ph.D. These statuses were coded 1 through 6 and are shown in the status variable.
- Set up the specification range and do the frequency distribution to count the number of students at each level.
- Set up the specification range and do the frequency distribution to count undergraduates versus graduates.

How to Lie with Statistics

Although a histogram is a good way to view data graphically, it is also one of the most common means of manipulating data. MegaStat automatically scales the vertical axis to be slightly larger than the largest percentage. However, the scaling can be changed (Learning Activity 3.1–3 explains how to do this). For example, if a realtor wanted to emphasize that the number of homes in each subdivision was relatively evenly distributed, he or she could expand the vertical axis to 100%. The resulting histogram, which is shown in Exhibit 3-2, de-emphasizes the differences between the heights of the bars.

However, if the realtor wanted to make it appear that Englewood had a lot more houses than the other subdivisions, the scaling could be compressed; in other words, one could look at it with a magnifying glass. Exhibit 3-3 scales the vertical axis from 10 to 32%, making it appear that Englewood has several times more houses than does Burbsville.

Exhibit 3-2 and Exhibit 3-3 are graphical representations of the same frequency distribution, but they give very different impressions. This scaling "trick" also applies to the quantitative frequency distributions that are discussed in the next section and also can be applied to boxplots.

Whenever you see a histogram or any graphical display, look at the scaling.

EXHIBIT 3-2
Axis scaled to deemphasize differences.

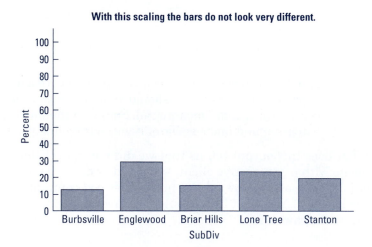

With this scaling the bars do not look very different.

EXHIBIT 3-3
Axis scaled to
emphasize
differences.

With this scaling Englewood appears to have a lot more houses.

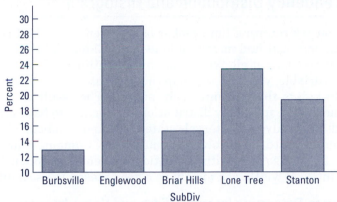

HOW TO LIE WITH STATISTICS (SCALING HISTOGRAMS)

Learning Activity **3.1–4**

- Use the output from Learning Activity 3.1–1 to replicate Exhibit 3-2 and Exhibit 3-3.
- You can rescale axes by
  - Right-clicking the vertical axis
  - Selecting Format Axis
  - Clicking the Scale tab and typing in the minimum and maximum values
    - Use 0 and 100 for Exhibit 3-2.
    - Use 10 and 32 for Exhibit 3-3.

PRACTICE WITH SCALING HISTOGRAMS

Learning Activity **3.1–5**

- Use the output from Learning Activity 3.1–2 to create histograms to deemphasize and emphasize the differences between the regions.
- Start by making two copies of the histogram:
  1. Right-click the original histogram and select Copy.
  2. Click in the cell below the histogram.
  3. Right-click Paste (you should now have two identical histograms).
- Scale the top histogram to deemphasize the differences and the bottom one to emphasize the differences.
- Look at the solution worksheet (**Solution_region_scaling**). Note that the histograms emphasize and deemphasize the differences even more by changing the aspect ratio of the histograms. See if you can replicate this with your output. (*Hint:* Click and drag the lower right corner.)
- If you want to be really manipulative, here is another trick:
  - Right-click one of the histogram bars and select Format Data Series.
  - Click the Options tab.
  - Make the gap width small on the "deemphasize" histogram and wider on the "emphasize" histogram.

3.2 Quantitative Frequency Distribution and Histogram

If you try counting the number of occurrences of the Price, LotSize, or SqrFt data, you will find mostly unique data values and thus will have not summarized the data at all. When you have quantitative data, usually from a continuous variable, you need to group the data into intervals and count the number of data points that fall into each interval. The result of this activity is called a quantitative frequency distribution. The goal is to have an appropriate interval width and have the intervals stated in round numbers. Getting the appropriate interval width can involve some judgment. Computers are great at calculations but are not so good with aesthetic judgments. Although MegaStat determines an interval width, you may have a good reason to use a different interval.

How to Determine Interval Width and Setup Intervals

The proper interval width for a quantitative frequency distribution is a round number that gives an appropriate number of intervals.

1. Calculate the range of the data.

   The range is the difference between the largest and smallest numbers. How do you find the range? One way is to examine the data visually to find the largest and smallest values. If you have access to Excel, you can sort the data or use the MAX( ) and MIN( ) functions, or you could use MegaStat's Descriptive Statistics option.

2. Determine an approximate number of intervals, k.

   What is a good value to use for the approximate number of intervals? There is no precise answer. It often turns out to be a number from 4 to 7, but it could be more or less. A good starting place is the 2^k rule based on the table in Exhibit 3-4.

   Find the value in the 2^k column that is closest to your sample size, and the approximate number of intervals will be k from the other column. For the **RealEstateData.xls,** the sample size is 124, which is closest to 128; therefore, we use k = 7.

   The 2^k rule is based on the idea that larger sample sizes can support more intervals, but it is a rough rule of thumb; it is a starting point, not a precise value.

   If you have a scientific or business calculator with an LN function, you can calculate k = LN(124)/LN(2) = 6.95, where 124 is the sample size.[1] The Excel function would be =LOG(124,2).

3. Divide the range by k.

   For the Price variable in **RealEstateData.xls,** you should verify that the range is 318.1. Dividing by k, we get 318.1/7 = 45.44.

4. The interval width is a round number near the value obtained in step 3.

   What is a round number? A general rule is that a round number is an even multiple of power of 10 times 1, 2, or 5.

   For our example, a round number near 45.44 would be 50. If you are using MegaStat, the number you determine at this step probably will be the same

2^k	k
16	4
32	5
64	6
128	7
256	8
512	9
1024	10

EXHIBIT 3-4
Values for the 2^k rule.

---

[1]This is really $\log_2(n)$, the base 2 log of the sample size, sometimes known as Sturge's rule.

number that MegaStat uses. It is easy to try different values with MegaStat and see which one looks best.

The important thing to remember is that having the roundest possible value for the interval width is more important than having any particular number of intervals. Although the 2^k rule looks like a precise calculation, it is really just a starting point; do not be afraid to deviate from it to get a nice round interval width.

5. **Set up the intervals.**

MegaStat sets up the intervals automatically, but you should be able to do them manually (e.g., on an examination). You start by determining the lower boundary of the first interval and then adding the interval width to it.

The lower boundary of the first interval usually should be a multiple of the interval width so that the interval includes the smallest number in the sample. In **RealEstateData.xls,** the smallest number is 192.9, and so the lower boundary of the first interval would be 100. The interval would be 100 to 200, which includes 192.9. The intervals formally would be $100 < 200$, $200 < 300$, and you would keep adding intervals until the upper boundary included the largest value.

The best way to learn about frequency distributions is to determine what intervals you think are best and then see if MegaStat agrees with you. It is also instructive to do frequency distributions with intervals that are too wide and too narrow. If the intervals are too narrow, the histogram looks uneven and there may be empty intervals; if the interval is too wide, the data are "over-summarized" and may not give much information.

Exhibit 3-5 shows a quantitative frequency distribution and histogram for the Price data in **RealEstateData.xls!Data.**

Notes Regarding Quantitative Frequency Distribution Output

- The "frequency" column is the actual frequency distribution. The frequencies also are shown as percents.
- Notice the $<$ symbol between the boundaries. For example, the first interval, $100 < 200$, reads "100 up to (but not including) 200." A house that cost exactly \$200,000 would be counted in the second interval. If you look at the cell on the MegaStat output that contains the 200, you will see it is really 199.999 rounded.
- The interval boundaries are multiples of the interval width.
- The midpoint of each interval is the mean of the upper and lower boundaries.
- The **cumulative frequency** is the number of observations in and below the interval. A plot of the cumulative percents is called an **ogive.**
- The interval boundaries (100, 200, etc.) are displayed at an angle on the MegaStat histogram horizontal axis to make them line up with the boundaries; Excel displays them in the middle.
- The vertical axis of the histogram is displayed in percent units to make it easier to compare to other histograms with different sample sizes.

TUTORIAL 4

EXHIBIT 3-5
Quantitative frequency distribution and histogram.

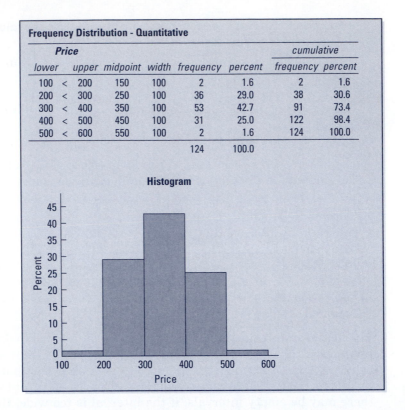

Frequency Distribution - Quantitative

Price						cumulative	
lower	upper	midpoint	width	frequency	percent	frequency	percent
100 <	200	150	100	2	1.6	2	1.6
200 <	300	250	100	36	29.0	38	30.6
300 <	400	350	100	53	42.7	91	73.4
400 <	500	450	100	31	25.0	122	98.4
500 <	600	550	100	2	1.6	124	100.0
				124	100.0		

Histogram

EXPLORING QUANTITATIVE FREQUENCY DISTRIBUTIONS

Learning Activity **3.2–1**

- Open **RealEstateData.xls!Data.**
- Use MegaStat I Frequency Distributions I Quantitative to replicate Exhibit 3-5.
  - Specify the Price variable (B2:B126) as the input range.
  - Type 100 as the interval width.
- Click on cell D6 of the Output sheet and note that the value is 199.999, not actually 200. Do the same thing for the other upper boundaries.
- Rerun, specifying 10 as the interval width. Note that this interval is too narrow and requires too many intervals and that the histogram has a ragged appearance.
- Rerun, specifying 250 as the interval width. This causes 90% of the observations to fall in one interval; thus, 250 is too wide.

Notes Regarding Exhibit 3-5

- Since most of the observations fall in three intervals, you could make the case that the interval width of 100 is too wide; in fact, MegaStat initially chose a width of 50. However, 100 is a very round number, and people often think of houses in units of a hundred thousand dollars ("How many $200,000 houses do you have?"). This emphasizes that there is an element of judgment and that there may be more than one valid way to summarize data.

- This output has the generic title "histogram." If you use this output in a report, you should change that to a more descriptive title.

Quantitative frequency distributions also can be displayed graphically with a frequency polygon that is a smoothed version of a histogram. A frequency polygon is what you get if you put a dot at the top-middle of each histogram bar and then connect the dots. A plot of the cumulative percentages is called an ogive.

Output Example Including a Frequency Polygon and Ogive

Exhibit 3-6 shows the MegaStat output for a quantitative frequency distribution for the Price variable of **RealEstateData.xls,** using the autoestimation option for interval width. If you replicate this output with MegaStat

EXHIBIT 3-6 **Quantitative frequency distribution output.**

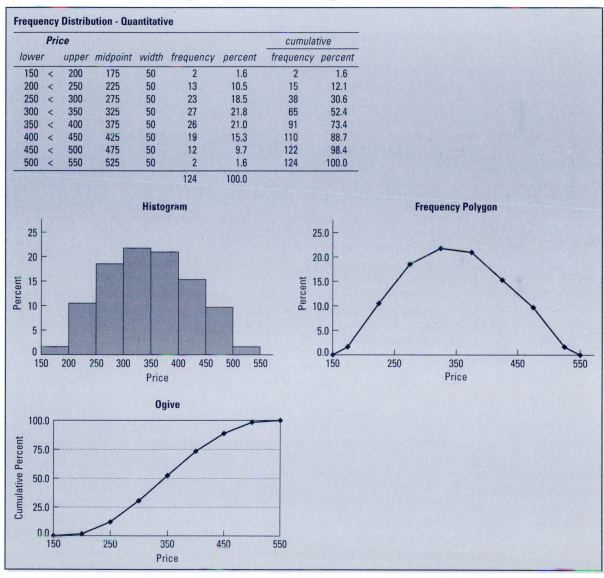

Frequency Distribution - Quantitative

Price						cumulative	
lower	upper	midpoint	width	frequency	percent	frequency	percent
150 <	200	175	50	2	1.6	2	1.6
200 <	250	225	50	13	10.5	15	12.1
250 <	300	275	50	23	18.5	38	30.6
300 <	350	325	50	27	21.8	65	52.4
350 <	400	375	50	26	21.0	91	73.4
400 <	450	425	50	19	15.3	110	88.7
450 <	500	475	50	12	9.7	122	98.4
500 <	550	525	50	2	1.6	124	100.0
				124	100.0		

PRACTICE WITH QUANTITATIVE FREQUENCY DISTRIBUTIONS (1)

Learning Activity **3.2–2**

- Open **RealEstateData.xls!Data.**
- Use MegaStat to do a quantitative frequency distribution on the LotSize, SqrFt, and Distance variables.
  - First determine the interval width and the lower boundary of the first interval by using the methods described in Section 3.2.
  - Next run the frequency distributions, letting MegaStat determine the intervals.
  - Compare your intervals with MegaStat's. If yours are different, do not necessarily assume that MegaStat's are better. See if you could defend your intervals.
- Rerun the distributions, specifying intervals that are too wide and too narrow, and note the effect.

PRACTICE WITH QUANTITATIVE FREQUENCY DISTRIBUTIONS (2)

Learning Activity **3.2–3**

Repeat the procedures below until you are comfortable with setting up frequency distributions, but do at least one of each type of distribution: uniform, normal, and exponential.

- Open a new Excel workbook.
- Use MegaStat | Generate Random Numbers to create a sample of random numbers.
  - Number of values: at least 30, up to several hundred.
  - Decimal places: whatever.
  - Use fixed values.
  - Select a distribution and specify the required inputs.

If you need more help with generating random numbers, see Module 7.A.

- Determine an appropriate interval width and set up the intervals.
- Use MegaStat | Frequency Distributions | Quantitative on the data (specify Histogram, Polygon, and Ogive).
  - Initially, let MegaStat do autoestimation for the intervals and see if the output agrees with yours. If necessary, force MegaStat to use your interval width.
  - If necessary, use custom intervals.

(recommended), you will find that the output is arranged in a slightly different manner. To fit more on a page, the output in the text may be rearranged and resized.

Compare this output with Exhibit 3-5, which uses an interval width of 100. Both interval widths are acceptable, depending on how much detail you want to have.

If you take a histogram, put a dot at the top-middle of each bar, and connect the dots, you will get a frequency polygon. This is a way to get a graphical display that reflects the fact that the data are from a continuous variable.

PRACTICE WITH QUANTITATIVE FREQUENCY DISTRIBUTION GRAPHICS

Learning Activity **3.2–4**

- Open **RealEstateData.xls!Data.**
- Use MegaStat | Frequency Distributions | Quantitative to replicate Exhibit 3-6.
  - Specify the Price variable (B2:B126) as the input range.
  - Type 50 as the interval width, or leave the field blank and MegaStat will determine 50 as the interval width.
  - Check the option boxes for Histogram, Polygon, and Ogive.
- Examine the graphical output and determine which values from the frequency distribution are being used for the graphic.
- Right-click the line on the Frequency Polygon | Format Data Series | Smoothed Line.
  - This shows how you can format the chart to make a smooth, curved line for the polygon.

The ogive plots the cumulative percents. It can be used to estimate quartiles, as shown in Module 3.C.

Module 3.A discusses ways to set up custom intervals if intervals of equal width are not adequate to handle your data, Module 3.B shows how capping the top interval is useful for certain types of data, and Module 3.C shows ways to estimate the median from a frequency distribution. Refer to these modules as needed or as required by your instructor.

Summary

In this chapter we discussed one of the most important tools of descriptive statistics: the frequency distribution. A frequency distribution counts the number of occurrences of data by counting individual occurrences (qualitative) or ranges of values (quantitative). The graphical representation of the frequencies shows the shape of the distribution.

If a sample consists of more than a few numbers, it is always useful to do a frequency distribution in addition to the descriptive measures discussed in Chapter 2.

Conceptual

- The concept of a frequency distribution and histogram
- Qualitative: counts individual occurrences
- Quantitative: counts occurrences of numbers in intervals
- Graphical representation of a frequency distribution
- Histogram: vertical bars corresponding to the frequencies
- Polygon: a smoothed version of a histogram
- Ogive: a plot of the cumulative frequencies

Applied

- Be able to set up the intervals for a quantitative frequency distribution.
- The appropriate interval width will produce a smooth histogram. The chapter shows how to start, but it may take a little "tweaking" to make the

histogram look good. It is important to use round numbers for the interval width and boundaries.

- If the interval width is too wide, most of the data will fall into one or two intervals; if the interval width is too narrow, there will be too many intervals, the histogram will be ragged, and there will be empty intervals.

Exercises

The exercises and data are found in **Ch_03_Frequency_Dist.xls** in the exercises folder of the CD.

No.	Content
1	Qualitative frequency distribution
2	Qualitative frequency distribution
3	Quantitative frequency distribution
4	Quantitative frequency distribution
5	Quantitative frequency distribution
6	Quantitative frequency distribution
7	Quantitative frequency distribution
8	Use RealEstateData to calculate frequency distributions

Modules for Frequency Distributions

3.A CUSTOM INTERVALS

When you are doing a frequency distribution, it is best to make each interval the same width, but occasionally there will be situations in which you need unequal interval widths. For example, if you do a frequency distribution on the LotSize variable in **RealEstateData.xls**, you will get the output shown in Exhibit 3-7.

Since there are only a few lots larger than 1 acre, you might want to combine all the lots that are 1 acre and larger in one interval. MegaStat does this with the Custom Intervals option. This option has you specify a bin range, which is a range of cells that contain the lower boundary for each interval except that the last cell contains the *upper* boundary for the last interval. The upper boundary would be a number larger than the largest data value. In this example, 3 was chosen to give an interval width of 2, which is a nice round number. The bin range is shown in Exhibit 3-8, and the resulting frequency distribution is shown in Exhibit 3-9.

Look at the width column and note that the last interval has a width of 2.

EXHIBIT 3-7
Frequency distribution for LotSize.

Frequency Distribution - Quantitative

LotSize						*cumulative*	
lower	*upper*	*midpoint*	*width*	*frequency*	*percent*	*frequency*	*percent*
0.20 < 0.40		0.30	0.20	23	18.5	23	18.5
0.40 < 0.60		0.50	0.20	38	30.6	61	49.2
0.60 < 0.80		0.70	0.20	28	22.6	89	71.8
0.80 < 1.00		0.90	0.20	11	8.9	100	80.6
1.00 < 1.20		1.10	0.20	7	5.6	107	86.3
1.20 < 1.40		1.30	0.20	3	2.4	110	88.7
1.40 < 1.60		1.50	0.20	9	7.3	119	96.0
1.60 < 1.80		1.70	0.20	3	2.4	122	98.4
1.80 < 2.00		1.90	0.20	0	0.0	122	98.4
2.00 < 2.20		2.10	0.20	2	1.6	124	100.0
				124	100.0		

Notice skew to the right

0.2
0.4
0.6
0.8
1.0
3.0

EXHIBIT 3-8
Bin range for custom intervals.

EXHIBIT 3-9
Frequency distribution showing custom intervals.

Frequency Distribution - Quantitative

LotSize						*cumulative*	
lower	*upper*	*midpoint*	*width*	*frequency*	*percent*	*frequency*	*percent*
0.20 < 0.40		0.30	0.20	23	18.5	23	18.5
0.40 < 0.60		0.50	0.20	38	30.6	61	49.2
0.60 < 0.80		0.70	0.20	28	22.6	89	71.8
0.80 < 1.00		0.90	0.20	11	8.9	100	80.6
1.00 < 3.00		2.00	2.00	24	19.4	124	100.0
				124	100.0		

Right interval (1 < 3) for lots larger than one acre.

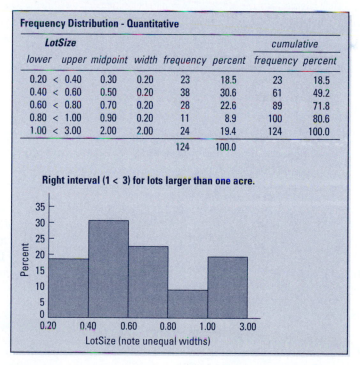

INTRODUCTION TO CUSTOM INTERVALS

- Open **RealEstateData.xls!Data.**
- Use MegaStat | Frequency Distributions | Quantitative to replicate Exhibit 3-7.
  - Specify C2:C126 as the input range, the LotSize variable.
  - Leave the Interval Width field blank, and MegaStat will determine .2 as the interval width.
- In the six blank cells type in the bin range shown in Exhibit 3-8.
- Select MegaStat | Repeat Last Option.
  - Click the Custom Intervals tab and select the six cells with the bin range.
- The output should look like Exhibit 3-9.
  - Note the values in the Width column.
- Run it again and also select the Polygon output.
  - Note that the polygon shows the wider interval but the histogram does not.

PRACTICE WITH CUSTOM INTERVALS

- Open **Income1.xls!Data.** This file contains a sample of the incomes of 94 families that live in an apartment complex.
- Use MegaStat | Frequency Distributions | Quantitative to do a frequency distribution. Leave the Interval Width field empty to let MegaStat determine the interval width.
- Note that a few large incomes cause the distribution to be skewed to the right.
- Determine appropriate custom intervals and use MegaStat to generate the frequency distribution and histogram.
  - The **Solution_frequencies** worksheet shows one possible solution.
  - Review the **Solution_descriptive** worksheet from Learning Activity 2.3–2. Compare the two and particularly note how the boxplot corresponds to the first frequency distribution.

3.B   CAPPING THE TOP INTERVAL

Exhibit 3-10 shows the frequency distribution of grade point averages for the freshman class of business students at a midwestern university (**GPAdata. xls**). In examining it, we see an anomaly. The upper interval of $4.00 < 4.50$ implies that there could be grade points higher than 4.0.

Why does this happen? It happens because the next to last interval, which looks like $3.50 < 4.00$, is actually $3.50 < 3.9999$, and so MegaStat has to open a new interval to include the four students who had a grade point average of 4.00. On the Options tab of the Quantitative Frequency Distributions dialog box there is a checkbox for "Close top interval." When you check it, the frequency distribution is as shown in Exhibit 3-11.

Note that the four students with perfect 4.00 grade points are included in the $3.5 \leq 4.0$ interval. Also note that the last interval has $\leq$ rather than $<$.

Closing the top interval can be useful in situations such as percentage data when there are values of 100%.

EXHIBIT 3-10
Frequency distribution of grade point averages.

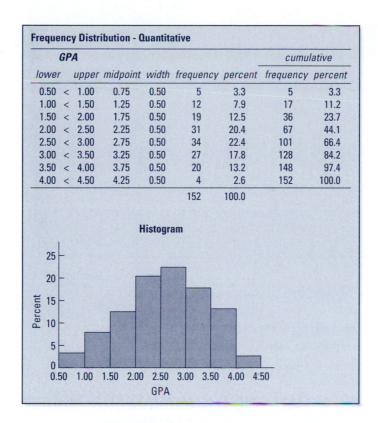

Frequency Distribution - Quantitative

GPA			midpoint	width	frequency	percent	cumulative	
lower		upper					frequency	percent
0.50	<	1.00	0.75	0.50	5	3.3	5	3.3
1.00	<	1.50	1.25	0.50	12	7.9	17	11.2
1.50	<	2.00	1.75	0.50	19	12.5	36	23.7
2.00	<	2.50	2.25	0.50	31	20.4	67	44.1
2.50	<	3.00	2.75	0.50	34	22.4	101	66.4
3.00	<	3.50	3.25	0.50	27	17.8	128	84.2
3.50	<	4.00	3.75	0.50	20	13.2	148	97.4
4.00	<	4.50	4.25	0.50	4	2.6	152	100.0
					152	100.0		

EXHIBIT 3-11
Frequency distribution with top interval capped.

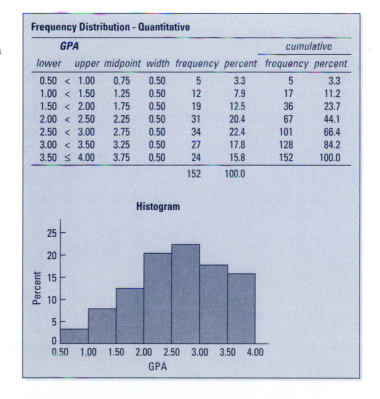

Frequency Distribution - Quantitative

GPA			midpoint	width	frequency	percent	cumulative	
lower		upper					frequency	percent
0.50	<	1.00	0.75	0.50	5	3.3	5	3.3
1.00	<	1.50	1.25	0.50	12	7.9	17	11.2
1.50	<	2.00	1.75	0.50	19	12.5	36	23.7
2.00	<	2.50	2.25	0.50	31	20.4	67	44.1
2.50	<	3.00	2.75	0.50	34	22.4	101	66.4
3.00	<	3.50	3.25	0.50	27	17.8	128	84.2
3.50	≤	4.00	3.75	0.50	24	15.8	152	100.0
					152	100.0		

INTRODUCTION TO CAPPED INTERVALS

Learning Activity **3.B–1**

- Open **GPAdata.xls!Data.**
- Use MegaStat | Frequency Distributions | Quantitative to replicate Exhibit 3-10.
- Use the MegaStat | Repeat Last Option | Options tab | Close top interval to replicate Exhibit 3-11.

PRACTICE WITH CAPPED INTERVALS

Learning Activity **3.B–2**

- Open **ExamScores.xls!Data.**
- Use MegaStat | Frequency Distributions | Quantitative to do a frequency distribution.
  ◦ Use an interval width of 10.
  ◦ Note that the upper interval implies percents greater than 100%.
- Rerun, selecting the "Close top interval" option.

3.C   ESTIMATING THE MEDIAN AND QUARTILES FROM A FREQUENCY DISTRIBUTION

Interpolated Median

Sometimes you need to estimate the median (or a quartile) from a frequency distribution. This is done by first determining which interval contains the median and then determining the proportion of the interval needed to get up to the halfway point. This sometimes is called the **interpolated median** or estimated median.

The method for calculating the interpolated median is shown in Equation [3.1]:

$$\text{Interpolated median} = L + w \left[\frac{\frac{1}{2}n - CF}{f} \right] \qquad \textbf{[3.1]}$$

Where:

L = lower limit of the interval containing the median

w = width of interval

n = total sample size

CF = cumulative frequency below the median interval

f = frequency of the median interval

At first glance this looks like a pretty imposing equation; however, it is expressing a very simple notion. By working through the example below, you should be able to understand what the equation does. If you are just trying to find numbers and substitute them ("plug and chug"), you do not understand the concept. Indeed, one of the main benefits of working with this equation is that you will become more familiar with the median and frequency distributions.

EXHIBIT 3-12
Frequency distribution annotated to show values used for the interpolated median.

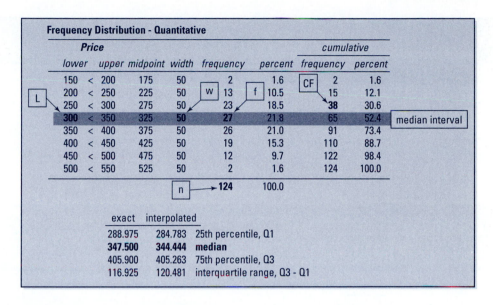

Exhibit 3-12 shows the frequency distribution for the Price variable of the **RealEstateData.xls** dataset, showing the values needed for Equation [3.1]. Since there are n = 124 numbers, the halfway point is 1/2*124 = 62. Looking at the frequency distribution, we see that the cumulative frequency for the fourth interval is 65 and the cumulative frequency for the third interval is 38; thus, the 62nd value would be somewhere in the fourth interval of 300 to 350. The lower limit of the median interval is L = 300, the cumulative frequency of the interval below the median interval is CF = 38, the frequency of the median interval is f = 27, and the interval width is w = 50. Substituting these values into Equation [3.1], we get

$$344.444 = 300 + 50 \left[\frac{\frac{1}{2}124 - 38}{27} \right] = 300 + 50 \left[\frac{24}{27} \right]$$

The ratio 24/27 = (62 − 38)/27 is the proportion of the interval width of 50 we need to add to 300 to get up to the halfway point.

MegaStat's Quantitative Frequency Distribution program has an option to calculate the interpolated median as well as the median from the actual data. You may wonder why you would want to calculate the interpolated median when you can get the actual median. One answer would be to verify your hand calculations. Although you rarely need to calculate an interpolated median, being able to do that calculation helps you understand the values in a frequency distribution.

By changing the 1/2 in the formula to 1/4 or 3/4, you also could calculate the interpolated quartiles. You also could estimate quintiles (5 divisions), deciles (10 divisions), or any other "ile" by using the appropriate value.

The exact median is the median as it is defined in Section 2.1, that is, the middle number or the average of the middle two numbers; it is calculated with Excel's MEDIAN() function. The exact median and the interpolated median rarely will be identical, but they should be pretty close. The interpolated

INTERPOLATED MEDIAN   Learning Activity **3.C–1**

- Open **RealEstateData.xls!Data.**
- Use MegaStat | Frequency Distributions | Quantitative on the Price variable to replicate Exhibit 3-6. Select Options | Interpolated Median and Quartiles.
- Use a calculator and/or Excel to replicate the calculation in Module 3.C. Your answer should match that of MegaStat.

PRACTICE WITH THE
INTERPOLATED MEDIAN   Learning Activity **3.C–2**

- Open **ExamScores.xls!Data.**
- Use MegaStat | Frequency Distributions | Quantitative to do a frequency distribution on the Score variable. Select Options | Interpolated Median and Quartiles.
- Calculate the interpolated median and quartiles with a calculator and/or Excel. Your answer should match that of MegaStat.
- For further practice, rerun any of the frequency distributions from this chapter. Select the option for an interpolated median and calculate the same value manually with Excel or a calculator.

EXHIBIT 3-13
An ogive with a vertical line estimating the median.

median depends on the values chosen for the interval width and interval boundaries and thus will change if you rerun the frequency distribution with a different interval width or starting value.

Estimating the Median from an Ogive

A plot of the cumulative percentages of a frequency distribution is called an ogive. If you draw a vertical line to the horizontal axis from the place where the 50% line intersects the ogive, it will intersect the horizontal axis at the interpolated median, as shown in Exhibit 3-13. The line intersects between the

ESTIMATING THE MEDIAN FROM AN OGIVE

- Open **RealEstateData.xls!Data.**
- Use MegaStat | Frequency Distributions | Quantitative on the Price variable to replicate Exhibit 3-13.
  - Use an interval width of 100.
  - Specify Ogive.
  - Use Options | Interpolated median and quartiles.
- Draw the vertical line to estimate the median.
  - You can draw the line with a rule or use Excel's drawing tools.
    - If you use Excel to draw a line or arrow, holding the shift key while drawing will give a perfectly vertical line.
- The median you estimate should be close to the value for the interpolated median.
- Draw lines to estimate the first and third quartiles.
- For further practice, use MegaStat to calculate the ogive for other data; use the interpolated median to check your answers.

340 and 350 tick marks, which corresponds to the interpolated median of 344.444 calculated in the previous section. The closest you could estimate graphically would be around 345. Note that the horizontal axis was rescaled to minor units of 10 to make it easier to read the value.

If you drop lines from the 25% and 75% points, you will estimate the first and third quartiles. To estimate quintiles or deciles, you would get the MegaStat output and right-click one of the gridlines and then format the gridlines to make the major unit 20 for quintiles or 10 for deciles.

CHAPTER FOUR

Probability Concepts

4.1 Introduction (p. 54)

4.2 Probability Terms and Definitions (p. 54)

4.3 Probability Concepts (p. 56)

   Summary (p. 60)

   Exercises (p. 60)

Modules for Chapter Four

4.A Probability versus Odds (p. 61)

4.B Counting Rules (p. 62)

4.1 Introduction

Probability concepts are the mathematical foundation of statistics. A basic understanding of probability is necessary for the study of statistics, but probability and statistics are different topics: A statistics course is not an advanced probability course.

If you ask people the definition of probability, they usually say it is the "likelihood of occurrence." Although this is correct in a general sense, in the study of probability and statistics, the term probability has a more precise definition:

Probability ≡ a number between 0 and 1 that measures likelihood

In other words, probability is not likelihood; it is a number that measures likelihood.

When talking about probability, people often refer to the odds of something happening, saying, for example, that "the odds are 3 to 1 that the Bulldogs will win the game Saturday." Probability and odds are two ways of stating the same thing, but statistics almost always uses probability terminology. Module 4.A discusses the relationship between odds and probability and explains how to convert from one expression to the other.

4.2 Probability Terms and Definitions

Experiment ≡ a process that leads to a well-defined outcome.

In probability courses experiments often are discussed in terms of simple **experiments** such as die tossing or drawing cards; in the real world events are more often assessments or measurements. For example, taking an examination or completing a questionnaire could be considered an experiment.

Outcome ≡ the result of an experiment.

Observing the number of dots on a die would be an **outcome.** A score for an examination also would be an outcome.

Event ≡ one or more outcomes.

An outcome is an **event,** but multiple outcomes also can qualify as an event. For example, if we defined an event as an even number of dots, a 2, 4, or 6 outcome would qualify for the even number event. If an examination score of 94 is needed for an A grade, any examination outcome with that score or higher would qualify for the event "grade of A."

Sample space ≡ a list of all possible events.

The **sample space** for tossing a die would be the numbers 1, 2, 3, 4, 5, 6; the sample space for tossing a coin would be heads and tails.

Mutually exclusive ≡ only one event can occur at a time.

The number of dots on each side of a die is **mutually exclusive;** one cannot simultaneously observe a 1 and a 3.

Collectively exhaustive ≡ includes all possible events.

The outcomes 1, 2, 3, 4, 5, and 6 are **collectively exhaustive** for the die toss experiment. The sum of probabilities for collectively exhaustive events is 1.

Complement ≡ all the events in sample space not included in any particular event.

The symbol ~ is used for the **complement,** and it reads "not." If the letter "A" refers to a particular event, say, an even number of dots when tossing a die, ~A (pronounced as "not A" or "A not") refers to the event of an odd number of dots.

Complementary events are, by definition, mutually exclusive and collectively exhaustive. In other words: $P(A) + P(\sim A) = 1$, which means that the probability of a complement is 1 minus the probability of the other event:

$$P(\sim A) = 1 - P(A)$$
$$\text{and} \quad P(A) = 1 - P(\sim A)$$

Assessing Probability

Since a probability is a number, how do we determine this number? It depends on the probability definition we are using.

Classical probability: the number of outcomes that qualify for any event relative to the number of possible outcomes.

For example, the probability of observing an even number when you toss a die is 3/6 since there are three ways of observing an even number out of the sample space of six possible outcomes.

The calculation of **classical probabilities** often involves counting rules (factorials, permutations, combinations), as discussed in Module 4.B.

Relative frequency probability: the number of times something has occurred relative to the total number of possible occurrences in the sample space.

In other words, any proportion or percentage could be thought of as a probability. If a news report says that 42% of small businesses fail during their first year, it means that in a given area the ratio of failures to start-ups is .42 P (failure during first year) = 84/200, which could be stated as .42.

Since relative frequency probabilities are based on observation, a different sample probably will give a different probability. In other words, **relative frequency probabilities** are estimates of the true population probability. The more observations you have, the closer the observed proportion will be to the true value; this is known as the "law of large numbers."

In a business environment the relative frequency method is the most common way to determine quantitative probabilities.

Subjective probability: probability assessment based on the degree of belief that an event will occur.

For example, if you are interviewing for a job, you think there is a "pretty good chance" you will get it. You probably would not say to your friend, "I think the probability I will get the job is .68," but there is still some number between 0 and 1 that represents the probability at any point in time. Thus, **subjective probability** does not negate the notion that a probability is a number.

Although subjective probabilities are not calculated and rarely are stated as precise numbers, you should not think they are just hunches or random guesses. A lot of research, knowledge, and thought can be involved in a subjective probability. The term *subjective* implies an emotional component. Perhaps a better term would be *nonnumeric or experiential probability*.

Most of the major decisions that affect people's lives are based on subjective probability: Personal, business, government, and sports decisions usually are based on subjective probabilities, and people make subjective probability assessments many times every day. For example, when you drive, you constantly make subjective probability estimates about the behavior of other drivers.

4.3 Probability Concepts

Basic probability terms and concepts are easy to illustrate by using a contingency table. A contingency table (sometimes called a joint frequency table) shows the joint occurrences of events. Assume that a market research company has a contract with an automobile manufacturer to determine whether marital status is related to the type of automobile a person owns. In probability terms, there are two "experiments." The first experiment is to ask what type of vehicle a person drives and classify the response as sport vehicle or nonsport vehicle; the second experiment is to ask the same person if he or she is married. The events represented by the rows and columns sometimes are called factors. In this example the factor represented by the rows is "Type of Vehicle"; the column factor is "Marital Status."

Let's assume the researchers asked 120 randomly selected people these two questions and got the contingency table results shown in Exhibit 4-1 (**Prob1.xls**). Here are some notes on this table:

- This is called a 2 by 2 table since there are two rows and two columns. These tables are very common, but a contingency table can have larger numbers of rows and columns, and the probability concepts would apply to larger tables.
- The events are labeled A and B. This will help you associate this table with the general probability expressions that use the letters A and B. The equations are stated in terms of A and B, but you could substitute ~A and ~B.
- Probabilities based on a contingency table usually are based on a sample and are thus relative frequency probabilities. In the business world, this is the most common way to determine numeric probabilities.

EXHIBIT 4-1
Contingency table showing type of vehicle and marital status.

		Marital Status		
		Married B	Not married ~B	
Type of vehicle	Sport vehicle A	14	27	41
	Non sport vehicle ~A	43	36	79
		57	63	120

EXHIBIT 4-2
Notation for marginal and intersection probability.

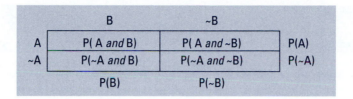

	B	~B	
A	P(A *and* B)	P(A *and* ~B)	P(A)
~A	P(~A *and* B)	P(~A *and* ~B)	P(~A)
	P(B)	P(~B)	

Let's use this table to examine probability terminology and concepts.

Marginal probability ≡ P(A)   also P(B), P(~A), P(~B)

This is the probability of an event occurring by itself without considering other events. In other words, a **marginal probability** is a probability calculated from the margins of the table. For example, the probability of being married would be a marginal probability, and it would be stated

$$P(\text{Married}) = P(B) = \frac{57}{120}$$

Intersection probability ≡ P(A *and* B)

This is the probability of two events occurring simultaneously.[1]

For example, the probability of owning a sports vehicle and being married would be an **intersection probability** and would be written P(A *and* B) = $\frac{14}{120}$. Intersection probabilities also can be calculated by using the multiplication rule shown in Equation [4.3].

Complementary events would not have any intersection since an event cannot simultaneously occur and not occur. In other words, P(A *and* ~A) = 0.

The notation for marginal and intersection probability for a 2 by 2 contingency table is shown in Exhibit 4-2.

Union probability ≡ P(A *or* B)

This is the probability of observing either or both of two events.

For example, the probability of owning a sports vehicle or being married (or both) would be a **union probability** and would be stated as P(A *or* B). It is tempting to add the number of people who own a sports vehicle to the number who are married, but if we did that, the intersection cell of 14 would be counted twice. Thus, the correct calculation is

$$P(A \text{ } or \text{ } B) = \frac{41 + 57 - 14}{120}$$

A more formal statement of union probability in probability terms is

$$P(A \text{ } or \text{ } B) = P(A) + P(B) - P(A \text{ } and \text{ } B) \qquad \textbf{[4.1]}$$

Conditional probability ≡ P(A | B)

This is a probability based on knowing that another event has occurred.

For example, the probability of owning a sports vehicle if a person is married would be a **conditional probability** and would be stated as P(A | B). The vertical bar | always reads "given" in probability notation.

---

[1]Some books use the symbols ∩ and ∪ for intersection and union; this book will use italicized *and* and *or*.

- Open **Prob1.xls!LA4.3-1**. It is always a good idea to make a copy of a worksheet before working with it.
- Use Excel or a calculator to determine the values in the shaded cells. The green cells correspond to values calculated in the text. You may put actual numbers or Excel formulas in the cells.
- The display in cell H31 will let you know when all your answers are correct.
- Check your answers in **Prob1.xls!Solution4.3-1**.
- *More practice:* Change the value in the upper left cell (14) to another value and redo the calculations. If you change the same cells in the **Solution4.3-1** worksheet, the solution values will be recalculated.

For our example, $P(A \mid B) = \frac{14}{57}$, meaning that 14 of the 57 married respondents own sports vehicles.

Conditional probabilities can be calculated by looking at the appropriate cells in a contingency table, but they also can be calculated from a more general equation:

$$P(A \mid B) = \frac{P(A \text{ and } B)}{P(B)} \quad \text{or} \quad P(B \mid A) = \frac{P(A \text{ and } B)}{P(A)} \quad \textbf{[4.2]}$$

Solving for the intersection probabilities in Equation [4.2] leads to the **multiplication rule** for intersection probabilities:

$$P(A \text{ and } B) = P(A) \cdot P(B \mid A) = P(B) \cdot P(A \mid B) \quad \textbf{[4.3]}$$

Statistical Independence

A special case of the multiplication rule leads to the most important concept in this chapter: the definition of **statistical independence.** Two events are said to be statistically independent if and only if the following equation is true:

$$P(A \text{ and } B) = P(A) \cdot P(B) \quad \textbf{[4.4]}$$

Since the statement of statistical independence is a special case of the multiplication rule, Equations [4.4] and [4.3] will be equal under the condition of independence:

$$P(A) \cdot P(B) = P(B) \cdot P(A \mid B)$$

If we cancel out the $P(B)$, on each side we are left with:

$$P(A) \cdot P(B) = P(B) \cdot P(A \mid B)$$

$$P(A) = P(A \mid B)$$

In others words, the probability of A is the same as the probability of A given B. This implies that A and B are independent because knowing that B has occurred does not change the probability of A occurring.

To see if two factors are independent, you can pick any cell from a contingency table and see if $P(A \text{ and } B) = P(A) \cdot P(B)$. For example, in the example above, we ask if $P(A \text{ and } B)$ equals $P(A) \cdot P(B)$. It turns out that $\frac{14}{120} \neq \frac{41}{120} \cdot \frac{57}{120}$. The decimal values are 0.1167 and 0.1623, which are not equal (verify these values with a calculator or Excel), and so type of car and marital status are not

EXPLORING STATISTICAL INDEPENDENCE

Learning Activity 4.3–2

- Open **Prob1.xls!LA4.3-2.**
- Use Excel or a calculator to determine the values in the shaded cells. The green cells correspond to the value calculated in the text.
- Check your answers in **Prob1.xls!Solution4.3-2.**
- Verify, by checking at least two cells, that A and B are independent in the following table.

	B	~B	
A	50	25	75
~A	30	15	45
	80	40	120

- Show P(A) = P(A|B).
- Show P(B) = P(B|A).
- Show P(~B) = P(~B|A).
- Try at least one more combination of A, B, ~A, and ~B.

EXPECTED FREQUENCIES WITH INDEPENDENCE

Learning Activity 4.3–3

- Open **Prob1.xls!LA4.3-3.**
- Use Excel or a calculator to determine the values in the shaded cells by multiplying the total sample size (120) by the probabilities expected under the assumption of independence (the bolded values in the table).
- Check your answers in **Prob1.xls!Solution4.3-3.**

MORE PRACTICE WITH PROBABILITY

Learning Activity 4.3–4

TUTORIAL 5

- Open **Prob1a.xls!Data.**
- Use Excel or a calculator to repeat Learning Activities 4.3–1, 4.3–2, and 4.3–3. Note that you can change the shaded values in **Prob1a.xls!Data** to create a new problem set and the solution pages will update.
- Check your answers with the solutions worksheets.

independent. However, since the values are fairly close, maybe they differ only because of sampling error.[2] If we took another sample of 120, maybe they would be closer. In Chapter 14 we examine a more powerful tool for studying statistical independence.

[2]Sampling error means sampling variation; in other words, every sample will be different. It does not mean error in the sense of making a mistake or doing something wrong.

Note that the previous paragraph said "not independent" rather than "dependent." Dependence could imply that one factor causes the other factor. Even if it is shown that a married person is much less likely to own a sports car, we cannot say that marital status causes a particular buying decision.

Summary

Probability is the mathematical foundation of statistics, and so you need to understand basic probability concepts. We started by emphasizing that a probability is not the likelihood of occurrence; it is a *number* between 0 and 1 that measures the likelihood of occurrence. We then looked at ways to determine this number.

This chapter took the approach of looking at probability from the perspective of a contingency table because that is an easy way to illustrate probability concepts and statistical independence. Later, in Chapter 14, when we have more tools at our disposal, we will take another look at contingency tables and independence.

Conceptual

- Probability as a number between 0 and 1 that measures the likelihood of occurrence.
- Methods of assessing probability:
  - Classical probability: counting occurrences in a sample space.
  - Relative frequency probability: treating a proportion as a probability.
  - Subjective probability: based on experience, not calculation.
- Basic probability terms and concepts (using the model of a contingency table):
  - Marginal probability, P(A), probability of any row; P(B), probability of any column.
  - Intersection probability, P(A *and* B), probability of any cell.
  - Union probability, P(A *or* B), probability of any row or column.
  - Conditional probability, P(A | B), probability of any cell given any row or column.
- Statistical independence: Two factors are independent if and only if the intersection probability equals the product of the marginal probabilities for any cell.

$$P(A \text{ } and \text{ } B) = P(A) \cdot P(B) \qquad \text{Equation [4.4]}$$

Applied

- For a contingency table, be able to
  - Calculate marginal, intersection, union, and conditional probabilities
  - Determine if the factors representing the rows and columns are statistically independent

Exercises

The exercises and data are found in **Ch_04_ Probability_Concepts.xls** in the exercises folder of the CD.

No.	Content
1	Probabilty concepts
2	Probabilty concepts
3	Probabilty concepts
4	Probabilty concepts
5	Probabilty concepts
6	Independence
7	Independence
8	Odds vs. probabilty
9	Odds vs. probabilty
10	Counting rules
11	Counting rules
12	Counting rules
13	Counting rules

Modules for Probability Concepts

4.A PROBABILITY VERSUS ODDS

In a nonstatistical context probability often is stated in terms of **odds.** For example, assume you have four blocks, one of which is shaded:

If you randomly selected a block, the odds would be 1 to 3 that it would be shaded since there are one shaded block and three white blocks. Sometimes the odds are written 1:3 instead of 1 to 3. In probability terms, the probability that a randomly selected block would be shaded is 1/4 since there is one shaded block out of four possible outcomes.

If a person says, "The odds are 1 in 4," he or she is using the term *odds* incorrectly; "1 in 4" and "1 out of 4" are probability statements.

How do you convert from one method to the other? If the odds are stated as A to B, the corresponding probability will be

$$P = \frac{A}{A + B}$$ [4.5]

For this example, A = 1 and B = 3, and so $P = \frac{1}{1+3} = \frac{1}{4}$.

If you wanted to convert a probability to odds, you would use the following relationship:

$$P \text{ to } (1 - P)$$ [4.6]

ODDS VERSUS PROBABILITY   Learning Activity **4.A–1**

- Open **Odds_vs._Prob.xls!**
- Enter 1 and 3 in cells A4 and C4 to replicate the text calculation.
- If a horse has 1 to 20 odds of winning a race, what is the probability? (Odds usually are stated as 20 to 1, but that would be the odds of *losing* the race.)

Solution:

$$P = \frac{1}{20+1} = .0476$$

This is the probability of the horse winning the race.

- Enter 1 and 20 in cells A4 and C4 to verify the solution.
- Look at the cell formulas and verify that they correspond to the text equations.
- What would the odds have to be for the probability to be p = .05?

Solution: The odds would be .05 to (1 − .05) or .05 to .95. Dividing both sides by .05, you get the odds as 1 to 19 in integer values. Verify, using the worksheet, by entering .95 in cell A13.

- *Excel exploration:* Look at the cell formulas in cell A13 and C13 to see how the odds are converted to one value equaling 1.

For this example, P = 1/4, and so the odds would be 1/4 to (1 − 1/4) or 1/4 to 3/4. By dividing both sides by the smaller value, we have the odds stated with one of the values being 1. For this example, if we divide both sides by 1/4, we get 1 to 3 odds. Odds usually are stated as integer numbers, often with one of the numbers being 1.

4.B   COUNTING RULES

In working with probability and probability distributions, you occasionally need to count the number of possible occurrences of events.

Fundamental Rule of Multiplication

Assume a statistics professor is getting dressed to go to campus. He has 16 shirts, 11 pairs of pants, and 8 pairs of shoes. How many different ways could he get dressed? The answer would be $(16)(11)(8) = 1408$. A more formal statement of the **fundamental rule** is shown in Equation [4.7]:

$$(k_1)(k_2)\ldots(k_n) \qquad \textbf{[4.7]}$$

where k_i is the number of possible outcomes for each trial and n is the number of trials.

For the example above, n = three trials and $k_1 = 16$, $k_2 = 11$, and $k_3 = 8$.

All the counting rules shown below are applications of the fundamental rule.

Special Case of the Fundamental Rule

If the number of outcomes is the same for each trial, the fundamental rule becomes

$$k^n \qquad \textbf{[4.8]}$$

If a password is made up of six characters and each character can be an uppercase or lowercase letter or a digit, how many passwords would be possible? n = 6, k = 62 (26 uppercase + 26 lowercase + 10 digits). Thus, $62^6 =$ 56,800,235,584.

Factorial

Assume there are six people and six chairs in a room. How many ways can the chairs be filled? There are six ways the first chair can be filled, five ways for the second, and so on, until there are only one person and one chair left. Applying the fundamental rule, we get

$$(6)(5)(4)(3)(2)(1) = 720$$

The product of all the integers from n down to 1 is called n **factorial** and is written

$$n! \qquad\qquad\qquad \text{[4.9]}$$

Equation [4.9] is formally called the number of permutations of n things taken n at a time.

Permutations

What happens in the example above if we have six people but only four chairs? Applying the fundamental rule, we get

$$(6)(5)(4)(3) = 360$$

The formal equation for the number of **permutations** of n things taken r at a time is

$$_nP_r = \frac{n!}{(n-r)!} \qquad\qquad\qquad \text{[4.10]}$$

For the example, n = 6 people and r = 4 chairs:

$$\frac{6!}{2!} = \frac{(6)(5)(4)(3)\cancel{(2)(1)}}{\cancel{(2)(1)}} = (6)(5)(4)(3) = 360$$

If r = n, Equation [4.10] is the same as Equation [4.9]. In other words, n! is the number of permutations of n things taken n at a time.

Combinations

If we don't care about how the four people are arranged in the chairs but only want to know how many ways we can select four people out of six, we divide the number of permutations by 4 factorial:

$$\frac{360}{4!} = \frac{360}{24} = 15$$

The formal equation for the number of **combinations** of n things taken r at a time is

$$_nC_r = \frac{_nP_r}{r!} = \frac{n!/(n-r)!}{r!} = \frac{n!}{r!(n-r)!} \qquad\qquad\qquad \text{[4.11]}$$

- *Computational note:* Factorials become very large numbers as n increases. The factorial 69! is the largest factorial most calculators can handle; 170! is the largest Excel can handle with the FACT() function. MegaStat can calculate factorials of 1000000! and larger.

REPLICATE TEXT COMPUTATION FOR COUNTING RULES
Learning Activity **4.B–1**

- Open a blank Excel workbook and calculate the values in the text by using the Excel functions FACT(), PERMUT(), and COMBIN().
- Calculate the same values by using MegaStat | Probability | Counting Rules.

PRACTICE WITH COUNTING RULES
Learning Activity **4.B–2**

- Calculate the following probabilities by using a calculator, Excel functions, and MegaStat:
  - If a new shopping center has seven store locations, how many arrangements of new businesses locate there? *Solution:* $7! = 5040$.
  - If seven businesses want to locate in a new shopping center but there are only five locations, how many arrangements could there be? *Solution:* $7 * 6 * 5 * 4 * 3 =$ the number of permutations of 7 things taken 5 at a time $= 7!/(7 − 5)! = 7!/2! = 2520$.
  - If seven businesses want to locate in a new shopping center but there are only five locations, how many different combinations of 5 could be selected? Solution: the number of combinations of 7 things taken 5 at a time $= 7!/((7 − 5)! * 5!) = 7!/(2! * 5!) = 21$.
- Try more calculations with other values. You can be fairly certain you have the right answer if your Excel calculations match those of MegaStat.

CHAPTER FIVE

Discrete Probability Distributions

5.1 Discrete Probability Distributions and Expected Value (p. 66)

5.2 Binomial Distribution (p. 68)

5.3 Using the Computer Output for the Binomial Distribution (p. 71)

5.4 Hypergeometric Distribution (p. 73)

5.5 Poisson Distribution (p. 75)

Summary (p. 77)

Exercises (p. 77)

Module for Chapter Five

5.A Discrete Distribution Simulation (p. 78)

This chapter extends probability concepts for use in calculating probabilities for events defined by a discrete variable. We saw in Chapter 1 that a discrete variable is defined by specific, discrete numerical values that in turn can be associated with discrete events. If we match each numerical value with a probability, we have a discrete probability distribution.

5.1   Discrete Probability Distributions and Expected Value

Let's start by looking at an insurance policy. Assume an insurance company sells a $10,000 one-year life policy for $250. This means that a person pays the insurance company $250, and if that person dies during the year, the insurance company pays the designated beneficiary $10,000. There are two discrete events—lives and dies—but to have a probability distribution, we need to assign numerical values to each outcome. If we look at it from the perspective of the insurance company, it makes $250 for each person who is alive at the end of the year and loses $9750 for each person who dies (pays out $10,000 − $250 premium). Let X represent the gain to the insurance company, and it is called a discrete random variable or, more formally:

> **random variable** ≡ a variable that by chance assumes numerical values based on the outcome of an experiment

If the experiment has discrete outcomes, the random variable is a *discrete* **random variable.** If the random variable could assume any of an infinite number of values along a continuous scale, it is called a *continuous* **random variable.**

In this example, the experiment is observing whether a person dies during the term of the policy. Obviously, this experiment has two discrete outcomes.

Next we need the probabilities for each of the outcomes. Later in this chapter we will see distributions where we can calculate the probabilities, but here the insurance company is using the relative frequency method of assessing probability. It determines the proportion of people in this category who died in the past. This sort of information is called a mortality table. Let's assume that the probability of dying is .02, which implies that the probability of being alive at the end of the year is .98.

Putting this together, we have the **discrete probability distribution** shown in Exhibit 5-1 (**Prob2.xls**):

EXHIBIT 5-1
Discrete probability distribution.

Event	X	P(X)
Lives	250	0.98
Dies	−9750	0.02
		1.00

Here we see the elements of any discrete probability distribution:

1. There is a discrete random variable.
2. Each value of the random variable is paired with a probability.
3. The probabilities sum to 1.

Note that rows are labeled "lives" and "dies," but these are not part of the probability distribution. If we had only the labels paired with probabilities, it would not be a probability distribution. There must be numeric values of a discrete random variable.

For any discrete probability distribution, we can calculate how much profit the insurance company should "average" for every policy it sells. This amount is called the mean or **expected value** of the distribution and is calculated as follows:

$$\mu = E(X) = \sum (X \cdot P(X)) \qquad \text{[5.1]}$$

For the example above the expected value would be $50 = 250^*.98 + (-9750)^*.02$. This means that if the insurance company sells a large number of policies, it should expect to average $50 per policy. Module 5.A shows an Excel simulation that illustrates the concept of expected value.

If we calculate the expected value of the squared deviations, we have the **variance** of the probability distribution, as shown in Equation [5.2]. The standard deviation, as always, is the square root of the variance:

$$\sigma^2 = E((X - \mu)^2) = \sum ((X - \mu)^2 \cdot P(X))$$
$$\sigma = \sqrt{\sigma^2} \qquad \text{[5.2]}$$

Three Discrete Probability Distributions

The example above is an empirical distribution because the probabilities are not calculated; they are observed relative frequencies. Discussed below are three discrete probability distributions that calculate the probability of a random variable representing the number of occurrences of an event.

REPLICATE TEXT DISCRETE DISTRIBUTION
Learning Activity **5.1–1**

- Use a calculator to calculate the expected value and variance for the distribution in the text.
- Open **Prob2.xls!Discrete** and calculate the expected value and variance by using Excel as a calculator (there are no Excel functions).
- See **Prob2.xlS!Solution1** for the solution.

EXPLORING EXPECTED VALUE
Learning Activity **5.1–2**

- If the insurance company sold 1000 policies and 2% of the policyholders died, 980 would live and 20 would die. If that happened, how much would the company average per policy? Try to figure it out with a calculator or by using Excel as a calculator.
- **Prob2.xls!Solution2** contains the solution.
- What has to happen for the calculation to be valid?
  Answer: Exactly 2% of the policyholders would have to die, and that is unlikely to happen.

Although the equations for these distributions are shown, our focus is not on calculating the probabilities since MegaStat is good at that. Instead, our focus is on determining when to use the distribution and interpreting the computer output. The computer output for all three distributions is similar, and Section 5.3 discusses how to use that output.

5.2   Binomial Distribution

The **binomial distribution** calculates the probability of X occurrences out of n trials when P is the probability of an occurrence on any given trial. For example, what is the probability of observing two heads if you toss six coins? There are two input values or parameters, n and p. For the example in Exhibit 5-2, n = 6 trials and p = .5.

The binomial distribution is the most important discrete distribution. The other two distributions (the hypergeometric and the Poisson) are actually special cases of the binomial, and the normal curve discussed in Chapter 6 is the continuous form of the binomial distribution. The formula for the binomial distribution is shown in Equation [5.3]:

$$P(X \mid n, p) = (_nC_X)p^X(1 - P)^{n-X} \qquad \textbf{[5.3]}$$

EXHIBIT 5-2
Binomial distribution for n = 6, p = 1/2.

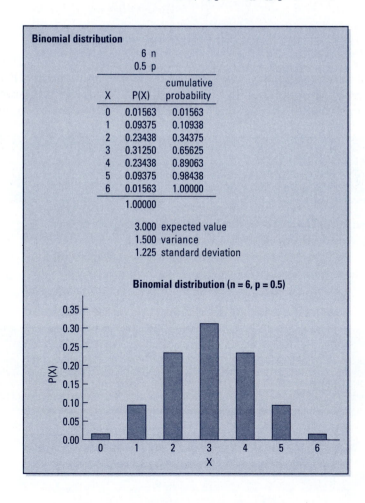

Where:

X = number of occurrences (X can range from 0 to n)

n = number of trials

p = probability of an occurrence on any trial

$_nC_X = \dfrac{n!}{X!(n - X)!}$ = number of combinations of X occurrences in n trials

The vertical bar after the X reads "given," and the values after the bar are the parameters of the distribution. The other discrete distributions also will have this form: the probability of X occurrences given certain parameters.

The formula is rather imposing; however, it is given here mainly to show that it exists. We let MegaStat do the calculations for us and focus on interpreting the output.

The expected value and the variance of the binomial distribution are shown in Equations (5.4) and (5.5):

$$\mu = np \qquad\qquad\qquad \textbf{[5.4]}$$

$$\sigma^2 = np(1 - p) \qquad\qquad \textbf{[5.5]}$$

Note that the expected value and the variance of the binomial distribution (and the hypergeometric and Poisson) also can be calculated by using Equations (5.1) and (5.2).

When Would You Use the Binomial Distribution?

The binomial distribution is used to calculate the probability of X occurrences when there are n trials each with a probability p of an occurrence on each trial.

Example 1

What is the probability of observing two heads if a coin is tossed six times?

n = 6; each toss is a trial.

p = 1/2, assuming it is an unbiased coin.

X = 2; 2 was chosen for this example; X could have been any value from 0 to 6. To calculate the entire distribution, you would have to calculate the probabilities for all the values of X.

The distribution is shown in Exhibit 5-2, and the probability of exactly two heads is .23438.

Example 2

What is the probability of a salesperson making four or more sales out of five sales calls if the probability of a sale on any call is .25?

n = 5; each sales call is a trial.

p = .25.

X = 4 and 5; X could have been any value from 0 to 5. To calculate the entire distribution, you would have to calculate the probabilities for all the values of X.

REPLICATE BINOMIAL DISTRIBUTION TEXT VALUES

Learning Activity **5.2–1**

TUTORIAL 6

- Open **Binomial.xls!Sheet1** and use MegaStat | Probability | Discrete Probability Distributions | Binomial. Use n = 6, p = 1/2 to replicate Exhibit 5-2.
- Experiment with running some other binomial distributions with other values of n and p (see **Binomial.xls! Solution1**).

PRACTICE WITH BINOMIAL DISTRIBUTION: REPLICATE EXAMPLE 2

Learning Activity **5.2–2**

- Open **Binomial.xls!Sheet1** and run MegaStat | Probability | Discrete Probability Distributions | Binomial. Use n = 5, p = 1/4.
- What is the probability of four or five sales (see **Binomial.xls!Solution2**)?

PRACTICE WITH EXPECTED VALUE OF BINOMIAL DISTRIBUTION

Learning Activity **5.2–3**

- Open **Binomial.xls!Sheet1** and run MegaStat | Probability | Discrete Probability Distributions | Binomial. Use n = 20, p = 1/4.
- The expected value of the distribution is np = (20)(1/4) = 5. Find this value on the output.
- Now calculate the expected value by using the expected value (Equation [5.1]). Do this by putting formulas in column E to multiply X by P(X) for each value of X. Sum the values. The result should equal 5.00000. Isn't it amazing how 21 fractional values can sum to a perfect integer? (The solution is shown in **Binomial.xls!Expected_value_solution**.)

Assumptions of the Binomial Distribution

- p is accurate and constant; that is, we have to know the probability of an occurrence on each trial, and it cannot change.
- The trials are independent. The outcome of a given trial is not dependent on prior trials and does not affect subsequent trials.

For the coin toss example, both of these assumptions are valid: The probability is always 1/2, and any toss is not influenced by the previous tosses and does not affect any subsequent outcomes.

These assumptions are less valid for the sales call example. Since each situation is different, the probability on any given trial will be different from the overall probability of 1/4. The independence assumption is also likely to be invalid. For example, if the salesperson had not made a sale on the first four sales calls of the day, he or she might try extra hard on the last one or just give up; in either case, the last trial would be influenced by the previous trials.

EXHIBIT 5-3
Binomial distribution output.

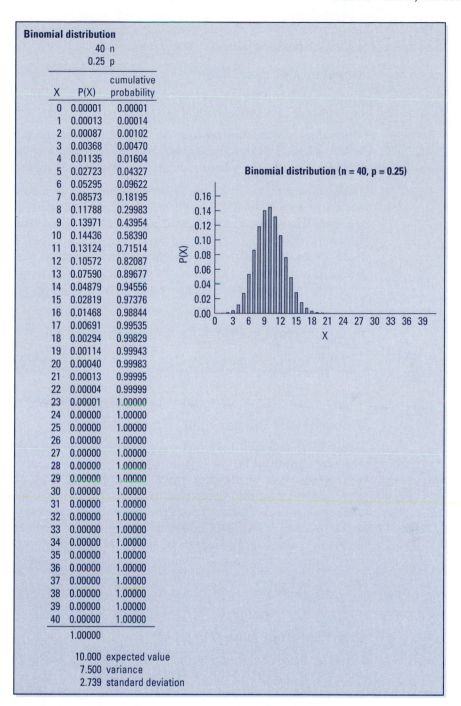

Binomial distribution

| | 40 | n |
| | 0.25 | p |

X	P(X)	cumulative probability
0	0.00001	0.00001
1	0.00013	0.00014
2	0.00087	0.00102
3	0.00368	0.00470
4	0.01135	0.01604
5	0.02723	0.04327
6	0.05295	0.09622
7	0.08573	0.18195
8	0.11788	0.29983
9	0.13971	0.43954
10	0.14436	0.58390
11	0.13124	0.71514
12	0.10572	0.82087
13	0.07590	0.89677
14	0.04879	0.94556
15	0.02819	0.97376
16	0.01468	0.98844
17	0.00691	0.99535
18	0.00294	0.99829
19	0.00114	0.99943
20	0.00040	0.99983
21	0.00013	0.99995
22	0.00004	0.99999
23	0.00001	1.00000
24	0.00000	1.00000
25	0.00000	1.00000
26	0.00000	1.00000
27	0.00000	1.00000
28	0.00000	1.00000
29	0.00000	1.00000
30	0.00000	1.00000
31	0.00000	1.00000
32	0.00000	1.00000
33	0.00000	1.00000
34	0.00000	1.00000
35	0.00000	1.00000
36	0.00000	1.00000
37	0.00000	1.00000
38	0.00000	1.00000
39	0.00000	1.00000
40	0.00000	1.00000
	1.00000	

10.000	expected value
7.500	variance
2.739	standard deviation

Binomial distribution (n = 40, p = 0.25)

5.3   Using the Computer Output for the Binomial Distribution

Discrete probability distributions are easy to calculate by using MegaStat |
Probability | Discrete Probability Distributions. Exhibit 5-3 shows the output for a
binomial distribution (**DiscreteDist.xls**) for someone who is guessing on a mul-
tiple-choice examination with 40 questions and four choices for each question
(n = 40, p = 1/4). Although this example uses the binomial distribution, the

outputs for the hypergeometric and Poisson distributions have the same format; in fact, without the label, you could not tell which distribution created the output.

Probability for Exact Value

The probability for any exact number of occurrences is read from the P(X) column. For example, the probability of getting exactly 10 answers correct is 0.14436.

The values are formatted to 5 decimal places on the output; however, if you look at the cell in the worksheet, you can see the value calculated to 15 digits. You may change the output formatting if you want more or fewer digits.

The values for 24 and higher show a probability of zero; however, the value is not truly zero, as you can see if you look at the exact cell values in the worksheet. Actually, the probability of getting all 40 correct by guessing is not zero. It is 8.27180612553022E-25; however, this is a number very close to zero. The E-25 at the end means to move the decimal point 25 places to the left, and so the actual number would have 24 leading zeros. The probability of getting all 40 correct by guessing would be equivalent to that for winning a state lottery over a trillion times.

Probability for Less Than (Cumulative Probability)

The probability for X or less correct is shown in the cumulative probability column. It is the sum of all the probabilities from 0 through X.

The probability of getting 12 or fewer answers correct is 0.82087.

Probability for Greater Than

What is the probability of eight *or more* correct answers? You could get the answer by summing $P(8) + P(9) + P(10) + \cdots P(40)$. If you were doing this from the output, you would stop when the probabilities reached zero, but still it would involve summing several five-digit numbers, which is time-consuming and error-prone. The faster way is to realize that the probability of eight or more correct answers is equal to 1 minus the probability of seven correct answers or less, and you can get that probability from the cumulative probability column. Thus the probability of 8 or more = $1 - 0.18195 = 0.81805$.

The general rule would be

$$P(X \text{ or more}) = 1 - \text{cumulative probability of } (X - 1)$$

Probability for Range of Values

What is the probability of 6 through 12 correct answers? You could sum $P(6) + P(7) + P(8) + P(9) + P(10) + P(11) + P(12)$. Using the worksheet, it would be easy to sum the cells, but you would not want to do it with a calculator.

If you experiment with the worksheet, you will see that the probability for the range is the cumulative probability of 12 minus the cumulative probability of 5. The probability of 6 through 12 correct answers would be $0.82087 - 0.04327 = 0.77759$.

The general rule would be

$$P(X1 \text{ through } X2, \text{ inclusive}) = \text{cumulative probability}(X2)$$
$$- \text{cumulative probability}(X1 - 1)$$

5.4   Hypergeometric Distribution

The **hypergeometric distribution** is used to calculate the probability of X occurrences in trials when you are sampling without replacement from a finite (and usually small) population.

The equation for the hypergeometric distribution involves combinations (Module 4.B) that in turn involve factorials. With a large population, the factorials become extremely large, and in years past the hypergeometric distribution often was approximated by other distributions. However, Excel and MegaStat can handle very large factorials, and the hypergeometric distribution probabilities now can be calculated accurately.

The formula for the hypergeometric distribution is shown in Equation [5.6]:

$$P(X \mid N, n, S) = \frac{({}_sC_x)({}_{N-s}C_{n-x})}{{}_NC_n}$$ [5.6]

Where:

X = number of occurrences (X can range from 0 to n, assuming S > n; otherwise the maximum value for X would be S)

N = population size

S = possible number of occurrences in the population

n = sample size

The C in the equation is the notation for the number of combinations as calculated from Equation [4.11]. The size of the factorials for any nontrivial problem can become very large, but, again, we are going to let the computer take care of the computations.

The expected value and the variance of the hypergeometric distribution are shown in Equations [5.7] and [5.8]. If you substitute p = S/N, these equations are very similar to the corresponding equations for the binomial distribution:

$$\mu = n\left(\frac{S}{N}\right)$$ [5.7]

$$\sigma^2 = n\left(\frac{S}{N}\right)\left(1 - \frac{S}{N}\right)\left(\frac{N-n}{N-1}\right)$$ [5.8]

When Would You Use the Hypergeometric Distribution?

The hypergeometric distribution is used to calculate the probability of X occurrences in n trials, just as in the binomial distribution. The difference is that the hypergeometric distribution assumes that you are sampling without replacement from a finite population. We see the effect of this in the first example below.

Example 1

Assume that a department with 12 people has four women employees. If a committee of three is chosen at random, what is the probability that the committee will have two women?

- N = 12, the size of the department.
- S = 4, the number of women employees.
- n = 3, the sample size, in this case the committee size.
- X = 2 for this example. X could be any value from 0 to 3.

In selecting the first person for the committee, the probability that it would be woman is 4/12; the probability that the second person would be a woman is either 3/11 or 4/11, depending on the first selection; and the probability that the third person would be a woman is 2, 3, or 4 out of 10, depending on the earlier selections. The probabilities change on subsequent trials because once a person is selected for the committee, that person no longer is eligible to be selected again. This is called sampling without replacement.

Example 2

A shipment of 1000 items contains 5% defectives. What is the probability that a sample of 10 will have one or more defectives?

- N = 1000, the number of items.
- S = 50, 5% of 1000.
- n = 10, the sample size.
- X = 1 through 10. To find the probabilities of one or more shipments, you would calculate and sum $P(1)$ through $P(10)$. A faster and easier way would be $1 - P(0)$ (See Section 5.3).

Once an item is selected for the sample, it is no longer available to be selected again. However, the sample size is so small relative to the population that sampling without replacement does not have much of an effect on the computations.

Assumptions of the Hypergeometric Distribution

- Sampling without replacement from a finite population. If the sample size is not at least 5% of the population, the binomial distribution with p = S/N will give almost the same answer. In the past this would have been important since older books included binomial tables. However, since MegaStat can handle large factorials, you may as well use the hypergeometric distribution when it is appropriate.
- True random sampling. Every object should have the same probability of being sampled. This means that in the second example you should not just open the door of the truck and take the first 10 items for the sample.

REPLICATE HYPERGEOMETRIC DISTRIBUTION TEXT VALUES

Learning Activity 5.4–1

- Open **Hypergeometric.xls!Sheet1** and run MegaStat I Probability I Discrete Probability Distributions I Hypergeometric. Use N = 12, S = 4, n = 3. Find the probability of X = 2 (see **Hypergeometric.xls!Solution1**).
- Open **Hypergeometric.xls!Sheet1** and run MegaStat I Probability I Discrete Probability Distributions I Hypergeometric. Use N = 1000, S = 50, n = 10. Find the probability of X = 1 or more by summing the probabilities of 1 through 10. Verify that you get the same answer by 1 − P(0) (see **Hypergeometric.xls!Solution2**).
- Experiment with running some other hypergeometric distributions with other values of N, S, and n.

5.5   Poisson Distribution

The Poisson distribution calculates the probability of X occurrences when there is a mean rate of occurrence. Usually the mean rate of occurrence is over time, but it could be another unit, such as area or distance. For example, what is the probability of 2 or more customers arriving at a bank teller's station in 1 minute if the mean arrival rate is 2.3 per minute? Thus, the Poisson distribution has only one parameter, μ, the mean rate of occurrence (for this example, $\mu = 2.3$).

The formula for the Poisson distribution is shown in Equation [5.9]:

$$P(X \mid \mu) = \frac{e^{-\mu}\mu^{X}}{X!} \qquad [5.9]$$

Where:

X = the number of occurrences (X starts at 0. There is no fixed upper limit for X; theoretically, X could approach infinity, but since the equation involves dividing by X!, the probabilities approach zero with fairly small values of X.) Also, in real-world situations there may be limits on how many occurrences actually could take place.

μ = mean rate of occurrence, usually over time.

e = mathematical constant 2.71828. . . .

The expected value Poisson distribution is the mean rate of occurrence, μ. The variance of the Poisson distribution is also μ.

When Would You Use the Poisson Distribution?

The **Poisson distribution** is used to calculate the probability of X occurrences over a period of time when there is a known mean rate of occurrence (μ). The Poisson distribution usually is used for low-frequency occurrences.

Assumptions of the Poisson Distribution

- The mean rate of occurrence must be accurate and constant. For the bank teller example, the overall rate of 2.3 per minute probably would be different for different times of the day.

Example 1

A teller's station in a bank has a mean arrival rate of 2.3 customers per minute. What is the probability of 2 or more arrivals for any given minute?

μ is 2.3.

You would sum the probabilities for $X = 2$ and larger until the probabilities approached zero. There also would be some physical limitation on how many people actually could get into the bank in 1 minute. Since this would require a large number of computations and since the upper limit of X is indefinite, it would be better to calculate $1 - P(0) - P(1)$. In other words, the probability of 2 or more is equal to 1 minus the probability of 1 or less.

Example 2

If an author averages .34 typographical error per page on a draft manuscript, what is the probability that a given page will have 1 or fewer errors?

μ is .34 (Usually μ would be over time; here it is per page.)

You would add the probabilities for $X = 0$ and $X = 1$.

REPLICATE POISSON DISTRIBUTION TEXT VALUES
Learning Activity 5.5–1

- Open **Poisson.xls!Sheet1** and run MegaStat I Probability I Discrete Probability Distributions I Poisson. Use $\mu = 2.3$. Find the probability of $X = 2$ or more (see **Poisson.xls!Solution1**).
- Open **Poisson.xls!Sheet1** and run MegaStat I Probability I Discrete Probability Distributions I Poisson. Use $\mu = .34$. Find the probability of $X = 1$ or less (see **Poisson.xls!Solution2**).
- Experiment with running some other Poisson distributions with other values of μ.

COMPARING THE BINOMIAL, HYPERGEOMETRIC, AND POISSON DISTRIBUTIONS
Learning Activity 5.5–2

- Open **Comparison.xls!Sheet1** and use MegaStat I Probability I Discrete Probability Distributions to run the following three distributions:
  - Binomial with $n = 20$, $p = .05$.
  - Hypergeometric with $N = 960$, $S = 48$, $n = 20$. Note that $S/N = .05 = p$. Any other large values of N and S with the same ratio would work.
  - Poisson with $\mu = 1$. Note that $\mu = 20 * .05 = np$.
- Compare the three distributions and note that they are very similar. Look at the **Solution** and **Side_by_side** worksheets.
- Experiment to show that the binomial and hypergeometric become more similar as N gets larger, for example with $N = 9600$ and $S = 480$.
- Experiment to show that the binomial and Poisson become more similar as n gets larger and p gets smaller, for example, with $n = 100$ and $p = .01$ and $\mu = 1$.

- The occurrences must be independent. This means that any occurrence should not be affected by previous occurrences and should not affect any subsequent occurrence. For the bank teller example, if there were enough people in line to discourage new customers, the previous occurrences would be affecting subsequent occurrences.

Summary

This chapter started by looking the notion of a discrete probability distribution that pairs numeric values (random variable) with the probability of occurrence and then looked at the concept of the expected value and the variance of such a distribution. It then looked at three probability distributions in which the random variable is the number of occurrences of some event.

Conceptual

- The concept of a discrete probability distribution.
- The concept of expected value:

$$\mu = E(X) = \sum (X \cdot P(X)) \qquad \text{Equation [5.1]}$$

- Three discrete distributions:
  - Binomial: for the number of occurrences in n trials with probability p of an occurrence on any given trial
  - Hypergeometric: for the number of occurrences in n trials with a finite population of size N, with S possible occurrences; sampling without replacement
  - Poisson distribution: for the number of occurrences during a unit of time (or space or distance) with a mean rate of occurrence, μ

Applied

- Be able to identify what distribution is appropriate for a given situation.
- Be able to interpret computer output.
- Be able to determine P(X) and the probability of below, above, and between given values.

Exercises

The exercises and data are found in **Ch_05_ Probability_Distributions.xls** in the exercises folder of the CD.

No.	Content
1	Expected value
2	Expected value
3	Binomial distribution
4	Binomial distribution
5	Hypergeometric distribution
6	Hypergeometric distribution
7	Poisson distribution
8	Poisson distribution
9	Poisson distribution
10	Compare distributions

Module for Discrete Probability Distributions

5.A   DISCRETE DISTRIBUTION SIMULATION

In the insurance company example (Section 5.1), we calculated the expected value to be 50; that meant that the insurance company should average $50 for every policy it sells. Let's see how this works by using an Excel worksheet to simulate the outcomes. Simulation is the procedure of using a random number generator to calculate a large number of values that represent possible outcomes. This module shows how easy it is to do simulation with Excel.

In this example, we want a cell in the worksheet to represent the outcome of an insurance policy such that 98% of the time the cell contains 250, meaning that the person was alive at the end of the term, and 2% of the time it contains −9750, which means that the person died during the term and the insurance company had to pay the death benefit. The trick is to use Excel's RAND() function, which calculates random numbers from 0 to 1. Every time you press the F9 function key, Excel calculates a new random number. Since every random number is equally likely, we check every value. If the value is less than or equal to .02, that means that the person died and we put −9750 in the cell; otherwise we put 250 in the cell. This is done with Excel's IF() statement. The statement looks like this:

$$=IF(RAND()<=0.02,-9750,250)$$

The first argument of the IF() statement is the logical condition that checks to see if the random value is less than or equal to .02. The next two arguments determine what to put in the cell if the logical condition is true or false, respectively.

If we copy this formula to a large number of cells, we have a simulation. **EV0.xls** shows the results of 1000 insurance policies in cells A1:E200. There is nothing magical about 1000; it is a large enough number to give a stable outcome. You can try using more or less. Every time the F9 function key is pressed, a new batch of 1000 policies is simulated. Cell G4 uses Excel's

---

DISCRETE DISTRIBUTION SIMULATION

Learning Activity 5.A–1

- Try creating the simulation in a new Excel workbook. If necessary, look at the formulas in **EV0.xls.** Even though you could copy/paste the formulas, there is value in creating the worksheet from scratch.
- Once you get it working, you can experiment with changing the number of cells and changing the values in the functions.
- **EV0.xls** is the solution worksheet.
- Open **EV1.xls**. This is the fancy version. Study how it works and play with it a bit.
  - *Excel note:* Click one of the green simulation cells and then select Format | Conditional Formatting on the Excel menu. Notice how the highlighted cells are formatted.

AVERAGE(A1:E200) function to calculate the mean outcome. If the expected value formula is correct, the mean outcome should be 50. Will it be? Only if exactly 20 out of the 1000 policies simulate a person dying. If you keep pressing F9, you occasionally will get an outcome of 50, but in general it will be some other number. However, the mean outcome will not be much different from 50, and if you record several mean outcomes, you will find that the mean of the means will be close to 50. Also, if you calculate more than 1000 simulated cells, the mean outcome will be closer to 50.

EV1.xls is a fancier version. It is prettier and more generalized and also calculates the variance and the standard deviation.

CHAPTER SIX

Normal Distribution

6.1 Normal Distribution (p. 82)

Summary (p. 90)

Exercises (p. 90)

Module for Chapter Six

6.A How to Determine Probabilities for a Normal Distribution (p. 91)

6.1 Normal Distribution

The normal distribution—the so-called bell curve—is an example of a **continuous probability distribution.** Instead of discrete values of X as we saw in Chapter 5, there is a continuous X axis. Each of the X values can be substituted into a mathematical function f(X) to plot a curve.

The mathematical function that describes a normal distribution is

$$f(X) = \frac{1}{\sigma\sqrt{2\pi}} e^{-\frac{1}{2}\left(\frac{X-\mu}{\sigma}\right)^2}$$ [6.1]

If we substitute many X values into this expression and plot them, we will have a normal curve. However, f(X) is just the height of the curve at any point; it is *not* a probability. Therefore, don't be concerned about the equation for the normal curve function. You never will have to calculate the height of the curve; the equation is displayed only to show that it exists. The center of the distribution is the population mean, μ. The X axis theoretically goes from $-\infty$ to $+\infty$ but as you can see in Exhibit 6-1, by the time you get up to 3 standard deviations away from the mean, the curve nearly touches the axis.

If f(X) is not a probability, what is? Probability corresponds to area under the curve. Just as the sum of discrete probabilities is 1, the total area under a continuous distribution equals 1. The area under a curve is calculated by numerical integration, which is a technique beyond the scope of this book. In this book, we use tables, Excel, and MegaStat.

EXHIBIT 6-1
Normal distribution.

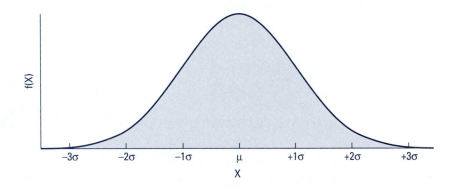

PLOTTING A NORMAL CURVE   Learning Activity **6.1–1**

The normal distributions displays in this chapter and throughout the book are done with MegaStat; however, it is instructive to see a normal curve plotted as a basic Excel chart.

- Open **z-plot.xls.**
- Click on the chart to see the source data highlighted.
- Click in one of the cells in column C. Compare the Excel formula to Equation [6.1] and see that they are the same.

PRACTICE WITH z-VALUES
Learning Activity **6.1–2**

- Open **z-demo.xls!Start.**
- Calculate the mean and the standard deviation of the X values by using the Excel functions AVERAGE() and STDEV().
- In column C calculate the z-value for each of the X values. Calculate the mean and the standard deviation of the z-values. The mean should be 0, and the standard deviation should be 1.
- It is good practice to repeat the calculations using only a calculator.
- Try changing one or more of the X values. You should find that the mean and the standard deviation of the z-values are still 0 and 1.
- Click on the **z-demo** worksheet tab. This worksheet generates random numbers for the X values.
  - Click on each of the named ranges in the Excel Name Box to see which cells are referenced with the names.
  - Examine the cell formulas (remember CTRL ~ toggles formula view).
- Click the Recalc button. Observe that the mean and the standard deviation of the z-values are always 0 and 1.

z-values

In working with the normal distribution, we convert our data to **z-values.** Sometimes this is called a z transformation or standardizing a variable. If we have a variable X, the equation for the corresponding z-value is

$$z = \frac{X - \text{mean}}{\text{stdev}}$$ [6.2]

The mean and the standard deviation referenced in Equation [6.2] can refer to population or sample values. Why is the z transformation useful? Because no matter what X values you have, the mean of the z-values is always 0 and the variance and the standard deviation are always 1. This is important because it allows us to use just one normal curve table.

Determining Normal Distribution Probabilities

Example 1

An IQ test is a standardized test that purports to measure intelligence. IQ scores are normally distributed[1] and standardized to have mean of $\mu = 100$ and a standard deviation of $\sigma = 16$. If you take an IQ test and get a score of 125, what is your percentile? In other words, what proportion of the population would be below you? The first step is to calculate the z-value. Substituting into Equation [6.2]:

$$z = \frac{125 - 100}{16} = 1.56$$ [6.3]

z-values usually are rounded to two decimal places to correspond to the tables. When you look up 1.56 in the table (see Module 6.A), you find that the probability is 0.9406: the probability of being below a z-value of 1.56 that corresponds to an IQ score of 125.

Thus, you could say an IQ score of 125 puts you at the 94th percentile (Exhibit 6-2), meaning that 94 percent of the population would be at or below an IQ score of 125. Module 6.A provides details on how to find normal curve probabilities by using tables, Excel, and MegaStat.

[1]No real-world variable is distributed in a *perfect* normal distribution, but IQ scores come as close as any.

EXHIBIT 6-2
The probability of an IQ score *less than* 125 is .9406.

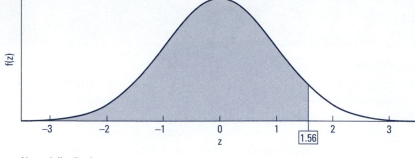

Normal distribution

P(lower)	P(upper)	z	X	mean	std.dev
.9406	.0594	*1.56*	125	100	16

EXHIBIT 6-3
The probability of an IQ score *greater than* 125 is .0594.

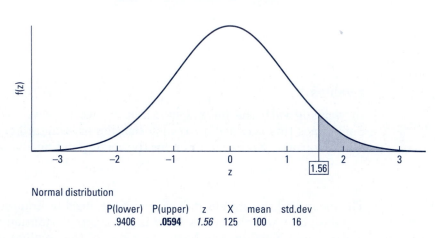

Normal distribution

P(lower)	P(upper)	z	X	mean	std.dev
.9406	**.0594**	*1.56*	125	100	16

The tables and Excel functions give the probability of being below a particular value. If you want the probability of being above, you subtract the probability from 1. The probability of having an IQ above 125 is $1 - .9406 = .0594$, as shown in Exhibit 6-3.

Example 2

What is the probability that an IQ score will fall between 90 and 125? To get the probability of being between two values, you calculate the z-values for each one and get the corresponding probabilities. Then you subtract the smaller probability from the larger. Note that you subtract the probabilities, not the z-values. You never subtract or add z-values. We saw above that the probability of being below 125 is .9406. An IQ score of 90 corresponds to a z-value of $-.63$, and the probability of being below $-.63$ is .2643. Subtracting the two probabilities, we find that the area between them is $.6763 = .9406 - .2643$ as shown in Exhibit 6-4.

Determining Values Corresponding to a Given Probability

Sometimes it is necessary to calculate the value that corresponds to a given probability. For example, if a school wants to place students in a accelerated class if they have an IQ score at the 92nd percentile or higher, to what IQ score does that correspond?

EXHIBIT 6-4
The probability of an IQ score between 90 and 125 is .6763.

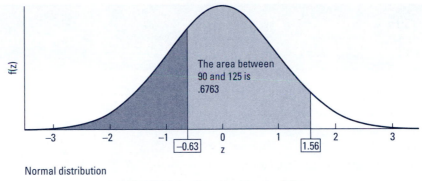

Normal distribution

P(lower)	P(upper)	z	X	mean	std.dev
.9406	.0594	*1.56*	125	100	16
.2643	.7357	*−0.63*	90	100	16
.6763					
difference					

REPLICATE TEXT VALUES FOR NORMAL DISTRIBUTION

Learning Activity **6.1–3**

Read Module 6.A before doing this activity.

- Replicate the values in the text by using all three methods:
  - Normal curve table
  - Excel function
  - MegaStat | Probability | Normal Distribution
- If the computer outcomes do not quite match the table values, use the rounding options to make them match.

Sometimes these are called inverse probability calculations. You can find inverse values by using tables, Excel, or MegaStat, as shown in Module 6.A. Using the tables, you find the probability as close as possible to .9200. You find that the closest probability is .9207 and that the corresponding z-value is 1.41. Substituting this into the z-value in Equation [6.2], we get

$$1.41 = \frac{X - 100}{16}$$

Solving this for X, we get the IQ score that would give a z-value of 1.41. The answer is $122.56 = 100 + (1.41)(16)$ and rounds to 123.

Solving Equation [6.2] for X, we get the general expression

$$X = \text{mean} + (z)(\text{stdev}) \qquad \text{[6.4]}$$

An Important Assumption

It is important to remember that normal curve probabilities are valid only to the extent to which population distribution is normal. When you are determining normal curve probabilities, you should always ask, Is the population

REPLICATE TEXT VALUES FOR INVERSE NORMAL DISTRIBUTION

Learning Activity **6.1–4**

Read Module 6.A before doing this activity.

- Replicate the values in the text by using all three methods:
  ◦ Normal curve table
  ◦ Excel function
  ◦ MegaStat | Probability | Normal Distribution
- If the computer outputs do not quite match the table values, use the rounding options to make them match.

distribution approximately normal? In the IQ example, the scores have been developed to be very close to a normal distribution, but that is not the case with many real-world variables. How would you know if a distribution was approximately normal? The first thing is to do a frequency distribution and see if it looks normal. If a distribution has a peak in the middle and sort of tapers down at both ends, it probably will be called approximately normal. (In Module 14.D we examine ways to test normality.) Although the probabilities are shown to four decimal places in the tables, no real-world distribution (not even IQ) is close enough to a perfect normal curve to justify that level of precision and certainly not to justify the 15 digit precision that Excel can calculate.

Benchmark z-values

We will see in the chapters on hypothesis testing (Chapters 9 and 10) that an unlikely occurrence usually is defined as something that happens less than 5% of the time; sometimes 1% or 10% is used. You should become familiar with the z-values corresponding to 1%, 5%, and 10%. These frequently used z-values are shown in Exhibit 6-5. The tables worksheet **(Tables.xls!Benchmark_z_values)** also shows the values. They are called benchmark values because they are used frequently, and if you become familiar with them, they provide a frame of reference for interpreting other z-values.

Let's look at the .05/.95 values in detail. Five percent of a normal curve would be above a z-value of +1.645 (and 95% would be below), and 5% of a normal curve would be below a z-value of −1.645 (and 95% would be above). If we split the 5% and put 2.5% in each tail (each end of the distribution is called a tail),

EXHIBIT 6-5
Benchmark z-values.

probability	One-Tail	Two-Tail
0.10/.90	+ or −1.28	+ and −1.645
0.05/.95	+ or −1.645	+ and −1.96
0.01/.99	+ or −2.33	+ and −2.58

95% of the distribution is between the z-values of −1.96 and +1.96. These values are shown in Exhibit 6-6. You should use inverse probability calculations to verify these values as well as the 1% and 10% values by using the tables, Excel, and MegaStat.

EXHIBIT 6-6
Upper, lower and two-tail 5%/95% probability.

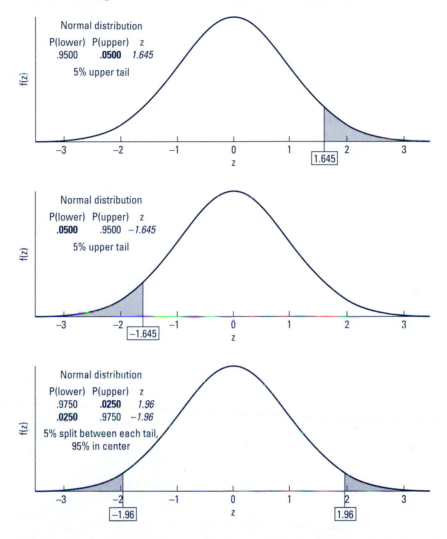

REPLICATE IMPORTANT z-VALUES   Learning Activity **6.1–5**

Read Module 6.A before doing this activity.

- Replicate the values in Exhibit 6-5 by using all three methods:
  - Normal curve table
  - Excel function
  - MegaStat | Probability | Normal Distribution
- If the computer outcomes do not quite match the table values, use the rounding options to make them match.

Empirical Rule

What percent of a normal distribution falls within 1 standard deviation of the mean? If you look up the probabilities for z = +1 and z = −1 and subtract them, you find that the answer is .6813, or roughly two-thirds. As we saw in the important z-values section (Exhibit 6-5), 95% of the distribution is within ±1.96 standard deviations, roughly ±2. Almost all (99.7%) of the distribution is within ±3 standard deviations.

Putting this together we have a rule of thumb called the **empirical rule** (Exhibit 6-7) that states: Approximately two-thirds of a normal curve is within 1 standard deviation of the mean, 95% is within 2 standard deviations, and almost all is within 3 standard deviations.

Why Is the Normal Curve Important?

Many things are approximately normally distributed. Although nothing in the real world can precisely match the exact mathematical shape of a normal

**EXHIBIT 6-7
The empirical
rule.**

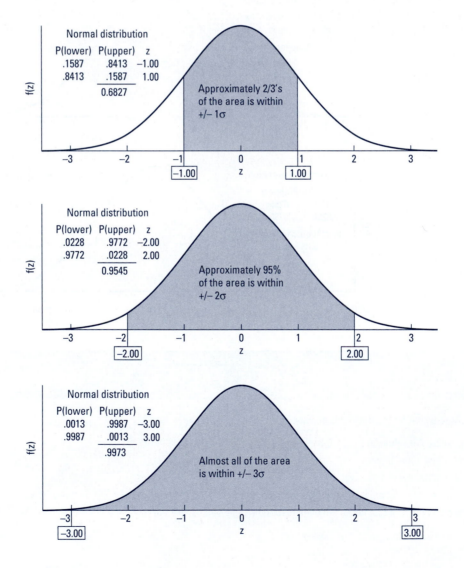

EMPIRICAL RULE   Learning Activity **6.1–6**

Read Module 6.A before doing this activity.

- Replicate Exhibit 6-7 by using MegaStat | Probability | Normal Distribution.
- Open **RealEstateData.xls!Data.**
- Run MegaStat | Descriptive Statistics.
  ○ Specify the Price *and* LotSize variables.
  ○ In addition to the default options, check Empirical Rule and Normal curve goodness of fit.

The empirical rule output shows how much of the data is within 1, 2, and 3 standard deviations. The closer the percents are to what the empirical rule predicts, the more normally distributed the data are. Again, you should see that the Price variable matches much better than does the LotSize variable.

We will not officially see the normal curve goodness test until much later (Chapter 14); however, the key item is the p-value. If it is less than .05 (and shown in yellow), it means the data probably are not normally distributed; the closer to 1.0, the better the fit.

Thus, we see in this case that the Price variable could be normally distributed and the LotSize variable probably is not. Run MegaStat | Frequency Distributions | Quantitative on both variables to verify that Price is roughly normal and LotSize is not.

distribution, many things have a more or less bell-shaped distribution. It is intuitive that in many instances the bulk of a population is near the center, with a lower probability of extremes at the high and low ends.

From a statistical analysis point of view, the normal curve is important because it provides a means for statistical inference. We will see this in Chapter 7.

Relationship between the Normal and Binomial Distributions

As a final note, recall that in Chapter 5 it was said that the binomial distribution is the most important discrete distribution and that the normal distribution is the continuous form of the binomial distribution. Exhibit 6-8 illustrates that by superimposing a normal curve on a binomial distribution with n = 1000. As you can see, the shape of the distributions is identical. It can be shown that as n approaches infinity, the binomial and normal distributions are

EXHIBIT 6-8
Normal curve superimposed on a binomial distribution.

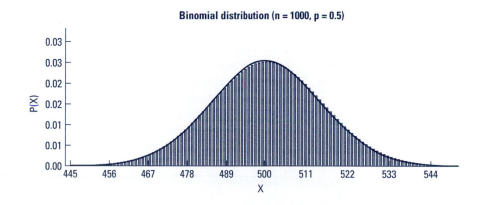

Binomial distribution (n = 1000, p = 0.5)

mathematically equivalent. When p = .5 the shape of a binomial distribution is very normal even with small sample sizes.

Summary

The normal distribution is important because many things are approximately normally distributed. As we will see in Chapter 7, the normal distribution is the foundation of much statistical theory.

Conceptual

- This chapter introduced the concept of a continuous probability distribution where probability is proportional to the area under a curve.
- The normal distribution is our first and primary example of a continuous probability distribution.
- z-Values always have a mean of 0 and a standard deviation of 1:

$$z = \frac{X - \text{mean}}{\text{stdev}} \qquad \text{Equation [6.2]}$$

- Empirical rule:
  - Approximately two-thirds s within ±1 standard deviation
  - Approximately 95% within ±2 standard deviations
  - Almost all within ±3 standard deviations

Applied

- Be familiar with (better yet, memorize) the z-values corresponding to 1%, 5%, and 10% in Exhibit 6-5.
- Be able to use tables, Excel, and MegaStat to find probabilities for below, above, and between.
- Given a probability, be able to find the corresponding X value.

Exercises

The exercises and data are found in **Ch_06_Normal_Distribution.xls** in the exercises folder of the CD.

No.	Content
1	Normal curve probabilities (above and below)
2	Normal curve probabilities (between)
3	Normal curve probabilities (inverse)
4	Normal curve probabilities (above and below)
5	Normal curve probabilities (between)
6	Normal curve probabilities (inverse)
7	Empirical rule practice
8	Benchmark z-values
9	Compare binomial and normal distributions
10	Create your own exercises

Module for Normal Distribution

6.A HOW TO DETERMINE PROBABILITIES FOR A NORMAL DISTRIBUTION

Using Tables

Tables.xls contains the tables used in this text. Click on the TOC (table of contents) worksheet and you will see links to worksheets that give the normal curve probabilities for negative and positive z-values.

EXHIBIT 6-9
Portion of normal curve table showing the probability for z = 1.56.

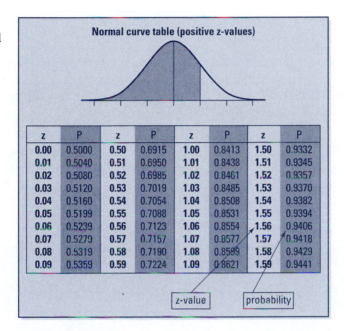

Normal curve table (positive z-values)

z	P	z	P	z	P	z	P
0.00	0.5000	0.50	0.6915	1.00	0.8413	1.50	0.9332
0.01	0.5040	0.51	0.6950	1.01	0.8438	1.51	0.9345
0.02	0.5080	0.52	0.6985	1.02	0.8461	1.52	0.9357
0.03	0.5120	0.53	0.7019	1.03	0.8485	1.53	0.9370
0.04	0.5160	0.54	0.7054	1.04	0.8508	1.54	0.9382
0.05	0.5199	0.55	0.7088	1.05	0.8531	1.55	0.9394
0.06	0.5239	0.56	0.7123	1.06	0.8554	1.56	0.9406
0.07	0.5279	0.57	0.7157	1.07	0.8577	1.57	0.9418
0.08	0.5319	0.58	0.7190	1.08	0.8599	1.58	0.9429
0.09	0.5359	0.59	0.7224	1.09	0.8621	1.59	0.9441

z-value   probability

Example 1

An IQ test is a standardized test that claims to measure intelligence. IQ scores are normally distributed and standardized to have a mean of $\mu = 100$ and a standard deviation of $\sigma = 16$. If you take an IQ test and get a score of 125, what is your percentile? In other words, what proportion of the population is below you? The first step is to calculate the z-value. Substituting into Equation [6.2]:

$$z = \frac{125 - 100}{16} = 1.56$$

Exhibit 6-9 shows a portion of the table containing the z-value of 1.56 and the corresponding probability of .9406.

To find inverse values, that is, the z-value corresponding to a given probability, you find the closest value in the probability column and then use the corresponding z-value to calculate the value, as shown in Section 6.1.

Example 2

If a university wanted to accept students at the 86th percentile on an entrance examination that had a mean of 400 and a standard deviation of 60, to what score would that correspond? Looking in the table segment in Exhibit 6-9, we see that the probability closest to 86% is .8599 and the corresponding z-value is 1.08. Substituting into Equation [6.4], we find

$$464.8 = 400 + 1.08 * 60$$

This rounds to 465.

Using Excel Functions

The Excel function NORMSDIST(z) calculates the normal curve probability when a z-value is the argument. For example, if a cell contains the formula =NORMSDIST(1.56), the cell value is .9406, assuming the cell was formatted to four decimal places. The NORMSDIST function was used to create the tables in **tables.xls.**

The Excel function NORMDIST(X, mean, stdev, 1) calculates the normal curve probability given some value X, a mean, and a standard deviation. For example, if a cell contained the formula =NORMDIST(125, 100, 16, 1), the display value would be .9409. This value is not quite the same as the one in the previous example

---

PRACTICE WITH THE NORMAL DISTRIBUTION

Learning Activity **6.A–1**

- Calculate the values below using the three methods:
  ○ Normal curve table
  ○ Excel function
  ○ MegaStat I Probability I Normal Distribution

  Assume an examination has a mean of 84.2 and a standard deviation of 10.9.
- What is the probability of being above 100?
- What is the probability of being between 77 and 97?
- If an examination score has to be at the 94th percentile to be an A, what score would that be?
- *Solution:*
  1. .0735 = 1 − .9265.
  2. .6244 = .8790 − .2546.
  3. The examination score would be 101.147, rounded to 101.

Detailed solutions are found in **Normal_practice.xls.**
  Remember that normal curve probabilities are accurate only to the extent to which the data are normally distributed.

because this function would use the z-value calculated to 15 decimal places, whereas the previous example used z rounded to 2 decimal places.

To calculate z or X given a probability (i.e., inverse values), you would use NORMSINV(p) or NORMINV(p, mean, stdev).

TUTORIAL 7

Using MegaStat

MegaStat | Probability | Normal Distribution calculates normal curve probabilities. See Tutorial 7, MegaStat help, or the *Getting Started Guide* for details on the options.

If you are working with z-values, set the mean = 0 and the standard deviation = 1. Otherwise use the mean and the standard deviation for the problem you are calculating.

To calculate z and X given a probability (inverse calculation), you would click "calculate z (or X) given P."

MegaStat has an option to round the computations to match the table values.

The exhibits in this chapter and the rest of the book were done with MegaStat.

CHAPTER SEVEN

Sampling and Sampling Distributions

7.1 Sampling Concepts (p. 96)

7.2 Sampling Distributions (p. 98)

Summary (p. 101)

Exercises (p. 102)

Modules for Chapter Seven

7.A Generating Random Numbers (p. 103)

7.B Central Limit Theorem Simulation (p. 106)

7.C A Proportion Is a Mean (p. 107)

This chapter provides the theoretical framework for statistics. Whereas most of this book focuses on "how" statistics works, this chapter focuses on "why."

7.1 Sampling Concepts

Samples and sampling techniques are important topics, but a detailed discussion of sampling is the purview of research methods or marketing research courses. Here we first take a brief look at some basic terms and concepts. The main things you need to know are the precise definitions of *population* and *sample* and what is meant by a simple random sample.

We defined the terms *population* and *sample* in Chapter 1 and already have used those terms (Sections 2.1, 2.2, and 6.1); however, like many terms, they have a slightly more precise meaning in statistics. Recall the definitions of population and sample from Chapter 1: In a general sense a population is the entire universe of objects we are studying, but since statistics works with data, we really are thinking about data associated with the physical objects. For example, if we are considering a population of college students, we really are considering the population of data associated with the students that we are interested in studying, such as their grade point average (GPA), income, and age.

A sample is a subset of a population. Why use a sample? If we are interested in a population, why not just do a census, that is, look at every item in the population? There are several reasons:

- In most cases the population is too large to assess every unit. Even the federal government with all its resources has difficulty doing a census of the U.S. population.
- Every unit in the population may not be identified, and so you would not know when you were done.
- The boundaries of some populations are vague. For example, if you were looking at a population of college students, there could be disagreement about whether certain institutions are colleges.
- Even if it was possible to do a census, the population probably would have changed by the time you were done.
- Another reason might be destructive sampling. For example, assume the population of interest was a truckload of items and you wanted to know how many were defective. The only way to know would be to open each item and perform a test that would destroy the item or make it unfit for retail sale. You might be willing to sacrifice a sample, but you would not want to destroy the entire shipment.
- Finally, a good sample can give good information and probably will be better than an incomplete attempt at a census. If you try to assess every item in a population, the ones you miss are likely to be systematically different from the ones you get. Thus, even though your final sample might be large, it probably would be biased.

The best type of sample is a **simple random sample,** in which every unit in the population has the same probability of being sampled. Although a simple random sample is simple in concept, it is frequently not simple to implement. To do a simple random sample, you would need a list of every item in the population.[1] Then you would have to generate a sample of random numbers that would tell you which items to use for your sample. The obvious problem is that most populations do not have such a list, and even if they did, you probably could not get access to them.

If you cannot do a simple random sample, **cluster sampling, systematic sampling, stratified sampling,** and **convenience sampling** are alternative methods that may approximate a simple random sample.

Cluster sampling is a method of efficiently approximating a simple random sample with a large population. Assume you wanted to interview a random sample of 100 people in the United States. Even if you had a list of every U.S. resident, the 100 people would be scattered across the country and it would require much traveling to interview them. Instead, you could take a small sample of states, within each state take a small sample of cities, and then within each city take a sample of people. The combined clusters of people in each city presumably would be a random sample of people in the country, but since the people in each cluster would be closer to one another, the interviewing would be easier. Cluster sampling is the best alternative if you cannot do a simple random sample.

Systematic sampling entails taking every nth item. For example, if you instructed your polling staff to get a random sample of surveys, it probably would not be very random; however, if you told them to get every third house on each block in a particular area, that presumably would be more random because there should be no particular characteristics associated with every third house.

Stratified sampling involves forcing certain elements into your sample. For example, if you were sampling undergraduates, you might try to make sure the sample had freshmen, sophomores, juniors, and seniors in approximately the same proportion as the population. Although this seems a logical thing to do, it should not be necessary. With a simple random sample, the different strata in a population should be represented proportionally in the sample.

Convenience sampling. If you take whatever sample is handy, it is a convenience sample. Much sampling is done this way, but it is not random. For example, if you give a questionnaire to a class of undergraduate statistics students, it will not be a random sample because they are at a particular school, probably are of similar age, and are mostly in the same academic program. The only population they would represent would be similar students, and even then, they would not be a random sample.

Creating a random sample often involves random numbers. Random numbers can be generated from tables of random numbers, but they can be generated faster and easier with Excel or MegaStat. Module 7.A shows how to generate random numbers for sampling purposes and how to generate random data for studying statistics.

---

[1]The technical name for such a list is a *frame.*

7.2   Sampling Distributions

One of the primary reasons for using statistics is to make decisions that are based on data; this is known as **statistical inference.** The remaining chapters deal with statistical inference; hypothesis testing, which is one of the primary tools of statistical inference, is based on the concept of a **sampling distribution.**

If you want to know the mean of a population, you estimate it from the mean of a sample. However, if you took another sample, you would get a different sample mean. If you took a large number of samples, recorded the mean of each sample, and looked at the frequency distribution of the means, that frequency distribution would approximate a sampling distribution. The continuous form of the distribution as the number of samples approaches infinity is a probability distribution known as a sampling distribution.

When we are considering the sampling distribution of sample means, we encounter an almost magical phenomenon known as the **central limit theorem,** which states that the sampling distribution of sample means will be normal. More formally:

> **Central limit theorem:** The sampling distribution of sample means approximates a normal distribution as the sample size becomes large no matter what the shape of the population is.

The last clause, "no matter what the shape of the population is," is what makes the central limit theorem so important. We can make precise probability statements about a population based on a sample even if we do not know the shape of the population distribution. This is the foundation of hypothesis testing, as we will see in Chapter 8.

TUTORIAL 8

What about the "as the sample size becomes large" phrase? A traditional rule of thumb states that a sample size of 30 or more results in a normal sampling distribution of means even if the population is fairly skewed. If the population distribution is symmetrical (i.e., uniform), a sample of around 15 gives a very normal sampling distribution; if the population is roughly normal (i.e., a peak in the middle), an even smaller sample is sufficient. Module 7.B presents a simulation that demonstrates the concept of a sampling distribution and shows the central limit theorem in action.

The mean of the sampling distribution of means is the population mean:

$$\mu_{\overline{X}} = \mu \qquad\qquad \textbf{[7.1]}$$

A more formal statement is that the sample mean is a point estimate of the population mean, meaning that it is a value that estimates a population parameter. It seems intuitively obvious that the mean of the means would be the population mean, and indeed it can be proved formally that the sample mean is an unbiased estimate of the population mean; however, the details of the proof are beyond the scope of this book.

When you take a sample and calculate the mean, the large values in the sample tend to "cancel out" or "average out" the small values. If you look at the central limit simulation (Module 7.B), you will see that although the individual observations range from 0 to 100, the values of the means tend to hover around 50. It seems intuitively obvious that a larger sample would make the sample means have even less variability. A formal statement of this is that the variance of the means is inversely proportional to the sample size:

$$\sigma_{\overline{X}}^2 = \frac{\sigma^2}{n} \qquad [7.2]$$

If we take the square root of the variance, we have the standard deviation of the means:

$$\sigma_{\overline{X}} = \sqrt{\sigma_{\overline{X}}^2} = \sqrt{\frac{\sigma^2}{n}} = \frac{\sigma}{\sqrt{n}} \qquad [7.3]$$

This often is called the **standard error of the mean.** *Standard error* means the standard deviation of a sampling distribution. As in *sampling error,* the word *error* here does not mean a mistake or something wrong; it is traditional statistical terminology.

Since we have a normal sampling distribution of means, we can use the normal curve skills we learned in Chapter 6 to calculate probabilities for means. The z-value equation for means is

$$z = \frac{\overline{X} - \mu}{\frac{\sigma}{\sqrt{n}}} \qquad [7.4]$$

Example

Assume that a standardized aptitude test is normally distributed with a mean of 800 and a standard deviation of 100.

a. What is the probability that one person selected at random from the population will have a score at or above 850?

Solution: This is a straightforward normal curve problem of the sort that we did in Chapter 6, using Equation [6.2]:

$$z = \frac{X - \mu}{\sigma} = \frac{850 - 800}{100} = .50$$

$$P(z \geq .50) = 1 - .6915 = .3085$$

b. What is the probability that a sample of 20 people selected at random from the population will have a *mean* score above 850?

Solution: Since the question is about the probability of a mean, we use the sampling distribution equation for calculating z (Equation [7.4]), where we divide by the standard error of the mean:

$$z = \frac{\overline{X} - \mu}{\frac{\sigma}{\sqrt{n}}} = \frac{850 - 800}{\frac{100}{\sqrt{20}}} = 2.24$$

$$P(z \geq 2.24) = .0125$$

What is the point of this? To show that it is not unusual to have one observation above 850 but that to get 20 that have a mean above 850 is pretty rare. Why? Because some of the sample probably will be below the population mean and pull the sample mean down. In other words, deviations from the population mean are much less likely than a deviation by a single observation. That is one reason we take a sample rather than make only one observation.

Would these computations be valid if the population was not normally distributed? Part a requires a normal population to be valid; part b is valid without a normal population because of the central limit theorem although a sample size of 30 or more would be better.

REPLICATE TEXT VALUES FOR SAMPLING DISTRIBUTION CALCULATIONS

Learning Activity **7.2–1**

Open a blank Excel workbook and calculate the z-values and probabilities in the example in Section 7.2. Use all three methods: tables, Excel, and MegaStat.

PRACTICE WITH SAMPLING DISTRIBUTION CALCULATIONS

Learning Activity **7.2–2**

- Assume a machine produces parts with a mean diameter of 60.2 and a standard deviation of 2.4. Calculate the answer by using a calculator and a normal curve table.
  - What is the probability that a randomly selected part will have a diameter greater than 62?
  - What is the probability that a sample of 17 parts will have a mean diameter greater than 62?

Solution: The solution is in **SampDist.xls!Solution**. Note that for the first part to be valid, you must assume a normal population distribution. The second part relies on the central limit theorem to provide a normal distribution.

- More practice: Open **SampDist.xls!Practice** and change any or all of the shaded cells. Use a calculator and a normal curve table to verify the calculated answers. (After using a calculator and tables, you may verify with Excel and/or MegaStat or check **SampDist.xls!Solution**.)

Proportions

A **proportion** is just a special case of a mean where the data are 0 and 1 to represent no and yes, respectively. Since a proportion is a mean, the central limit theorem applies to proportions, and the equation for the standard deviation of the proportions, that is, the **standard error of the proportion,** is

$$\sigma_p = \sqrt{\frac{\pi(1-\pi)}{n}} \qquad [7.5]$$

This is a computational equation that results from the numbers being 0's and 1's. These formulas are useful because we often do not have the raw data.

Since we are using lowercase Greek letters to represent population values, it makes sense to let p represent a sample proportion and π (lowercase Greek p) represent a population proportion. The only problem with this is that π usually

PRACTICE WITH PROPORTIONS

- Use a calculator or Excel to convert the following to ratios:
  - 28.3% of 120
  - 30% of 37
- Solution:
  - 33.96/120 → 34/120, and so the unrounded proportion is 28.3333 . . . %.
  - 11.1/37 → 11/37, and so the unrounded proportion is 29.7297297 . . . %.

is used to represent the mathematical constant 3.14159. Just remember that in the context of statistics, π means population proportion, *not* the mathematical constant.[2]

Module 7.C shows how a proportion is a mean. It also gives an example of how the standard error of the proportion can be calculated with Equation [7.5] as well as with the formula for the mean (Equation [7.3]).

If you have a sample proportion stated as a ratio, for example, 35/62, you should try to keep it in that form. Once you convert it to a decimal and round, you lose some accuracy. If a proportion is reported as a fraction, say, 56% of 62 ($p = .56$, $n = 62$), you can multiply $np = (62)(.56) = 34.72$ and round to the nearest integer to see that the ratio is actually 35/62 and the actual proportion is 0.564516129032258. Admittedly, you do not need this much accuracy for any real-world calculation, but the difference between .56 and .5645 could be important. In using a computer or calculator, it is a good rule to carry as much accuracy as possible and round only the final answer. Learn to use the memory registers in your calculator for intermediate results. Rounding and writing down intermediate results and reentering them not only sacrifices accuracy but also are time-consuming and error-prone.

Summary

Sampling is necessary because we rarely have access to an entire population. The best sample is a simple random sample in which every item in the population has an equal chance of being selected. However, that is difficult or impossible to accomplish in practice, and other types of samples are compromises that attempt to emulate a true random sample.

Samples are used to estimate population values. For example, the sample mean is used to estimate the population mean. If sampling is repeated many times, the distribution of sample values is a sampling distribution. The central limit theorem states that the sampling distribution of means will be normal with a large enough sample even when the population is not normal.

Conceptual

- Sampling concepts and types of samples.
- Simple random sample, systematic sampling, stratified sampling, cluster sampling, and convenience sampling.

[2]One exception: In Chapter 6, the equation for the normal curve function shows π (pi), and that is the traditional 3.14159 use of π.

- Concept of a sampling distribution: the probability distribution of sample values.
- Central limit theorem: sampling distribution of means will be normal if the sample is large enough.
  - The mean of a sampling distribution of means is the population mean:

$$\mu_{\overline{X}} = \mu \qquad \text{Equation [7.1]}$$

  - The variance of a sampling distribution of means is inversely proportional to the sample size:

$$\sigma_{\overline{X}}^2 = \frac{\sigma^2}{n} \qquad \text{Equation [7.2]}$$

  - The standard deviation of a sampling distribution is called the standard error of the mean:

$$\sigma_{\overline{X}} = \frac{\sigma}{\sqrt{n}} \qquad \text{Equation [7.3]}$$

  - Since a sampling distribution of means is normal, we can calculate normal curve probabilities for means by using a z-value based on the standard error of the mean:

$$z = \frac{\overline{X} - \mu}{\dfrac{\sigma}{\sqrt{n}}} \qquad \text{Equation [7.4]}$$

- The proportion is a special case of the mean, and the standard error of the proportion is

$$\sigma_p = \sqrt{\frac{\pi(1 - \pi)}{n}} \qquad \text{Equation [7.5]}$$

Applied

- Be able to calculate normal curve probabilities for a sampling distribution.

Exercises

The exercises and data are found in **Ch_07_Sampling_Distributions.xls** in the exercises folder of the CD.

No.	Content
1	Sampling distribution calculations
2	Sampling distribution calculations
3	Proportions
4	Proportions
5	Proportions
6	Proportions
7	Random numbers
8	Random numbers
9	Random numbers
10	Random numbers—randomization

Modules for Sampling and Sampling Distributions

7.A GENERATING RANDOM NUMBERS

In selecting random samples, it is necessary to generate random numbers. Random numbers also are used for simulations and can be used to create sample datasets. Many older books contain a table of random numbers, but Excel can create random numbers easily without the use of tables.

The Excel function for creating random numbers is RAND(). It creates random numbers between 0 and 1. If you put =RAND() into a worksheet cell and press the F9 function key, you will see random values.

If you want random numbers larger than 1, multiply the random number function by a constant. For example, =RAND()*100 gives random numbers between 0 and 100. If you want integer random numbers, put the function inside an INT() function. The formula =INT(RAND()*100) gives random numbers between 0 and 99. The largest value is 99 rather than 100 because RAND() will not give a value equal to 1.0; the largest is .9999. . . . Thus, multiplying by 100 gives a maximum value of 99.99999 . . . , and the integer portion is 99. The formula =INT(RAND()*100)+1 gives integers from 1 to 100.

To get multiple random numbers, you copy the formula to multiple cells. Pressing the F9 function key generates new values. Doing other operations in the worksheet also will trigger a recalculation and generate new values. If you want to "lock in" a particular batch of random numbers, select the range, copy, and then do an Edit | Paste Special | Values. You can paste into a new range or overwrite the original range.

Random Numbers with MegaStat

TUTORIAL 10

MegaStat's Generate Random Numbers option automates and expands random number generation. You specify how many values you want, the number of decimals of rounding (if any), and whether you want fixed values or functions that can be recalculated. In addition to uniformly distributed random numbers, you also may specify normal or exponentially distributed values. Exponentially distributed numbers give a skewed distribution.

Exhibit 7-1 shows the output from MegaStat | Generate Random Numbers, specifying a sample size of 28, zero decimal places, live functions, and normally distributed values with a mean of 100 and a standard deviation of 16. The program calculates the mean and the standard deviation of the randomly generated sample. Since it is a random sample, the actual mean and standard deviation are not exactly 100 and 16; however, if you press F9 a number of times, you will find that the values are generally close to the input parameters.

Randomizing Data

Sometimes you want to rearrange a column of existing values randomly, that is, shuffle them. For example, if you wanted to take a random sample

EXHIBIT 7-1
Sample of 28 normally distributed random numbers.

Normally Distributed Random Numbers (Press F9 to recalculate values.)

parameters	
Mean	100
Stdev	16
Dec places	0

calculated	
mean	99.86
std. dev.	13.30
n	28
min	71
max	126

Normal
89
105
91
110
100
101
108
83
119
106
82
71
110
105
94
126
98
96
109
91
98
103
100
113
102
92
122
72

of 25 from 100 values, you would shuffle the values and then take the first 25.

The procedure for shuffling data is to put a column of RAND() functions next to the column (or columns) to be shuffled. Click any cell in the random number column and then click the Sort Ascending button on Excel's toolbar. Sorting the random numbers has the effect of randomizing the contiguous columns of data. Note that the random numbers will not appear to be sorted because immediately after they are sorted, a recalculation is triggered that gives a new batch of random numbers. Typically, the random number column is deleted after it serves its purpose of shuffling the values.

GENERATING RANDOM NUMBERS
Learning Activity 7.A–1

- Open **RandomNumbers.xls!Start.**
- Create a sample of 20 random integers between 1 and 100 in cells A2:A21 by using the RAND() function as described in the text.
- Use the ROUND function to round the values to one decimal place in cells B2:B22. Solution: **RandomNumbers.xls!RandInt.**
- Use MegaStat | Generate Random Numbers to replicate Exhibit 7-1. Specify the following input:
  - There are 28 numbers to be generated.
  - Click the spin button to specify 0 decimal places.
  - These are live functions.
  - These are normally distributed numbers with a mean of 100 and a standard deviation of 16.
- Your output will look similar to Exhibit 7-1, but your numbers will be different. Press the F9 function key to generate different values. Notice how the samples will have a mean near 100 and a standard deviation near 16. Your output should look similar to that of the **Solution** worksheet.
- Look at the cell formulas to see if you can figure out how the normally distributed numbers are generated.
  - *Solution:* It probably is not important that you know how the numbers are generated; the trick is to assume that the values from RAND() are random probabilities that are input into the NORMINV() function to create the normally distributed random numbers.
- Select the 28 random numbers and do Copy and then Paste Special | Values in the same cells or a different location. Examine the values in the cells to note that the formulas were changed to actual numbers. This is how you freeze a particular batch of random numbers.
- Do MegaStat | Frequency Distributions | Quantitative to see if the distribution looks normal. If you create a larger batch of numbers, the distribution will be more likely to look like a normal distribution.
- Select cells B5:B44. Drag the "copy corner" of cell B44 two columns to the right to copy the formulas to columns C and D.
- Change the values in cells C5:D7 to get different normal distributions in columns B, C, and D. This shows how the formulas can be copied to create new variables. The bottom row also could be copied downward to increase the number of rows.
- Experiment with creating uniform and exponentially distributed random numbers and do frequency distributions to look at the shape.

RANDOMIZING DATA
Learning Activity 7.A–2

- Open **RandomNumbers.xls!PriceData.** This worksheet contains the Price variable from **RealEstateData.xls.** This Learning Activity shows how to select a random sample of values from data. To select a random sample from a column of numbers, the trick is to rearrange randomly (i.e., shuffle) the values and then pick the first n values, in this example the first 25. To shuffle the numbers, place random numbers in the column adjacent to the one (or ones) you want and then sort the random number column. The effect is to rearrange any contiguous columns randomly. Here are the steps:
- Type =RAND() in cell C2 and copy it down through C101.
- Click anywhere in the random number range C2:C126 and then click Excel's Sort Ascending or Sort Descending button and notice how the Price values are shuffled. You can click Sort more than once, but once is enough.
  - Note that the random numbers do not appear to be sorted. Actually, they were briefly sorted, but the sort operation triggered a recalculation that created a new batch of random numbers.
- If you now take the first 25 values, they will be a random sample. **RandomNumbers.xls!PriceData_shuffled** is the solution worksheet. Any 25 values will be a random sample, but if you allow that, you open up the possibility of someone looking for a batch of 25 that have a particular characteristic.
- If you wanted to put the numbers back in their original order, you could sort the No. variable. (Try it.) If you want to get numbers back into their original sequence, you need to include a sequential number variable; otherwise there is no easy way to undo the shuffling.

7.B   CENTRAL LIMIT THEOREM SIMULATION

CLT.xls is an Excel workbook that shows how the central limit theorem works. Each row in the body of the worksheet shows a random sample of size 15 from a uniform population. For example, cells A4:O4 represent the first sample. Each cell contains the formula =ROUND(RAND()*100,1), which generates random numbers from 0 to 100 and rounds them to one decimal place (see Module 7.A). Cell P4 calculates the mean of the sample. Why a sample size of 15? It is a small but not tiny value, and 15 columns fit on most computer screens. Any sample size could have been used. Larger samples would make the central limit theorem work even better.

The sampling then is repeated for 600 rows. Why 600? There is nothing magical about 600; it is a moderately large number that will produce enough outcomes to have a stable distribution but not so large that it will make the file too large or slow down recalculation times.

If you click the View Summary button or scroll to the bottom of the worksheet, you will see the charts summarizing the simulation. Every time you click the Recalc button, you get a new batch of 600 samples each of size 15. Exhibit 7-2

EXHIBIT 7-2   One output from the central limit theorem simulation.

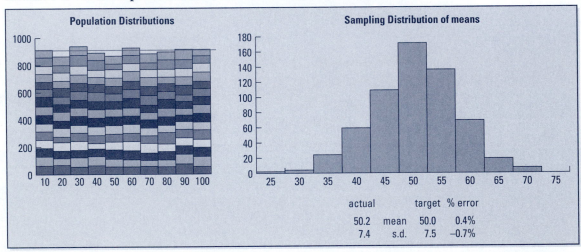

	actual		target	% error
	50.2	mean	50.0	0.4%
	7.4	s.d.	7.5	−0.7%

CENTRAL LIMIT THEOREM SIMULATION   Learning Activity 7.B–1

- Open **CLTs.xls.** This Excel workbook contains 600 random samples from a uniform distribution and summarizes the distribution of the population and the distribution of the means: the sampling distribution.
- Examine the worksheet and the formulas; however, it is more important to see what this illustrates than to see the details of how it works. Note how the individual observations vary from 0 to 100 and the means hover around 50. Why is that?
  - *Answer:* For a mean to be very large, say, above 90, most of the values in the sample have to be above 90, and that is unlikely. In other words, small values cancel large values, and the result tends to be near the mean most of the time.
- Click on the View Summary button or scroll to the bottom to view the summary charts. Press F9 or click the Recalc button several times to see how the sampling distribution is always nearly normal even though the population is essentially flat.

1
0
0
0
1
1
0
1
0
1
0
0
0
1
0
1
0
0
1
1
0
0
0
1
1

Do you own or rent?

1 = own
0 = rent

EXHIBIT 7-3
Rent versus own data to illustrate a proportion.

shows the results of one iteration. The left chart shows the population distribution. Because Excel's FREQUENCY() function gets the frequencies from each of the 15 columns, the colored bars show the 15 frequencies stacked. The red line shows where they would line up with a perfectly uniform distribution.

The right-hand chart shows the distribution of the means column. As you click the Recalc button, you find the distribution of means to be approximately normal even though the population is essentially flat, just as the central limit theorem states.

7.C   A PROPORTION IS A MEAN

A graduate school professor wants to estimate the proportion of MBA students who own their own homes. Using his statistics class as a sample,[3] he asks each student if he or she owns or rents and codes the data 1 = own, 0 = rent, with the results shown in Exhibit 7-3.

There are 25 students in the class, and 11 of them own their homes. Therefore, the proportion is

$$p = \frac{count}{n} = \frac{11}{25} = .44$$

Now notice what happens when we calculate the mean of the data by using Equation [2.1]:

$$\overline{X} = \frac{\sum X_i}{n} = \frac{11}{25} = .44.$$

REPLICATE TEXT VALUES FOR PROPORTION AS A MEAN
Learning Activity **7.C–1**

- Open **Proportions.xls!Start.**
- Replicate the values in Module 7.C.
- Check the solution and cell formulas in **Proportions.xls!Solution1.** Note that the solution worksheet shows three different methods of calculating the proportion.

PRACTICE WITH PROPORTION AS A MEAN
Learning Activity **7.C–2**

- Open **Proportions.xls!Practice.** This worksheet identifies whether families in a neighborhood own an SUV (0 = no, 1 = yes).
- Calculate the proportion and the mean. Verify they are the same.
- Check the solution and cell formulas in **Proportions.xls!.**
- **Solution2.** Note that the solution worksheet shows three different methods for calculating the proportion.

---

[3]This obviously is a convenience sample rather than a true random sample, but that is not relevant to the concept being illustrated.

Both give the same results. Why? Because when you sum 0's and 1's, the sum is the same as counting the 1's. Thus, a proportion is a mean of data values that are 0's and 1's.

If you calculate the standard error of the proportion using Equation [7.5], you get

$$\sigma_p = \sqrt{\frac{.44(1-.44)}{25}} = .0993$$

If you then calculate the standard error of the mean from the raw data in Exhibit 7-3 by using Equation [7.3], you get the same answer.

CHAPTER EIGHT

Confidence Intervals

8.1 Confidence Intervals (p. 110)

8.2 Sample Size Estimation (p. 114)

Summary (p. 117)

Exercises (p. 118)

Modules for Chapter Eight

8.A Equations for Confidence Intervals and Sample Size (p. 118)

8.B Confidence Interval Simulation (p. 120)

8.1   Confidence Intervals

We saw in Chapter 7 that the best estimate of the population mean is the sample mean, but the sample mean is rarely exactly the same as the population mean. Using the concept of a sampling distribution, we can calculate a **confidence interval** that is a range of numbers around the mean that lets us "hedge our bet" and say that it is likely that the interval contains the true mean. Confidence intervals can be calculated for any statistic, and we will see some in later chapters, but the **confidence interval for the mean** is the most common.

Confidence Interval: Mean

We start by finding a 95% confidence interval and later see how to change to 99% or other levels. Remember from the discussion in the normal distribution chapter of common z-values (Exhibit 6-5) that 95% of the curve falls within ±1.96 standard deviations from the mean. This means that the probability is .95 that a z-value sampled at random from a normal distribution will be between plus and minus 1.96 (see Exhibit 6-6). Stated more formally:

$$P(-1.96 \le z \le +1.96) = .95 \qquad \text{[8.1]}$$

If we substitute the sampling distribution version of z, Equation [7.4],

$$P\left(-1.96 \le \frac{\overline{X} - \mu}{\sigma/\sqrt{n}} \le +1.96\right) = .95 \qquad \text{[8.2]}$$

and do some algebra (shown in Module 8.A) to get μ by itself in the middle, we end up with a confidence interval:

$$P\left(\overline{X} - 1.96\frac{\sigma}{\sqrt{n}} \le \mu \le \overline{X} + 1.96\frac{\sigma}{\sqrt{n}}\right) = .95 \qquad \text{[8.3]}$$

The confidence interval is a probability statement. It says that the probability is .95 that the interval contains the true population mean, μ, somewhere in the range between two numbers, the sample mean minus and plus a quantity. Confidence intervals usually are stated as two numbers: the lower limit and the upper limit. However, you always should think of a confidence interval as a probability statement: There is a 95% chance that any given confidence interval includes the true mean, μ.

People often misinterpret a confidence interval and say that it means that 95% of the population falls within the interval, but that is incorrect because the confidence interval is a statement about the mean. It is also incorrect to say, "There is a 95% chance that the mean will be in the interval." That implies that the interval is fixed and the mean is the variable. However, it is the other way around: The population mean is fixed, and the probability statement is a statement about the interval. A confidence interval puts brackets around the *sample* mean and says that there is a 95% chance that the *population* mean is contained in the interval.

TUTORIAL 9

Module 8.B discusses a worksheet that starts with the central limit theorem simulation worksheet from Module 7.B. It then calculates a confidence interval for each sample and checks to see if the interval contains the population mean. Note that as you recalculate the simulation, approximately 95% of the intervals contain the population mean.

EXHIBIT 8-1
A confidence interval is the sample mean plus and minus the margin of error.

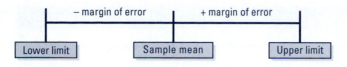

A general expression for confidence intervals often is stated as

$$\text{Sample value} \pm \text{margin of error} \qquad \textbf{[8.4]}$$

The quantity that is added and subtracted—the **margin of error**—is z times the standard error. It sometimes is also called the half-width because the total width of the interval is the distance that is added on one side and subtracted on the other (see Exhibit 8-1).

Restating Equation [8.3] in this form, we get the general expression for the confidence interval for a mean:

$$\overline{X} \pm z \frac{\sigma}{\sqrt{n}} \qquad \textbf{[8.5]}$$

To change a 95% confidence interval to a different percentage, we change the z-value. For example, a 99% confidence would use z = 2.58 (see common z-values in Exhibit 6-5). Being 99% confident that the mean is in our interval seems better than being 95% confident, but there is a trade-off, namely, that the confidence interval is wider. Indeed, we could have a 100% confidence interval by saying the population mean is between plus and minus infinity, but obviously that would not give us any information.

In developing the equation for the confidence interval, we started with the equation for a z-value for a sampling distribution (Equation [7.4]):

$$z = \frac{\overline{X} - \mu}{\dfrac{\sigma}{\sqrt{n}}}$$

This equation assumes we know the population standard deviation, σ, but what happens when we don't know σ, which is almost always the case? Since we have a sample, we can use the sample standard deviation as an estimate of the population standard deviation. The sample version of the standard error of the mean is (review Equation [7.3])

$$s_{\overline{X}} = \frac{s}{\sqrt{n}} \qquad \textbf{[8.6]}$$

Thus, even though Equation [8.5] is the proper definition of a confidence interval for the mean, that interval usually is calculated by using the sample standard deviation:

$$\overline{X} \pm z \frac{s}{\sqrt{n}} \qquad \textbf{[8.7]}$$

When the sample size is moderately large, around 30 or larger, substituting s for σ works fine. It also is acceptable for smaller sample sizes if the population distribution is even roughly normal.[1]

---

[1]In Chapter 10 we will revisit confidence intervals and see how to handle smaller sample sizes when using s instead of the population standard deviation.

Example 1

A man recently subscribed to a cable-based Internet service. At a party Saturday night he wants to brag that he is getting a download speed of 2000 kilobits per second (Kbs). Having taken a statistics class, however, he wants to be precise about his statement. First he collects a sample of 28 download readings by using http://www.pcpitstop.com/internet/Bandwidth.asp.

The results are shown in Kbs.xls, and the MegaStat Descriptive Statistics output is shown in Exhibit 8-2.

EXHIBIT 8-2   MegaStat Descriptive Statistics output for confidence interval example.

Descriptive statistics	
	Kbs
count	28
mean	2,005.54
sample standard deviation	184.27
sample variance	33,955.29
confidence interval 95.% lower	1,937.28
confidence interval 95.% upper	2,073.79
margin of error	68.25
z	1.96

Let's now show how these numbers were calculated. First we calculate the standard error of the mean by using Equation [8.6]:

$$s_{\bar{x}} = \frac{s}{\sqrt{n}} = \frac{184.27}{\sqrt{28}} = 34.824$$

The z-value for this calculation is 1.96 (95%, two-tail). Multiplying z times the standard error gives the margin of error:

$$\text{Margin of error} = z \cdot s_{\bar{x}} = 1.96 * 34.824 = 68.25$$

Subtracting and adding the margin of error to the mean gives the lower and upper confidence limits:

$$\text{Lower limit} = \text{mean} - \text{margin of error} = 2005.54 - 68.25 = 1937.28$$

$$\text{Upper limit} = \text{mean} + \text{margin of error} = 2005.54 + 68.25 = 2073.79$$

Thus, at the party he says, "Hey, I'm getting 2000 kilobits per second with my new cable modem. Well, actually I'm getting an average of 2005.54 kilobits per second from a sample of size 28, and the 95% confidence interval goes from about 1937 to 2074, meaning that there is a 95% chance the true mean is between those values."

CONFIDENCE INTERVAL FOR A MEAN   Learning Activity **8.1–1**

- Open **Kbs.xls!Data.**
- Calculate the mean and standard deviation of the Kbs variable by using AVERAGE() and STDEV().
- Use a calculator (or Excel as a calculator) to replicate the 95% confidence interval for the mean shown in Example 1 in Section 8.1. Calculate the confidence interval by using MegaStat I Confidence Intervals I Sample Size I Confidence Interval— Mean.
- Calculate the confidence interval by using MegaStat I Descriptive Statistics.
- See **Kbs.xls!Solution1** for the solution.
- Now calculate the 99% confidence interval by using a calculator and with MegaStat.
- Compare the 95% and 99% confidence intervals.
  - You will find that the 99% confidence interval is over 31% wider to increase the confidence by 4% (**Kbs.xls!Solution1a**).

Confidence Interval: Proportion

To calculate the **confidence interval for a proportion,** you substitute the standard error for the proportion. The equation then becomes

$$p \pm z\sqrt{\frac{p(1-p)}{n}} \qquad\qquad [8.8]$$

Notice that the standard error of the proportion is calculated by using the sample proportion, p, instead of the population proportion, π, that was shown in Equation [7.5] because we do not know π and have to estimate it from the sample. Indeed, if we knew π, we would not have any reason to calculate a confidence interval.

Example 2

The research department for a news magazine reports that 56% of its sample of 756 people think a particular political candidate is trustworthy. What is the 95% confidence interval?

Since the 95% two-tail z-value is 1.96, the margin of error is as follows:

$$\text{Margin of error} = z\sqrt{\frac{p(1-p)}{n}} = 1.96\sqrt{\frac{.56(1-.56)}{756}} = .035$$

Thus, the margin of error as reported in many polls is actually the half-width of a confidence interval. Subtracting and adding the margin of error gives the lower and upper confidence interval:

$$\text{Lower limit} = p - \text{margin of error} = .56 - .035 = .525$$
$$\text{Upper limit} = p + \text{margin of error} = .56 + .035 = .595$$

There is a 95% chance that the true proportion falls between .525 and .595.

8.2   Sample Size Estimation

Since sampling is often expensive and time-consuming, it is useful to know approximately what size sample we need for a given level of accuracy.

Sample Size: Mean

We approach the problem of **sample size estimation for the mean** similarly to the development of the confidence interval by starting with a z-value for a sampling distribution as shown in Equation [7.4]:

$$z = \frac{\overline{X} - \mu}{\frac{\sigma}{\sqrt{n}}}$$

By doing some simple algebra (Module 8.A) to solve for n, we get

$$n = \left(\frac{z\sigma}{E}\right)^2 \qquad \textbf{[8.9]}$$

Where:

 z = z-value corresponding to the confidence level, e.g., 1.96 for 95%.
 σ = population standard deviation.
 E = **error tolerance,** namely, how close we want our estimate to be to the population mean. E represents the absolute value of $\overline{X} - \mu$ in the expression for z.

In calculating n, we get to choose z and E; the challenge is to come up with a reasonable value for σ. If we knew enough about a population to know its standard deviation, we probably also would know its mean and would not be trying to determine a sample size to estimate the mean. So what do you do? One approach would be to make a reasonable guess at the standard deviation or look at similar data. You also could take a small sample from the population and use the sample standard deviation as an estimate of σ. If you did proper random sampling, you could use the data values from your pilot study as part of the final sample. When you take the final sample, you should see if its standard deviation is close to the pilot value. If it is smaller, your sample probably was larger than necessary. If the actual standard deviation is considerably larger than the pilot value, you might consider increasing the sample size by using the standard deviation from the sample.

Example 3

An Internet-based computer accessory company wants to estimate the mean amount each customer purchases within $2 with 95% confidence. A small pilot sample indicates that the standard deviation is about 5.5. Substituting into Equation [8.9], you get

$$n = \left(\frac{z\sigma}{E}\right)^2 = \left(\frac{1.96 * 5.5}{2}\right)^2 = 29.05$$

which is rounded up to a sample size of 30. Sample size calculations usually are rounded up because a slightly larger sample size will give a better estimate.

Learning Activity 8.2–1 shows how changing the input values affects the sample size. You will find that if you want a precise estimate (E) with a high degree of confidence (z) in a population with a lot of variance (σ), you will need a large sample size.

SAMPLE SIZE FOR A MEAN — Learning Activity **8.2–1**

- Open **SampleSize.xls!Start.**
- Use a calculator (or Excel as a calculator) to replicate the sample size calculation for the mean shown in Example 3 in Section 8.2.
- Calculate the confidence interval by using MegaStat | Confidence Intervals | Sample Size | Sample Size—Mean
- See **SampleSize.xls!Solution1** for the solution.
- Experiment with changing the error tolerance, confidence level, and standard deviation and note the effect on the sample size.

Sample Size: Proportion

The equation for **sample size estimation for proportions** is similar to the one for means:

$$n = \pi(1 - \pi)\left(\frac{z}{E}\right)^2 \qquad \text{[8.10]}$$

This equation really is a catch-22 because you are calculating what sample size would be needed to estimate π, but π is a part of the equation. As with σ, you can take a pilot sample or use historical data to estimate π; however, there is another option you can use. If you try multiplying different values of π by $(1 - \pi)$, you will find that the product is largest when $\pi = .5$. Thus, a conservative (i.e., larger) sample size is calculated by using $\pi = .5$. This is probably the best approach unless you have a good reason to believe π is near 0 or 1.

Example 4

A political polling company wants to estimate with a margin of error of 4% the proportion of people who will vote for a candidate, using a 95% confidence level. Since the company does not know the true proportion, it should use $\pi = .5$. Substituting into Equation [8.10], you get

$$.5(1 - .5)\left(\frac{1.96}{.04}\right)^2 = 600.25$$

which would round to 601. Remember that this is not a precise calculation since we do not know the true population proportion. However, we do know that a sample size of 60 would be too small and a sample size of 6000 would be unnecessarily large.

SAMPLE SIZE FOR A PROPORTION   Learning Activity **8.2–2**

- Open **SampleSize.xls!Start.**
- Use a calculator (or Excel as a calculator) to replicate the sample size calculation for the proportion shown in Example 4 in Section 8.2.
- Calculate the confidence interval by using MegaStat | Confidence Intervals | Sample Size | Sample Size—p.
- See **SampleSize.xls!Solution2** for the solution.
- Experiment with changing the error tolerance, confidence level, and standard deviation and note the effect on the sample size.

WHY p = .5 IS THE DEFAULT VALUE   Learning Activity **8.2–3**

- Open **SampleSize.xls!Why p of .5.**
- In calculating a sample size for a proportion, a value of .5 is used for the estimate of the population proportion if there is no evidence that another value is the correct value. Study this worksheet to see why p = .5 gives the most conservative, that is, largest, sample size relative to any other value of p.

Relationship between Sample Size Estimation and Confidence Intervals

If you take a sample of the size calculated by the sample size equation, the margin of error of the confidence interval calculated from the sample should be close to the error tolerance used to calculate the sample size.

Referring to Example 3, if we calculate the margin of error for a confidence interval by using 5.5 as the standard deviation and 29.05 (the calculated sample size before rounding) as the sample size, we get a margin of error of 2.000 that is exactly the specified error tolerance:

$$\text{Margin of error } = 1.96 \frac{5.5}{\sqrt{29.05}} = 2.000$$

In practice, it will not turn out to be exactly 2.000 because the sample size will have to be an integer number, in this case rounded up to 30. Of course, the standard deviation from the sample will not be the same as the value we used for the sample size estimation, although it should be relatively close; if it very different, you should review the sample size calculation. The margin of error of the confidence interval should be relatively close to the error tolerance. The point is this: When you specify the error tolerance (E) for the sample size estimation, you are indicating what you want the margin of error to be for a confidence interval calculated from the resulting sample.

CONFIDENCE INTERVAL AND SAMPLE SIZE PRACTICE

Learning Activity **8.2–4**

- Open **Population.xls!Data.** This worksheet contains 10,000 values in column B that we will consider to be a population. Our first task is to estimate the mean of the population based on a sample of 30 items from the population.
- Click any of the values in Column A and then click Excel's Sort Ascending button. This will shuffle the values in Column B. (See Module 7.A for details on randomization.)
- After the values in Column B are shuffled, the first 30 values in cells B2:B31 are a random sample from the population. Click the dropdown arrow in Excel's Name Box in **Population.xls!Data** and then click Sample to see that the named range "Sample" refers to these cells.
- Calculate the 95% confidence interval with a calculator and by using Excel as a calculator. Verify your answer with MegaStat. Check by clicking the **Solution** worksheet.
- Go to the **Population.xls!Data** worksheet. In cell E23 calculate the sample size needed to estimate the mean within ±20 with 95% confidence. Use the standard deviation from your sample of 30. Verify your calculations with MegaStat.
- Shuffle Column B again by sorting column A. Select a sample of the size calculated in the previous step (use the Excel status bar to count the cells; review Learning Activity 2.1–2). Copy/paste the values into **Sheet3**. Use MegaStat I Descriptive Statistics to calculate the 95% confidence interval (check the "z" box for the confidence interval option). Verify that the margin of error of the confidence interval is approximately 20, the error tolerance specified in the sample size calculation.
- Why is the margin of error not exactly 20?
  - *Answer:* (1) Because we are sampling, and (2) because the standard deviation used in the sample size calculation may not be very close to the population standard deviation, leading to a sample size that is not optimal.

Summary

Chapter 7 on sampling distributions showed that the sample mean is the best estimate of the population mean. This chapter extended that idea to confidence intervals. A confidence interval for a mean is the mean plus and minus the margin of error, where the margin of error is the z-value corresponding to the confidence level times the standard error of the mean.

A confidence interval is actually a probability statement. It says there is a 95% chance that any given confidence interval includes the population mean.

The flip side of confidence intervals is sample size estimation. By letting E, the error tolerance, represent how precise we want the sample to be, we can estimate approximately the sample size we need. Calculations of sample size are not very precise because the formulas require us to specify values we can only estimate (σ in Equation [8.9] and π in Equation [8.10]).

Conceptual

- Although the confidence intervals in this chapter were for means and proportions, you can calculate a confidence interval for any statistic if you have an expression for the standard error:

$$\text{Sample value} \pm \text{margin of error} \qquad \text{Equation [8.4]}$$

- Confidence interval for a mean (using s to estimate σ):

$$\overline{X} \pm z\frac{s}{\sqrt{n}} \qquad \text{Equation [8.7]}$$

- Confidence interval for a proportion:

$$p \pm z \sqrt{\frac{p(1-p)}{n}} \qquad \text{Equation [8.8]}$$

- Sample size estimation for a mean:

$$n = \left(\frac{z\sigma}{E}\right)^2 \qquad \text{Equation [8.9]}$$

- Sample size estimation for a proportion:

$$n = \pi(1-\pi)\left(\frac{z}{E}\right)^2 \qquad \text{Equation [8.10]}$$

- Relationship between confidence intervals and sample size estimation: The error tolerance (E) in the sample size equations corresponds to the margin of error in a confidence interval. If we take a sample of the size calculated, the margin of error should be close to the error tolerance.

Applied

- Be able to calculate and interpret confidence intervals for means and proportions
- Be able to estimate sample sizes for means and proportions

Exercises

The exercises and data are found in **Ch_08_Confidence_Intervals.xls** in the exercises folder of the CD.

No.	Content
1	Confidence interval—mean
2	Confidence interval—mean (create your own)
3	Confidence interval—proportion
4	Confidence interval—proportion (create your own)
5	Sample size—mean
6	Sample size—mean
7	Sample size—mean (create your own)
8	Sample size—proportion
9	Sample size—proportion
10	Sample size—proportion (create your own)

Modules for Confidence Intervals

8.A   EQUATIONS FOR CONFIDENCE INTERVALS AND SAMPLE SIZE

This section shows the development (dare we say derivation?) of the equations for confidence intervals and sample size. Starting with the equation for a z-value, we do some fairly simple algebra and end up with a confidence interval. It probably is not necessary for you to be able to replicate the algebra, but this material does show that a confidence interval is based on a simple probability statement about a z-value.

Confidence Interval

In Section 8.1 we said that we could start with a probability statement about z-values from a normal distribution

$$P(-1.96 \leq z \leq +1.96) = .95$$

and do some algebra to end up with a confidence interval. Here is where we see the algebra.

First, we substitute the sampling distribution version of z (Equation [7.4]). Let's also drop the probability notation to make things cleaner and put it back at the end:

$$-1.96 \leq \frac{\overline{X} - \mu}{\frac{\sigma}{\sqrt{n}}} \leq +1.96$$

If we can get μ by itself in the middle, we end up with a confidence interval.

Multiply by $\dfrac{\sigma}{\sqrt{n}}$:

$$-1.96 \frac{\sigma}{\sqrt{n}} \leq \overline{X} - \mu \leq +1.96 \frac{\sigma}{\sqrt{n}}$$

Subtract $\overline{X}$

$$-\overline{X} - 1.96 \frac{\sigma}{\sqrt{n}} \leq -\mu \leq -\overline{X} + 1.96 \frac{\sigma}{\sqrt{n}}$$

Now all we need to do is get rid of the minus sign in front of μ. This is done by multiplying by -1, which changes the signs and changes the $\leq$ symbols to $\geq$:

$$\overline{X} + 1.96 \frac{\sigma}{\sqrt{n}} \geq \mu \geq \overline{X} - 1.96 \frac{\sigma}{\sqrt{n}}$$

Flipping the inequality again and putting the probability notation back in place, we have our confidence interval:

$$P\left(\overline{X} - 1.96 \frac{\sigma}{\sqrt{n}} \leq \mu \leq \overline{X} + 1.96 \frac{\sigma}{\sqrt{n}}\right) = .95$$

The confidence interval for proportions can be developed in the same way. Just substitute p for $\overline{X}$ and the standard error of the proportion for the standard error of the mean.

Sample Size

The formula for sample size is developed in a manner similar to that for confidence intervals. First we start with the z-value formula for a sampling distribution and solve for n:

$$z = \frac{\overline{X} - \mu}{\frac{\sigma}{\sqrt{n}}}$$

The absolute value of the numerator part is called the error tolerance: how close we want the sample mean to be to the population mean. The numerator is replaced by E, representing the error tolerance:

$$z = \frac{E}{\frac{\sigma}{\sqrt{n}}}$$

Simplify the right side with an invert and multiply:

$$z = \frac{E\sqrt{n}}{\sigma}$$

Multiply by σ/E to cancel out on right side:

$$\frac{z\sigma}{E} = \sqrt{n}$$

Square both sides and flip left and right:

$$n = \left(\frac{z\sigma}{E}\right)^2$$

Thus, we have the equation for sample size estimation.

8.B   CONFIDENCE INTERVAL SIMULATION

CLT-CI.xls is a worksheet (Exhibit 8-3) that illustrates the concept of confidence intervals. It is similar to the worksheet from Module 7.B except that it uses a sample size of 30 and for each sample calculates the 95% confidence interval. The lower and upper bounds of each confidence interval are shown in columns AF and AG. Since we are sampling from a uniform population, we can determine the true value of σ; that value is shown in cell AF2. (The formula used for finding σ isn't important here—just accept it.)

In column AH, an IF() statement places a 1 in the cell if the confidence interval contains the population mean of 50 and a 0 if it does not. Note that the confidence intervals in rows 11, 13, and 20 do not include 50.

The percent in cell AH5 is the proportion of the 600 confidence intervals that contain the population mean. Since we calculated 95% confidence intervals, the value should be around 95%. When you open the workbook and press the F9 function key, you will find that although the percent varies, it always will be pretty close to 95%. The simulation output captured in Exhibit 8-3 shows that 95.2% of the confidence intervals include the population mean.

A confidence interval says that there is a 95% chance that any given confidence interval contains the true population mean. That was illustrated with this simulation.

EXHIBIT 8-3
A portion of the confidence interval simulation worksheet.

	AB	AC	AD	AE	AF	AG	AH	AI	AJ
1					1.96 = z		95% confidence level		
2					28.87 = σ				
3					10.33 = margin of error				
4									
5							**94.8%**		
6	X28	X29	X30	mean	lower	upper	OK?		
7	28.0	70.3	89.3	48.9	38.6	59.2	1		
8	31.4	42.5	40.0	51.0	40.7	61.3	1		
9	71.2	65.5	59.1	59.7	49.3	70.0	1		
10	84.1	46.0	26.5	50.4	40.0	60.7	1		
11	26.6	76.3	34.7	36.8	26.5	47.2	0		
12	50.7	98.2	50.2	48.9	38.5	59.2	1		
13	68.6	10.4	68.5	60.8	50.5	71.1	0		
14	46.8	98.8	23.9	47.7	37.4	58.0	1		
15	53.0	80.4	48.8	45.8	35.5	56.1	1		
16	7.7	50.7	42.1	50.4	40.1	60.7	1		
17	46.7	45.3	52.0	48.2	37.9	58.5	1		
18	11.4	71.6	74.6	58.0	47.7	68.4	1		
19	62.2	51.7	48.0	53.7	43.3	64.0	1		
20	85.1	69.3	19.6	38.4	28.0	48.7	0		
21	82.4	27.1	43.6	49.6	39.2	59.9	1		
22	51.4	60.0	27.2	53.0	42.6	63.3	1		
23	63.5	37.6	92.4	52.7	42.3	63.0	1		

CONFIDENCE INTERVAL SIMULATION   Learning Activity 8.B–1

- Open **CLT-CI.xls.** This worksheet is similar to the central limit theorem worksheet from Module 7.B except that it uses a sample size of 30 instead of 15. Click on the View Summary button and click Recalc a few times to see that a large sample size gives an even more normal sampling distribution than a sample of size 15 did.

- Move to the top of the worksheet and scroll right so that you can see columns AF through AH. For each of the samples, the 95% confidence interval is calculated.

- Examine cell AF3 to see how the margin of error is calculated. Compare this cell formula to the right-hand side of Equation [8.5]. Examine the cells in columns AF and AG to see that the confidence interval is the sample mean plus and minus the margin of error.

- Examine the IF() statement in column AG to see how a 1 is placed in the cell if the confidence interval includes the true mean of 50; otherwise, a 0 is placed in the cell.

- Press the F9 function key a few times and notice that the percent of confidence intervals that include population mean of 50 is around 95%.

- Scroll down and find one confidence interval where the mean is too small and one where the mean is too large.

- Change cell AH1 to 99% and press F9 a few times to see that the observed percent is around 99%. Try this also with the 90% and 50%.

- Bonus Challenge Learning Activity: Add the columns to calculate a sample standard deviation for each sample and calculate the confidence interval based on the sample standard deviation, s. Add the IF() statement column and see if the percents are similar to the percents using the margin of error based on the populaton standard deviation, σ. You should find that around 95% of the intervals contain the population mean, perhaps a bit less (solution: **CLT-CI2.xls**).

- Double Bonus Challenge Learning Activity: From the worksheet in the previous step, calculate the confidence interval based on a sample size of 15 or less. You should find that as the sample size gets smaller, fewer than 95% of the intervals will contain the population mean.

CHAPTER NINE

Hypothesis Testing Concepts

9.1 Introduction to Hypothesis Testing (p. 124)

9.2 Steps of Hypothesis Testing (p. 124)

   Summary (p. 132)

   Exercises (p. 133)

Module for Chapter Nine

9.A Hypothesis Testing Simulation (p. 133)

9.1   Introduction to Hypothesis Testing

Earlier we defined statistics as the concepts and tools used to make decisions from data. Now we finally are going to see how this is done with a statistical procedure known as **hypothesis testing.** Everything we have looked at up until now has prepared us for this chapter, and the rest of the book will consist of variations on the theme introduced here. Descriptive statistics techniques (frequency distributions, central tendency, and variation) are useful for summarizing data, but they also provide tools for more advanced analysis. The chapters on probability, sampling distributions, and confidence intervals provided the background necessary for this chapter; indeed, when you calculate a confidence interval, you are close to doing a **hypothesis test.**

Since all the previous chapters have led to hypothesis testing, it must be a difficult topic. Not really; in fact, it is a simple notion and something you implicitly do whenever:

- You make a statement about something.
- You collect sample data relating to the statement.
- If given that the statement is true, the sample outcome is unlikely, you realize that the statement probably is not true.

For example, assume you want to know if a particular coin is fair. Your statement (hypothesis) is that it is a fair coin. You toss the coin 20 times and get heads 18 times. Since that is an unlikely outcome given that it is a fair coin, you reject the hypothesis that it is a fair coin.

We now proceed to formalize this process. However, if you keep this example in mind, you will be able to keep things in perspective.

9.2   Steps of Hypothesis Testing

Hypothesis tests are best performed by explicitly going through the seven steps of the procedure:

- Step 1: Specify the null hypothesis and the alternative hypothesis.
- Step 2: What level of significance?
- Step 3: Which test and test statistic?
- Step 4: State the decision rule.
- Step 5: Use the sample data to calculate the test statistic.
- Step 6: Use the test statistic to make a decision.
- Step 7: Interpret the decision in the context of the original question.

The rest of this chapter discusses these steps in detail. In the specific tests in later chapters, we go through the steps for particular applications.

After you do several hypothesis tests, it is tempting to jump to the "bottom line"—the calculation step—but the steps are always implicitly there and always should be listed in a formal report.

To guide us through the steps, let us use the following example. Assume that a grade school teacher has a class of 28 students. If she can demonstrate that the students are "above average," she can get extra resources to teach the class.

She uses IQ scores as a measure of intelligence. IQ scores are standardized to have a population mean of 100 and a standard deviation of 16.

Step 1: Specify the Null Hypothesis and the Alternative Hypothesis

The **null hypothesis, H$_0$,** is the statement we are interested in testing. The word *null* implies "nothing" or "nonexistent." It indicates what would happen by chance or what would happen if there was no difference or no treatment effect. If you were testing whether a coin was fair, the null condition would be that it is fair; in the classroom example, the null condition is that the students have an average IQ.

The **alternative hypothesis, H$_1$,** is the statement that we accept if our sample outcome leads us to reject the null hypothesis. In the coin toss example, the alternative hypothesis would be that the coin is not fair; in the classroom example, the alternative hypothesis is that the average IQ of the students is greater than 100.

A formal statement of the hypotheses for the classroom example is as follows:

H$_0$: $\mu = 100$ (the students have an average IQ)
H$_1$: $\mu > 100$ (the students have an above-average IQ)

Here are some notes:

- The null hypothesis could have been written $\mu \leq 100$ (many books show it that way), but the equal condition is what we are interested in testing. If it turns out that the students' mean IQ is less than 100, that certainly would not provide evidence that they are above average. The important thing here is that the null hypothesis always includes the equal condition.

- Why is the alternative hypothesis greater than rather than less than or unequal to? Because the teacher is interested only in and has reason to believe the notion that the students are above average. She certainly could have tested whether they were below average; if she wanted to know if they were either above *or* below average, she could have done a "two-tailed" test. We will see examples of these tests in Chapter 10.

- The hypotheses are written in the form shown here, with a population parameter on the left and a numeric value on the right:

  H$_0$: $\mu = \mu_0$
  H$_1$: $\mu > \mu_0$
  μ_0 = the hypothesized value, 100 in this example

Step 2: What Level of Significance?

The **level of significance** is the probability of rejecting the null hypothesis by chance alone. How could that happen? It could result from sampling error (i.e., sampling variation): Every sample is different, and occasionally we get a sample just by chance that would lead to the rejection of the null hypothesis even though it is the correct hypothesis. For example, in the coin toss example, it is possible to get 18 out of 20 heads with a perfectly fair coin.

In the introduction to this chapter, we said that we would reject the null hypothesis if the sample result was unlikely given that it was true. The level of significance is our operational definition of *unlikely*. The traditional definition of *unlikely* is 5% of the time or less.

What Significance Level Should You Use?

A hypothesis is rejected if the sample result is unlikely given that the null hypothesis is true. We traditionally define unlikely as less than 5% of the time.

However, if, on the basis of the test, we are going to commit to an action that is expensive or health-related or could have legal consequences, we want to be more certain that we are not falsely rejecting the null hypothesis and reduce the significance level to .01 or even lower. We could make the significance level even smaller so that we almost never would falsely reject the null hypothesis, but there would be no point to doing a test if it was nearly impossible ever to reject the null hypothesis.

For example, if a company was going to commit a large amount of money to develop and market a product, it would want to make sure the decision was not based on a sampling error, and so it might make sense for that company to change the significance level from 5% to 1%. In contrast, if we are doing a pilot study or just want to have some indication of an effect, we might let the significance level be 10%. When in doubt, it is best to use the standard 5% level.

Type I and Type II Errors

The significance level sometimes is referred to as the probability of a Type I error. A **Type I error** occurs when you falsely reject the null hypothesis on the basis of sampling error. A **Type II error** occurs when you fail to reject the null hypothesis when it is false.

Exhibit 9-1 shows a classification of Type I and Type II errors. When you perform a hypothesis test, you make a decision: You reject or fail to reject the null hypothesis.

The null hypothesis is either true or false, as shown by the columns in the table. We do not know if the null hypothesis is true or false. If we did, we would not have to be doing a hypothesis test, but in fact, one of the columns is the true condition.

If we fail to reject the null hypothesis and the null hypothesis is true, we are in the upper left-hand cell and have made a correct decision. In the IQ example, this would mean that we said the class was average and it actually was.

If we reject the null hypothesis and it is false, we are in the lower right-hand cell and have made a correct decision. This would mean that we said the class was *above* average and it actually was.

EXHIBIT 9-1
Type I and Type II errors.

Decision:	Actual situation: H_0 is true	H_0 is false
Fail to Reject H_0	Correct decision	Type II error
Reject H_0	Type I error	Correct decision

If we reject the null hypothesis and it is actually true, we are in the lower left-hand cell and have made an incorrect decision, a Type I error. In the IQ example, this would mean that we said the class was *above* average and it actually was not. This could happen because of a sampling error; occasionally we get a sample that is above average even if the population is not. The probability of a Type I error is specified as the significance level of the test.

If we fail to reject the null hypothesis when we should have, we are in the upper right-hand cell and have made an incorrect decision, a Type II error. In the IQ example, this would mean that we said the class was *not* above average and it actually was. This could happen because of a sampling error; occasionally we get a sample that is average even if the population is above average. To calculate the probability of a Type II error, we need to make an assumption about how far the population mean is from the hypothesized value. Calculation of Type II errors is beyond the scope of this text.

Module 9.A discusses a simulation worksheet that lets you take repeated samples and actually see Type I and Type II errors occur. It probably would be best to look at it after reading the rest of this chapter.

Back to Our Example

alpha, lowercase Greek "a" (α) is used to represent the level of significance, and so this step would be listed as follows:

$$\alpha = .05$$

Step 3: Which Test and Test Statistic?

The **test statistic** is the value calculated from the sample to determine whether to reject the null hypothesis. If we can assume a normal sampling distribution of means, we can calculate a z-value for a sampling distribution. Can we make this assumption? Yes, since a sample of 28 is enough for the central limit theorem to be valid, especially since we have reason to believe that the population distribution of IQs is close to normal.

For our test we would state this step as mean versus hypothesized value, z-test.

The test statistic is

$$z = \frac{\overline{X} - \mu_0}{\frac{\sigma}{\sqrt{n}}} \qquad \text{[9.1]}$$

This equation is the same as Equation [7.4], a z-value from a sampling distribution. Note that this expression requires that we know the population standard deviation, σ; in this instance, we have the rare case of knowing σ since IQ tests have been developed and standardized to have a standard deviation of $\sigma = 16$. Chapter 10 shows the more commonly used test based on a sample standard deviation.

Step 4: State the Decision Rule

The **decision rule** is always of the following form:

Reject H_0 if . . .

We reject the null hypothesis if the test statistic is larger than a **critical value** corresponding to the significance level in step 2. Since the significance level is $\alpha = .05$, we find that in the table of common z-values (see Exhibit 6-5, Exhibit 6-6, or **Tables.xls! Common_z-values**) the z-value corresponding to .05 in the upper tail of the normal curve is 1.645. Thus, the decision rule would be stated as follows:

Reject H_0 if $z > 1.645$

The decision rule is shown graphically in Exhibit 9-2.

In this example we were testing whether the IQ scores are greater than 100. We also could have been interested in whether the mean is less than 100, or maybe we want to reject the hypothesis if the mean is either greater than *or* less than 100, that is, a two-tailed test. Exhibit 9-3 shows the decision rules for the three types of tests for a 5% significance level z-test; however, the general form is the same for different test statistics and different significance levels.

The z-values for the two-tail (not equal) test are $+1.96$ and -1.96 because the 5% significance level is split between both ends (tails) of the distribution.

When you are setting up a hypothesis test, always make sure the form of your decision rules corresponds to your hypothesis. Use Exhibit 9-3 as a guide.

EXHIBIT 9-2
Graphical representation of the decision rule.

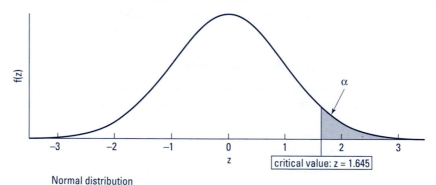

Normal distribution

P(lower)	P(upper)	z
.9500	.0500	1.645

EXHIBIT 9-3
Decision rules for different alternative hypotheses.

Alternative Hypothesis	Decision Rule
$H_1: \mu > \mu_0$ (greater than)	Reject H_0 if $z > 1.645$
$H_1: \mu < \mu_0$ (less than)	Reject H_0 if $z < -1.645$
$H_1: \mu \neq \mu_0$ (not equal)	Reject H_0 if $z > 1.96$ or $z < -1.96$

FIND z-VALUES FOR DIFFERENT HYPOTHESES

Learning Activity **9.1–1**

- Refer to Exhibit 6-6 and find the z-values in Exhibit 9-3.
- Note how the z-values correspond to .05 upper, .05 lower, and .05 split between both tails.

Step 5: Use the Sample Data to Calculate the Test Statistic

We still do not know the mean IQ of the students, and ideally you should set up the first four steps before you look at your data. In practice, you probably would already know the general outcome before you did a formal hypothesis test, but you should never let the results influence the choices you make in steps 1 through 4. You should not design or revise a test on the basis of the outcome of your data.

Assume that the mean IQ of the students is 105.6. If we substitute this into the equation for the test statistic, we get

$$z = \frac{\overline{X} - \mu_0}{\frac{\sigma}{\sqrt{n}}} = \frac{(105.6 - 100)}{\frac{16}{\sqrt{28}}} = 1.85$$

Exhibit 9-4 shows the MegaStat hypothesis test output, and Exhibit 9-5 shows a graphical representation of the output.

Step 6: Use the Test Statistic to Make a Decision

When we compare the result of step 5 to the decision rule in step 4, we see that 1.85 is greater than 1.645, and so we reject the null hypothesis.

Curiously, students often do everything correctly until this step but then make the wrong decision. If you explicitly compare the test statistic from step 5 to the decision rule in step 4, you should never get it wrong.

EXHIBIT 9-4
MegaStat output for hypothesis test.

	Hypothesis Test: Mean vs. Hypothesized Value
100.000	hypothesized value
105.600	mean IQ
16.000	std. dev.
3.024	std. error
28	n
1.85	z
.0320	p-value (one-tailed, upper)

EXHIBIT 9-5
Graphical representation of the hypothesis test.

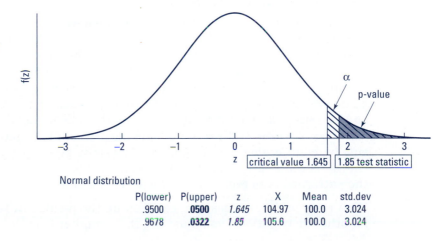

P(lower)	P(upper)	z	X	Mean	std.dev
.9500	.0500	1.645	104.97	100.0	3.024
.9678	.0322	1.85	105.6	100.0	3.024

Another observation is that students sometimes think that rejecting the null hypothesis is not a good outcome since the word *reject* has a negative connotation. In a strictly scientific context, we should not think in terms of good and bad outcomes, but in fact, we probably are doing the test because we want to show something or make some point and can do that only by rejecting the null hypothesis. Thus, in a hypothesis testing context, rejection usually is considered good.

Step 7: Interpret the Decision in the Context of the Original Question

At this step, you would go back and review why you have been doing the test and what the test tells us. In this example, the teacher would have statistical evidence that her class was above average.

Also at this step, you would want to carefully review the test: play "devil's advocate" if it is your test or critically examine someone else's test. Look for what I call "ya-buts"–"yes, the test is significant, but. . . ."

One question you always should ask if there is a significant result is whether the result is actually useful. To say that a result is "statistically significant" sounds impressive, but all it really means is that it is more than by chance alone. It does not imply real-world significance in terms of being large, practical, meaningful, or important. That is a decision that must be made without the help of statistics. Indeed, with a large sample size, trivial differences can become statistically significant. Remember: Significance is not necessarily significant.

Whether the mean of 105.6 is really meaningfully greater than 100 would have to be determined by the parties involved. Also, if you were a school administrator and did not want to come up with extra resources, you might question whether an IQ test is an appropriate measure of intelligence. It also would be valid to point out that the test is for the mean of the class. Even though the mean is significantly higher than 100, there could be several students near or below the mean. It would be useful to look at the actual data to see if there are one or more high outliers pulling up the mean.

We will see various ya-buts in later tests. Do not get so involved with the technical details that you forget to take a commonsense look at the test.

The Concept of a p-value

In step 5 we calculated z = 1.85, and in step 6 we rejected the null hypothesis because 1.85 was larger than the decision rule critical value of 1.645, meaning that it could have happened less than 5% of the time by chance alone. However, since we have calculated a z-value and can assume a normal distribution, we can find the exact probability of the result occurring by chance alone. What is the probability of a z-value greater than 1.85? Using the tables or with Excel or MegaStat, you should be able to verify that the probability is .0322. This is called the **p-value** of the test, and it is the probability of getting the sample result by chance alone if the null hypothesis is actually true. The p-value is shown as the upper shaded area in Exhibit 9-5, and the area is smaller than the patterned area representing the level of significance.

With tests using z-values, you can look up the p-value in the table. However, for other distributions, you must use the computer to calculate p-values.

When you are studying statistics, you should state the decision rule in terms of a critical value. However, as you become more experienced (and especially when you are using MegaStat, which always calculates the p-value for a test), you can use a more general form for the decision rule:

Reject H_0 if the p-value is less than α

(α typically would be .05 but could be any other significance level you deem appropriate for the test.)

Another advantage of this procedure is that the comparison is always "less than," never "greater than." If you are doing a "not equal" (two-tail) test, you double the one-tail p-value before comparing it to α because it is a two-tail test. MegaStat does this automatically.

Test Statistic versus p-value

The test statistic approach to hypothesis testing and the p-value approach are two ways of doing the same thing. Both methods require the calculation of a test statistic. The test statistic approach compares the value of the calculated test statistic to a critical value from a table; the p-value approach calculates the probability of the test statistic and compares it to the significance level, α (which is the critical value with this approach).

The test statistic approach has been the traditional method since it was developed before there was easy access to computers, and it still is used when computers are not available (e.g., on examinations). Assuming you have access to a computer and statistical software, the p-value approach is more efficient because you do not have to look up a critical value in a table. However, you are still using the significance level as a critical value, and you should choose a significance level before running the test.

With the p-value approach, instead of just rejecting the null hypothesis (or not rejecting it), you can get a sense of how significant (or not significant) the results are. For example, if a test has a p-value of .000035, it is very unlikely

REPLICATE TEXT HYPOTHESIS TEST CALCULATIONS
Learning Activity 9.1–2

- Open **Htest1.xls!Data**.
- Use a calculator to replicate the z-value in the text section.
- Determine the p-value by using the three methods discussed in Module 6.A.
- Replicate the z-value and the p-value by using MegaStat | Hypothesis Tests | Mean vs. Hypothesized Value.
  - Click "Summary Data" and select cells B3:B6 as the input range.
  - Select other options and values necessary to replicate the text z-value and p-value (Exhibit 9-4).
- Use MegaStat to replicate the normal distribution graphics in Exhibit 9-2 and Exhibit 9-5. Specify mean = 100 and std.dev = 100/SQRT(28), the standard error of the mean.
  - To get your output to look exactly like that in the exhibits, you will have to click in the label text boxes to add text and then move the boxes with the arrow keys or the mouse.

to have happened by chance alone; in contrast, if the p-value is .6849, it did not even come close to being significant. You still need to specify a significance level so that you can make a yes/no decision, but the p-value provides additional information. Of course, you can do a similar procedure with the test statistic approach by seeing how close the calculated test statistic is to the critical value, but that is not as precise since it is not stated in probability terms.

Remember that we said that you should set up steps 1 through 4 before looking at the data and not change the steps on the basis of your results. For example, if you had set up a 5% alpha level and your p-value turned out to be .000035, it would not be ethical to report the test with an alpha level of 1% or .1%, implying that you knew ahead of time that you thought your results were going to be significant at that level.

Hypothesis Testing as a Sampling Process

One of the hardest statistical ideas to comprehend is the concept of sampling. It is sometimes difficult to think of a class of 28 students as a sample. Can't we just treat them as a population and look at their mean IQ and see if it is greater than 100? However, the IQ scores are indeed a sample of all the possible IQ scores we could have observed. If we could "rewind the world" and start over, we would have a different batch of IQ scores.

Summary

- Try to keep in mind the basic idea of hypothesis testing:
  - Make a statement about something.
  - Collect sample data relating to the statement.
  - If the sample outcome is unlikely given that the statement is true, the statement probably is not true.
- The chapter used a z-test to test a mean versus a hypothesized value; however, the real-world version has a slight difference that we will see in Chapter 10 when we start looking at specific hypothesis testing applications.
- The main focus of this chapter was the introduction of the seven steps of hypothesis testing. As a summary, the seven steps are reviewed below with just the essential information for the example discussed above, with a few notes inserted. If you were answering a hypothesis testing question on an examination, this would give you a grade of 100.

Step 1: Specify the Null Hypothesis and the Alternative Hypothesis
H_0: $\mu = 100$ (the students have an average IQ)
H_1: $\mu > 100$ (the students have an above-average IQ)

Step 2: What Level of Significance?
$\alpha = .05$ (upper tail)   default value
(Know the difference between Type I and Type II errors. Module 9.A discusses a simulation worksheet that lets you take repeated samples and actually see Type I and Type II errors occur.)
(Know when you might use a value other than .05.)

Step 3: Which Test and Test Statistic?
Mean versus hypothesized value, z-test

The test statistic is

$$z = \frac{\overline{X} - \mu_0}{\frac{\sigma}{\sqrt{n}}}$$

Step 4: State the Decision Rule
Reject H_0 if z > 1.645 because 1.645 is the z-value associated with .05 (upper)

Step 5: Use the Sample Data to Calculate the Test Statistic

$$z = \frac{\overline{X} - \mu_0}{\frac{\sigma}{\sqrt{n}}} = \frac{(105.6 - 100)}{\frac{16}{\sqrt{28}}} = 1.85$$

Step 6: Use the Test Statistic to Make a Decision
Reject H_0 because 1.85 is greater than the critical value of 1.645

Also, reject it because the p-value of .0322 is less than .05 (know what a p-value is).

Step 7: Interpret the Decision in the Context of the Original Question
Look for issues and alternative explanations: ya-buts.

The class appears to be above average, but

1. The mean of 105.6 does not seem to be meaningful distance above 100.
2. IQ may not be the appropriate measure.
3. Maybe there are just few high outlier IQs that are inflating the mean.

Exercises

The exercises and data are found in **Ch_09_HTest_Intro.xls** in the exercises folder of the CD. This is mostly a conceptual chapter, and so there are only a couple of exercises.

No.	Content
1	Intro hypothesis testing
2	Intro hypothesis testing

Module for Hypothesis Testing Concepts

9.A HYPOTHESIS TESTING SIMULATION

HtestSim1.xls shows a simulation corresponding to the example we looked at in this chapter. As you click the Recalc button or press the F9 function key, new samples of students are displayed in the 28 blue cells. If you want to increase your Excel knowledge, look at the equations and see if you can "reverse engineer" the way in which values are simulated.

EXHIBIT 9-6
Output from hypothesis testing simulation.

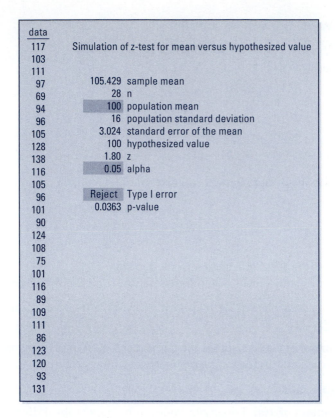

data	
117	Simulation of z-test for mean versus hypothesized value
103	
111	
97	105.429 sample mean
69	28 n
94	100 population mean
96	16 population standard deviation
105	3.024 standard error of the mean
128	100 hypothesized value
138	1.80 z
116	0.05 alpha
105	
96	Reject Type I error
101	0.0363 p-value
90	
124	
108	
75	
101	
116	
89	
109	
111	
86	
123	
120	
93	
131	

The green cells are values you can change. Since we are testing whether the mean is equal to 100, we rarely will reject the hypothesis when the population mean is set equal to 100, and when we do reject the hypothesis, it is an example of a Type I error (rejecting based on a lucky sample). If you change the population value to something larger, say, 107, you will find that the null hypothesis is rejected most of the time, and when it is not, you are looking at a Type II error (failing to reject when you should have since the population mean is greater than 100).

The output captured in Exhibit 9-6 shows a Type I error because the sample led to rejecting the null hypothesis even though the population mean was 100.

HYPOTHESIS TESTING SIMULATION   Learning Activity **9.A–1**

- Open **HtestSim1.xls.**
- Every time you click the Recalc button, you get a new sample of data. Keep clicking until you get a sample that leads to rejecting the null hypothesis, which is an example of Type I error—a significant result by chance alone.
- Click the Recalc button 100 times and count the number of Type I errors. It should be approximately five.
- Change the population mean in cell D7 to 103. Nonsignificant results are Type II errors: samples that do not lead to rejection of the null hypothesis even though the null hypothesis is false.
- Change the population mean in cell D7 to 105. As you continue to click Recalc, you will see relatively few Type II errors because the true mean is large enough that most samples will lead to rejecting the null hypothesis.

CHAPTER TEN

Hypothesis Testing Applications

10.1 Introduction (p. 136)

10.2 Mean versus Hypothesized Value (Test #1) (p. 136)

10.3 Compare Two Independent Groups (Test #2) (p. 140)

10.4 Paired Observations (Test #3) (p. 146)

10.5 Proportion versus Hypothesized Value (Test #4) (p. 151)

10.6 Compare Two Independent Proportions (Test #5) (p. 154)

10.7 Tests for Variance (p. 158)

10.8 Confidence Intervals Revisited (p. 158)

Summary (p. 160)

Exercises (p. 161)

Modules for Chapter Ten

10.A The t-Distribution (p. 161)

10.B Issues Related to Paired Observations (p. 164)

10.C Proportion versus Hypothesized Value Using the Binomial Distribution (p. 167)

10.1 Introduction

Chapter 9 introduced the concept of hypothesis testing and examined the seven steps of hypothesis testing. This chapter discusses applications of hypothesis testing for testing means and proportions.

The tests introduced in this chapter and the rest of the book are numbered Test #1, Test #2, and so on, referring to their numbers in the **TestSummaries .xls** workbook and in Appendix B. When you open the Test Summaries workbook, use the table of contents (TOC) worksheet page to locate the test you need.

In this chapter we look at the five most common one- and two-group tests. We will examine three tests for means (mean versus hypothesized, two groups, and paired observations) and two tests for proportions (proportion versus hypothesized and comparing two proportions).

10.2 Mean versus Hypothesized Value (Test #1)

Data form: one sample of data that is compared to a hypothesized value.

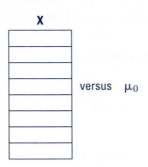

In the rest of the book, the data form for each test is shown in this form, where the cells represent worksheet cells that would contain data. The number of cells represented will vary.

In Chapter 9, the concept of hypothesis testing was introduced with a z-test. The test statistic was

$$z = \frac{\overline{X} - \mu_0}{\frac{\sigma}{\sqrt{n}}}$$

However, that test requires that you know the population standard deviation, σ. When you do not know σ, which is almost always the case, you can substitute the sample standard deviation, s. If the sample is moderately large, you can still treat the result as a z-value, but what you actually have calculated is a **t-value.** The test statistic then becomes

$$t = \frac{\overline{X} - \mu_0}{\frac{s}{\sqrt{n}}} \qquad \text{[10.1]}$$

Note that t and z are calculated the same way; however, they involve the use of different tables. Every t-calculation has an associated value called degrees of

EXHIBIT 10-1
Sample data for mean versus hypothesized with descriptive statistics.

	Bulb Life
	2023
	2048
	2081
	2236
	2042
	2174
	2002
	1942
	2207
	2145

Descriptive statistics

	Bulb Life
count	10
mean	2090.00
sample standard deviation	96.25

freedom, which is abbreviated d.f. or df. For this test, the degrees of freedom is $n - 1$, the same as the denominator in the calculation of the sample variance (see Equations [2.6] and [2.8]). Module 10.A describes the t-distribution and explains how to use it.

Example of Mean versus Hypothesized

A company has a device that purports to increase the life of lightbulbs. To test this, you purchase a sample of 10 lightbulbs that have an advertised life of 2000 hours and see how long they last with the use of the device. Why a sample size of 10? It is a small sample that could be done with a calculator; in the real world, you probably would want a somewhat larger sample. You want to know if the lightbulbs last longer than 2000 hours with the device. Exhibit 10-1 shows the results (**HtestExamples.xls!Mean_vs.**).

Now we use the seven-step hypothesis test.

> **Step 1: Specify the null hypothesis and the alternative hypothesis.**
> H_0: $\mu = 2000$ (the mean advertised life of the lightbulbs)
> H_1: $\mu > 2000$ (greater than test because we have reason to believe the mean should be larger than 2000)

> **Step 2: What level of significance?**
> $\alpha = .05$ (upper tail) (we are using .05 because it is the standard default value)

> **Step 3: Which test and test statistic?**
> Mean versus Hypothesized value, t-test (Test #1)

The test statistic is Equation [10.1] with $df = n - 1$

> **Step 4: State the decision rule.**
> Reject H_0 if $t_9 > 1.833$ (from t-table, MegaStat, or Excel)
> or
> Reject if p-value < .05

EXHIBIT 10-2
MegaStat output for Mean versus Hypothesized test.

Hypothesis Test: Mean versus Hypothesized Value

2,000.00	hypothesized value
2,090.00	mean Bulb Life
96.25	std. dev.
30.44	std. error
10	n
9	df
2.96	t
.0080	p-value (one-tailed, upper)

EXHIBIT 10-3
Graphical illustration of Mean versus Hypothesized Value t-test.

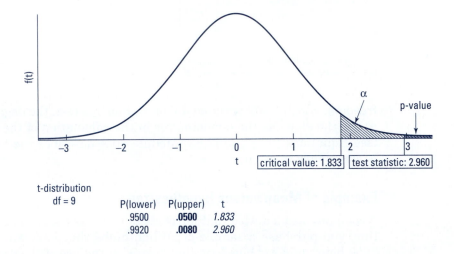

t-distribution
df = 9

P(lower)	P(upper)	t
.9500	.0500	1.833
.9920	.0080	2.960

Step 5: Use the sample data to calculate the test statistic.

Calculate t with Equation [10.1]:

$$t = \frac{2090 - 2000}{\frac{96.25}{\sqrt{10}}} = 2.96$$

Exhibit 10-2 shows the MegaStat output. Exhibit 10-3 provides a graphical representation of this test.

Step 6: Use the test statistic to make a decision.

Reject H_0 because 2.96 is greater than the critical value of 1.833

Also, the p-value of .0080 is less than .05.

Unlike the normal distribution, you cannot look up a p-value for the t-distribution because it would require a whole page of values for every possible degree of freedom. You need to have a computer to calculate the p-value: MegaStat or the Excel TDIST function (Appendix A).

Step 7: Interpret the decision in the context of the original question.

The result is statistically significant, which means that the result is unlikely to be due to sampling. Not only is the p-value under 5%, it is also less than 1%.

However, we should always examine our results with a critical eye. In this case, we have a classic ya-but: Even though the result is clearly significant, it is probably not meaningful. The increase from 2000 to 2090 is only a 4.5% improvement that probably would not justify the cost of the device. Remember: Significance is not necessarily significant.

The randomness of the sample also could be an issue. If you just walked in a store and bought 10 bulbs, they all probably would be from the same production run. If you bought one bulb from each of 10 different stores in widely different locations, they would be more likely to be representative of all bulbs.

You also might wonder if the mean life of 2000 hours is accurate. Maybe the bulbs would have lasted longer than 2000 hours without the device. It would be better to compare two samples of bulbs with and without the device. That is what the next test illustrates.

MEAN VERSUS HYPOTHESIZED TEXT REPLICATION
Learning Activity **10.2–1**

- Open **HtestExamples.xls!Mean_vs.**
- Use Excel or a calculator to replicate the calculations in the text.
- Replicate the t-value and the p-value by using MegaStat | Hypothesis Tests | Mean vs. Hypothesized Value.

MEAN VERSUS HYPOTHESIZED PRACTICE
Learning Activity **10.2–2**

- A shopping center developer wants to build a small shopping area in a particular neighborhood only if the average income of the surrounding homes is well above $50,000. The results from a sample of 18 homes are shown in **Htest2a.xls!Data.**
- Perform the appropriate hypothesis test. Do the calculations first with a calculator or Excel and verify with MegaStat.
- Following is the solution.

Step 1: Specify the Null Hypothesis and the Alternative Hypothesis
H_0: $\mu = 50$ [the mean income is 50,000 (or less)]

H_1: $\mu > 50$ (greater than test because the developer is interested only in whether the income level is greater than 50,000)

Step 2: What Level of Significance?
$\alpha = .05$ (upper tail) (we are using .05 because it is the standard default value)

Step 3: Which Test and Test Statistic?
Mean versus hypothesized value, t-test (Test #1)

The test statistic is Equation [10.1], with df $= n - 1 = 18 - 1 = 17$

Step 4: State the Decision Rule
Reject H_0 if $t_{17} > 1.740$

or

Reject if p-value $< .05$

Continued

Step 5: Use the Sample Data to Calculate the Test Statistic
Calculate t with Equation [10.1]:

$$t = \frac{53.5 - 50}{\frac{9.064}{\sqrt{18}}} = 1.638$$

Exhibit 10-4 shows the MegaStat output.

EXHIBIT 10-4   MegaStat Output for Mean versus Hypothesized Value.

Hypothesis Test: Mean versus Hypothesized Value

50.000	hypothesized value
53.500	mean Normal
9.064	std. dev.
2.136	std. error
18	n
17	df
1.638	t
.0599	p-value (one-tailed, upper)

Step 6: Use the Test Statistic to Make a Decision
Fail to reject H_0 because 1.638 is less than the critical value of 1.740

Also, the p-value of .0599 is greater than .05.

Step 7: Interpret the Decision in the Context of the Original Question
The result is not statistically significant, which means that the result could be due to chance alone; however, it is close to being significant. If the developer is the only person using this data and doesn't have to prove his case to someone else, he might say "close enough," especially if he has other reasons to believe it is a good project.

• Since it is close, maybe there are a few low values that are pulling the mean down. Use MegaStat Descriptive Statistics (median, boxplot, etc.) to see if there are some low values and then rerun the analysis.

10.3   Compare Two Independent Groups (Test #2)

Data form: two independent samples of data.

Group 1	Group 2

The groups are shown as different sizes to indicate that they do not have to be the same size (although they can be). The space between the groups implies that they are independent.

Often we are more interested in comparing the means of two groups than in comparing a mean to a hypothesized value. By independent groups, we mean that the same person (or other unit of observation) could not be in both groups. The groups do not have to be the same size, although it is best if one group is not greatly larger than the other.

If we extend the expression for a z-value to two groups, it looks as follows:

$$z = \frac{\overline{X} - \mu_0}{\frac{\sigma}{\sqrt{n}}} \quad \text{becomes} \quad z = \frac{(\overline{X}_1 - \overline{X}_2) - D_0}{\sqrt{\frac{\sigma^2}{n_1} + \frac{\sigma^2}{n_2}}}$$

This is still of the general form of observed minus hypothesized divided by a standard error. Instead of a sample mean, we have the difference between two sample means. The hypothesized value, μ_0, becomes the hypothesized difference, D_0, which is just a change of notation; the standard error of the difference comes from adding the variances of the two groups.

Of course, the equation still has the problem of requiring the usually unknown population standard deviation, σ. By now we hope you are thinking, "No problem; just substitute s for σ and call it t instead of z." Good thought, but there is one difficulty: We do not have a sample standard deviation. Instead, we have *two* of them, one from each group: s_1 and s_2. We need to combine (i.e., pool) the two sample variances into a pooled variance, s_p^2. How do we do that? By adding the sum of squared deviations (SSX) for each group and dividing by the combined degrees of freedom:

$$s_p^2 = \frac{SSX_1 + SSX_2}{df_1 + df_2} \tag{10.2}$$

If you are working one of these problems with a calculator and are given a mean, a standard deviation, and n for each group, how do you find the SSX? Recall that the sample variance is as shown in Equation (2.8):

$$s^2 = \frac{SSX}{n - 1}$$

where $n - 1$ is the degrees of freedom. If you solve for SSX, you get $SSX = (n - 1)s^2$.

Substituting this into the equation above, we get

$$s_p^2 = \frac{(n_1 - 1)s_1^2 + (n_2 - 1)s_2^2}{(n_1 - 1) + (n_2 - 1)} \tag{10.3}$$

If we substitute s_p^2 for σ, we get the test statistic for comparing two independent groups shown in Equation [10.4]. This can be treated as a z-value if the sample sizes are large, but here it is a t-value since the pooled variance came from combining the sample variances:

$$t = \frac{(\overline{X}_1 - \overline{X}_2) - D_0}{\sqrt{\dfrac{s_p^2}{n_1} + \dfrac{s_p^2}{n_2}}}$$ [10.4]

Since -1 appears twice in the denominator, the total degrees of freedom is written $n_1 + n_2 - 2$.

Note that the hypothesized difference, D_0, is usually zero. However, it is good practice to write the "minus zero" even though it does not affect the value of the computation.

Example of Comparing Two Independent Groups

A statistics instructor wants to know if her 11 a.m. section is different from her 10 a.m. section on the first examination. Exhibit 10-5 shows the data (**HtestExamples.xls!TwoGroup**).

Now we use the seven-step hypothesis test.

Step 1: Specify the null hypothesis and the alternative hypothesis.

H_0: $\mu_{10} - \mu_{11} = 0$ (the classes have the same mean)

H_1: $\mu_{10} - \mu_{11} \neq 0$ (the classes have a different mean)

We are doing a two-tail (not equal) test because the instructor wants to know if the groups are different and has no a priori reason to know which group would have the higher mean.

EXHIBIT 10-5
Sample data for comparing two groups.

	10:00	11:00
	148	143
	149	137
	152	147
	157	151
	153	146
	148	155
	160	147
	154	150
	154	147
	148	138
		145
		144
		155
		156
		138

Descriptive statistics

	10:00	11:00
count	10	15
mean	152.30	146.60
sample standard deviation	4.138	6.116
deviation sum of squares (SSX)	154.10	523.60

Since we are doing a two-tail test it does not make any difference whether we subtract $\mu_{11} - \mu_{10}$ or $\mu_{10} - \mu_{11}$, but since we see the 10:00 class has a higher mean, we may as well subtract to get a positive difference.

Step 2: What level of significance?

$\alpha = .05$ (two-tail; not equal)

We are using the default value of .05 because there is no context for doing otherwise.

Step 3: Which test and test statistic?

Compare Two Independent Groups (Test #2)

Test statistic-Equation [10.4]

Degrees of freedom $= (n_1 - 1) + (n_2 - 1) = n_1 + n_2 - 2$

Step 4: State the decision rule.

Reject H_0 if $t_{23} > 2.069$ or $t_{23} < -2.069$

A more compact way of stating this would be to see if the absolute value of t is greater than the critical value:

Reject H_0 if $|t_{23}| > 2.069$

or

Reject H_0 if the two-tail p-value is less than .05 (a two-tail p-value is a one-tail p-value doubled)

Step 5: Use the sample data to calculate the test statistic.

First calculate the pooled variance with Equation [10.3]:

$$s_p^2 = \frac{(10-1)4.138^2 + (15-1)6.116^2}{(10-1)+(15-1)} = \frac{154.1 + 523.6}{9 + 14} = 29.465$$

Then calculate t by substituting the pooled variance into Equation [10.4]:

$$t = \frac{(152.3 - 146.6) - 0}{\sqrt{\frac{29.465}{10} + \frac{29.465}{15}}} = 2.57$$

Computational note: The calculations shown here and all the calculations shown in this book assume that the calculations have been done with Excel with the full accuracy of the data. For example, the standard deviation of 4.138 shown is really 4.13790070231539. If you try to replicate the results with a calculator using the output above (which is a good idea), your answer will be close but not exact, especially if you round the intermediate results. If you want to replicate the result exactly (which is an even better idea), do the calculations with Excel, starting with the raw data.

Exhibit 10-6 shows the MegaStat output. Exhibit 10-7 provides a graphical representation of this test.

EXHIBIT 10-6
MegaStat output for comparing two independent groups.

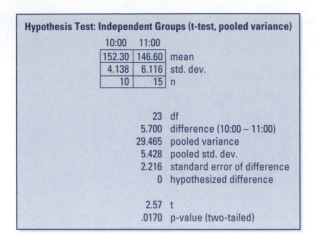

Hypothesis Test: Independent Groups (t-test, pooled variance)

	10:00	11:00	
	152.30	146.60	mean
	4.138	6.116	std. dev.
	10	15	n

23	df
5.700	difference (10:00 – 11:00)
29.465	pooled variance
5.428	pooled std. dev.
2.216	standard error of difference
0	hypothesized difference
2.57	t
.0170	p-value (two-tailed)

EXHIBIT 10-7
Graphical illustration of Two Independent Groups Test.

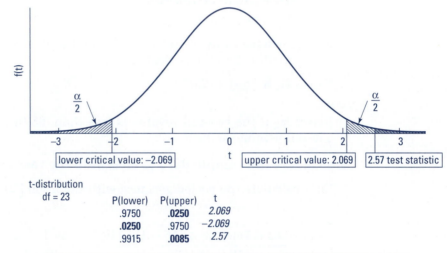

lower critical value: –2.069

upper critical value: 2.069   2.57 test statistic

t-distribution
df = 23

P(lower)	P(upper)	t
.9750	.0250	2.069
.0250	.9750	–2.069
.9915	.0085	2.57

0.0170   Since this is a two-tail test, the upper tail probability doubled is the p-value.

Step 6: Use the test statistic to make a decision.

Reject H_0 because 2.57 is greater than the critical value of 2.069.

Also, the p-value of .0170 is less than .05.

TUTORIAL 11

Step 7: Interpret the decision in the context of the original question.

The groups appear to be different. There is not enough of a context in this example to know if it is a meaningful difference.

COMPARE TWO GROUPS TEXT REPLICATION

Learning Activity **10.3–1**

- Open **HtestExamples.xls!Two-group.**
- Use Excel or a calculator to replicate the calculations in the text.
- Replicate the t-value and p-value by using MegaStat | Hypothesis Tests | Compare Two Independent Groups.

PRACTICE COMPARING TWO GROUPS   Learning Activity **10.3–2**

- A sales manager wants to know if the sales productivity of her east region is greater than the sales productivity of her west region. The results from a sample of 12 salespersons from the east region and 16 salespersons from the west region are shown in **Htest2b.xls!Data.**
- Perform the appropriate hypothesis test. Do the calculations first with a calculator or Excel and verify with MegaStat.
- Here is the Solution.

Step 1: Specify the Null Hypothesis and the Alternative Hypothesis

H_0: $\mu_{East} - \mu_{West} = 0$ (the regions have the same mean)

H_1: $\mu_{East} - \mu_{1West} > 0$ (the east region has a larger mean)

We are doing a one-tail test because the manager wants to know only if the east region has a greater mean than does the west region.

Step 2: What Level of Significance?

$\alpha = .05$ (one-tail; greater than)

We are using the default value of .05 because there is no context for doing otherwise.

Step 3: Which Test and Test Statistic?

t-test for comparing two independent groups (Test #2)

Test statistic-Equation [10.4]

Degrees of freedom $= (n_1 - 1) + (n_2 - 1) = n_1 + n_2 - 2$

Step 4: State the Decision Rule

Reject H_0 if $t_{26} > 1.706$

or

Reject H_0 if the p-value is less than .05

Step 5: Use the Sample Data to Calculate the Test Statistic

First calculate the pooled variance with Equation [10.3]:

$$s_p^2 = \frac{(12-1)7.596^2 + (16-1)10.100^2}{(12-1)+(16-1)} = \frac{634.71 + 1530.29}{11 + 15} = 83.2691$$

Then calculate t by substituting the pooled variance into Equation [10.4]:

$$t = \frac{(79.933 - 65.975) - 0}{\sqrt{\dfrac{83.2691}{12} + \dfrac{83.2691}{16}}} = 2.28$$

Exhibit 10-8 shows the MegaStat ouput.

Note that the output also includes the test for equality of variance. If the groups have different variances, a different test (beyond the scope of this text) should be used. We have not studied the F-distribution yet, but the p-value greater than .05 indicates that the variances are not close to being different even though one is nearly twice the other one.

Step 6: Use the Test Statistic to Make a Decision

Reject H_0 because 2.28 is greater than the critical value of 1.706

Also, the p-value of .0154 is less than .05.

Step 7: Interpret the Decision in the Context of the Original Question

The east region appears to have a larger mean sales than does the west region.

Continued

EXHIBIT 10-8   MegaStat output for comparing two independent groups.

Hypothesis Test: Independent Groups (t-test, pooled variance)

East	West	
73.933	65.975	mean
7.596	10.100	std. dev.
12	16	n

26	df
7.9583	difference (East – West)
83.2691	pooled variance
9.1252	pooled std. dev.
3.4847	standard error of difference
0	hypothesized difference

2.28	t
.0154	p-value (one-tailed, upper)

F-test for equality of variance

102.019	variance: West
57.701	variance: East
1.77	F
.3440	p-value

10.4   Paired Observations (Test #3)

Data form: pairs of data.

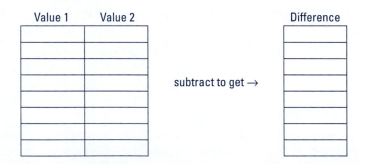

The contiguous columns imply pairing. The pairing can represent various things, but the key factor is that the values in each pair of values have some meaningful connection to each other, for example, before–after or pre–post. This test sometimes is called paired comparisons, dependent samples, or paired differences.

To compare the pairs, we look at the difference between each pair. However, once we subtract each pair, we have one sample representing the differences between the pairs. (You can subtract either way, but if you know which column is going to have the larger values, you might as well subtract to have positive differences.) Since we want to compare these numbers to the hypothesized value of zero, we are back to test #1, Mean versus Hypothesized Value. Paired Observations is listed as a separate test here and has a separate MegaStat menu item because the data are in pairs, but when we look at the equation that is used for Paired Observations,

$$t = \frac{\bar{d} - D_0}{\dfrac{s_d}{\sqrt{n}}}$$ [10.5]

we see that it is the same as Equation [10.1] for test #1 except for notational differences: $\bar{d}$ is substituted for $\bar{X}$, and s_d is the standard deviation of some values that happen to be differences. The hypothesized difference, D_0, is typically zero. The degrees of freedom is $n - 1$, where n is the number of pairs.

The Paired Observations test can be a powerful test if the pairing makes a difference, that is, if the pairs are correlated: Large values tend to be paired with large, and small with small. If the pairs are uncorrelated and the pairing is essentially random, the Paired Observations test confers no benefit. After studying the example below, see Module 10.B for a discussion of issues related to paired observations.

Example of Paired Observations

A large real estate company has a department that assesses the market value of homes that are listed for sale. To become an assessment specialist, a candidate has the following examination procedure: The candidate and an experienced manager both look at a sample of houses and independently determine the assessed value. The pairing of the Paired Observations comes from the fact that each pair of assessments involves the same house.

If the assessment of the manager and the trainee are not significantly different, the trainee passes the course and is certified; if there is a significant difference, the trainee must take another six weeks of training. Exhibit 10-9 shows the results of the assessments (data represents assessment to the nearest $1000) for one examination (**HtestExamples.xls!PairedObsv**).

EXHIBIT 10-9
Sample data for Paired Observations.

Manager	Trainee	Difference
247	239	8
283	273	10
205	215	−10
247	223	24
205	195	10
269	265	4
235	229	6
245	231	14
198	181	17
255	241	14

Descriptive statistics

	Manager	Trainee	Difference
count	10	10	10
mean	238.90	229.20	9.70
sample standard deviation	28.41	28.23	9.02

Now we use the seven-step hypothesis test.

Step 1: Specify the null hypothesis and the alternative hypothesis.

H_0: $\mu_d = 0$ (the manager and trainee assessments are the same)

H_1: $\mu_d \neq 0$ (the manager and trainee assessments are different)

Step 2: What level of significance?

$\alpha = .01$ (two-tail; not equal)

We use a two-tailed test because we want know if the trainee is higher *or* lower in his or her assessments.

This is our first example of using a significance level other than .05. Since making the trainee do another six weeks of training is expensive for the company and probably not pleasant for the trainee, we want to be more certain that the result is not a Type I error. A .01 alpha level would be even more important if the company planned to terminate or reassign the trainee if he or she failed.

If the result of rejecting a null hypothesis could lead to expensive, unpleasant, legal, or health-related action, it may be appropriate to use a lower significance level. Although lowering the alpha level reduces the probability of a Type I error, it increases the probability of a Type II error. If you make the significance level so low that you almost never will reject the null hypothesis, there is no point doing the test.

Step 3: Which test and test statistic?

Paired observations t-test (Test #3)

Test statistic-Equation [10.5]

df $= n - 1$ (where n is the number of pairs, $n = 10$ for our example; although we have 20 data values, we are testing the 10 differences)

Step 4: State the decision rule.

Reject H_0 if $|t_9| > 3.250$

or

Reject if p-value $< .01$ (two-tailed)

Step 5: Use the sample data to calculate the test statistic.

$$t = \frac{9.7 - 0}{\frac{9.02}{\sqrt{10}}} = 3.40$$

Exhibit 10-10 shows the MegaStat output. Exhibit 10-11 provides a graphical representation of this test.

Step 6: Use the test statistic to make a decision.

Reject H_0 because 3.40 is greater than the critical value of 3.250

Also, the p-value of .0079 is less than .01.

Note that since the t-value is just slightly above the critical value, the p-value is just slightly below .01.

Step 7: Interpret the decision in the context of the original question.

Since the hypothesis was rejected, the company has evidence that the trainee needs to remain in training. However, if the trainee saw the data, he or she

EXHIBIT 10-10
MegaStat output for Paired Observations.

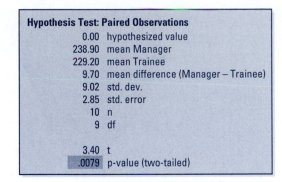

Hypothesis Test: Paired Observations

0.00	hypothesized value
238.90	mean Manager
229.20	mean Trainee
9.70	mean difference (Manager – Trainee)
9.02	std. dev.
2.85	std. error
10	n
9	df
3.40	t
.0079	p-value (two-tailed)

EXHIBIT 10-11
Graphical illustration of Paired Observations test.

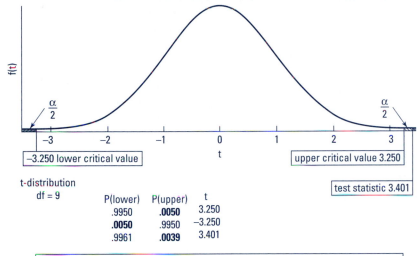

−3.250 lower critical value

upper critical value 3.250

test statistic 3.401

t-distribution
df = 9

P(lower)	P(upper)	t
.9950	**.0050**	3.250
.0050	.9950	−3.250
.9961	**.0039**	3.401

0.0079   Since this is a two-tail test, the upper tail probability doubled is the p-value.

probably would say, "Hey, except for that fourth house where I was off by $24,000, I was pretty close." It also should be noted that if a trainee was way above on some of the assessments and way below on others, his or her mean difference with the manager might be pretty close even though most of his or her assessments were not accurate. To avoid this, it would be better to test whether the *absolute* differences were greater than zero.

A larger sample of houses also would give a more accurate result.

PAIRED OBSERVATIONS TEXT REPLICATION

Learning Activity **10.4–1**

- Open **HtestExamples.xls!PairedObsv.**
- Use Excel or a calculator to replicate the calculations in the text.
- Replicate the t-value and the p-value by using MegaStat I Hypothesis Tests I Paired Observations.
- Use MegaStat I Hypothesis Tests I Mean versus Hypothesized Value on the Difference variable to get the same outcome as the paired observations test.

PAIRED OBSERVATIONS PRACTICE   Learning Activity **10.4**–2

- An automobile manufacturer recommends premium fuel for one of its models but says that regular fuel also may be used, although with lower performance. A consumer organization wants to know if using premium fuel gives better mileage. A sample of five test drivers each drove a sample of four automobiles with premium and regular fuel, giving 20 pairs of observations. They drove the cars as similarly as possible, and the data recorded are the miles per gallon for 500 miles of driving. The results are shown in **Htest2c.xls!Data**.

- Perform the appropriate hypothesis test. Do the calculations first with a calculator or Excel and verify with MegaStat.

- Here is the Solution.

Step 1: Specify the Null Hypothesis and the Alternative Hypothesis
H_0: $\mu_d = 0$ (the mileage with premium fuel and regular fuel is the same)

H_1: $\mu_d \neq 0$ (the mileage with premium fuel is greater than the mileage with regular fuel)

Step 2: What Level of Significance?
$\alpha = .05$ (one-tail; greater than)

One-tailed because there is reason to believe that autos with premium fuel will get better mileage.

Step 3: Which Test and Test Statistic?
Paired observations t-test (Test #3)

Test statistic-Equation [10.5]

$df = n - 1$ (where n is the number of pairs, n = 20 for our example; although we have 40 data values, we are testing 20 differences)

Step 4: State the Decision Rule
Reject H_0 if $t_{19} > 1.729$

or

Reject if p-value < .05   (two-tailed)

Step 5: Use the Sample Data to Calculate the Test Statistic
$$t = \frac{.45 - 0}{\frac{1.1325}{\sqrt{20}}} = 1.78$$

Exhibit 10-12 shows the MegaStat output.

EXHIBIT 10-12   MegaStat output for Paired Observations test.

Hypothesis Test: Paired Observations	
0.0000	hypothesized value
20.7000	mean Premium
20.2500	mean Regular
0.4500	mean difference (Premium − Regular)
1.1325	std. dev.
0.2532	std. error
20	n
19	df
1.78	t
.0458	p-value (one-tailed, upper)

Step 6: Use the Test Statistic to Make a Decision
Reject H_0 because 1.78 is greater than the critical value of 1.729

Also, the p-value of .0458 is less than .05.

Step 7: Interpret the Decision in the Context of the Original Question
The mileage is significantly better with premium fuel, but only barely. The .45 mile per gallon is not a large difference, and looking at the differences, 6 of the 20 observations had better mileage with regular fuel.

Even though the drivers tried to drive the cars the same way, it would not be possible for the observations to be identical.

10.5   Proportion versus Hypothesized Value (Test #4)

Data form: sample proportion, $p = X/n$, where X is the number of occurrences in a sample of size n.

This test compares a sample proportion to a hypothesized value. Thus, it is similar to Mean versus Hypothesized value. The test statistic is

$$z = \frac{p - \pi_0}{\sqrt{\dfrac{\pi_0(1 - \pi_0)}{n}}} \qquad\qquad [10.6]$$

where p is the observed sample proportion and π_0 is the hypothesized value. Note that the hypothesized value is used to calculate the standard error of the proportion because we want to see how likely our sample result is given that the hypothesized value is true.

Note that this test uses a z-value even though a proportion is a sample value. This is done because the standard error uses the hypothesized proportion rather than the sample proportion. Also, proportions usually come from large samples, and so t and z will be very similar.

This test actually uses the normal curve to approximate a binomial distribution. Whenever you have a proportion versus hypothesized value, you can use the binomial distribution to do a more accurate test. (Refer to Module 10.C after studying the example below.)

Example of Proportion versus Hypothesized Value

A marketing research department wants to determine if consumers can detect a minor change in product labeling such as a font change, a color change, or the addition of a warning label on the package. One way to do this is with a "triangle test," in which people are shown three items very briefly and asked to say which one of the three is different.

Assume that 90 people are shown the items and that 40% (36/90) are able to detect the different item.

Step 1: Specify the null hypothesis and the alternative hypothesis.

H_0: $\pi = 1/3$ (the participants cannot identify the different item; this would be the proportion correct if the three items were actually identical and we arbitrarily picked one as the correct one)

H_1: $\pi > 1/3$ (the participants are doing better than guessing; this has to be a one-tailed test because doing significantly worse than guessing would imply that the participants can detect the different item but are choosing another one)

Step 2: What level of significance?

$\sigma = .05$ (upper tail)

Step 3: Which test and test statistic?

Proportion versus hypothesized value, z-test (Test #4)

Test statistic-Equation [10.6]

Step 4: State the decision rule.

Reject H_0 if z > 1.645

or

Reject if p-value < .05

Step 5: Use the sample data to calculate the test statistic.

$$z = \frac{\dfrac{36}{90} - \dfrac{1}{3}}{\sqrt{\dfrac{\dfrac{1}{3}\left(1 - \dfrac{1}{3}\right)}{90}}} = 1.34$$

Exhibit 10-13 shows the MegaStat output. Exhibit 10-14 provides a graphical representation of this test.

EXHIBIT 10-13
MegaStat output for Proportion versus Hypothesized value.

Hypothesis Test for Proportion versus Hypothesized Value		
Observed	Hypothesized	
0.4	0.3333	p (as decimal)
36/90	30/90	p (as fraction)
36.	30.	X
90	90	n
	0.0497	std. error
	1.34	z
	.0899	p-value (one-tailed, upper)

EXHIBIT 10-14
Graphical illustration of Proportion versus Hypothesized value.

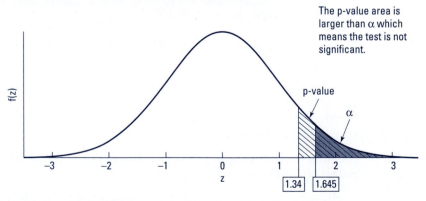

The p-value area is larger than α which means the test is not significant.

p-value

α

1.34   1.645

Normal distribution

P(lower)	P(upper)	z
.9500	.0500	1.645
.9101	.0899	1.34

Step 6: Use the test statistic to make a decision.

Fail to reject H_0 because 1.34 is less than the critical value of 1.645

Also fail to reject because the p-value of .0899 is greater than .05. (if you look up the p-value in the normal distribution table, you will get $1 - .9099 = .0901$, which is slightly different because of rounding z to two places)

Note: It is better to say "fail to reject H_0" than "accept H_0" because saying that you accept the null hypothesis might imply that you have proved that the participants are truly guessing, and you have not proved that. One can never prove a null hypothesis.

Step 7: Interpret the decision in the context of the original question.

It appears that people cannot identify the change in the packaging. It is interesting to note that if people were truly guessing, we would expect 30 out of 90. Although 36 out of 90 is not enough to reject, it is closer than you might think (the p-value was under .10).

PROPORTION VERSUS HYPOTHESIZED TEXT REPLICATION
Learning Activity **10.5–1**

- Calculate the z-value and find the p-value of the text example by using Excel and/or a calculator.
- Verify your calculations with MegaStat | Hypothesis Tests | Proportion versus Hypothesized Value.

PROPORTION VERSUS HYPOTHESIZED PRACTICE
Learning Activity **10.5–2**

An entrepreneur wants to put a children's clothing store in a shopping center only if more than 40% of the nearby households have children under age 8. What would be his decision if a sample of 180 households showed that 45% had children under age 8?

- Perform the appropriate hypothesis test. Calculate the z-value and find the p-value of the text example by using Excel and/or a calculator.
- Verify your calculations with MegaStat | Hypothesis Tests | Proportion versus Hypothesized Value.
- Here is the solution.

Step 1: Specify the Null Hypothesis and the Alternative Hypothesis
$H_0: \pi = .4$

$H_1: \pi > .4$ (it is greater than because that is what we are interested in testing)

Step 2: What Level of Significance?
$\alpha = .05$ (upper tail)

Step 3: Which Test and Test Statistic?
Proportion versus hypothesized value, z-test (Test #4)

Test statistic-Equation [10.6].

Continued

(*Continued*)   Learning Activity **10.5–2**

Step 4: State the Decision Rule

Reject H_0 if $z > 1.645$

or

Reject if p-value $< .05$

Step 5: Use the Sample data to Calculate the Test Statistic.

$$z = \frac{.45 - .4}{\sqrt{\dfrac{.4(1 - .4)}{180}}} = 1.37$$

Exhibit 10-15 shows the MegaStat output.

EXHIBIT 10-15 **MegaStat output for proportion versus hypothesized.**

Hypothesis Test for Proportion versus Hypothesized value		
Observed	Hypothesized	
0.45	0.4	p (as decimal)
81/180	72/180	p (as fraction)
81.	72.	X
180	180	n
0.0365		std. error
1.37		z
.0855		p-value (one-tailed, upper)

Step 6: Use the Test Statistic to Make a Decision

Fail to reject H_0 because 1.37 is less than the critical value of 1.645

Also, fail to reject because the p-value of .0855 is greater than .05.

Step 7: Interpret the Decision in the Context of the Original Question

Although the proportion is greater than .4, it is not quite significantly greater than .4.

- How much greater would the proportion have to be significant at the .05 level?
  - *Answer:* By trial and error with Excel or MegaStat, you will find that 83/180 would be enough to make the p-value less than .05.

10.6   Compare Two Independent Proportions (Test #5)

Data form: two sample proportions, p_1 and p_2, from independent groups.

When you examine the test statistic for comparing two proportions

$$z = \frac{(p_1 - p_2) - D_0}{\sqrt{\dfrac{p_c(1 - p_c)}{n_1} + \dfrac{p_c(1 - p_c)}{n_2}}} \qquad \text{[10.7]}$$

you see it is parallel to the test for two means: observed difference minus hypothesized difference divided by the standard error of the difference. As with the test for means, *independent* means that the groups need to be completely separate: The same person could not be in both groups. This test is only valid when the hypothesized value, D_0, equals zero; however that is usually the case.

The standard error of the difference uses a value, p_c, that is similar to the pooled variance. The c stands for "combined," and p_c is the estimate of the population proportion derived by combining the two sample proportions; that is, it is calculated by adding the sum of the two numerators divided by the sum of the two denominators. If $p_1 = X_1/n_1$ and $p_2 = X_2/n_2$,

$$p_c = \frac{X_1 + X_2}{n_1 + n_2}$$ [10.8]

If the data are reported as proportions (or percents) and not ratios, you need to find the numerator X by multiplying n by p:

$$p_c = \frac{n_1 p_1 + n_2 p_2}{n_1 + n_2}$$ [10.9]

where $n_1 p_1$ and $n_2 p_2$ are rounded to the nearest integer.

Example of Comparing Two Independent Proportions

It is found that 57.8% of 244 men say they will vote for a particular candidate and 48.1% of 156 women say they will vote for that candidate. Are these proportions significantly different?

By multiplying n by p and rounding, we can state the proportions in ratio form: $p_1 = 141/244$ and $p_2 = 75/156$.

Hypothesis Testing Steps (Short Form)

Now that we have seen the formal presentation of the seven steps, we start using a more compact form to save space. The seven steps are still used and are numbered. This would be a good format for examination answers or report presentation, except that it would be better to write out the equations than to refer to equation numbers. After you have done several hypothesis tests, it is tempting to go directly to step 5 and start calculating a test statistic. However, in reporting the results, it is always a good idea to list the seven steps.

Step 1. $H_0: \pi_1 - \pi_2 = 0$

$H_1: \pi_1 - \pi_2 \neq 0$ (two-tailed because you want to know if they are "different"; for a one-tail test, you would have to know a priori which proportion would be larger)

Step 2. $\alpha = .05$ (default)

Step 3. Test: compare two independent proportions (Test #5)

Step 4. Decision rule: Reject H_0 if $|z| > 1.96$ or p-value $< .05$

Step 5. Calculation of test statistic using Equations [10.8] and [10.7]:

$$p_c = \frac{141 + 75}{244 + 156} = \frac{216}{400} = .54$$

$$z = \frac{\left(\frac{141}{244} - \frac{75}{156}\right) - 0}{\sqrt{\frac{.54(1 - .54)}{244} + \frac{.54(1 - .54)}{156}}} = 1.90$$

EXHIBIT 10-16
MegaStat output for comparing two proportions.

Hypothesis Test for Two Independent Proportions			
p1	p2	p_c	
0.5779	0.4808	0.54	p (as decimal)
141/244	75/156	216/400	p (as fraction)
141.	75.	216.	X
244	156	400	n
	0.0971	difference	
	0.	hypothesized difference	
	0.0511	std. error	
	1.90	z	
	.0574	p-value (two-tailed)	

EXHIBIT 10-17
Graphical illustration of hypothesis test for comparing two proportions.

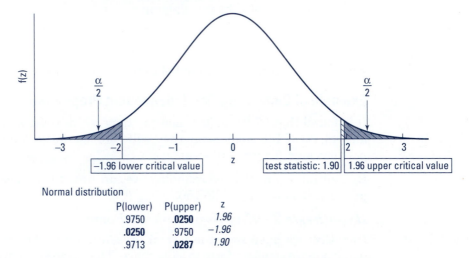

Normal distribution

	P(lower)	P(upper)	z
	.9750	**.0250**	*1.96*
	.0250	.9750	*−1.96*
	.9713	**.0287**	*1.90*

0.0574   Since this is a two-tail test, the upper tail probability doubled is the p-value.

Computational note: Since p_c was a round value (.5400 . . .), the decimal version was used in the equation. If you had to round and truncate the decimal, it would be better to stay with the ratio version.

Exhibit 10-16 shows the MegaStat output. Exhibit 10-17 shows a graphical representation of this test.

Step 6. Decision: Fail to reject because 1.90 < 1.96 and .0574 > .05

Step 7. Interpretation: The groups are not significantly different, but they are close to being significant. See if one person changing his or her mind could have made the difference significant.

COMPARE TWO PROPORTIONS
TEXT REPLICATION

Learning Activity **10.6–1**

- Calculate the z-value and find the p-value of the text example by using Excel and/or a calculator.
- Verify your calculations with MegaStat | Hypothesis Tests | Compare Two Independent Proportions.

PRACTICE COMPARING TWO PROPORTIONS

Learning Activity **10.6–2**

A statistics instructor has 20 sophomores in her morning class of 43 students (46.5%) and 35 sophomores of 51 (68.6%) in afternoon class. Is the proportion greater in the afternoon class?

- Perform the appropriate hypothesis test. Calculate the z-value and find the p-value of the text example by using Excel and/or a calculator.
- Verify your calculations with MegaStat | Hypothesis Tests | Compare Two Independent Proportions.
- Here is the Solution.

Step 1. H_0: $\pi_1 - \pi_2 = 0$

H_1: $\pi_1 - \pi_2 > 0$ (one-tailed because the instructor is interested in testing whether the afternoon proportion is greater; let p_1 be the larger proportion)

Step 2. $\alpha = .05$ (default)

Step 3. Test: Compare two independent proportions (Test #5)

Step 4. Decision rule: Reject H_0 if z > 1.645 or p-value < .05

Step 5. Calculation of test statistic using Equations [10.8] and [10.7]:

$$p_c = \frac{35 + 20}{51 + 43} = \frac{55}{94} = .585$$

$$z = \frac{\left(\frac{35}{51} - \frac{20}{43}\right) - 0}{\sqrt{\frac{\frac{55}{94}\left(1 - \frac{55}{94}\right)}{51} + \frac{\frac{55}{94}\left(1 - \frac{55}{94}\right)}{43}}} = 2.17$$

Exhibit 10-18 shows the MegaStat output.

EXHIBIT 10-18   MegaStat output for comparing two proportions.

Hypothesis Test for Two Independent Proportions

p1	p2	p_c	
0.6863	0.4651	0.5851	p (as decimal)
35/51	20/43	55/94	p (as fraction)
35.	20.	55.	X
51	43	94	n
	0.2212		difference
	0.		hypothesized difference
	0.102		std. error
	2.17		z
	.0151		p-value (one-tailed, upper)

Step 6. Decision: Reject because 2.17 > 1.645 and .0151 < .05

Step 7. Interpretation: The groups are significantly different.

If we could have justified a one-tail test, the result would have been significant, but you cannot go back and restate the hypothesis after you see the results.

10.7   Tests for Variance

Since tests for variance are not particularly common, I have chosen not to include them in my "dirty-dozen" list. However, MegaStat can test variances.

If you want to compare a variance to a hypothesized value, there is a Chi-square Variance Test at the end of the Hypothesis Testing menu. Its operation is the same as that of the mean versus hypothesized test. The test utilizes the chi-square distribution (Module 14.A), or you can rely on the p-value for now.

If you want to compare two variances, use the Compare Two Independent Groups test and check the box for "Test for equality of variances." If you are not interested in the mean differences, ignore that portion of the output; delete it if you wish. The test utilizes the F-distribution (Module 11.C), or you can rely on the p-value for now.

Tests for variance assume a normal population and are sensitive to violations of that assumption. Therefore, you should test variances only if you are certain the population is fairly normal.

10.8   Confidence Intervals Revisited

When we discussed confidence intervals in Section 8.1, we saw that the general form for a confidence interval is the mean plus and minus the margin of error, as shown in Equation [8.5] and repeated here:

$$\overline{X} \pm z \frac{\sigma}{\sqrt{n}}$$

We noted that when σ is unknown, one substitutes the sample standard deviation, s. Although this is fine for larger samples, now that we have seen that we should use the t-distribution in hypothesis testing when the sample standard deviation is used, we should do the same thing for confidence intervals. Thus, the expression for a confidence interval for the mean when one is using the sample standard deviation is

$$\overline{X} \pm t \frac{s}{\sqrt{n}} \qquad\qquad \text{[10.10]}$$

where t has $n - 1$ degrees of freedom.

The calculation for the margin of error for Example 1 in Section 8.1 is

$$2005.54 \pm 2.052 \frac{184.27}{\sqrt{28}}$$

The 2.052 is the t-value for 27 degrees of freedom (.05, two-tailed). The resulting lower and upper confidence limits are 1934.08 and 2076.99. Since t-values are always larger than their corresponding z-values, the margin of error using the sample version of the confidence limit equation will always be larger. Exhibit 10-19 shows a comparison of confidence limits calculated with z and with t.

EXHIBIT 10-19
Confidence limits calculated with z and t.

Descriptive statistics	
	Kbs
count	28
mean	2,005.54
sample standard deviation	184.27
sample variance	33,955.29
confidence interval 95.% lower	1,937.28
confidence interval 95.% upper	2,073.79
margin of error	68.25
z	1.96
confidence interval 95.% lower	1,934.08
confidence interval 95.% upper	2,076.99
margin of error	71.45
t(df = 27)	2.052

EXHIBIT 10-20
Hypothesis test output showing confidence interval.

Hypothesis Test: Mean versus Hypothesized Value	
2,000.000	hypothesized value
2,090.000	mean Bulb Life
96.247	std. dev.
30.436	std. error
10	n
9	df
2.96	t
.0160	p-value (two-tailed)
2,021.149	confidence interval 95.% lower
2,158.851	confidence interval 95.% upper
68.851	margin of error

Note that the calculation of confidence intervals for proportions uses z despite the fact that we should use t in working with sample data. Strictly speaking, the equation for confidence intervals should use t and divide by n − 1, but traditionally that usually is not done for proportions. The rationale is that if a sample is large enough to have a stable estimate of a proportion, the difference between the t and z versions is negligible since t values converge to z as the sample size increases.

Relationship between Confidence Intervals and Hypothesis Testing

Exhibit 10-20 shows the example from Section 10.2 done as a two-tailed test. It also shows the confidence interval calculated when the confidence interval box is checked. The confidence interval is the same one you would get using MegaStat | Descriptive Statistics | Confidence Interval (specifying t).

The relationship between hypothesis testing and confidence intervals is as follows: If a two-tailed hypothesis test rejects the null hypothesis at the 5% level, the 95% confidence interval will not contain the hypothesized value. This could be generalized to any other significance level, for example, 1% and 99%. Notice that for this example, the confidence interval does not include 2000 since we rejected the hypothesis that the mean is equal to 2000.

CONFIDENCE INTERVALS USING THE t-DISTRIBUTION

Learning Activity **10.8–1**

- Open **HtestExamples.xls!Mean_vs.**
- Replicate the two-tail test (not equal) in Exhibit 10-20. Check the confidence interval option.
- Use MegaStat | Descriptive Statistics to calculate a 95% confidence interval. Check both the t and z checkboxes for the confidence interval.
  - Note that the margin of error for the t interval is slightly larger.
  - Note that the t confidence interval is the same as the hypothesis test output.
  - Note that the interval does not include the hypothesized value of 2000.
- Use MegaStat | Descriptive Statistics to calculate a 99% confidence interval. Check the t checkbox for the confidence interval.
  - Note that the 99% interval does include 2000 because the hypothesis test was significant at the 5% level but not at the 1% level.

CONFIDENCE INTERVAL VERSUS HYPOTHESIS TEST

Learning Activity **10.8–2**

- Review Example 1 in Section 8.1, where a man wanted to brag that he was getting a 2000-Kbs download speed with his cable modem. Instead of calculating a confidence interval, let's say that he does a hypothesis test with $H_0 = 2000$. If he does not reject the hypothesis with a two-tailed test, that provides the evidence that his result was not significantly different from 2000.
- Open **Kbs.xls!Data.**
- Use MegaStat | Hypothesis Tests | Mean versus Hypothesized Value. Specify Hypothesized value: 2000; Alternative: not equal, t-test. Check the confidence interval box.
- See **Kbs.xls!Solution1b** for the solution. Since the result was not close to being significant, that supports his statement that he was getting a 2000-Kbs download rate.
  - Note that the confidence interval from the hypothesis test checkbox is the same as the one calculated in Exhibit 10-19 using Descriptive Statistics.
  - If his sample had rejected the hypothesis, his confidence interval would not have contained the hypothesized value.

Summary

Conceptual

This chapter presented the most commonly used one- and two-sample hypothesis tests. Summaries of the individual tests are in Appendix B. The tests there are numbered Test #1 through Test #12; the first 5 were covered in this chapter.

This chapter also introduced the t-distribution. The t-distribution is similar to the normal distribution but is used when the sample standard deviation is used to estimate the population standard deviation.

It also was noted that the t-distribution also should be used for calculating confidence intervals when one is using the sample standard deviation, especially if the sample size is small.

Know When and How to Use These Tests

- Mean versus hypothesized value (Test #1)
- Compare Two Independent Groups (Test #2)
- Paired Observations (Test #3)
- Proportion versus Hypothesized Value (Test #4)
- Compare Two Independent Proportions (Test #5)

Exercises

The exercises and data are found in **Ch_10_HTest_Apps.xls** in the exercises folder of the CD.

No.	Content
1	t-Distribution
2	Mean versus hypothesized
3	Mean versus hypothesized
4	Compare two groups
5	Compare two groups
6	Paired observations
7	Paired observations
8	Proportion versus hypothesized
9	Proportion versus hypothesized
10	Compare two proportions
11	Compare two proportions
12	Confidence interval

Modules for Hypothesis Testing Applications

10.A   THE t-DISTRIBUTION[1]

The t-distribution is a continuous probability distribution that is shaped similarly to the normal distribution; in fact, it is like a normal distribution that is pushed down on top and flattened out to the sides. The shape of the t-distribution is based on a value known as the degrees of freedom. There is a different t-distribution for every possible degree of freedom. The larger the degrees of freedom, the more nearly the t-distribution looks like a normal distribution.

Exhibit 10-21 shows a t-distribution with 9 degrees of freedom with a dashed-line normal curve superimposed that shows that even with fairly small degrees of freedom, the normal distribution and t-distribution are very similar. When the degrees of freedom gets up around 30, the two distributions are nearly indistinguishable.

[1]Sometimes this distribution is referred to as Student's t-distribution from the pseudonym used by William Sealy Gossett, who developed the distribution in 1908.

EXHIBIT 10-21
Normal versus t-distribution for df = 9.

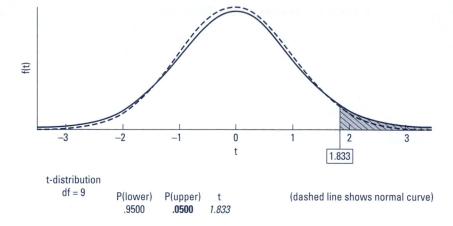

t-distribution
df = 9

	P(lower)	P(upper)	t	(dashed line shows normal curve)
	.9500	**.0500**	*1.833*	

EXHIBIT 10-22
Portion of t-table showing t-value for df = 9, one-tailed.

t Distribution					
	One-tailed				
	0.1	**0.05**	0.025	0.01	0.005	0.0005
	Two-tailed					
df	0.20	0.10	0.05	0.02	0.01	0.001
1	3.078	6.314	12.706	31.821	63.656	636.578
2	1.886	2.920	4.303	6.965	9.925	31.600
3	1.638	2.353	3.182	4.541	5.841	12.924
4	1.533	2.132	2.776	3.747	4.604	8.610
5	1.476	2.015	2.571	3.365	4.032	6.869
6	1.440	1.943	2.447	3.143	3.707	5.959
7	1.415	1.895	2.365	2.998	3.499	5.408
8	1.397	1.860	2.306	2.896	3.355	5.041
9	1.383	1.833	2.262	2.821	3.250	4.781
10	1.372	1.812	2.228	2.764	3.169	4.587
11	1.363	1.796	2.201	2.718	3.106	4.437
12	1.356	1.782	2.179	2.681	3.055	4.318
13	1.350	1.771	2.160	2.650	3.012	4.221
14	1.345	1.761	2.145	2.624	2.977	4.140
15	1.341	1.753	2.131	2.602	2.947	4.073
16	1.337	1.746	2.120	2.583	2.921	4.015
17	1.333	1.740	2.110	2.567	2.898	3.965
18	1.330	1.734	2.101	2.552	2.878	3.922
19	1.328	1.729	2.093	2.539	2.861	3.883
20	1.325	1.725	2.086	2.528	2.845	3.850

t-Table

Since the t-distribution is based on degrees of freedom, there could be a table like the normal curve table for every possible degree of freedom. Since that would take a lot of space, t-tables show only the values for common probability levels that are used for confidence intervals and hypothesis testing.

Exhibit 10-22 shows a portion of the t-table from **Tables.xls!t-dist** with the t-value highlighted for 9 degrees of freedom and a 5% probability level. **Tables.xls!t-dist** shows the highlighting when you click a row, column, or cell.

When you look at the t-values for larger degrees of freedom, you see that they get close to z-values. In the last row in the table for df $= \infty$, the values are actually z-values.

Excel t-Functions

TDIST(t, df, tails) is Excel's t-distribution function. The tails argument must be either 1 or 2. The function does not allow negative values of t even though t can be negative. =TDIST(1.833, 9, 1) is the function that corresponds to the table example in Exhibit 10-22.

TINV(probability, df) gives the t-value corresponding to a probability. The function assumes that it is a two-tailed probability. To get a one-tailed inverse value, double the probability value. =TINV(.05*2, 9) corresponds to the table in Exhibit 10-22.

USING THE t-DISTRIBUTION   Learning Activity **10.A–1**

- Determine the t-value to be used for a 95% confidence interval with 14 degrees of freedom by using all three methods:
  - t-table
  - Excel function: TINV
  - MegaStat
- If the computer outputs do not quite match the table values, use the rounding options to make them match.
- *Solution:* The t-value is 1.833.

COMPARING t AND NORMAL DISTRIBUTIONS   Learning Activity **10.A–2**

- Open **Normal_vs_t.xls!Data**. Do not be concerned about how the plotted values are calculated. If you are curious, you can click in cell F8 and columns C and D to see the cell formulas.
  - Enter 14 in the shaded df cell (F3) and then click the **Graph** worksheet. Notice that with even with this fairly small value for degrees of freedom, the normal distribution and t-distribution are not dramatically different.
- Enter 30 in the shaded df cell (F3) and then click the graph worksheet. Textbooks traditionally state that anything above 30 is considered a large sample, and you will see that with df = 30, the normal distribution and t-distribution are very similar.
- Enter 5 in the shaded df cell (F3) and then click the graph worksheet. With df this small, the normal distribution and t-distribution are somewhat different.
- What is the smallest df that can be used?
- Use MegaStat | Probability | t-Distribution and run outputs for various degrees of freedom. Check the "Show normal curve" box.

MegaStat t-Distribution

MegaStat | Probability | t-Distribution allows the calculation of t-probabilities and inverse probabilities as well as the generation of a graphical plot. MegaStat handles negative t-values and has a rounding option to match table values. The MegaStat output in Exhibit 10-21 corresponds to the table in Exhibit 10-22.

10.B   ISSUES RELATED TO PAIRED OBSERVATIONS

A company that sells a tutoring course for the SAT wants to advertise that its course significantly improves SAT scores. It randomly selects 15 students and has them take the SAT. Then they take the tutoring course, and then they take the SAT examination again.

The data are in **PairedObs.xls!Data** and are shown in Exhibit 10-23, along with the MegaStat output.

Since the mean difference of after–before is positive and the p-value is under 5%, the company can advertise that its product "significantly improves SAT scores." Can you think of any ya-buts?

What would have happened if the company had mistakenly performed a Compare Two Independent Groups test on this data? Exhibit 10-24 shows the results.

Even though the data are the same and the mean difference is the same, this test is not close to being significant (the p-value is much larger than .05). Why is this the case? Note that the standard error of the difference is 21.398, and from Exhibit 10-23, the standard error of the Paired Observations test is only 3.659. The Paired Observations test looks only at the variance of the differences, whereas the Independent Groups test looks at the variance of the actual data. Thus, the paired differences test can be more powerful; that is, it is more likely to show a significant difference.

EXHIBIT 10-23 Paired observations data with MegaStat output.

Paired Observations Data: SAT scores before and after a tutoring course

before	after	difference		
480	475	−5		
517	531	14	**Hypothesis Test: Paired Observations**	
621	614	−7	0.000	hypothesized value
550	570	20	530.133	mean after
489	517	28	518.800	mean before
499	516	17	11.333	mean difference (after – before)
503	493	−10	14.171	std. dev.
374	390	16	3.659	std. error
501	531	30	15	n
540	537	−3	14	df
600	633	33		
577	598	21	3.10	t
528	528	0	.0039	p-value (one-tailed, upper)
510	512	2		
493	507	14		
518.800	530.133	11.333	mean	
57.940	59.255	14.171	stdev	

EXHIBIT 10-24
Independent groups test of paired observation data.

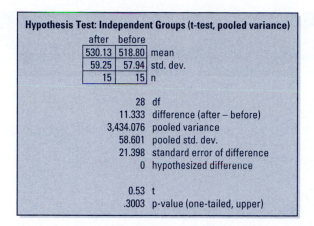

Hypothesis Test: Independent Groups (t-test, pooled variance)

	after	before	
	530.13	518.80	mean
	59.25	57.94	std. dev.
	15	15	n

28	df
11.333	difference (after – before)
3,434.076	pooled variance
58.601	pooled std. dev.
21.398	standard error of difference
0	hypothesized difference
0.53	t
.3003	p-value (one-tailed, upper)

EXHIBIT 10-25
Paired observations test with shuffled data.

paired observations data: SAT scores before and after a tutoring course
(the 'after' column has been randomized to de-pair the data)

before	after	diff		
480	531	51		
517	570	53		**Hypothesis Test: Paired Observations**
621	633	12	0.000	hypothesized value
550	531	−19	530.133	mean after
489	390	−99	518.800	mean before
499	537	38	11.333	mean difference (after – before)
503	516	13	63.159	std. dev.
374	507	133	16.308	std. error
501	614	113	15	n
540	512	−28	14	df
600	517	−83		
577	598	21	0.69	t
528	493	−35	.2492	p-value (one-tailed, upper)
510	528	18		
493	475	−18		

518.800	530.133	11.333	mean
57.940	59.255	63.159	stdev

Is it true that the Paired Difference test is always more powerful than company independent groups test? Not necessarily. Exhibit 10-25 (and **PairedObs.xls!Shuffled**) shows the data after randomizing (i.e., shuffling) the "after" variable.

Note that the Paired Observations test is not close to being significant even though the data are the same and thus the mean difference is still the same. Why is this the case? In the original data, larger "before" values tended to go with larger "after" values, and smaller ones go with smaller; in other words, the variables were somewhat correlated. When data were shuffled, it had the effect of "depairing" the data. Since the variables were uncorrelated, the differences were larger and had more variation. (Note the differences column in Exhibit 10-23 versus that in Exhibit 10-25). The Paired Observations test is more powerful if the variables are correlated; if the variables are not correlated, Paired Observations and compare independent groups tests will give approximately the same results.

PAIRED OBSERVATIONS IN DEPTH — Learning Activity **10.B–1**

- Open **PairedObsv.xls.**
- Use MegaStat to replicate the output in Exhibit 10-23.
- Can you think of any alternative explanations for the results (ya-buts)?
  - *Answer:* They might have done better on the second test even without the tutoring course because they would have been more familiar with the test environment and might have learned things other than what was provided by the tutoring course. And even though the test was quite significant, it hardly seems that an 11-point improvement is very meaningful, especially when some of it could be due to the retest effect.
- Use MegaStat to replicate the output in Exhibit 10-24.
  - Even though the mean difference is the same, the Compare Independent Groups test is not close to being significant.
- Copy/paste the after data into another worksheet, shuffle the values (see Module 7.A), and copy/paste the shuffled values back to their original location. Rerun the paired observations test.
  - Your results should look similar to Exhibit 10-25 but will not be identical. If there is still a significant result, reshuffle the data.
  - This output shows that the Paired Observations test is beneficial only if the two variables are correlated (i.e., small values tend to be paired with small, and large with large).

PAIRED OBSERVATIONS EXPLORATION — Learning Activity **10.B–2**

- Open a blank Excel workbook.
- Use MegaStat | Generate Random Numbers to create a sample of 15 normally distributed numbers with a mean of 85 and a standard deviation of 10. Create fixed values with one decimal place. (If necessary, review Module 7.A for creating random numbers.)
- Copy/paste the numbers to B3:B17 in Sheet 1 and label them "Pre" in cell B2.
- Use MegaStat | Generate Random Numbers to create another a sample of 15 normally distributed numbers with a mean of 80 and a standard deviation of 10. Create fixed values with one decimal place.
- Copy/paste the numbers to D3:D17 in Sheet 1 and label them "Post" in cell D2.
- Use MegaStat | Hypothesis Tests | Paired Observations to compare the groups.
  - Unless you got unusual samples, there should not be a significant difference. If you do get a significant difference, repeat the sampling for one or both groups.
- Sort both groups ascending and repeat the paired observations test.
  - By sorting, you pair small with small and large with large, and you should see a significant (or at least much smaller) p-value.
  - In the real world, you would have to use the data as you found it; you could not sort this way. This was a "what-if" exercise to show that the paired observations test is powerful if the data are paired.

It should be emphasized that performing a compare independent groups test on paired data and randomizing the data were "what-if" analyses to show how the tests work. In the real world, if you have paired data, you should do a Paired Observations test. Obviously, you could not change the pairing.

EXHIBIT 10-26
Portion of binomial distribution for n = 90, p = 1/3.

Binomial distribution		
	90	n
	1/3	p

X	P(X)	cumulative probability
25	0.04909	0.15707
26	0.06136	0.21843
27	0.07273	0.29116
28	0.08182	0.37297
29	0.08746	0.46043
30	0.08892	0.54935
31	0.08605	0.63540
32	0.07933	0.71473
33	0.06971	0.78444
34	0.05843	0.84287
35	0.04675	0.88962
36	0.03571	0.92533
37	0.02606	0.95139
38	0.01817	0.96956
39	0.01211	0.98168
40	0.00772	0.98940
41	0.00471	0.99411
42	0.00275	0.99686
43	0.00153	0.99839
44	0.00082	0.99921
45	0.00042	0.99963
	1.00000	

30.000	expected value
20.000	variance
4.472	standard deviation

10.C   PROPORTION VERSUS HYPOTHESIZED VALUE USING THE BINOMIAL DISTRIBUTION

In Section 10.5 we saw in testing an observed proportion of 36/90 versus a hypothesized value of 1/3 that the difference was not significant when the sample size was 90. To do the same test with the binomial distribution, we would answer the question, How unlikely is the result of 36 outcomes out of 90 if the true proportion is 1/3? To answer this, we run a binomial distribution with MegaStat with n = 90 and p = 1/3. The result is shown in Exhibit 10-26 (some of the probabilities are not displayed to save space).

The probability of 36 or more occurrences is equal to 1 − P(35 or less). (See Section 5.3 to review reading probability distribution output.)

$$1 - P(35 \text{ or less}) = 1 - 0.88962 = 0.11038$$

We find that 0.11038 is the p-value of the test. Since the p-value is greater than .05, we fail to reject the null hypothesis, which is the same conclusion as in the z-test. In Exhibit 10-13, you can see that the p-value for the z test is .0899, which is reasonably close to the binomial value.[2]

---

[2]You can make the z-test p-value closer to the binomial p-value by using 35.5 instead of 36 as the observed value when you run the test. This is called a continuity correction.

PROPORTION VERSUS HYPOTHESIZED WITH BINOMIAL DISTRIBUTION

Learning Activity **10.C–1**

- Use MegaStat | Probability | Discrete Probability Distributions | Binomial to replicate Exhibit 10-26 and calculate the p-value in the example.

Which is the correct value? The binomial distribution gives the true p-value. The z test uses the normal curve to approximate a binomial distribution. If the binomial test is the more accurate test, why do we present the z-test version? The answer is tradition. This goes back to a time (not many years ago) when computer software was not able to calculate binomial distributions accurately for a large number of trials.

Analysis of Variance

11.1 One-Factor ANOVA (Test #6) (p. 170)

11.2 Randomized Blocks ANOVA (Test #7) (p. 176)

11.3 ANOVA Compared to t-Tests (p. 181)

11.4 Two-Factor ANOVA (Test #8) (p. 181)

Summary (p. 182)

Exercises (p. 183)

Modules for Chapter Eleven

11.A Partitioning the Sum of Squares (p. 183)

11.B Worksheet Showing Partitioning (p. 184)

11.C Using the F-Distribution (p. 186)

11.D ANOVA Simulation (p. 188)

11.E Post Hoc Analysis (p. 190)

11.F ANOVA versus t-Tests (p. 194)

11.G Randomized Blocks Compared to One-Factor ANOVA (p. 198)

11.H Example of Two-Factor ANOVA Showing Interaction (p. 201)

In Chapter 10, we saw how to compare means from two groups, but what do we do if there are three or more groups? **Analysis of variance** compares multiple groups. Analysis of variance (often abbreviated ANOVA) refers to a family of similar methods; an ANOVA book could cover at least 20 variations.

This chapter discusses three ANOVA procedures. We explore the concept of ANOVA in some detail with the most common form, One-Factor ANOVA, and then we see when and how to use Randomized Blocks ANOVA and Two-Factor ANOVA.

11.1   One-Factor ANOVA (Test #6)

One-Factor ANOVA is used when you want to compare the means of three or more independent groups. However, the concept of analyzing variance is a useful procedure that we will use in a different context in later chapters.

Data form: multiple independent groups.

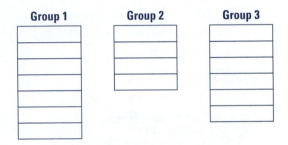

This example shows three groups. Is there a limit to the maximum number of groups we can compare? There is no official upper limit, but ANOVA usually is used for a relatively small number of groups, typically six or less. Does ANOVA also work with only two groups? We will explore that later. As the example shows, the groups do not have to be the same size, but it is best if they are not extremely different in size. The groups are shown with space between them to imply that they are independent, but in MegaStat the columns have to be touching (*contiguous* is the technical term).

Early in this book, when we were discussing measures of variation, we introduced the concept of the sum of the squared deviations from the mean (SSX) as our primary measure of variation. Values in a sample may differ from each other because of sampling error, but they also may differ because they come from different treatment groups. If we can attribute some of the total variation to group differences, we have explained some of the variability. In other words, not all variation is bad. In this chapter, we see how to separate the explained variance and unexplained variance; if the explained part is large enough relative to the unexplained part, we can say that the groups are significantly different from each other.

Remember the expression for the sample variance (Equations [2.6] and [2.8]):

$$s^2 = \frac{\sum (X_i - \overline{X})^2}{n - 1} = \frac{SSX}{df}$$

When we talk about analysis of variance, we really are analyzing the SSX (review Equation [2.7]).

In discussing ANOVA, SSX becomes SSTotal:

$$\text{SSTotal} = \sum (X_{ij} - \bar{\bar{X}})^2 \qquad \text{[11.1]}$$

where X_{ij} is the ith observation in the jth group and $\bar{\bar{X}}$ is the grand mean, the mean of numbers in all the groups combined. X with a double bar could be interpreted as the mean of the group means, but that does not give the correct value unless all the groups are the same size.

ANOVA involves partitioning (i.e., splitting) SSTotal into two parts: SSE (SS Error, the unexplained part) and SST (SS Treatment, the explained part):

$$\text{SSTotal} = \text{SSE} + \text{SST}$$

$$\sum (X_{ij} - \bar{\bar{X}})^2 = \sum (X_{ij} - \bar{X}_j)^2 + \sum (\bar{X}_j - \bar{\bar{X}})^2 \qquad \text{[11.2]}$$

where $\bar{X}_j$ is the mean of the jth group.

Module 11.A shows the partitioning of the sum of squares. The partitioning looks a little messy at first glance, but it is just basic algebra. You do not need to memorize or be able to replicate the algebra, but it is worth taking a look at it.

> SSTotal is based on how much each number deviates from the grand mean; just like SSX that we saw back in Chapter 2 (Equation [2.7]).
>
> SSE is the error portion. It is based on how much the numbers in each group deviate from the mean of that group. We hope that the numbers in each group will be relatively close to each other; to the extent that they are not, we hope it is a result of a random error.
>
> SST is the treatment portion. It is based on how much the group means deviate from the grand mean. The extent to which the means are different can be attributed to whatever defines the groups.

We talk about "treatment" effect because ANOVA was developed for agricultural research, where the treatment might have been a particular pesticide or fertilizer. In a business setting, the treatment is rarely an actual treatment but instead refers to whatever defines the groups.

Module 11.B discusses a worksheet that shows the partitioning for a specific example. Look at the equations and see how closely they match Equation [11.2]. Better yet, see if you can replicate the worksheet from scratch. MegaStat's ANOVA tests have an option for displaying the partitioned output.

Now we do a seven-step example of an ANOVA test. Steps 3 and 4 introduce the F-distribution and the **F-ratio** as a test statistic. This ratio is the ratio of the good variation to the bad variation, and if that ratio becomes large enough, we say there is a significant difference among the groups. ANOVA test results are presented formally with an ANOVA table, as discussed in step 5.

Example of One-Factor ANOVA

A fleet manager wanted to determine the best replacement tire for the corporate automobiles. He selected four tires that are called Alpha, Beta, Gamma, and Delta and had a set of each of them installed on eight randomly selected

EXHIBIT 11-1
Sample data for
One-Factor
ANOVA.

Alpha	Beta	Gamma	Delta
46	73	65	44
55	61	50	50
49	67	58	48
44	54	61	41
61		56	53
		68	45
		71	

EXHIBIT 11-2
ANOVA table for
One-Factor
ANOVA.

ANOVA Table				
Source	SS	df	MS	F
Treatment	SST	$k-1$	$\dfrac{SST}{k-1}$	$\dfrac{MST}{MSE}$
Error	SSE	$N-k$	$\dfrac{SSE}{N-k}$	
Total	SSTotal	$N-1$		

automobiles. He then recorded the mileage (in thousands of miles) when the tires were due for replacement. At the end of the study, he had the data shown in Exhibit 11-1 (**ANOVA-OneFactor.xls**).

Note that although he started with eight automobiles for each tire, some of the cars were not available by the end of the study for various reasons. Although it is desirable to have nearly equal sample sizes, that is not a requirement for One-Factor ANOVA.

What would be his recommendation? Before you look at the results below, examine the data and see if you can predict what the result will be.

Hypothesis Testing Steps (Short Form)

1. H_0: $\mu_1 = \mu_2 = \mu_3 = \mu_4$ (the group means are equal).

   H_1: $\mu_1 \neq \mu_2 \neq \mu_3 \neq \mu_4$ (the group means are not equal; ANOVA tests are always two-tailed)

2. $\alpha = .05$ (default).

3. Test: One-Factor ANOVA (Test #6).

The test statistic is an F-ratio[1] that is presented formally in an ANOVA table, as shown in Exhibit 11-2.

Since the F-value is a ratio, it has degrees of freedom for the numerator $(k - 1)$ and the denominator $(N - k)$, where k is the number of groups and N is the total sample size for all groups and is displayed as F_{N-k}^{k-1}.

4. Decision rule: See Module 11.C to learn how to use the F-distribution table. For this example, $k = 4$ groups and $N = 22$.

   Reject H_0 if $F_{18}^{3} > 3.16$ (the 3 and the 18 are the notation for the degrees of freedom; they are not a superscript and subscript)

   or

   Reject H_0 if the p-value $< .05$

---

[1]The "F" in the F-ratio comes from the British statistician Sir R. A. Fisher.

EXHIBIT 11-3
MegaStat output for One-Factor ANOVA.

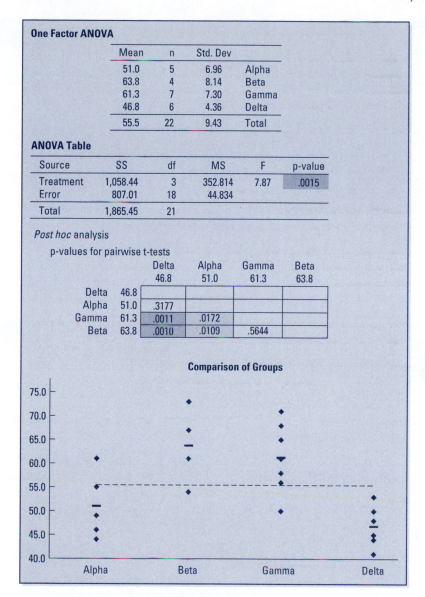

One Factor ANOVA

Mean	n	Std. Dev	
51.0	5	6.96	Alpha
63.8	4	8.14	Beta
61.3	7	7.30	Gamma
46.8	6	4.36	Delta
55.5	22	9.43	Total

ANOVA Table

Source	SS	df	MS	F	p-value
Treatment	1,058.44	3	352.814	7.87	.0015
Error	807.01	18	44.834		
Total	1,865.45	21			

Post hoc analysis

p-values for pairwise t-tests

		Delta 46.8	Alpha 51.0	Gamma 61.3	Beta 63.8
Delta	46.8				
Alpha	51.0	.3177			
Gamma	61.3	.0011	.0172		
Beta	63.8	.0010	.0109	.5644	

Comparison of Groups

5. Calculation of test statistic: F = 7.87, as shown in Exhibit 11-3 and Module 11.B.

6. Decision: Reject the null hypothesis since the calculated value of 7.87 is greater than the critical value of 3.16 and the p-value is less than .05.

7. Interpretation: The significant F-ratio tells us that the tires are more different than we would expect by chance alone, but the manager still has to make a decision about which tire to select. Is every tire different from every other tire, is one tire a clear winner, or are there groups or clusters? The MegaStat output shown in Exhibit 11-3 gives more information than does the significance test.

First, look at the graphical output showing the comparison of the groups. The chart shows each data value; the horizontal bar in each group represents the group means, and the horizontal line going through all the groups is the grand mean. The spread within each group represents the error variance, and the distance of the group means away from the grand mean

ONE-FACTOR ANOVA TEXT REPLICATION AND SIMULATION

Learning Activity **11.1–1**

- Open **ANOVA-OneFactor.xls.**
- Look up the .05 and .01 critical F-values in the table.
- Replicate Exhibit 11-3 by using MegaStat I Analysis of Variance I One-Factor ANOVA.
- After reading Module 11.D, open **ANOVA-sim.xls!Data.**
- Press the F9 function key until you get a significant result. This is an example of a Type I error: a significant outcome resulting from chance alone.
- Try changing some of the group means and note the effect on the chart. The **Chart** worksheet gives a more detailed view of the chart.
- Make one of the standard deviation values larger, say 20. As you press F9, you will see that the "spread" for that group is larger than that for the other groups.
- Use the method discussed in Module 11.D to use MegaStat to do a one-factor ANOVA on one of the simulated datasets.

ONE-FACTOR ANOVA PRACTICE

Learning Activity **11.1–2**

Using the real estate dataset, answer this question: Are the lot sizes different in the different subdivisions? If so, how are they different?
- First you need to get the lot sizes in groups for each subdivision. You do that with the following steps:
  - Open **RealEstateData.xls!Data.**
  - Sort the Subdivision variable.
  - Copy the lot sizes corresponding to each of the subdivision numbers and paste them side by side in a separate area of the worksheet.
  - Copy the subdivision names as variable labels.
  - Copy the five groups to a new worksheet and close **RealEstateData.xls** without saving.
- **LotSize.xls!Data** shows what the data should look like.
- Do the full hypothesis test.
- The Solution is as follows.

Hypothesis Testing Steps

1. $H_0: \mu_1 = \mu_2 = \mu_3 = \mu_4 = \mu_5$ (the group means are equal)

   $H_1: \mu_1 \neq \mu_2 \neq \mu_3 \neq \mu_4 \neq \mu_5$ (the group means are not equal; ANOVA tests are always two-tailed)

2. $\alpha = .05$ (default)

3. Test: one-factor ANOVA (Test #6)

The test statistic is an F-ratio that is presented formally in an ANOVA table, as shown in Exhibit 11-2.

4. Decision rule: Reject H_0 if $F^4_{119} > 2.45$ (note that the table does not have a row for 119 degrees of freedom, but you can get the exact value with MegaStat or the Excel function FINV). Or you can reject H_0 if the p-value $< .05$.

5. Calculation of test statistic: $F = 21.42$, as shown in Exhibit 11-4.

6. Decision: Reject the null hypothesis since the calculated value of 21.42 is greater than the critical value of 2.45 and the p-value is less than .05.

7. Interpretation: The post hoc analysis and the graphical comparison of groups show that the Stanton subdivision clearly stands out from the others. The remaining four subdivisions are not significantly different from each other.

EXHIBIT 11-4.
ANOVA output
for Learning
Activity 11.1–2.

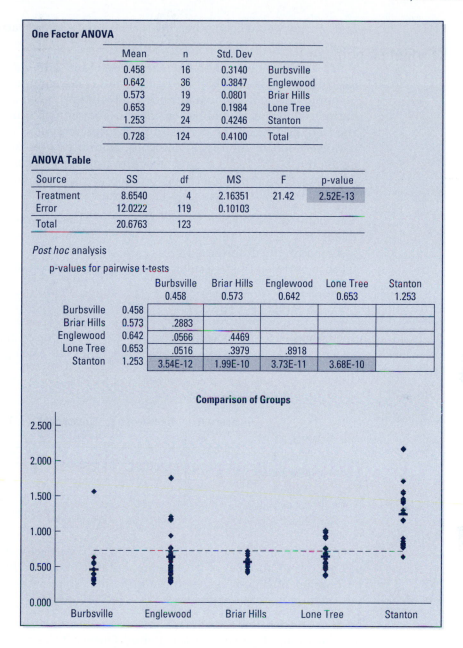

One Factor ANOVA

	Mean	n	Std. Dev	
	0.458	16	0.3140	Burbsville
	0.642	36	0.3847	Englewood
	0.573	19	0.0801	Briar Hills
	0.653	29	0.1984	Lone Tree
	1.253	24	0.4246	Stanton
	0.728	124	0.4100	Total

ANOVA Table

Source	SS	df	MS	F	p-value
Treatment	8.6540	4	2.16351	21.42	2.52E-13
Error	12.0222	119	0.10103		
Total	20.6763	123			

Post hoc analysis

p-values for pairwise t-tests

		Burbsville 0.458	Briar Hills 0.573	Englewood 0.642	Lone Tree 0.653	Stanton 1.253
Burbsville	0.458					
Briar Hills	0.573	.2883				
Englewood	0.642	.0566	.4469			
Lone Tree	0.653	.0516	.3979	.8918		
Stanton	1.253	3.54E-12	1.99E-10	3.73E-11	3.68E-10	

Comparison of Groups

shows the treatment effect. It appears that Beta and Gamma are better than Alpha and Delta.

TUTORIAL 12

Module 11.D describes an ANOVA simulation model. This worksheet helps you understand how ANOVA works and allows you to specify different group means to practice interpreting **post hoc analyses.**

Next examine the post hoc analysis, which helps identify the ways in which the groups are different. Module 11.E gives more information for interpreting post hoc output, but basically we see in the p-values for the pairwise tests that the p-value for comparing Beta and Gamma (.5644) is not under .05 and thus is not significant, and so Beta and Gamma would be a cluster. We also see that Alpha and Delta are not different from each other, and so they would be another cluster. The more conservative Tukey post hoc output shows the same general pattern.

What does this mean to the manager? Beta and Gamma are clearly the better tires. Beta has the highest mileage but is not significantly different from Gamma, and so if Gamma has other advantages (such as a lower price or a better vendor), it should be considered. The manager also should note that the Beta group had the highest dropout rate (only four of the eight original cars were left in the test at the end). Not only is the sample size for Beta small, but he might try to find out if the tires were responsible for any of the dropouts. Also, the standard deviation of the Beta group is the largest, and that means that the Beta tires have more variation.

The point is as follows: Do not blindly select the group with the highest mean. Let the data tell its story. Also, always ask if a significant difference is a meaningful difference. In this case, there is over a 13,000-mile mean difference between the two clusters, and that is surely a meaningful effect.

11.2   Randomized Blocks ANOVA (Test #7)

In the hypothesis testing chapter, we discussed the paired observations test for paired data. Randomized Blocks ANOVA extends the concept of pairs to blocks of data.

Data form: blocks of data.

	Treatment A	Treatment B	Treatment C	Treatment D
Block 1				
Block 2				
Block 3				
Block 4				
Block 5				
Block 6				

This example shows four treatments. As with One-Factor ANOVA, there is no fixed maximum number of treatments, but it is usually a fairly small number. The number of Blocks can be quite large and should be substantially larger than the number of treatments.

The data in each row (i.e., block) have to "go together" just as there has to be some meaningful pairing in the Paired Observations test. Often each block represents data from the same person, but there could be other ways for the data to go together.

Randomized Blocks ANOVA sometimes is called Two-Factor ANOVA without Replication or Repeated Measures ANOVA. In some older books, it is called Randomized Plots ANOVA from agricultural research, where each block could be a plot of soil split into different treatments.

The SSTotal for this model can be partitioned in a manner similar to that used in the One-Factor ANOVA, but this is not shown because it is fairly complex and does not really increase our understanding. However, MegaStat has an option for showing the partitioned output.

It appears that machine C has the highest mean, and the post hoc analysis confirms that machine C is significantly different from the other machines. Machines A, B, and D are not significantly different from each other, and so they would constitute a second cluster.

The operators are even more different than are the machines. Is this good? It means that the machines are different even with a wide range of operator ability, and this is probably good because it implies that the results can be generalized to a wide range of workers. However, if the manager was hoping to find a machine that would work best for a particular skill level, she would not have wanted to find a significant difference for the operators.

11.3   ANOVA Compared to t-Tests

ANOVA was introduced in this chapter as a test for comparing three or more groups, but One-Factor ANOVA also works for comparing two independent groups. As the examples in Module 11.F show, you get exactly the same p-value with the t-test and the ANOVA, assuming that you did a two-tail t-test and $t^2 = F$. Also, if you examine the MegaStat output, you will see that the pooled variance for the t-test is the same as the mean square error for the ANOVA test.

In the same way that a One-Factor ANOVA can be used for an independent groups t-test, a Randomized Blocks ANOVA with two treatments is equivalent to doing a Paired Comparisons hypothesis test (see Module 11.F).

If you can justify a one-tailed test, the t-test is slightly more powerful (i.e., more likely to reject the null hypothesis) than the ANOVA, but other than that, they are identical. You might ask, If they are identical, why do we have both? The answer is more a matter of tradition than of merit. If you are going to use just one procedure, the ANOVA is more general because it can handle more than two groups, but many courses do not cover ANOVA; thus, the hypothesis testing is introduced with the t-test.

It is interesting to note that you can use Randomized Blocks ANOVA to do a Mean versus Hypothesized test. If you create pairs of values in which one value is the data and the paired value is the hypothesized value and then run a Randomized blocks ANOVA, you get the same result as you would doing the t-test for Mean versus Hypothesized. (See the example in Module 11.F.)

There is no particular reason to do the test with ANOVA, but it does show that any test that can be done with a t-test also can be done with an ANOVA.

11.4   Two-Factor ANOVA (Test #8)

As the name implies, Two-Factor ANOVA is an extension of One-Factor ANOVA to test two different treatment factors. For example, if one factor is gender (Male, Female) and the other factor is type of machine (A, B), the data form will look like this:

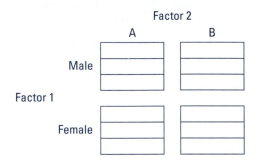

In this example, each factor has two levels and each cell has three values (replications). The number of levels of each factor can be larger, and each cell typically would have more than three replications. Every cell has to have the same number of replications, and there can be no missing data. The cells are shown with space between them to indicate that they are independent, but in setting up the data for MegaStat, there would be no space.

As you probably have guessed, there is an F-ratio for each factor, but what makes this test especially useful is a third F-ratio for interaction. It could turn out that there is no difference between Male and Female or between machines A and B, but if, for example, men do better on machine B and women do better on machine A, there will be a significant interaction effect (Module 11.H).

Although the two-factor ANOVA is a useful test, it is somewhat limited in practice by the fact that it requires exactly the same number of observations in each cell.

Summary

Conceptual

This chapter extended hypothesis testing from two groups to multiple groups, but it also introduced a new way of looking at group differences. The main theme was that not all variability is bad. Variance can be partitioned into explained and unexplained components; if the variance attributable to group differences is sufficiently larger than the error component, there is a significant difference between the groups.

ANOVA test results are summarized in an ANOVA table.

- If an ANOVA test is significant, post hoc procedures can be used to determine which group differences have caused the significant result.
- Although ANOVA usually is thought of as a method for testing three or more groups, it also works with two groups and gives the same result as the corresponding t-test.

Applied

- The three most commonly used ANOVA models were discussed in the chapter. Know when each would be used and be able to interpret the computer output for the ANOVA table. See Appendix B for a more detailed summary of the individual tests:

- One-Factor ANOVA for independent groups (Test #6)
- Randomized Blocks ANOVA for blocked data (Test #7)
- Two-Factor ANOVA for two independent factors (Test #8)

Exercises

The exercises and data are found in **Ch_11_ANOVA.xls** in the exercises folder of the CD.

No.	Content
1	F-distribution
2	One-Factor
3	One-Factor
4	One-Factor
5	One-Factor—RealEstateData
6	One-Factor—create your own
7	One-Factor—two groups
8	Randomized Blocks
9	Randomized Blocks
10	Randomized Blocks
11	Randomized Blocks—transpose
12	Randomized Blocks—compare to One-Factor
13	Randomized Blocks—paired obsv.
14	Two-Factor
15	Two-Factor

Modules for Analysis of Variance

11.A PARTITIONING THE SUM OF SQUARES

In Section 11.1, we started with

$$\text{SSTotal} = \sum (X_{ij} - \overline{\overline{X}})^2$$

and said that it could be split into

$$\sum (X_{ij} - \overline{\overline{X}})^2 = \sum (X_{ij} - \overline{X}_j)^2 + \sum (\overline{X}_j - \overline{\overline{X}})^2$$

$$\text{SSTotal} = \text{SSE} + \text{SST}$$

In this module, we see how that is done. Although the subscripts and sigmas make it look messy, it is just high school–level algebra.

Start with

$$\text{SSTotal} = \sum (X_{ij} - \overline{\overline{X}})^2$$

Then rewrite with some space in the center:

$$= \sum (X_{ij} \qquad - \overline{\overline{X}})^2$$

In the space, subtract and then add the group means. If you subtract and add the same thing, they cancel and there is still an equality:

$$= \sum (X_{ij} - \overline{X}_j + \overline{X}_j - \overline{\overline{X}})^2$$

Group with parentheses:

$$= \sum ((X_{ij} - \overline{X}_j) + (\overline{X}_j - \overline{\overline{X}}))^2$$

Note that what we have is of the form $(a + b)^2 = a^2 + b^2 + 2ab$. If we expand the square, we get

$$\sum (X_{ij} - \overline{X}_j)^2 + \sum (\overline{X}_j - \overline{\overline{X}})^2 + 2 \sum (X_{ij} - \overline{X}_j)(\overline{X}_j - \overline{\overline{X}})$$

Since, as we have seen, the sum of deviations from the mean will always equal zero, the 2ab part will drop out, leaving us with

$$\text{SSTotal} = \sum (X_{ij} - \overline{X}_j)^2 + \sum (\overline{X}_j - \overline{\overline{X}})^2$$

which is what we wanted—the total variation split into two parts: error and treatment.

11.B   WORKSHEET SHOWING PARTITIONING

Exhibit 11-8 shows the ANOVA partitioning worksheet in **ANOVA-One Factor.xls!Defn_method.** The worksheet is the Excel version of the partitioning shown in Equation [11.2] and Module 11.A. Note that for each observation the total deviation is equal to the error part plus the treatment

WORKSHEET PARTITIONING— EXAMINE   Learning Activity **11.B–1**

- Open **ANOVA-OneFactor.xls!Defn_method** and note that it corresponds to Exhibit 11-8.
- Study the worksheet until you see how it partitions the SSTotal into error and treatment components. Look at the cell formulas (remember CTRL ~ toggles formula view).
  - Compare total, error, and treatment columns to Equation [11.2] (columns F, G, and H). Do you see the correspondence? Could you explain it to one of your fellow classmates who could not see it?
    - *Answer:* The three columns correspond to the three components of the equation. F = G + H. You can see it best in formula view.

EXHIBIT 11-12   ANOVA simulation showing groups B and D with higher means.

ANOVA Simulation

mean	80	90	80	90	80	population means (try changing them)
sd	8	8	8	8	8	

	A	B	C	D	E
	82	98	81	87	80
	56	98	89	101	76
	80	99	86	92	76
	88	90	71	94	69
	89	87	72	92	89
	91		84		80
	75		84		
			78		

	A	B	C	D	E
84.32 GM	80.14 MeanA	94.40 MeanB	80.63 MeanC	93.20 MeanD	78.33 MeanE
	12.05	5.50	6.93	5.07	6.59

0.0025 p-value

Recalc

data cells. As you press the F9 function cell, you will see new values calculated and displayed in the chart. The p-value for the ANOVA is displayed above the chart. The worksheet also displays the ANOVA partitioning and the full ANOVA table.

With the means all set equal to the same value, you would not expect significant group differences; however, if you keep pressing the F9 key, you occasionally will get a significant result, that is, a p-value less than .05. When this happens, you are observing a Type I error: a significant outcome resulting from sampling error even though the means are equal.

Typically, you would leave the standard deviations all the same. However, if you make one of them larger, you can see that group generally will have more within-group variation on the chart.

The simulation is most useful when you change the means and note the result on the chart and the other values in the table. It is especially useful for practicing analysis of post hoc output. Exhibit 11-12 shows what the simulation looked like when it generated the data for Module 11.E and Exhibit 11-13. Note how the population means for groups B and D are set to 90 and those for A, C, and E are set to 80.

To do MegaStat analysis on the data, do the following steps:

- Select the colored data cells, including the column headings.
- Copy.
- Click on the template worksheet.
- Click cell A1.
- Edit | Paste Special | Values.
- Run MegaStat | One Factor ANOVA using cells A1:E9 of the template worksheet as the input range.

ANOVA SIMULATION   Learning Activity **11.D–1**

- Open **ANOVA-sim.xls!Data.**
- Make sure all the means in cells B3:F3 are 80 and the standard deviations below are 20.
- Click the Recalc button or press the F9 function key and observe the chart and the p-value in cell H8. Keep clicking Recalc until you get a p-value under .05; this is a Type I error—a significant resulting from chance alone. Look at the chart and determine which group or groups caused the significant result.
- Change mean B and D to 90.
- Click Recalc. The output should look similar to that in Exhibit 11-12. Outputs that have a p-value greater than .05 are Type II errors because they do not show a significant result even though the group means are different.
- Run MegaStat | Analysis of Variance | One-Factor ANOVA using the procedure discussed in Module 11.D.

11.E   POST HOC ANALYSIS

A significant result (i.e., a p-value $< .05$) from an ANOVA test just means that the groups are somehow different from each other but does not say how they are different. For example, if you have four groups, every group may be different from every other group, but maybe one group is different from the other three or maybe two are high and two are low or some other combination.

There are various methods for post hoc analysis that help you identify how the groups are different. The obvious thing to do is to compare the groups pairwise, in other words, do an independent groups t-test for every possible pair of variables. What you are looking for are clusters: variables that are not different from each other but are different from the other variables.

Although pairwise comparisons are a good way to see where the action is in a set of data, it can be shown the pairwise p-values are not independent. If you have three groups—A, B, and C—and you compare A versus B and A versus C, the tests are not independent because A is common to both comparisons. Since the p-values are not independent, they should not be used for formal hypothesis testing. MegaStat does the Tukey simultaneous comparison test, which is one of the post hoc tests that address this issue. The Tukey test shows the same general patterns as the pairwise comparisons but will be more conservative.

Use the pairwise comparisons to look for patterns in your data. Use the Tukey output if you need to show more conclusive proof of the patterns.

Exhibit 11-13 shows the data and MegaStat output for a five-group one-factor ANOVA. The overall p-value is very small, and so the groups are different from each other, but how are they different? Looking at the data, the group means, and the graphical output, it appears that groups B and D have higher means than do groups A, C, and E. Let's see how this is shown with the post hoc analysis.

The top part of the post hoc output shows the pairwise t-tests. This is where your main focus should be. Note that the groups are sorted from low to high and that each cell contains the p-value for a t-test comparing the groups. For

EXHIBIT 11-13   MegaStat ANOVA output with post hoc analysis.

A	B	C	D	E
87	111	71	99	82
82	109	69	96	80
74	96	82	88	71
103	102	87	101	82
73	87	81	91	79
78		80		79
78		79		
		74		

One Factor ANOVA

Mean	n	Std. Dev	
82.1	7	10.35	A
101.0	5	9.82	B
77.9	8	6.06	C
95.0	5	5.43	D
78.8	6	4.07	E
85.5	31	11.47	Total

Comparison of Groups

ANOVA Table

Source	SS	df	MS	F	p-value
Treatment	2,463.18	4	615.794	10.77	2.77E-05
Error	1,486.57	26	57.176		
Total	3,949.74	30			

Post hoc analysis

p-values for pairwise t-tests

		C	E	A	D	B
		77.9	78.8	82.1	95.0	101.0
C	77.9					
E	78.8	.8163				
A	82.1	.2855	.4386			
D	95.0	.0005	.0016	.0074		
B	101.0	1.29E-05	.0001	.0002	.2208	

Tukey simultaneous comparison t-values (d.f. = 26)

		C	E	A	D	B
		77.9	78.8	82.1	95.0	101.0
C	77.9					
E	78.8	0.23				
A	82.1	1.09	0.79			
D	95.0	3.97	3.53	2.90		
B	101.0	5.36	4.84	4.26	1.25	

critical values for experimentwise error rate:

0.05	2.93	
0.01	3.63	

example, if you do a two-tailed independent groups t-test comparing E and C, you get a value that is close to the .8163 shown in the table. If you actually do the test (a good idea), you will get a p-value of .7445. Why are they not identical? When you do the t-test, the pooled variance is calculated from the two groups involved in the test, whereas the post hoc procedure uses the mean square error from the ANOVA table as the variance estimate for all the pairwise tests.

EXHIBIT 11-14
Post hoc analysis showing clusters circled.

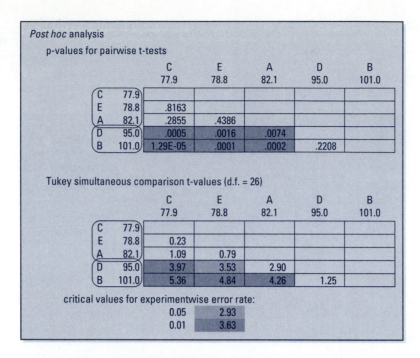

Post hoc analysis
p-values for pairwise t-tests

		C 77.9	E 78.8	A 82.1	D 95.0	B 101.0
C	77.9					
E	78.8	.8163				
A	82.1	.2855	.4386			
D	95.0	.0005	.0016	.0074		
B	101.0	1.29E-05	.0001	.0002	.2208	

Tukey simultaneous comparison t-values (d.f. = 26)

		C 77.9	E 78.8	A 82.1	D 95.0	B 101.0
C	77.9					
E	78.8	0.23				
A	82.1	1.09	0.79			
D	95.0	3.97	3.53	2.90		
B	101.0	5.36	4.84	4.26	1.25	

critical values for experimentwise error rate:
0.05	2.93
0.01	3.63

The important thing to remember here is that a shaded cell indicates that the group means represented by that cell are probably different from each other and that nonshaded cells are probably not different. You can look at the actual p-values to see if they are close to .05. A group of variables that are not different from each other is considered a cluster. In our preliminary look at the data, it appeared that groups A, C, and E were pretty close to each other, and the p-values for A–C, A–E, and C–E confirm that. Thus, you would circle those variables, as indicated in Exhibit 11-14. In the same way, groups B and D form a cluster. A, C, and E are all pairwise different from B and D, and so the clusters in this example are clear and nonoverlapping. In the Learning Activities that follows, you will see examples that are not as obvious.

Whenever you identify a cluster, you should confirm it on the graphical output, as shown in Exhibit 11-15.

EXHIBIT 11-15
ANOVA chart with post hoc clusters circled.

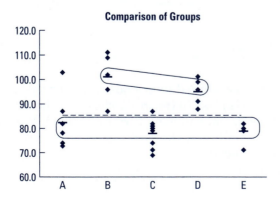

ANOVA VERSUS t-TEST—TWO GROUPS

Learning Activity **11.F–1**

- Open **Htest2b.xls!Data.**
- Use MegaStat | Hypothesis Testing | Compare Two Independent Groups to compare East versus West doing a two-tail (not equal) test.
- Compare East and West by using One-Factor ANOVA. You will need to move one of the groups so that the East and West variables are contiguous.
- Note that the p-values are the same for both tests and $t^2 = F$.

ANOVA VERSUS t-TEST—PAIRED OBSERVATIONS

Learning Activity **11.F–2**

- Open **Htest2c.xls!Data.**
- Use MegaStat | Hypothesis Testing | Paired Observations to compare Premium versus Regular doing a two-tail (not equal) test.
- Compare Premium versus Regular using Randomized Blocks ANOVA.
- Note that the p-values are the same for both tests and $t^2 = F$.

ANOVA VERSUS t-TEST—MEAN VERSUS HYPOTHESIZED

Learning Activity **11.F–3**

- Open **Htest2a.xls!Data.**
- Use MegaStat | Hypothesis Testing | Mean vs. Hypothesized to test the hypothesis that the mean is equal to 50 doing a two-tail (not equal) test.
- Set up the data as discussed in Module 11.F and do a Randomized Blocks ANOVA.
- Note that the p-values are the same for both tests and $t^2 = F$.

you get the same result you would from doing the t-test for mean versus hypothesized. The data from Exhibit 10-1 with the paired values and the output from the t-test and ANOVA are shown in Exhibit 11-18.

There is no particular reason to do a mean versus hypothesized test in this manner. It is shown here to demonstrate that ANOVA can perform any one- or two-group hypothesis test.

As with the other examples above, the p-values are the same and $t^2 = F$. Note that the t-test was done as a two-tailed test to make the p-value correspond to the ANOVA output.

EXHIBIT 11-18
Randomized Blocks ANOVA used to do Mean versus Hypothesized Test.

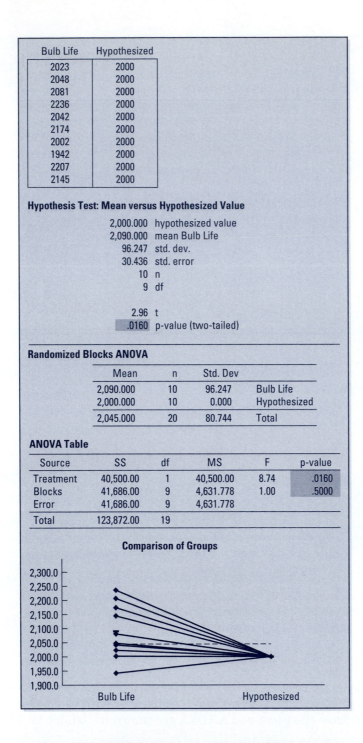

Bulb Life	Hypothesized
2023	2000
2048	2000
2081	2000
2236	2000
2042	2000
2174	2000
2002	2000
1942	2000
2207	2000
2145	2000

Hypothesis Test: Mean versus Hypothesized Value

2,000.000	hypothesized value
2,090.000	mean Bulb Life
96.247	std. dev.
30.436	std. error
10	n
9	df
2.96	t
.0160	p-value (two-tailed)

Randomized Blocks ANOVA

Mean	n	Std. Dev	
2,090.000	10	96.247	Bulb Life
2,000.000	10	0.000	Hypothesized
2,045.000	20	80.744	Total

ANOVA Table

Source	SS	df	MS	F	p-value
Treatment	40,500.00	1	40,500.00	8.74	.0160
Blocks	41,686.00	9	4,631.778	1.00	.5000
Error	41,686.00	9	4,631.778		
Total	123,872.00	19			

Comparison of Groups

(graph: y-axis from 1,900.0 to 2,300.0 in increments of 50.0; x-axis categories: Bulb Life, Hypothesized)

11.G   RANDOMIZED BLOCKS COMPARED TO ONE-FACTOR ANOVA

The Randomized Blocks data in Exhibit 11-5 and the output in Exhibit 11-6 show a significant treatment effect. What would happen if someone mistakenly ran the data as a One-Factor ANOVA (a fairly common mistake)? The results are shown in Exhibit 11-19, along with the Randomized Blocks output for

EXHIBIT 11-19
One-Factor
ANOVA on
randomized
blocks data.

One Factor ANOVA

	Mean	n	Std. Dev	
	86.8	6	12.43	A
	89.5	6	12.69	B
	96.8	6	8.75	C
	88.2	6	10.30	D
	90.3	24	11.13	Total

ANOVA Table

Source	SS	df	MS	F	p-value
Treatment	359.33	3	119.778	0.96	.4303
Error	2,492.00	20	124.600		
Total	2,851.33	23			

Randomized Blocks ANOVA

	Mean	n	Std. Dev	
	86.833	6	12.432	A
	89.500	6	12.693	B
	96.833	6	8.750	C
	88.167	6	10.304	D
	79.500	4	6.557	Joe
	88.750	4	5.123	John
	93.000	4	7.659	Dan
	100.000	4	3.162	Frank
	103.500	4	3.109	Susan
	77.250	4	7.042	Harry
	90.333	24	11.134	Total

ANOVA Table

Source	SS	df	MS	F	p-value
Treatments	359.33	3	119.778	7.74	.0024
Blocks	2,259.83	5	451.967	29.20	3.18E-07
Error	232.17	15	15.478		
Total	2,851.33	23			

comparison. To save space, the post hoc analysis and data plots are not shown; you can run them if you wish.

Even though the Randomized Blocks test shows a clear treatment effect, the One-Factor ANOVA using the same data does not come close to being significant. If we look at the sums of squares, we see why this is the case. First note

RANDOMIZED BLOCKS EXPLORATION (1)

Learning Activity **11.G–1**

- Open **ANOVA-Rblock.xls!Data.**
- Replicate Exhibit 11-19, using MegaStat | Analysis of Variance | One-Factor ANOVA.
- Open **ANOVA-Rblock2.xls!Data.**
- Run MegaStat | Analysis of Variance | One-Factor ANOVA and compare the results to that of the Randomized Blocks.

RANDOMIZED BLOCKS EXPLORATION (2)

Learning Activity **11.G–2**

- Open **ANOVA-Rblock.xls!Data.**
- Randomly shuffle each of the treatment groups. You do this by copying each treatment to a new location, shuffling by using the technique discussed in Module 7.A, and copy/pasting back to the original location.
- Run a randomized blocks ANOVA using MegaStat and compare the results to Exhibit 11-6.
  - *Solution:* With the data "unblocked," you should not have a significant result. The SSTotal will be the same, but the SSBlocks will be smaller and the SSError will be greater.

that the treatment and the total sums of squares are the same for both ANOVAs; however, the Error SS of the one-factor ANOVA is split between blocks *and* error in the Randomized Blocks ANOVA. To the extent that some of the variation can be attributed to the blocks, the error portion is correspondingly smaller, and that in turn makes the F-ratio larger.

In Module 10.B, we saw that the Paired Observations test is useful only if the pairs are correlated. The same concept is true for Randomized Blocks. If you randomly shuffled each column of randomized blocks data, you would find that a Randomized Blocks ANOVA has about the same p-value as a One-Factor ANOVA. Randomized blocks is a more powerful test only if the data in each block are relatively consistent.

EXHIBIT 11-20 Sample data for Two-Factor ANOVA.

	A	B
Male	46.0	84.6
	58.2	89.7
	28.3	64.0
	64.1	49.3
	63.3	88.3
	36.3	77.6
	33.5	56.3
	51.3	70.7
	28.0	72.2
	48.5	64.4
Female	81.4	30.9
	60.7	51.3
	83.9	63.9
	82.1	56.8
	61.1	46.0
	73.8	57.6
	73.5	35.7
	55.5	55.8
	70.6	40.2
	86.3	44.2

12.2   Scatterplot

X	Y
12	35.7
14	21.1
17	56.9
18	27.6
23	32.9
24	65.9
28	29.5
32	60.0
33	90.1
36	49.7
37	84.0
42	63.6
43	107.2
45	77.9
49	92.7
52	82.4
54	124.3
57	129.9
62	129.3
65	139.3

EXHIBIT 12-1
X = number of sales calls, Y = sales.

Since we have X,Y pairs, it makes sense to plot them to see the relationship graphically with a scatterplot. The data in Exhibit 12-1 represent the number of sales calls a salesperson makes in a month (X) and the corresponding sales in thousands of dollars (Y) (**Regr1.xls!Scatterplot**).

By plotting the X,Y pairs, we get the scatterplot shown in Exhibit 12-2.

Note that as X gets larger, so does Y; thus, we would say that there is a moderately strong relationship between X and Y. Below, we will see more details regarding the line and the strength of the relationship.

Open **RegrSim1.xls** and select the "Graph" worksheet. Repeatedly press the F9 function key to see randomly created scatterplots.

Before you do any regression analysis, you should do a scatterplot. If the points do not fall more or less on a straight line, linear regression will not work very well. If the points seem to follow a curved line, there are advanced techniques to fit a nonlinear regression line.

You also should examine the scatterplot for outliers: points that do not go along with the others. There is a more detailed discussion of outliers below (p. 216).

EXHIBIT 12-2   Scatterplot output showing linear regression line.

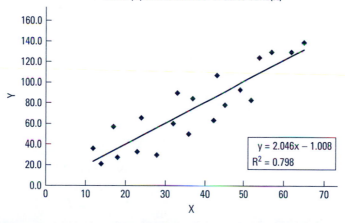

Sales (Y) versus Number of Sales Calls(X)

$y = 2.046x - 1.008$
$R^2 = 0.798$

REPLICATE SCATTERPLOT   Learning Activity **12.2–1**

- Open **Regr1.xls!Data**
- Use MegaStat I Correlation/Regression I Scatterplot to replicate Exhibit 12-2.
- Add the heading shown in Exhibit 12-2.
- Locate a few of the data points on the scatterplot.
- Find the slope and intercept values on the scatterplot.

- Open **RegrSim1.xls!Graph.**
- Click the Recalc button or press F9 to create different random scatterplots. Keep pressing F9 until you can guess fairly accurately what the number at the bottom will be by looking at the scatterplot.
- Keep clicking until you get a value greater than .95 and less than .05.
- If you are curious, click the **Data** worksheet to see how the charts are created.

12.3   Regression Line

On the scatterplot in Exhibit 12-2 and on the randomly generated scatterplot in Learning Activity 12.2–2, there is a line that goes through the "middle" of the scatterplot. Regression analysis allows us to determine this best-fitting line, which officially is called the *least-squares* **regression line**. Later we will see what is meant by *best fitting* and *least squares*.

Let's briefly review what is meant by a line or, more formally, a linear function. The equation for the regression line is

$$Y' = bX + a \qquad \textbf{[12.1]}$$

Where:

     Y' = **predicted value** (some books use $\hat{Y}$ or Y_C)
     b = slope (how much Y' changes for each unit change in X)
     a = intercept (height of the line when $X = 0$)
     X = value of the independent variable

If b and a are the slope and the intercept for the best-fitting straight line, how are these values determined? By applying calculus procedures that are beyond the scope of this book, we get the following equations:

$$b = \frac{n\left(\sum XY\right) - \left(\sum X\right)\left(\sum Y\right)}{n\left(\sum X^2\right) - \left(\sum X\right)^2} \qquad \textbf{[12.2]}$$

$$a = \frac{\sum Y}{n} - b\frac{\sum X}{n} = \overline{Y} - b\overline{X} \qquad \textbf{[12.3]}$$

These are computational equations, and thus we usually let the computer calculate the values. Computers are great at multiplying, squaring, summing, and the like.

The regression equation for the sample data is

$$Y' = 2.046(X) - 1.008$$

This was calculated with the MegaStat regression option. **Regr1.xls! Partition** also shows the coefficients calculated with Excel's SLOPE() and INTERCEPT() functions. These values also are shown on the scatterplot in Exhibit 12-2.

CALCULATE SLOPE AND INTERCEPT BY USING EXCEL

Learning Activity **12.3–1**

- Open **Regr1.xls!Data.**
- Use Excel's SLOPE() and INTERCEPT() functions to find the slope and the intercept.
- Verify that the values match the slope and the intercept on the scatterplot (Exhibit 12-2).

Recall that X is the number of sales calls and Y is sales. Thus, the slope of 2.046 means that we would predict slightly over $2000 of sales for every additional sales call a person makes.

If the person makes no sales calls, we would expect zero sales; however, the intercept is not zero. The reason the intercept is not zero is that we are fitting the regression to the observed data. The intercept is mathematically correct, and if you look at the scatterplot, you will see that it crosses at nearly zero and that there are no data points near zero. There is a MegaStat and Excel option for forcing the intercept to be exactly zero, but the regression line is then no longer the best-fitting regression line; it is the best-fitting regression line given that its intercept is zero.

12.4 Measuring Strength of Relationship

In the Chapter 11, we saw how to partition total variability to see how much can be attributed to group differences. In this module, we partition total variability to see how much can be attributed to the regression line.

The total variation for the dependent variable Y is

$$SSTotal = \sum (Y_i - \overline{Y})^2 \qquad \text{[12.4]}$$

Note that this is the same as SSX with X changed to Y. If we do some algebra on this similar to what we did in Chapter 11 (see Module 12.A), we end up with

$$SSTotal = \sum (Y_i - Y'_i)^2 + \sum (Y'_i - \overline{Y})^2$$

$$= SSE + SSR$$

$$= SSError + SSRegression$$

$$= \text{unexplained variance} + \text{explained variance} \qquad \text{[12.5]}$$

The SSE component is based on the deviations of Y from Y' (the predicted value, i.e., the height of the line). In other words, the closer the points are to the line, the smaller SSE will be. The SSR component is based on how far the predicted values, Y', are from the mean of Y, $\overline{Y}$. In other words, the steeper the line is, the larger SSR will be. The "Partition" worksheet of **Regr1.xls!Partition** shows the worksheet version of the partitioning. Study it and look at the underlying equations. You will see that it has columns corresponding to total, error, and regression.

The following three exhibits show the three different types of variation. The first type is total variation (Exhibit 12-3). The horizontal line is the mean of Y. Note how the vertical lines go from the mean of Y to each point. If you squared those distances, you would have the total sum of squares error: $\text{SSTotal} = \sum (Y_i - \overline{Y})^2$.

EXHIBIT 12-3
Total deviations from the mean of Y.

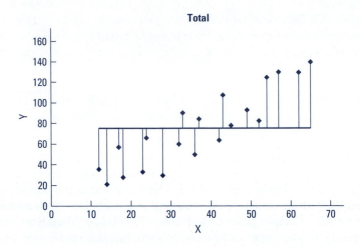

EXHIBIT 12-4
Regression component of total deviations.

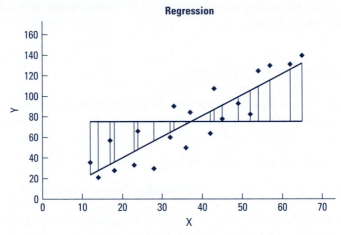

EXHIBIT 12-5
Error (residual) component of total deviations.

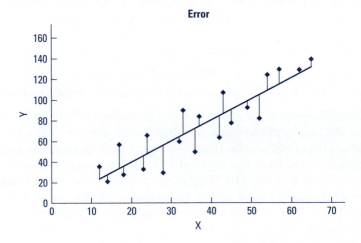

Next, we put in the regression line and draw lines from the mean to the line at each data point (Exhibit 12-4). Since both the mean and the regression line are straight lines, the lines between them are neat and orderly. That is why the regression variation (the squared distances) $\text{SSR} = \sum (Y_i' - \overline{Y})^2$ is called "good" or "explained" variation.

Exhibit 12-5 shows the deviations of each point from the regression line. Since these points are what is left over from the total variation after we account for as much as we can with the regression line, these lines sometimes are called **residuals** or error deviations. The squared distances are the sum of squares error: $\text{SSE} = \sum (Y_i - Y_i')^2$.

When we are doing least-squares regression, this is the quantity we are trying to minimize by choosing a slope and an intercept that make the error lines shown in Exhibit 12-5 as short as possible.

Regr1-SSplot.xls is the worksheet that was used to create these exhibits. If you quickly click between the worksheets for SSTotal, SSR, and SSE, you can get an even better understanding of the different components of variation.

Notice how the regression bars are generally longer than the error bars in this example. That implies that most of the total variation is explained variation and that we have good predictability. Since we have partitioned the total sum of squared deviations, we can get a measure of the strength of relationship by looking at the ratio of the good variability (SSR) to the total variability (SSTotal). This value is called r-squared (r^2):

$$r^2 = \frac{\text{SSR}}{\text{SSTotal}}$$ [12.6]

Sometimes called the *coefficient of determination,* r^2 is the proportion of explained variability of the dependent variable and can range from 0, meaning no relationship between X and Y, to 1, meaning a perfect relationship (i.e, the points fall on a straight line). See the "Partition" worksheet in **Regr1.xls** to see the partitioning and the calculation of r^2.

How large does r^2 need to be to be considered good? It depends on the context, but generally an r^2 of .7 or larger can be considered a moderately strong relationship. On the scatterplot simulation (**RegrSim1.xls**), the number at the bottom is r^2. Run it some more and note what the scatterplot looks like for different values of r^2.

STUDY REGRESSION PARTITIONING   Learning Activity **12.4–1**

- Open **Regr1-SSplot.xls!Intro**.
- Follow the instructions on the "Intro" page to cycle through the chart.
- Select the SSTotal worksheet. Focus on one error bar and then click CTRL-s to see how it splits between regression and error segments. Repeat until you see how it works.
- *Exploration:* Go to the **Data** worksheet. In column I the data sort ascending t, and in column K the data are randomly shuffled. Paste each of these values into column B and note the effect on the scatterplots.

EXPLORING PARTITIONING: WHAT DOES *LEAST SQUARES* REALLY MEAN?   Learning Activity **12.4–2**

- Open **Regr1.xls!Partition.**
- Examine the worksheet.
  - Note how it is similar to the ANOVA partitioning.
  - Compare the worksheet to the equations.
  - If you really want to see how it works, re-create it from scratch.
- Now we will see what really is meant by least-squares regression. Click on the **Partition2** worksheet. This worksheet is similar to the "Partition" worksheet except that the slope and the intercept are entered as constants so that they can be changed.
  - Change the slope in cell A26 to 2.0. This value is used to calculate the SS columns. Note that the SSE value is larger than it was before; the difference is shown in cell E31.
  - Try using other values for the slope and the intercept. No matter what values you use, the SSE will be larger than it is when you are using the values calculated by regression Equations [12.2] and [12.3]. This is why it is called least-squares regression.
  - The least-squares slope and intercept are in cells A37:A38 if you want to paste them in to get the minimum SSE again.

r^2 is a good measure of strength of relationship, but we also need a way to determine whether the relationship is statistically significant. Since we have partitioned the variance, this is done with an ANOVA test. Module 12.B shows a detailed hypothesis test for regression that has the ANOVA table for regression in step 5.

12.5   Regression Computer Output

TUTORIAL 13

Exhibit 12-6 shows the MegaStat output for linear regression.

First of all, note that the r^2 (.798), the slope (2.046), and the intercept (-1.008) that were shown on the scatterplot and discussed above are included in this regression output. Let's take a look at this full regression output.

EXHIBIT 12-6
Regression output.

Regression Analysis

r^2	0.798		n	20
r	0.893		k	1
Std. Error of Estimate	17.139		Dep. Var.	Y

Regression Output

variables		coefficients	std. error	t (df=18)	p-value	95% lower	95% upper
Intercept	a =	−1.008	9.790	−0.103	.9192	−21.577	19.561
X	b =	2.046	0.243	8.437	1.14E-07	1.536	2.555

confidence interval

ANOVA Table

Source	SS	df	MS	F	p-value
Regression	20,907.155	1	20,907.155	71.18	1.14E-07
Residual	5,287.225	18	293.735		
Total	26,194.380	19			

REPLICATE TEXT
REGRESSION OUTPUT

Learning Activity **12.5–1**

- Open **Regr1.xls!Data.**
- Use MegaStat | Correlation/Regression | Regression to replicate Exhibit 12-6.
- Find the values discussed in the text.

r^2 and the Correlation Coefficient (r)

As we saw in Section 12.4 and Equation [12.6], r^2 is the primary measure of strength of relationship. That is why it is shown on the scatterplot[1] and is often the first value displayed on regression output.

The square root of r^2 is obviously r, which is called the **correlation coefficient.** Since we can look at the positive or negative square root, r can be negative. If the regression slope is negative, r is negative, and that is its advantage: With one value, we can have a measure of strength of relationship *and* direction of relationship. r can range from -1.00 (perfect negative relationship) through 0.00 (no relationship) to $+1.00$ (perfect positive relationship). However, since r is calculated via a square root, it is not a linear proportion. For example, a correlation of .7 seems like a moderately strong relationship, but if we square it to get r^2, we see that the proportion of variance accounted for is only .49.

If you want to get an idea about the relationship among several variables, you can look at all possible pairwise correlations. This is called a correlation matrix, and we see its use in Chapter 13.

r^2 is a better descriptive measure of strength of relationship because it ranges from 0 to 1 and can be interpreted as a simple percentage.

Standard Error of Estimate

The **standard error of estimate** is a measure of variation around the regression line. It is calculated as follows:

$$s_{y \cdot x} = \sqrt{\frac{\sum (Y_i - Y_i')^2}{n-2}} = \sqrt{\frac{SSE}{n-2}} = \sqrt{MSE} \qquad [12.7]$$

Since the standard error of estimate measures variability around the regression line, the smaller, the better. However, as a descriptive measure by itself, the standard error of estimate is not particularly useful. If someone reported a standard error of estimate of 17.143 with no other information, you would have no way of knowing whether that was a good or a bad value. However, the standard error of estimate is important because it is used in other regression calculations.

[1] On the scatterplot, Excel refers to r^2 with a capital "R" even though R^2 generally is used for multiple regression. Excel also calls the regression line a trendline, but strictly speaking, a trendline is special case of a regression line when the independent variable is time-sequenced.

ANOVA Table (Test #9)

The ANOVA table was discussed above. Module 12.B shows the hypothesis test for regression that includes the ANOVA table for regression. It is test Test #9 on the test summaries worksheet.

Slope and Intercept

The slope and intercept also appear on the scatterplot output. They are discussed in Section 12.3.

t-Test for Slope (Test #10)

On the same line as the slope there is a t-value (df $= n - 2$) with its corresponding p-value. This is the test statistic you would use if you were testing the hypothesis that the slope is equal to zero. The t-value is found by dividing the slope by the standard error of the slope. The equation for the standard error of the slope can be found in more advanced books; we let MegaStat calculate it for us.

Note that the p-value for this test is the same as the p-value for the ANOVA test. You also can verify that $t^2 = F$. See test #10 in the test summaries worksheet.

If the ANOVA and the t-test give the same results, why are both shown? We will see in Chapter 13 that you can have more than one independent variable, and in that case there will be a t-test for each variable.

t-Test for Intercept

There is also a t-value to test whether the intercept is equal to zero. In the example in this chapter, we saw that the intercept should be zero because you would expect zero sales with zero sales calls. We saw that the intercept did not have to be exactly zero with the best-fitting straight line, but it is good that it is not significantly different from zero.

Confidence Interval for Slope and Intercept

When you run a regression analysis, the slope is a statistic, that is, a value calculated from a sample that estimates the true population value; in other words, it is a point estimate, our best guess of the population slope. The confidence interval for the slope calculates a range of values, and we are 95% confident that the interval contains the population slope. The equation for the confidence interval is $b \pm t_{(n-2)}s_b$, where t is the 95% two-tailed table value for $n - 2$ degrees of freedom and s_b is the standard error of the slope shown on the same line of the output.

The confidence interval for the intercept also is shown. It is calculated in a parallel manner.

Note that the confidence interval for the slope in this example does not include zero. This corresponds to the fact that the t-test is significant; the confidence level for the intercept does include zero, and that means that its t-test is not significant.

12.6   Making Predictions with Regression

We noted at the beginning of this chapter that regression analysis should be called prediction analysis and that if there is a significant relationship between X and Y in the future, we can use new values of X to predict Y. How do we do that? By substituting an X value into the regression equation. We saw above that the regression equation for our sample data was $Y' = 2.046(X) - 1.008$. If we wanted to predict what sales would be for 25 sales calls, we would substitute 25 for X and calculate Y':

$$Y' = 2.046 * 25 - 1.008 = 50.141$$

When you run the MegaStat regression option, you can specify X values for prediction. Exhibit 12-7 shows the output for X = 25 (**Regr1.xls!Prediction**). (Note the MegaStat value of 50.141 is slightly different from the calculated value of 50.142 that you get if you do the rounded values with a calculator.)

Exhibit 12-8 shows some more predictions. First, note that when X = 0, the predicted value is the intercept because that is how we define the intercept: the predicted value when X is zero. When X = 37.15 (the mean of X), the predicted value is 75 (the mean of Y). That will always be the case:

$$\overline{Y} = b\overline{X} + a$$

Exhibit 12-8 also contains predictions for values of X at the ends of the data range and beyond. These issues are discussed in the extrapolation section (p. 216).

Confidence Intervals for Prediction

The predicted value is a sample statistic. If you took another sample, you would get a different regression equation and thus a different predicted value. If you repeated the process many times, you would get a sampling distribution of predicted values, and the predicted value we just calculated is a point

EXHIBIT 12-7
Predicted value and confidence intervals.

Predicted Values for: Y

			95% Confidence Interval		95% Prediction Interval		
X	Predicted		lower	upper	lower	upper	Leverage
25	50.141		39.985	60.298	12.730	87.553	0.080

EXHIBIT 12-8
More predictions.

Predicted Values for: Y

		95% Confidence Intervals		95% Prediction Intervals		
X	Predicted	lower	upper	lower	upper	Leverage
0	−1.008	−21.577	19.561	−42.476	40.460	0.326
12	23.544	8.410	38.677	−15.514	62.602	0.177
37.15	75.000	66.949	83.051	38.104	111.896	0.050
64	129.934	114.061	145.808	90.584	169.285	0.194
65	131.980	115.666	148.295	92.450	171.511	0.205
80	162.670	139.401	185.939	119.798	205.541	0.418

EXHIBIT 12-9
Plot of 95% confidence interval for prediction.

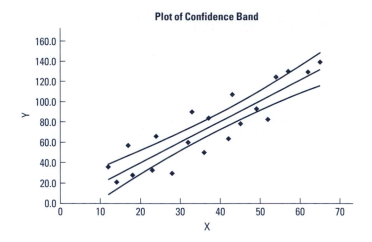

estimate of the mean of that sampling distribution. If we have a sampling distribution, we can calculate a confidence interval, and we see from the output that two intervals are calculated. The confidence interval says that there is a 95% chance that the interval includes the true *mean* predicted value of many people with an X value of 25. The second confidence interval, which is called a prediction interval, says that there is a 95% chance that that interval includes the true predicted value for *one individual*.

Since means have less variability than do individual observations, the prediction interval is always wider than the confidence interval. In fact, in this example, even with a very significant regression and a good r^2 of .798, the upper limit of the prediction interval is over twice as large as the lower limit.

Exhibit 12-9 shows a plot of the lower and upper confidence limits for prediction. (See **ConfBand.xls!Data** if you are curious about how the extra lines were added.) What it shows is the intuitively obvious notion that predictions have less variability near the center of the data and are less stable at the ends. A plot of the prediction interval would have a similar shape.

PRACTICE WITH PREDICTED VALUES   Learning Activity **12.6–1**

- Open **Regr1.xls!Data**.
- Calculate the predicted value in the text by using a calculator.
  - Run MegaStat | Correlation/Regression | Regression to replicate Exhibit 12-7. In the center of the Regression dialog box, click the dropdown menu, select "Type in predictor values," and type in 25.
- Now we do some more predictions: Use MegaStat | Correlation/Regression | Regression to replicate Exhibit 12-8.
  - In cells B32:B37 of the **Data** worksheet, type the X values shown in Exhibit 12-8.
  - Run MegaStat | Correlation/Regression | Regression. In the center of the Regression dialog box, click the dropdown menu, select "Predictor values from worksheet cells," and select cells B32:B37.
- For each of the predictions, calculate the upper confidence interval limit minus the lower confidence interval limit to get the width of the confidence interval. Note that the width is smallest for the mean and larger for values farther from the mean. (You can do the same thing for the prediction intervals.) Also note that the leverage value is smaller when X is in the center. The MegaStat output is shown in **Regr1.xls!Prediction**.

Module 12.C shows the equations for the confidence intervals for prediction. (The leverage value is discussed in Module 12.D and in the extrapolation section below.)

12.7   Other Issues Related to Regression

Assumptions of Regression

In our example, every X value was paired with a Y value. If we took another sample with the same X values, the corresponding Y values would not be the same as as they were in the first sample. If we repeated the sampling many times, we would get a distribution of Y values for each X value. These distributions are called conditional distributions. Exhibit 12-10 shows conditional distributions.

Assumption 1: The means of the conditional distributions are centered on the regression line.

Assumption 2: The conditional distributions are normal.

Assumption 3: All the conditional distributions have the same standard deviation, and it is estimated by the standard error of estimate, $s_{y \cdot x}$.

Assumption 4: The values of the error terms $(Y - Y')$ are independent. This means that if you look at a plot of the errors (i.e., residuals), they should look random. This assumption is critical when the X values are time-related; this assumption is examined in the time series chapter.

Assumption 5: The values of the independent variable (X) are fixed and known. In other words, X should not be a random variable.

How do you know if your data meet these assumptions? The last assumption is ignored routinely, and in most cases you do not know if the other assumptions are valid. The good news is that regression analysis is fairly robust; in other words, unless the assumptions are violated extremely, the impact on regression is minimal.

These assumptions also apply to multiple regression, which is discussed in Chapter 13.

Correlation Does Not Imply Causation

The fact that two variables are related does not imply that X causes Y. It is obvious that in general you will make more sales if you make more sales calls,

EXHIBIT 12-10
Conditional distributions for four values of X.

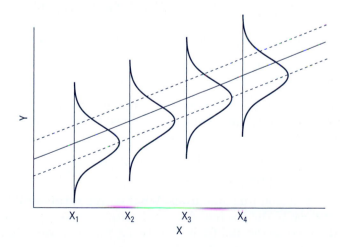

but we cannot say that a sales call causes a sale. A lot of things happen during a sales call, and there may be other factors related to the sale.

Extrapolation

If we wanted to predict sales for 80 sales calls, we could do the calculation $Y' = 2.046(80) - 1.008 = 162.67$ (or about \$163,000), but we could not be very confident about our prediction. Why? Look at the scatterplot in Exhibit 12-2. The largest X value is 65. To make a prediction for $X = 80$, we would have to assume that the regression line would keep going up at the same slope, but we do not have data to support that assumption. Indeed, if someone tries to make too many sales calls, his or her sales may level off or even drop.

You usually can extrapolate a little above or below your data range. However, the farther you extrapolate, the more cautious you should be about your prediction.

In the MegaStat output for predicted values (Exhibit 12-8), we saw a value labeled "Leverage." **Leverage** is a measure of **extrapolation.** If the leverage value is shaded (blue if you have color), it means that your X value is outside the range of the original data. Note that the leverage value for $X = 64$ is not shaded, but it is shaded for 65. The leverage for the smallest X value of 12 is not significant, but it would be significant for smaller values. Module 12.C discusses details regarding the leverage value.

Outliers

What if there are one or more data values that do not go along with the pattern of the others? These values are called outliers. For example, in our sample dataset, the last data pair is (65, 139.3). What if someone mistyped the 139.3 as 9.3?

Think of a physical model of regression in which the regression line is a bar, the scatterplot points are nails in a wall, and the points are connected to the regression line with rubber bands. (It would look like the Error scatterplot shown in Exhibit 12-5). If you took the 139.3 value and pulled it down to 9.3, the rubber band would pull the regression bar (line) down and the slope would be less. Since we are pulling down a point at the right side of the scatterplot, we might expect that the regression bar would rotate up a bit at the other end. Therefore, we would expect the slope to be less and the intercept to be higher; of course, the r^2 will be lower since we are taking a point near the line and pulling it away. This is shown in **Regr1.xls!Outlier Scatterplot** and in Exhibit 12-11.

Comparing Exhibit 12-11 with Exhibit 12-2, we see that the r^2 is less than half of what it was, the slope is less, and the intercept is greater, as predicted.

Outliers usually make r^2 less than it would be without an outlier. However, outliers sometimes can lead to a spuriously high r^2, as shown in Module 12.D and Exhibit 12-17.

MegaStat has a residuals diagnostic option that helps you detect outliers and extrapolation values, as discussed in Module 12.D.

Let's assume you find an outlier: What do you do about it? The best procedure is to go back to the original data and see if it represents some sort of recording or data entry error and fix it. If it turns out to be valid data, you have to live

**EXHIBIT 12-11
Scatterplot
showing an
outlier.**

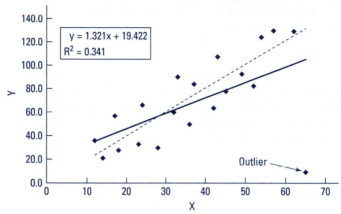

Sales (Y) versus Number of Sales Calls (X) with Outlier
(dashed line shows original regression line)

$y = 1.321x + 19.422$
$R^2 = 0.341$

Outlier

with it. But, you say, "I would have such a nice scatterplot without that point. Can't I just get rid of it or replace it with 'what it should have been'?" If your analysis is subject to review for publication or academic credit, any deletions or modifications of data should be well documented and justified; by definition, outliers are only a small proportion of your total data. If you cavalierly change large amounts of data, you can make your analysis show anything.

Using Regression to Test Group Means

By setting up an independent variable consisting of 0's and 1's, you can use regression to compare group means. This type of variable is called a dummy variable, indicator variable, or binary variable. Module 12.E shows how to set up an indicator variable and demonstrates that regression can give the same results as ANOVA or a hypothesis test for means.

Indicator variables often are included with other variables in multiple regression. There is no particular reason to do a group comparison with bivariate regression, but this makes it easier to see how indicator variables work in bivariate regression.

The procedure of comparing group means with regression sometimes is called the general linear model approach.

EXPLORING OUTLIERS   Learning Activity **12.7–1**

- Open **Regr1.xls!Outlier_data.**
- Compare the scatterplots with and without the outlier.
- Change the 9.3 value back to 139.3 and then create other outliers. Practice until you can predict the general effect on the slope, intercept, and r^2.
    - Try this method of creating outliers by dragging values on the scatterplot:
        - Click one of the data points to select the data.
        - Click one of the selected data points, and a double-arrow mouse pointer will appear.
        - Drag the double arrow to change the value. When you release the arrow, note that the original data value has changed.

Summary

Regression analysis is one of the most widely used techniques for business statistics because it can be used for making predictions and for studying the relationship between two variables.

Conceptual

- The relationship between two variables is shown with a scatterplot. A scatterplot should always be a part of a regression analysis.
- The concept of the best-fitting regression line (least-squares fit).
- Partitioning total variance into regression and error components:
  - An ANOVA test is used as significance test for regression (Test #9).
  - A t-test is used to see whether the slope of the regression line is different from zero (Test #10).
    - Both of these tests give the same p-value.
- Strength of relationship is measured with r^2, the proportion of explained variance.

Applied

Be able to do the following:

- Interpret scatterplot and regression output
- Make predictions with the regression equation
- Interpret confidence and prediction intervals for prediction
- Identify outliers and extrapolation.

Exercises

The exercises and data are found in **Ch_12_Regression.xls** in the exercises folder of the CD.

No.	Content
1	Linear regression
2	Linear regression
3	Linear regression
4	Linear regression
5	Linear regression
6	Linear regression
7	Linear regression
8	Linear regression
9	Linear regression
10	Linear regression, create your own
11	Outlier
12	Experiment
13	Linear transformation
14	Variables reversed
15	Indicator variables
16	Indicator variables

Modules for Linear Regression

12.A PARTITIONING THE SUM OF SQUARES

In Section 12.4 we started with

$$\text{SSTotal} = \sum (Y_i - \overline{Y})^2$$

and said it could be split into

$$\text{SSTotal} = \sum (Y_i - Y_i')^2 + \sum (Y_i' - \overline{Y})^2$$
$$= \quad \text{SSE} \quad + \text{SSR}$$

In this module, we see how this is done. Note that this section is identical to Module 11.A except for notation changes.

We start as follows:

$$\text{SSTotal} = \sum (Y_i - \overline{Y})$$

Rewrite this with some space in the center:

$$= \sum (Y_i \qquad - \overline{Y})^2$$

In the space, subtract and then add the group means. If you subtract and add the same thing, they cancel and we still have an equality:

$$= \sum (Y_i - Y_i' + Y_i' - \overline{Y})^2$$

Here is the group with parentheses:

$$= \sum ((Y_i - Y_i') + (Y_i' - \overline{Y}))^2$$

Note that what we have is of the form $(a + b)^2 = a^2 + b^2 + 2ab$. If we expand the square, we get

$$\sum (Y_i - Y_i')^2 + \sum (Y_i' - \overline{Y})^2 + 2\sum (Y - Y_i')(Y_i' - \overline{Y})$$

Since, as we have seen, the summation of deviations from the mean will always equal zero, the 2ab part will drop out, leaving

$$\text{SSTotal} = \sum (Y_i - Y_i')^2 + \sum (Y_i' - \overline{Y})^2$$

which is what we wanted, the total variation split into two parts: error and regression.

EXHIBIT 12-12
Regression partitioning with Excel.

X	Y	Y′	Total	Error	Regression
12	35.7	23.5	−39.300	12.156	−51.456
14	21.1	27.6	−53.900	−6.536	−47.364
17	56.9	33.8	−18.100	23.126	−41.226
18	27.6	35.8	−47.400	−8.220	−39.180
23	32.9	46.0	−42.100	−13.150	−28.950
24	65.9	48.1	−9.100	17.805	−26.905
28	29.5	56.3	−45.500	−26.779	−18.721
32	60.0	64.5	−15.000	−4.463	−10.537
33	90.1	66.5	15.100	23.591	−8.491
36	49.7	72.6	−25.300	−22.947	−2.353
37	84.0	74.7	9.000	9.307	−0.307
42	63.6	84.9	−11.400	−21.323	9.923
43	107.2	87.0	32.200	20.231	11.969
45	77.9	91.1	2.900	−13.161	16.061
49	92.7	99.2	17.700	−6.545	24.245
52	82.4	105.4	7.400	−22.983	30.383
54	124.3	109.5	49.300	14.825	34.475
57	129.9	115.6	54.900	14.287	40.613
62	129.3	125.8	54.300	3.458	50.842
65	139.3	132.0	64.300	7.320	56.980
37.15	75.00		0.000	0.000	0.000
			26,194.380	5,287.225	20,907.155
			SSTotal	SSE	SSR

2.046 slope
−1.008 intercept

ANOVA Table for Regression

Source	SS	df	MS	F	p-value
Regression	20907.155	1	20907.155	71.18	0.000000114
Error	5287.225	18	293.735		
Total	26194.380	19	1378.652		

Exhibit 12-12 shows the partitioning done with Excel. The "Total," "Error," and "Regr" columns correspond to the equation above.

12.B EXAMPLES OF HYPOTHESIS TESTS FOR REGRESSION

Regression analysis has two hypothesis tests: an ANOVA test for testing the significance of the relationship and a t-test for testing whether a slope is equal to zero. In bivariate regression, the tests are equivalent (both have the same p-value and $t^2 = F$). In the multiple regression chapter, we see that each variable will have a t-test associated with it.

ANOVA Test

The test shown here also is used for multiple regression in Chapter 13. The only difference is that the number of independent variables is $k = 1$ for bivariate regression and $k > 1$ for multiple regression. This example refers the sample output for bivariate regression (Exhibit 12-6), but it can be generalized to multiple regression.

Hypothesis Testing Steps (Short Form)

1. H_0: no predictability.

   H_1: more predictability than by chance alone.
2. $\alpha = .05$ (default).
3. Test: ANOVA test for regression (Test #9).

The test statistic is an F-ratio that is presented formally in an ANOVA table, as shown in the following ANOVA table:

Source	SS	df	MS	F
Regression	SSR	k	$\frac{SSR}{k}$	$\frac{MSR}{MSE}$
Residual	SSE	n − k − 1	$\frac{SSE}{n-k-1}$	
Total	SSToal	r − 1		

This table corresponds to the ANOVA table output in Exhibit 12-6. Since the F-value[2] is a ratio, it has degrees of freedom for the numerator (k) and the denominator (n − k − 1), where k is the number of independent variables and n is the total sample size for all groups. F is displayed as: F_{n-k-1}^{k}. Since k = 1 for bivariate regression, the test value is displayed as: F_{n-2}^{1}.

4. Decision rule: Reject H_0 if $F_{18}^{1} > 4.41$.

   or

   Reject H_0 if the p-value $< .05$.

5. Calculation of ANOVA table: see Exhibit 12-6.

6. Decision: Reject the null hypothesis since the calculated F of 71.13 is greater than the decision rule value of 4.41.

7. Interpretation: There appears to be more predictability than by chance alone, but

   ○ Look for alternative explanations of the relationship.

   ○ Even if the relationship is significant, is it large enough to be meaningful?

   ○ Remember that correlation does not imply causation.

t-Test for Slope

This example refers to the sample output for bivariate regression (Exhibit 12-6). For multiple regression, there would be a test for each slope. The test for intercept would be performed in a similar manner.

Hypothesis Testing Steps (Short Form)

1. H_0: $\beta = 0$ (slope is flat).

   H_1: $\beta \neq 0$ (slope is positive or negative).

   (Note: β is a lowercase Greek "b" that refers to the population slope.)

2. $\alpha = .05$ (default).

3. Test: t test for regression slope (Test #10):

$$t = \frac{b - 0}{s_b} \quad \text{where } s_b = \sqrt{\frac{MSE}{SSX}}$$

   where s_b is the standard error of the slope and df $= n - k - 1$.

4. Decision rule: Reject H_0 if $|t| > 2.101$.

---

[2]If you did not cover analysis of variance in Chapter 11, refer to Module 11.C for details on using the F-distribution.

5. Calculation of test statistic (find the values on the computer output):

$$t = \frac{2.046}{.243} = 8.420$$

(The MegaStat t-value without rounding is 8.437.)

6. Decision: Reject the null hypothesis since $8.420 > 2.101$.

7. Interpretation: There appears to be more predictability than by chance alone, but
   - Look for alternative explanations of the relationship.
   - Even if the relationship is significant, is it large enough to be meaningful?
   - Remember that correlation does not imply causation.

12.C EQUATIONS FOR THE CONFIDENCE INTERVALS FOR PREDICTION

Equations [12.8] and [12.9] show the equations for the confidence interval and the prediction interval for bivariate regression:

$$\text{Confidence interval:}\quad Y' \pm t(s_{y \cdot x}) \sqrt{\frac{1}{n} + \frac{(X - \overline{X})^2}{SSX}} \qquad \textbf{[12.8]}$$

$$\text{Prediction interval:}\quad Y' \pm t(s_{y \cdot x}) \sqrt{1 + \frac{1}{n} + \frac{(X - \overline{X})^2}{SSX}} \qquad \textbf{[12.9]}$$

Where:

Y' = predicted value

t = two-tailed 95% t-value with df $= n - 2$ (other levels can be specified with MegaStat)

$s_{y \cdot x}$ = standard error of estimate

n = sample size

SSX = sum of squared deviations for the independent variable

The part under the square root,

$$\frac{1}{n} + \frac{(X - \overline{X})^2}{SSX} \qquad \textbf{[12.10]}$$

is called the *leverage*, a term used in Module 12.D, which discusses regression diagnostics.

A Closer Look

At first glance, these two equations look very similar. There is only a minor difference: the 1 just inside the square root. However, that 1 makes a big difference because the other two quantities under the square root are small. $1/n$ is small, especially as n gets large, and $(X - \overline{X})^2/SSX$ is also small since it is one squared deviation relative to all the squared deviations. For values where X is near the mean, the second term becomes negligible, so let's ignore it for a moment. The formula for the prediction interval then becomes

$$Y' \pm t(s_{y \cdot x}) \sqrt{1 + \frac{1}{n}}$$

Bringing $s_{y \cdot x}$ under the square root, we get an expression that shows the two components of a prediction interval: the variance *around* the regression line and the variance *of* the regression line:

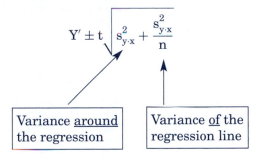

$$Y' \pm t \sqrt{s_{y \cdot x}^2 + \frac{s_{y \cdot x}^2}{n}}$$

| Variance <u>around</u> the regression | Variance <u>of</u> the regression line |

Thus, we see that the prediction interval is always wider than the confidence interval since it accounts for the variation of the individual observation as well as the variation of the line.

12.D   REGRESSION DIAGNOSTICS

Leverage

The leverage value measures extrapolation, that is, X values that are out of the range of the input data. Equation [12.10] shows the computation of the leverage value, although this is a value that rarely would be calculated. Our interest is in the interpretation of the computer output. If a MegaStat leverage value is shaded blue, it means that it is more than twice the mean of all the leverage values; that corresponds to a value greater than $2(k + 1)/n$, where k is the number of independent (X) variables, $k = 1$ for bivariate regression. For the sample data in this chapter, n is 20, and so the critical value of leverage is $2(1 + 1)/20 = 4/20 = .200$.

In Exhibit 12-14, you can see that the last data value is shaded, but the value of .205 is just barely over the critical value of .200 and there are other values near it; thus, it is nothing to be concerned about. It is not unusual for data values at each end of the range to be shaded.

Leverage values are more useful for detecting extrapolation when one is making predictions. Exhibit 12-13 shows predictions for two values of the independent variable. For X = 37.15 (the mean of X), the leverage is .05, its minimum value. However, predicting for X = 80 is clearly an extrapolation since the largest data value is 65. The extrapolation is clearly indicated by the leverage value of .418 that is shaded in Exhibit 12-13.

EXHIBIT 12-13
Regression predictions with leverage diagnostics.

Predicted Values for: Y						
		95% Confidence Intervals		*95% Prediction Intervals*		
X	Predicted	lower	upper	lower	upper	Leverage
37.15	75.000	66.949	83.051	38.104	111.896	0.050
80.00	162.670	139.401	185.939	119.798	205.541	0.418

EXHIBIT 12-14   **MegaStat residual diagnostics.**

Observation	Y	Predicted	Total =	Residual +	Regression	Leverage	Studentized Residual	Studentized Deleted Residual	Cook's D
1	35.70	35.27	−32.80	0.43	−33.23	0.177	0.015	0.015	0.000
2	21.10	37.92	−47.40	−16.82	−30.58	0.157	−0.599	−0.588	0.034
3	56.90	41.88	−11.60	15.02	−26.62	0.131	0.527	0.516	0.021
4	27.60	43.20	−40.90	−15.60	−25.30	0.123	−0.545	−0.534	0.021
5	32.90	49.81	−35.60	−16.91	−18.69	0.090	−0.580	−0.569	0.017
6	65.90	51.13	−2.60	14.77	−17.37	0.085	0.505	0.494	0.012
7	29.50	56.41	−39.00	−26.91	−12.09	0.067	−0.911	−0.907	0.030
8	60.00	61.70	−8.50	−1.70	−6.80	0.055	−0.057	−0.056	0.000
9	90.10	63.02	21.60	27.08	−5.48	0.053	0.911	0.906	0.023
10	49.70	66.98	−18.80	−17.28	−1.52	0.050	−0.580	−0.569	0.009
11	82.00	68.30	15.50	15.70	−0.20	0.050	0.527	0.516	0.007
12	63.60	74.91	−4.90	−11.31	6.41	0.055	−0.381	−0.371	0.004
13	107.20	76.23	38.70	30.97	7.73	0.057	1.043	1.046	0.033
14	77.90	78.87	9.40	−0.97	10.37	0.062	−0.033	−0.032	0.000
15	92.70	84.15	24.20	8.55	15.65	0.078	0.291	0.284	0.004
16	84.40	88.12	13.90	−5.72	19.62	0.094	−0.197	−0.191	0.002
17	124.30	90.76	55.80	33.54	22.26	0.107	1.161	1.173	0.081
18	129.90	94.72	61.40	35.18	26.22	0.129	1.233	1.252	0.112
19	129.30	101.33	60.80	27.97	32.83	0.174	1.007	1.007	0.106
20	9.30	105.29	−59.20	−95.99	36.79	0.205	−3.523	−6.145	−1.603
			0.00	0.00	0.00	Sum			
			25,531.38	16,814.63	8,716.75				
			SSTotal =	SSE +	SSR				

Residual Diagnostics

The two columns in Exhibit 12-14 titled "Studentized Residual" and "Studentized Deleted Residual" detect outliers with respect to their Y values. A Studentized residual converts a residual to a t-value by dividing each residual by a standard error (hence the term *Studentized* for Student's t-distribution). The standard error of a residual is roughly the standard error of estimate; the actual formula is beyond the scope of this text, and besides, we are focusing on the computer output.

As a rule of thumb, absolute values of Studentized values greater than 2 possibly could indicate an outlier. MegaStat calculates the exact inverse t-value at the 5% and 1% levels (df = n − k − 2, two-tailed) and shades the values light blue and darker blue, respectively. Exhibit 12-14 shows the MegaStat residual diagnostics output using the outlier from **Regr1.xls!Outlier_data.** The Outlier is indicated by the shading in the last row.

REPLICATE TEXT RESIDUAL DIAGNOSTICS

Learning Activity **12.D–1**

- Open **Regr1.xls!Outlier_data.**
- Use MegaStat to replicate Exhibit 12-13, Exhibit 12-14, and Exhibit 12-15.
  - You will need to do predicted values for X = 37.15 and 80.
  - In the regression dialog box, check "Diagnostic and Influential Residuals" and "Plot Residuals by Observation."

EXHIBIT 12-15
Residuals plot
(note the outlier).

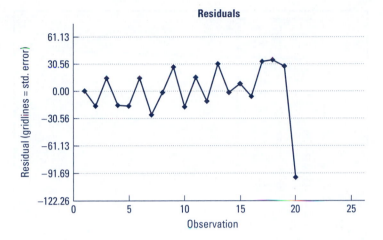

What is the Studentized *Deleted* Residual? Since least-squares regression gives the best fit for all the data values, an outlier influences the calculation and pulls the slope toward it. We saw that in Module 12.7 (see Exhibit 12-2 versus Exhibit 12-11). A deleted residual is calculated by using all the data *except* the value being considered.

Studentized deleted residuals can be quite different from Studentized Residuals, especially in a small sample in which one data point can make a difference. In Exhibit 12-14, the Studentized Deleted Residual is considerably larger than the Studentized Residual, although both are shaded darker blue.

MegaStat also has an option for plotting the residuals, as shown in Exhibit 12-15. There we see that the outlier observation is identified clearly.

Influential Values

An **influential value** is one that would cause a noticeable difference in the regression analysis if it were removed from the data.

Influential observations are detected by using Cook's D value on the MegaStat regression diagnostic output. Cook's D is actually an F-ratio but its calculation is beyond the scope of this text. Suffice it to say that light blue shading and darker blue shading indicate different levels of influence.

Outliers, especially fairly extreme outliers, are usually influential, but a value can be influential without being an outlier. Influential values sometimes can cause a spuriously high r^2. Exhibit 12-16 shows a scatterplot of two variables made up of random numbers. As expected, the r^2 is nearly zero. If we change one

PRACTICE WITH RESIDUAL DIAGNOSTICS

Learning Activity 12.D–2

- Open **Regr1.xls!Outlier_data**.
- Use MegaStat to create other outliers and run "Diagnostic and Influential Residuals" and "Plot Residuals by Observation."
- Repeat until you can predict what the output will show.

**EXHIBIT 12-16
Scatterplot
showing no
relationship.**

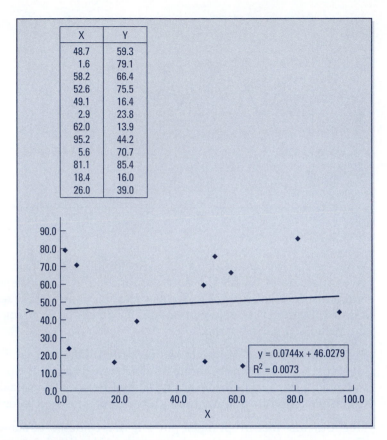

of the data pairs, it can make a dramatic difference. Let's arbitrarily pick the eighth pair (95.2, 44.2) and increase each value by a factor of 10 to (952, 442).

The result is shown in Exhibit 12-17. When we change one value to a value that is far out on the regression line, r^2 is increased to over 94%. If you just ran the regression and looked at r^2, you would think that you had a really good relationship when, in fact, there is no relationship for most of the data. That is why it is important to look at the scatterplot.

REPLICATE INFLUENTIAL VALUE OUTPUT

Learning Activity **12.D–3**

- Open a blank workbook.
- Use MegaStat to create two variables (labeled X and Y) of 10 uniformly distributed random numbers between 0 and 100 (fixed values). If necessary, review Module 7.A for generating random numbers.
- Run a scatterplot. The result should show a very low r^2 similar to that in Exhibit 12-16.
- On the scatterplot, drag one of the points out on the X axis and up on the Y axis. (If you don't remember how to drag data points, enter large values for one of the data pairs.) Your scatterplot should end up looking similar to the one in Exhibit 12-17.
- Run a regression on the data, specifying "Diagnostics and Influential Residuals." You should find that the value you changed will have a large leverage value and be influential (Cook's D); however, it should not be an outlier because it is near the regression line.

EXHIBIT 12-17
Exhibit 12-16 with one data value changed to increase r^2.

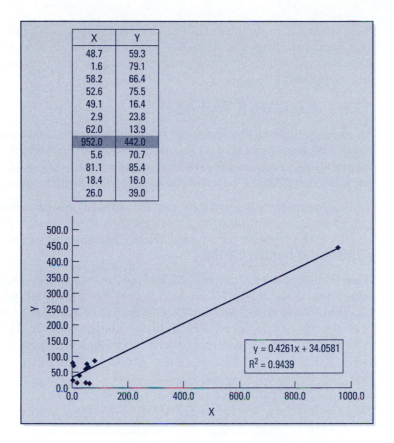

X	Y
48.7	59.3
1.6	79.1
58.2	66.4
52.6	75.5
49.1	16.4
2.9	23.8
62.0	13.9
952.0	442.0
5.6	70.7
81.1	85.4
18.4	16.0
26.0	39.0

$$y = 0.4261x + 34.0581$$
$$R^2 = 0.9439$$

EXHIBIT 12-18   **Regression diagnostics for the data in Exhibit 12-17.**

Observation	Y	Predicted	Total	= Residual	+ Regression	Leverage	Studentized Residual	Studentized Deleted Residual	Cook's D
1	59.32	54.81	−22.97	4.51	−27.48	0.089	0.163	0.155	0.001
2	79.06	34.76	−3.23	44.30	−47.53	0.099	1.614	1.781	0.144
3	66.36	58.84	−15.93	7.52	−23.45	0.087	0.272	0.259	0.004
4	75.50	56.47	−6.79	19.02	−25.81	0.088	0.689	0.670	0.023
5	16.38	55.00	−65.91	−38.62	−27.29	0.089	−1.399	−1.480	0.095
6	23.83	35.28	−58.46	−11.45	−47.01	0.099	−0.417	−0.399	0.010
7	13.88	60.48	−68.41	−46.60	−21.80	0.087	−1.686	−1.891	0.135
8	442.00	439.72	359.71	2.28	357.43	0.991	0.842	0.829	40.105
9	70.70	36.44	−11.58	34.27	−45.85	0.098	1.248	1.288	0.085
10	85.40	68.62	3.12	16.79	−13.67	0.085	0.607	0.586	0.017
11	16.02	41.88	−66.27	−25.87	−40.40	0.095	−0.940	−0.934	0.046
12	39.00	45.14	−43.29	−6.15	−37.14	0.093	−0.223	−0.212	0.003

Although this is an extreme example, it easily could happen if a decimal point was missed or entered incorrectly. This effect also can happen in more subtle ways and with a less dramatic impact. Again, always do a scatterplot before doing regression computations. In Module 12.D, we see a MegaStat regression option that will help detect this sort of situation.

The regression diagnostics in Exhibit 12-18 show a very large Cook's D value of 40.105 for the influential observation. The leverage value is also large because the X value of the influential observation is far larger than the rest of the X values. But notice that the Studentized residual is quite small because the observation is near the regression line. It is very influential but technically not an outlier.

12.E   INDICATOR VARIABLES

In Section 10.3, we discussed the *t*-test for comparing two independent groups. Review that section and note the example data in Exhibit 10-5 and the output in Exhibit 10-6. Then, in Module 11.F, we saw that two groups also could be compared by using ANOVA. Review that section and note the output in Exhibit 11-16.

In this module, we see another way to compare groups using regression analysis. This is done by placing the data for the two groups in one column and placing 0's in the adjacent column next to one group and 1's next to the other group, as shown in Exhibit 12-19.

The 0–1 variable is called an **indicator variable,** dummy variable, or -binary variable. It is arbitrary which group is associated with a 0 or a 1. Note that the labels shown at the side and the boxes around the groups are for clarity and are not required. The data in this form are in **HtestExamples.xls! Sheet4.** Running a scatterplot and regression analysis using Group as the

EXHIBIT 12-19
Two groups set up with indicator variables.

	Group	Score
10:00	0	148
	0	149
	0	152
	0	157
	0	153
	0	148
	0	160
	0	154
	0	154
	0	148
11:00	1	143
	1	137
	1	147
	1	151
	1	146
	1	155
	1	147
	1	150
	1	147
	1	138
	1	145
	1	144
	1	155
	1	156
	1	138

EXHIBIT 12-20
Two groups compared using regression analysis.

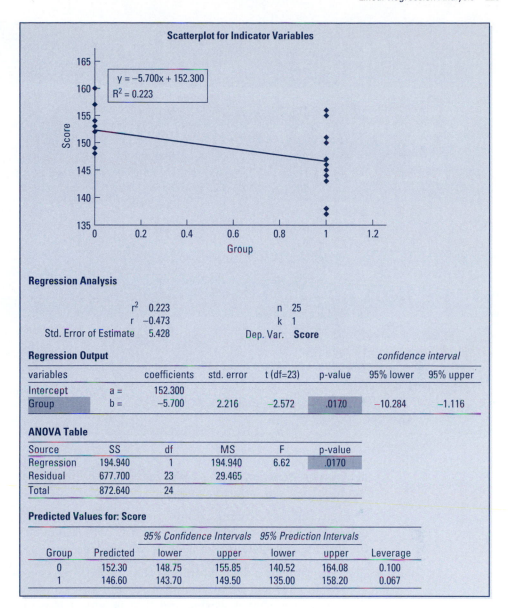

Scatterplot for Indicator Variables

$y = -5.700x + 152.300$
$R^2 = 0.223$

Regression Analysis

	r^2	0.223		n	25
	r	−0.473		k	1
Std. Error of Estimate		5.428		Dep. Var.	**Score**

Regression Output   *confidence interval*

variables		coefficients	std. error	t (df=23)	p-value	95% lower	95% upper
Intercept	a =	152.300					
Group	b =	−5.700	2.216	−2.572	.0170	−10.284	−1.116

ANOVA Table

Source	SS	df	MS	F	p-value
Regression	194.940	1	194.940	6.62	.0170
Residual	677.700	23	29.465		
Total	872.640	24			

Predicted Values for: Score

		95% Confidence Intervals		*95% Prediction Intervals*		
Group	Predicted	lower	upper	lower	upper	Leverage
0	152.30	148.75	155.85	140.52	164.08	0.100
1	146.60	143.70	149.50	135.00	158.20	0.067

independent variable and Score as the dependent variable, we get the output shown in Exhibit 12-20.

Comparing Exhibit 12-20 with Exhibit 11-16, we see that the t-value, F-value, and p-values for regression correspond to the t-test and ANOVA. Thus, regression can be used to compare group means.

How would you compare three groups using regression? It is tempting to say, "Add a 2 to go with the 0 and the 1." However, since 0 and 1 mean no and yes, respectively, in the question "Is this person in the 11 a.m. class?" a 2 would have no meaning. The correct procedure is to add another column and use patterns of 0's and 1's to identify the groups. Multiple regression will be needed to do the analysis. Indicator variables often are introduced in a multiple regression context, but as we have seen, in the simplest case they are used in

REPLICATE INDICATOR
VARIABLE OUTPUT

Learning Activity **12.E–1**

- Open **Htest2b.xls!Data.**
- Use MegaStat to compare the groups using the two-group hypothesis test and ANOVA. The output should look like that in Exhibit 11-16.
- Click **Sheet4** to see the data in regression form.
- Run the regression. Do predicted values X = 0 and 1. The output should look like that in Exhibit 12-20.

PRACTICE WITH
INDICATOR VARIABLES

Learning Activity **12.E–2**

- Open **HtestExamples.xls!Two-Group.**
- Run the two group hypothesis test (two-tailed test).
- Compare the groups using one-factor ANOVA.
- Set up the groups with an indicator variable and run the regression. Do predicted values for X = 0 and 1.
- *Solution:* The p-values should be the same on all three versions and t^2 = F.

bivariate regression. In multiple regression, indicator variables can be used in combination with other variables.

This procedure of doing group comparisons using regression sometimes is called the general linear model approach. With sufficiently complex patterns of 0's and 1's, any ANOVA can be done with regression.

Perhaps you have been thinking that something is a little strange in this approach: How can we use qualitative data in a multiple regression analysis? One answer is that it works, and that is why it is called a dummy variable. Another answer is that the 0 and the 1 really are quantitative. If that is the case, what do they measure? They measure the degree of eleven-o'clockness of each observation: 0% or 100%.

One more comment on the output in Exhibit 12-20 involves the predicted values. Since the only valid data values are 0 and 1, those are the only values that may be used for prediction. When X = 0 is used, the prediction is 152.3 (the intercept), which is also the mean of the 10 a.m. class. When X = 1, the prediction is 146.6, the mean of the 11 a.m. class. The slope (−5.7) is the difference between the means for the 10 a.m. class and the 11 a.m. class. As X increases 1 unit (from 0 to 1), the predicted value decreases by −5.70 units.

CHAPTER THIRTEEN

Multiple Regression

13.1 Introduction to Multiple Regression (p. 232)

13.2 Interpreting Multiple Regression Computer Output (p. 235)

Summary (p. 244)

Exercises (p. 245)

Modules for Chapter Thirteen

13.A What Is the Multiple Correlation, R? (p. 246)

13.B Exploring Standardized Regression Coefficients (p. 247)

13.1 Introduction to Multiple Regression

As the name implies, multiple regression is the procedure that is used when there are two or more independent variables. Multiple regression is conceptually similar to bivariate regression. What you learned in Chapter 12 applies to multiple regression; in fact, bivariate regression is a special case of multiple regression.

Data form: One dependent variable, Y, and two or more independent variables that usually are shown on the right.

Y	X1	X2

Is there a limit to the number of independent variables? Yes; mathematically, the number of rows in the table must be larger than the number of independent variables. In practice, the number of observations (sample size) should be several times larger than the number of variables. We will see later that although there can be several independent variables, it is rare to find more than three that all contribute meaningfully to predicting Y.

The bivariate regression equation

$$Y' = bX + a \qquad \text{[13.1]}$$

expands to

$$Y' = b_1X_1 + b_2X_2 + a \qquad \text{[13.2]}$$

for two variables and to

$$Y' = b_1X_1 + b_2X_2 + \cdots + b_kX_k + a \qquad \text{[13.3]}$$

for k variables.

The coefficients indicate the slope for each variable with the other variable(s) held constant. The regression model finds the coefficients that work best together to predict Y. It may be the case, and indeed often is, that variables that work well individually in bivariate regression to predict Y do not work well together in multiple regression. Conversely, a variable that does not predict very well by itself can be useful in combination with other variables.

EXHIBIT 13-1
Three-dimensional scatterplot.

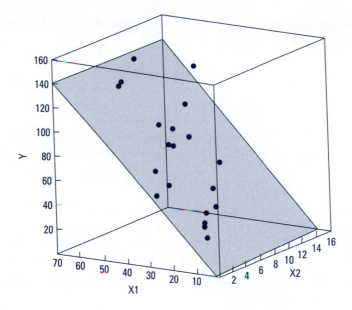

Equations

In Chapter 12 we saw equations for the slope and the intercept. Are there corresponding equations for multiple regression? Although it is possible to do multiple regression algebraically with a calculator, there is no good reason for doing that. The process is messy, slow, and error-prone and has no educational benefit. With the availability of computers and software such as Excel and MegaStat, most textbooks have stopped showing how to do even two-variable multiple regression calculations. Multiple regression is actually a matrix algebra model, and although the algebraic expression is complex, the equations are elegantly simple when stated in matrix algebra terms.

Graphical Representation

With bivariate regression, the relationship between X and Y is shown with a scatterplot. With three variables, one could envision a three-dimensional model with the X1 and X2 being plotted on a horizontal surface and with Y being the vertical distance. You then would have a "scattercloud" of data points, and the concept of a regression line will become a regression plane as if you were fitting a sheet of paper among the cloud of data points so that the vertical distances from the points to the plane are minimized. Exhibit 13-1 shows a three-dimensional scatterplot and the regression plane. When you add more variables, the three-dimensional space becomes "hyperspace" and it is no longer possible to have a graphical model of the relationship even though the mathematical model is still valid.

Correlation Matrix as a Prelude to Multiple Regression

In Chapter 12, we discussed the correlation coefficient, r, which measures the strength and direction of relationship. Before doing a multiple regression analysis, it is advisable to do a **correlation matrix** that shows the correlation between all possible pairs of variables. If you had five variables, the dependent variable, and four independent variables, the correlation matrix would look like this:

	Y	X1	X2	X3	X4
Y	1.00				
X1		1.00			
X2			1.00		
X3				1.00	
X4					1.00

Each cell would contain a correlation coefficient. The main diagonal contains 1.00's because any variable correlated with itself is a perfect correlation. Typically, only the lower half of the matrix is shown because the table is symmetrical; the correlations in the top half are the same as those in the bottom half.

Why calculate the correlation matrix? The ideal pattern you are looking for is shown in Exhibit 13-2.

Since we are trying to predict Y, we would expect some of the independent variables to have moderate to high correlations with Y. Remember that a negative correlation can predict as well as a positive one can. The most important thing you are looking for, however, is relatively low correlations among the predictor variables. Why? Look at an extreme situation first: What if X1 and X2 were perfectly correlated? Then variable X2 could not add any information for predicting Y that was not already contained in X1. This problem is called **multicollinearity,** and it exists to the degree that the independent variables are correlated with each other.

When variables are extremely highly correlated, say, $r = .999$ or greater, it also can lead to computational inaccuracies, but that largely has been fixed with current software. If two variables are correlated highly enough to cause computational problems, you should not be using both of them anyway.

The correlation coefficient is a shorthand summary value indicating direction and strength of relationship. For an important analysis, it might be worthwhile to run all the pairwise scatterplots that the correlations summarize to look for patterns and outliers.

The purpose of the correlation matrix is to give you an idea of what problems you may face. However, since the computer will be doing the work, it makes sense to go ahead with the initial regression analysis even if problems are indicated and use the correlation matrix to help decide which variables to keep for subsequent regression runs.

EXHIBIT 13-2
Ideal correlation pattern for multiple regression.

	Y	X1	X2	X3	X4
Y	1.00				
X1	High	1.00			
X2	High	Low	1.00		
X3	High	Low	Low	1.00	
X4	High	Low	Low	Low	1.00

13.2   Interpreting Multiple Regression Computer Output

The example for this chapter is shown in **Mregr1.xls.** The data build on the bivariate regression data in Chapter 12 that related sales (Y) to number of sales calls (X1) and add three independent variables: number of year's sales experiences (X2), mean driving distance to each sales call (X3), and an indicator variable for whether the salesperson is using a new high-tech computerized sales system (X4).

Correlation Matrix

First we look at the correlation matrix (Exhibit 13-3). Does it have the pattern we were looking for in Exhibit 13-2? Yes, it looks about as good as you typically could find. The correlation between Y and X3 is low ($-.079$). However, on a first analysis you should not throw out variables because they do not correlate with Y. In multiple regression we are looking for patterns of variables, and maybe it will work better in combination with other variables.

The correlations among the predictor variables look good. Only one correlation is significant, and it is not extremely high. Therefore, we proceed with the multiple regression, as shown in Exhibit 13-4.

The output looks similar to the output for bivariate regression. Unless noted otherwise, any discussion of bivariate regression applies to multiple regression as well; in particular, the assumptions of bivariate regression also apply to multiple regression.

If we wrote out the formal regression equation using the values from the computer output, it would read as follows:

$$Y' = 2.010X_1 - 1.009X_2 - 2.047X_3 + 18.026X_4 + 14.871$$

TUTORIAL 14

Each coefficient shows how much each additional unit of the variable changes Y with the other variables held constant.

R^2 and Multiple R

R^2 is the percent of explained variance. Verify that SSR/SSTotal $= R^2$. Note that a capital "R" typically is used in multiple regression.

R is the **multiple correlation** and is the square root of R^2. R is actually the correlation of the dependent variable (Y) and the prediction of it (Y') using the original independent variables. If we are able to predict Y well, there

**EXHIBIT 13-3
Correlation
matrix.**

Correlation Matrix

	Y	X1	X2	X3	X4
Y	1.000				
X1	.893	1.000			
X2	.514	.591	1.000		
X3	−.079	.159	.081	1.000	
X4	.589	.419	.435	−.103	1.000

20 sample size

± .444 critical value .05 (two-tail)

± .561 critical value .01 (two-tail)

EXHIBIT 13-4   Multiple regression output.

Regression Analysis

R^2 0.893		
Adjusted R^2 0.865	n	20
R 0.945	k	4
Std. Error of Estimate 13.656	Dep. Var.	Y

Regression Output

confidence interval

variables		coefficients	std. error	t (df=15)	p-value	95% lower	95% upper	std. coeff.	VIF
Intercept	a =	14.871	9.924	1.499	.1547	−6.280	36.023	0.000	
X1	b1 =	2.010	0.250	8.045	8.03E-07	1.477	2.542	0.877	1.671
X2	b2 =	−1.009	1.142	−0.883	.3909	−3.444	1.426	−0.096	1.646
X3	b3 =	−2.047	0.958	−2.137	.0495	−4.089	−0.006	−0.186	1.065
X4	b4 =	18.026	7.233	2.492	.0249	2.610	33.442	0.244	1.346
									1.432
									mean VIF

ANOVA Table

Source	SS	df	MS	F	p-value
Regression	23,396.960	4	5,849.240	31.36	3.99E-07
Residual	2,797.420	15	186.495		
Total	26,194.380	19			

Predicted Values for: Y

					95% Confidence Intervals		95% Prediction Intervals		
X1	X2	X3	X4	Predicted	lower	upper	lower	upper	Leverage
48.00	10.0	10.000	1.0	98.790	86.501	111.079	67.195	130.386	0.178
20.00	12.0	5.000	1.0	50.741	29.302	72.180	14.590	86.892	0.542
37.15	6.8	.7.265	0.4	75.000	68.491	81.509	45.173	104.827	0.050
0.00	0.0	0.000	0.0	14.871	−6.280	36.023	−21.110	50.853	0.528

REPLICATE TEXT OUTPUT   Learning Activity **13.2–1**

- Open **Mregr1.xls!Data.**
- Run the multiple regression to predict Y using X1 − X4.
- Find the values referenced in the text.

should be a strong relationship between Y and Y′ and R will be large (approaching 1); if we cannot predict Y, R will be 0. The multiple R cannot be negative. Module 13.A illustrates this and shows some other interesting relationships.

Adjusted R^2

If you add a variable to a regression model (e.g., go from four to five independent variables), R^2 can never decrease even if the new variable does not add much to the prediction. The following equation for **adjusted R^2** allows you to compare the relative effectiveness of regression models with a different number of independent variables (k). The adjusted R^2 is always less than R^2 and can decrease as the number of variables increases.

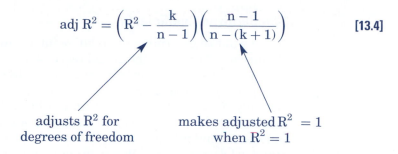

$$\text{adj } R^2 = \left(R^2 - \frac{k}{n-1} \right)\left(\frac{n-1}{n-(k+1)} \right) \qquad \text{[13.4]}$$

adjusts R^2 for
degrees of freedom

makes adjusted $R^2 = 1$
when $R^2 = 1$

Use adjusted R^2 to compare regression models with different numbers of predictors. However, the standard R^2 that represents the proportion of variance accounted for is a better descriptive measure for any given regression.

Overall ANOVA (Test #9) and Test for Each Slope (Test #10)

For bivariate regression, we saw that the ANOVA test and the t-test for the slope are redundant; both give the same p-value. For multiple regression, ANOVA tests whether there is an overall significant amount of predictability and the t-test for each slope indicates whether each variable is significant. The t-test indicates how well each variable works in combination with the other variables; it does not give any information about how well it might work by itself in a bivariate regression.

For the example data shown above, ANOVA shows a strong degree of overall predictability for the model (p-value = 0.0000004). The individual t-values show some interesting findings.

Mregr1.xls!Bivariate Regressions shows the four individual bivariate regressions using X1 through X4 to predict Y. The p-values correspond to the correlations in the correlation matrix shown in Exhibit 13-2; X1 and X4 are significant at less than .01, X2 is significant at less than .05, and X3 is not significant at all. The multiple regression output (Exhibit [13-4]) using all four variables shows a different pattern: X1 remains quite significant; X4 also remains significant, but its p-value is not nearly as low. Interestingly, X2, which was significant by itself, is not close to being significant in combination with the other variables, and X3, which had almost no correlation by itself, becomes significant in combination with other variables.

X2 is not effective in the multiple regression because of its correlation with X1. When two predictor variables are correlated, usually one of them prevails in the multiple regression and the other "washes out." The correlation between X1 and X2 was not especially strong, but it was strong enough that they did not work well together. You can see this better if you run the regression with only X1 and X2.

X3 was able to become significant because it somehow related to variance that the other variables did not account for. In other words, it "picked up the leftovers."

Variable X4 is an indicator or dummy variable for whether the salesperson was using the new computerized sales system. The coefficient of 18.026 indicates that a person using the new system should have sales slightly more than $18,000 greater than those of a person who does not use the system (keeping the level of the other variables constant).

Standardized Coefficients

If you want to determine the relative importance of the variables in predicting Y, you cannot compare the actual regression slopes. For example, the coefficient for X1 is 2.010 and the coefficient for X4 is 18.026, but we cannot infer that X4 is 9 times more important than X1 just because its coefficient is 9 times larger. Actually, X1 is more important since it has a lower p-value than does X4. Regression coefficients cannot be compared directly because the variables have different standard deviations: X4 has a large coefficient because it has a small standard deviation, and the coefficient adjusts for that.

To compare the relative importance of variables, check the Standardized Coefficients option. The relative size of the **standardized coefficients** (sometimes called betas) corresponds to their relative impact on the regression equation. The standardized coefficients are the coefficients you would get if you ran the regression with standardized data, that is, all variables with a mean of 0 and a standard deviation of 1 (see **Mregr1-z.xls**). Recall that the coefficients show the change in Y′ for a unit of change in one of the X variables with the others held constant. With all the variables having the same standard deviation, the standardized coefficients are comparable. In the example, X1 has a standardized coefficient of .877 versus .244 for X4; this means that a unit change in X1 has over three times as much impact as does a unit change in X4. Note that X2 and X3 have smaller standardized coefficients, which means they are less important.

Notes: (1) When comparing standardized coefficients, look at the absolute value. (2) Standardized coefficients are typically less than 1.0, but they do not have to be; however, if you get a standardized coefficient greater than 1.0, it probably means there is something unusual about your data.

Module 13.B converts the example dataset to z-values (i.e., standardizes it) and runs the regression to show that the standardized coefficients are indeed the coefficients you would get with standardized data.

Variance Inflation Factors

Correlation among predictor variables is a common problem in multiple regression analysis. This often is called multicollinearity. Checking the **Variance Inflation Factor** box in MegaStat gives a measure of multicollinearity (VIF). The equation for VIF is

$$VIF_j = \frac{1}{1 - R_j^2}$$ [13.5]

where R_j^2 is the R^2 from predicting variable j from the remaining independent variables. For example, if $j = 2$, the R^2 would be for predicting variable X2 using X1, X3, and X4.

If a variable is not related to any of the other variables, R^2 will be 0 and VIF will be 1. As the relationship among the predictor variables approaches 1, the denominator will approach 0 and VIF will become very large. Thus, the ideal situation would be VIF values near 1.

On the MegaStat output, the VIF is shaded light blue if the VIF is greater than 3⅓, which would result from an R^2 of .7 and would indicate a moderate degree of multicollinearity. The VIF is shaded darker blue if the VIF is greater than

EXPLORING VIF

- Open **Mregr1.xls!Data.**
- Run the multiple regression to predict X1 using X2, X3, and X4.
- Use a calculator or Excel to calculate the VIF for variable X1 using Equation [13.5].
- *Solution:* See **Mregr1.xls!VIF_calc.**
- *Practice:* Calculate at least one more VIF.

10, which would result from an R^2 of .9 and would indicate a strong degree of multicollinearity.

In the sample output, we see that the VIFs are relatively small. Even so, we saw above that the relationship between X1 and X2 caused X2 to be nonsignificant in the multiple regression.

Prediction

Predictions are made the same way bivariate regression is done: by substituting values into the regression equation. Suppose you wanted to make a prediction for a salesperson who made 48 sales calls, with 10 years of work experience, with an average driving distance of 10 miles to each sales call, and using the new computerized system (1). The prediction would be as follows:

$$98.790 = 2.010 * 48 - 1.009 * 10 - 2.047 * 10 + 18.026 * 1 + 14.871$$

This prediction is shown in the multiple regression output in Exhibit 13-4. Note that the output also includes a prediction interval for the mean prediction and the prediction interval for one particular prediction. See the discussion of prediction intervals in Section 12.6.

The next prediction shown in the output is for 20 sales calls, 12 years of experience, 5 miles of driving distance, and using the computerized sales system. Note the leverage value is shaded blue. We saw in Section 12.7 that a larger leverage value indicates extrapolation: an independent variable value not in the range of the original data. However, if you look at the X values for this prediction, you will see that all of them are well within the range of the input data. What causes the high leverage value? It results from the fact that there is no *set* of values that matches or is near the set of predictor values. This is called **multivariate extrapolation.** You could make the prediction, but you would not be as confident of it. You also can verify that the confidence and prediction intervals are wider with a larger leverage value.

The third prediction shown in the output uses the means of the independent variables for prediction. When we do this, it should be no surprise that the predicted value is the mean of Y. (If you want to use a fancy word, the point in hyperspace representing the mean of all the variables is called the *centroid*.)

The last prediction shown just verifies that if we predict using all zeros, the prediction is the intercept. With zero sales calls and zero for the other variables, we would expect zero sales. However, as we saw in Section 12.5, it does not

PREDICTION   Learning Activity **13.2–3**

- Open **Mregr1.xls!Data** and replicate the regression in Exhibit 13-4 (if you do not already have it).
- Calculate the first prediction with a calculator, using the values in the computer output. You should find that the predicted value is 98.817 versus the value of 98.790 in the computer output. Why the difference? The computer uses the full accuracy of the coefficients, not values as they are formatted in the output.
- Calculate the predicted values with Excel, using the cell references of the coefficients. You should get the same values that MegaStat gets.
- Use MegaStat | Correlation/Regression | Regression to replicate the predictions at the bottom of Exhibit 13-4. In the center of the Regression dialog box, click the dropdown menu, select "Predictor values from worksheet cells," and select cells C29:F32.
- Try experimenting with other predictions. Try typing in the independent variables and entering them in the worksheet. Determine values that will give both low- and high-leverage calculations.

WHAT DOES *HELD CONSTANT* MEAN?   Learning Activity **13.2–4**

- Open **Mregr1A.xls!Data.** These data are the same as those in Mregr1.xls from previous Learning Activities.
- Use MegaStat to repeat the multiple regression using all four variables. Click on "Predictor values from worksheet cells" and select cells C26:F36.
  ◦ Note that each prediction increases X1 by 1 unit while X2, X3, and X4 stay the same, that is, are held constant.
- On the output sheet, subtract each predicted value from the one just prior to it. You would start by subtracting the first predicted value from the second one. Put the calculations in Column K.
  ◦ You should find that the values you get are b_1, the slope for X1. In other words, as X1 increases by 1 unit, the prediction increases by the amount of the slope (with the other variables staying the same, i.e., held constant).
  ◦ Check the solution in **Mregr1A.xls!Solution.**
- *Exploration:* Set X1 at a fixed value, say, 35, and change X2 to go from 15 to 25 in steps of 1. When you do the subtraction, you should get the slope of X2.

have to be exactly zero and we see that the intercept is not significantly different from zero.

Analysis of Residuals: Looking for Outliers

In Chapter 12, we saw that outliers can have a dramatic effect on regression. The same thing applies to multiple regression except that it is more difficult to detect outliers with multiple regression since we do not have a scatterplot. Module 12.D from Chapter 12 discusses ways to interpret MegaStat's residual diagnostics output. The concepts discussed there apply to multiple regression as well.

Model Building and Stepwise Selection

If you have several variables, how do you select the best subset of them for prediction? In other words, how do you build a model for prediction? In general, the goal is to get R^2 as high as possible and have all the variables in the model have significant p-values. The discussion below takes this approach; however,

ANALYSIS OF RESIDUALS · Learning Activity **13.2–5**

- Open **Mregr1.xls!outlier_data.** This is a copy of the data that can be changed without messing up the original data.
- Run the multiple regression to predict Y using X1 − X4, specifying "Diagnostics and Influential Residuals." What is your interpretation of the output?
  - *Answer:* None of the values is shaded blue, indicating that there are no problems.
- Change data value 17 from 124.3 to 170 to create an outlier and rerun the regression. You should be able to identify the outlier. Notice that the outlier also has a significant Cook's D value, meaning that it is also influential. This is common. If a value is far enough away from the line to be an outlier, it is likely to be influential. The leverage value, however, does not change since it is based on the independent variables.
- Change other data values (independent and dependent) and try to predict what the diagnostics will show.

you always should keep in mind the context of your analysis and know which variables are important from a theoretical point of view. It would not be reasonable to throw out a variable that makes a lot of sense conceptually in favor of another variable just because it increases R^2 a little. One common misuse of multiple regression is to throw in a bunch of variables and see if some combination happens to work. This sort of fishing expedition probably will result in the selection of variables that capitalize on chance patterns within the sample. The result will be a regression model that does not reflect real relationships in the population and probably will not show the same relationships in another sample, that is, will not replicate.

It is also advisable to look at the regressions using each variable individually and, better yet, also look at the scatterplots before doing multiple regression. You should be familiar with your data and have some rationale for using a variable other than that you hope it works.

With those caveats, how do we proceed? Although MegaStat (and most other statistical packages) provides a means to automate the process, it is best to proceed manually at first. In other words, do a bivariate regression with the variable you consider most important and then add other variables, using multiple regression to try other combinations until you have a subset of variables that seem to work well together.

When you are finished selecting variables for the model, it is interesting to examine all possible regression models. The number of possible regression models is $2^k - 1$, where k is the number of independent variables. In our sample data, we have four independent variables that give 15 regression models. This is shown in Exhibit 13-5 from MegaStat's "All Possible Regressions" option.

Each row is a summary of a regression output. In the cells are the p-values for the variables in the model. Also listed for each model are the adjusted R^2, R^2, standard error of estimate(s), and overall p-value. The models initially are sorted ascending by the adjusted R^2; however, in Excel you can sort on any of the columns. What does this output tell us? Probably the most obvious thing is that X1 is included in all the better models (better implies a higher Adj R^2 and a smaller s). The other variables all have significant coefficients in some models, but there is no model in which X2 is significant along with X1.

EXHIBIT 13-5
"All Possible Regressions"
output from MegaStat.

Regression Analysis—All Possible Regressions

20 observations
Y is the dependent variable

p-values for the coefficients

Nvar	X1	X2	X3	X4	Adj. R^2	R^2	s	p-value
3	.0000		.0442	.0313	.867	.888	13.562	8.04E-08
4	.0000	.3909	.0495	.0249	.865	.893	13.656	3.99E-07
2	.0000			.0205	.837	.854	14.990	7.81E-08
3	.0000	.3999		.0167	.835	.861	15.102	4.43E-07
2	.0000		.0294		.831	.849	15.277	1.08E-07
3	.0000	.8301	.0343		.821	.849	15.724	8.40E-07
1	.0000				.787	.798	17.139	1.14E-07
2	.0000	.8738			.775	.798	17.622	1.22E-06
2		.1365		.0408	.362	.429	29.667	.0086
3		.1406	.7560	.0539	.326	.432	30.485	.0253
1				.0063	.310	.347	30.833	.0063
2			.9254	.0084	.270	.347	31.718	.0267
1		.0205			.223	.264	32.726	.0205
2		.0214	.5635		.194	.279	33.336	.0622
1		.7401			.000	.006	38.028	.7401

The second row with all four variables corresponds to the full regression model we examined above. Which model is best? One obvious criterion would be to use the model with the highest Adj R^2 in which all the coefficients are significant, and that would be the first model listed. There might, however, be situations in which you have an interest in a particular variable, and you might be willing to go with a lower R^2 in order to use a model that includes that particular variable. When you determine the model you want to use, run the full regression output to get more detail using those variables.

If you have selected a regression model manually, locate its line in the output. See if there are models near it that might represent an improvement. Your model ideally will be somewhere near the top. If it is not, that does not mean that you should discard it. However, you might consider some of the other models, especially if they have dramatically higher adjusted R^2 values.

As the number of variables increases, the number of possible regression models increases exponentially. MegaStat handles all possible regressions for 12 variables, but it generates 4095 lines of output. Sifting through that much output is tedious, and generally you are interested in only the best model of any given size. MegaStat's **"Stepwise Selection"** option shows the one best model of each size, as shown in Exhibit 13-6.

The rows are sorted by the number of variables (Nvar). The first row is the best single-variable model, the second row is the best two-variable model, and so forth. Each row in the stepwise selection table also is listed in the All Possible Regressions table. The output is more manageable, especially as the number of variables increases. In the Excel sheet, you can sort on s or Adj R^2 to find the best model.

The output also includes a chart that shows how Adj R^2 increases as variables are added to the regression model. This chart shows a very typical pattern: Adding a second variable often helps the prediction; adding a third variable

EXHIBIT 13-6
Stepwise selection output.

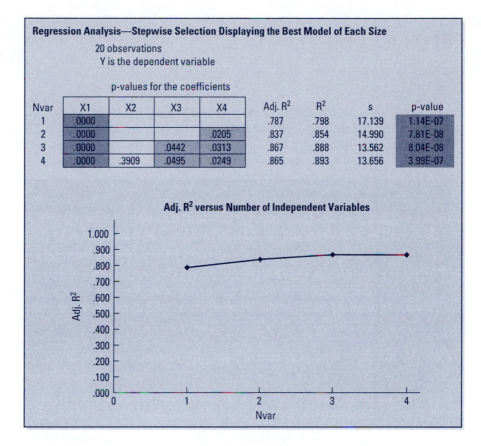

Regression Analysis—Stepwise Selection Displaying the Best Model of Each Size

20 observations
Y is the dependent variable

p-values for the coefficients

Nvar	X1	X2	X3	X4	Adj. R^2	R^2	s	p-value
1	.0000				.787	.798	17.139	1.14E-07
2	.0000			.0205	.837	.854	14.990	7.81E-08
3	.0000		.0442	.0313	.867	.888	13.562	8.04E-08
4	.0000	.3909	.0495	.0249	.865	.893	13.656	3.99E-07

Adj. R^2 versus Number of Independent Variables

helps less. In this case, adding a fourth variable actually decreases Adj R^2. Whenever you work with multiple regression data, run Stepwise Selection and you almost always will find this "diminishing returns" pattern. No matter how many variables you start with, it is rare to find a situation in which the fourth variable (or more) adds appreciably to Adj R^2, and you often do not find much improvement with a third variable.

Admittedly, All Possible Regressions and Stepwise Selection lend themselves to fishing expeditions, but they are good for exploration and confirmation. The chart that accompanies "Stepwise Selection" is especially useful for illustrating

STEPWISE SELECTION: REPLICATE TEXT OUTPUT

Learning Activity **13.2–6**

- Open **Mregr1.xls!Data.**
- Use "All Possible Regressions" and "Stepwise Selection" to replicate Exhibit 13-5 and Exhibit 13-6.
- As an exercise in how to lie with statistics, right-click the vertical axis of the stepwise selection chart and rescale it with a minimum value of .75. It will now appear that including a second variable and adding a third variable will add much more than they actually do. That is why the axis is scaled 0 to 1.

MULTIPLE REGRESSION PRACTICE Learning Activity 13.2–7

- Open **RealEstateData.xls!Data.**
- Use MegaStat to calculate the correlation matrix for all variables except "No." Which variables look promising for multiple regression for predicting Price?
  - ○ *Answer:* As seen in the **Correlation_Matrix** worksheet, Basement and Distance do not have particularly large correlations with Price. Subdiv appears to be a promising variable with a correlation of .837 with Price; however, SubDiv is a qualitative variable and the numbers do not measure anything, and so it should not be used in regression. The association of the numbers with the subdivision is arbitrary, and they could have been chosen to give a small correlation. SqrFt and Bedrooms appear to be the two best variables.
    - The multicollinearity among the predictor variables is not as low as we might like, but it is fairly typical.
- Run the multiple regression using the eight variables SqrFt through Rating. How does it look?
  - ○ *Answer:* As seen in the Regression_Output worksheet, SqrFt and Bedrooms are significant and Bathrooms also is significant.
- Use the same eight variables and run "All Possible Regressions." What can you make of the output?
  - ○ *Answer:* As you scan through all the possible regressions in the All Possible Regressions worksheet, you see that SqrtFt, Bedrooms, and Bathrooms are yellow on most of the lines, indicating that they are the dominant variables.
- Suppose you were particularly interested in the Rating variable. To see if it is useful with any combination of variables, click in the Rating column and Sort Ascending. What does this tell you?
  - ○ You see that it is significant with several combinations of variables; however, the R^2 is not as large as it is using SqrFt and Bedrooms.
- Run the Stepwise Selection option. What does this tell you?
  - ○ *Answer:* The Stepwise Selection worksheet shows that SqrFt is clearly the single best variable. Adding Bedrooms increases the adjusted R^2 from .691 to .858. Adding more variables does not improve the prediction much even though Bathrooms is significant.
    - The chart at the bottom shows that the adjusted R^2 levels off after the second variable and even starts to decrease with the last two variables.

the futility of trying to improve a prediction by adding more and more independent variables.

One common outcome of model building in multiple regression is to end up with a bivariate regression model. It is often difficult to improve much on bivariate regression, especially if one variable does fairly well by itself. The problem is that variables that relate to the dependent variable also tend to be related to each other.

Summary

Multiple regression is an extension of bivariate regression and uses multiple independent variables to predict the dependent variable. Although multiple regression can be run with several independent variables, it is rare to find more than three variables that contribute substantially to the prediction.

Conceptual

- The relationship between two or more variables and a dependent variable:
  - ○ A variable that is not significant in multiple regression can be significant when used by itself in bivariate regression.
  - ○ A variable that does not work well by itself can be significant when used in multiple regression.

- Be able to conceptualize the graphical representation of multiple regression with two independent variables.
- The multiple R is the correlation between Y and Y′.

Applied

- A correlation matrix should be run as a preliminary to regression analysis. Look for
  - Moderate to high correlations between the dependent and independent variables
  - Low to moderate correlation among the independent variables
- Multiple regression output:
  - Regression equation coefficients show how much 1 unit of the variable will increase the dependent variable with the other variables held constant.
  - R^2, Adj R^2, and R measure strength of relationship.
  - An ANOVA test (Test #9) is used to measure overall significance, and t-tests (Test #10) are used for the individual variables.
  - Standardized coefficients show the relative importance of the variables.
  - VIFs measure multicollinearity.
- Be able to interpret confidence intervals for prediction, prediction interval, and leverage.
- Analysis of residuals can be used to look for outliers:
  - Be able to calculate a predicted value given a regression equation and values for X.
  - All Possible Regressions and/or Stepwise Selection can be used to select the best variables for a multiple regression model.

Exercises

The exercises and data are found in **Ch_13_Mult_Regression.xls** in the exercises folder of the CD

No.	Content
1	Example 1—correlation matrix
2	Example 1—regression
3	Example 1—prediction
4	Example 1—stepwise
5	Example 2—correlation matrix
6	Example 2—regression
7	Example 2—prediction
8	Example 2—stepwise
9	Longley data—regression
10	Longley data—correlation
11	Create your own data

Modules for Multiple Regression

13.A   WHAT IS THE MULTIPLE CORRELATION, R?

Exhibit 13-7 shows the sample multiple regression data with two variables added: the predicted value (Y′) and the residual (Y − Y′). These values were copy/pasted from MegaStat multiple regression output with the Output Residuals option box checked. Exhibit 13-8 shows the correlation matrix of these variables.

The box indicates the original correlation matrix from Exhibit 13-3. The correlation between Y and "Predicted" (.945) is the multiple correlation.[1]

Recall that R^2 is the percent of variance that is accounted for. If we squared the correlation (.327) of Y and the residual, we would get the proportion of variance *not* accounted for; thus, $.945^2 + .327^2 = 1.000$.

EXHIBIT 13-7
Multiple regression data with predicted and residual variables added.

Y	X1	X2	X3	X4	Predicted	Residual
35.7	12	2	7.5	0	21.61	14.09
21.1	14	3	7.6	0	24.42	−3.32
56.9	17	5	3.8	0	36.21	20.69
27.6	18	4	11.8	0	22.85	4.75
32.9	23	6	4.8	0	45.21	−12.31
65.9	24	1	5.3	1	69.27	−3.37
29.5	28	9	13.4	0	34.62	−5.12
60.0	32	11	8.3	1	69.11	−9.11
90.1	33	7	4.3	1	83.34	6.76
49.7	36	3	7.2	0	69.45	−19.75
84.0	37	6	2.5	0	78.05	5.95
63.6	42	5	4.9	0	84.19	−20.59
107.2	43	10	4.4	1	100.21	6.99
77.9	45	8	9.3	0	78.19	−0.29
92.7	49	8	4.9	1	113.26	−20.56
82.4	52	11	11.1	0	85.54	−3.14
124.3	54	15	3.7	1	118.70	5.60
129.9	57	5	6.6	0	110.86	19.04
129.3	62	7	14.0	1	121.76	7.54
139.3	65	10	9.9	1	133.16	6.14

EXPLORING MULTIPLE R   Learning Activity **13.A–1**

- Open **Mregr1.xls!Data**
- Run the multiple regression to predict Y using X1 − X4. Check the "Output Residuals" option.
- Copy the Predicted variable and the Residual variable to the data worksheet, as shown in Exhibit 13-7.
- Run the correlation to replicate the output in Exhibit 13-8.
- Find the multiple R and the other values discussed in the text.
- Run a scatterplot with the Predicted and Residual variables. Since the correlation is zero, what will the scatterplot look like?
- Create the same output using **RealEstateData.xls!Data** and find R.

[1]The correlation .945 of **X1** and **Y** in the cell to the right is just a coincidence. In fact, the values are not equal beyond three decimal places.

EXHIBIT 13-8
Correlation matrix showing multiple R.

Correlation Matrix

	Y	X1	X2	X3	X4	Predicted	Residual
Y	1.000						
X1	.893	1.000					
X2	.514	.591	1.000				
X3	−.079	.159	.081	1.000			
X4	.589	.419	.435	−.103	1.000		
Predicted	.945	.945	.544	−.084	.623	1.000	
Residual	.327	.000	.000	.000	.000	.000	1.000

R 20 sample size

± .444 critical value .05 (two-tail)

± .561 critical value .01 (two-tail)

EXHIBIT 13-9
Original data and standardized data.

	Original data					Data converted to z-values				
Y	X1	X2	X3	X4		zY	zX1	zX2	zX3	zX4
35.7	12	2	7.5	0		−1.06	−1.55	−1.36	0.07	−0.80
21.1	14	3	7.6	0		−1.45	−1.43	−1.08	0.10	−0.80
56.9	17	5	3.8	0		−0.49	−1.24	−0.51	−1.03	−0.80
27.6	18	4	11.8	0		−1.28	−1.18	−0.80	1.34	−0.80
32.9	23	6	4.8	0		−1.13	−0.87	−0.23	−0.73	−0.80
65.9	24	1	5.3	1		−0.25	−0.81	−1.65	−0.58	1.19
29.5	28	9	13.4	0		−1.23	−0.56	0.63	1.82	−0.80
60.0	32	11	8.3	1		−0.40	−0.32	1.19	0.31	1.19
90.1	33	7	4.3	1		0.41	−0.26	0.06	−0.88	1.19
49.7	36	3	7.2	0		−0.68	−0.07	−1.08	−0.02	−0.80
84.0	37	6	2.5	0		0.24	−0.01	−0.23	−1.41	−0.80
63.6	42	5	4.9	0		−0.31	0.30	−0.51	−0.70	−0.80
107.2	43	10	4.4	1		0.87	0.36	0.91	−0.85	1.19
77.9	45	8	9.3	0		0.08	0.48	0.34	0.60	−0.80
92.7	49	8	4.9	1		0.48	0.73	0.34	−0.70	1.19
82.4	52	11	11.1	0		0.20	0.92	1.19	1.14	−0.80
124.3	54	15	3.7	1		1.33	1.04	2.33	−1.06	1.19
129.9	57	5	6.6	0		1.48	1.22	−0.51	−0.20	−0.80
129.3	62	7	14.0	1		1.46	1.53	0.06	1.99	1.19
139.3	65	10	9.9	1		1.73	1.72	0.91	0.78	1.19
75.00	37.15	6.80	7.27	0.40	mean	0.00	0.00	0.00	0.00	0.00
37.13	16.21	3.52	3.38	0.50	stdev	1.00	1.00	1.00	1.00	1.00

Another interesting thing to note in the correlation matrix is the correlation of zero between Predicted and Residual. This will always be the case. If this correlation was greater than zero, it would imply that there was some predictability remaining. Even more interesting is the fact that each of the components of the predicted value (X1 − X4) individually correlates zero with the predicted value.

13.B   EXPLORING STANDARDIZED REGRESSION COEFFICIENTS

Exhibit 13-9 shows the sample multiple regression data on the left and the standardized values on the right.

The top half of Exhibit 13-10 shows the regression output with the standardized coefficients box checked. The bottom half shows the multiple regression using the standardized data. From this we see that the standardized coefficients are simply the regression coefficients you get when using standardized data.

EXHIBIT 13-10
Standardized coefficients and regression using standardized data.

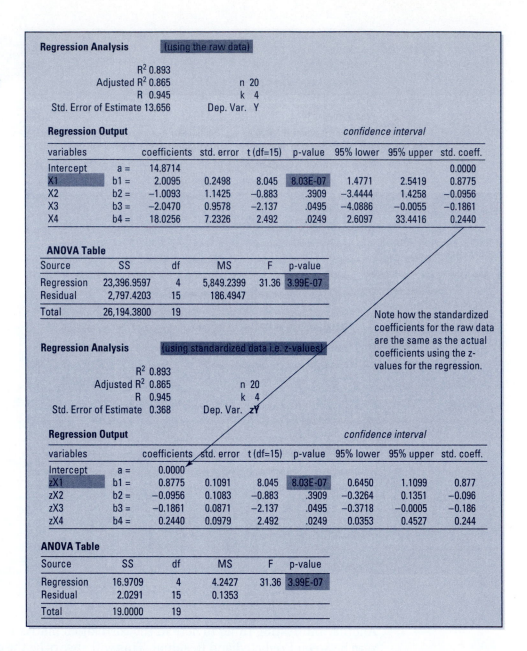

Regression Analysis (using the raw data)

R^2 0.893
Adjusted R^2 0.865   n 20
R 0.945   k 4
Std. Error of Estimate 13.656   Dep. Var. Y

Regression Output   *confidence interval*

variables		coefficients	std. error	t (df=15)	p-value	95% lower	95% upper	std. coeff.
Intercept	a =	14.8714						0.0000
X1	b1 =	2.0095	0.2498	8.045	8.03E-07	1.4771	2.5419	0.8775
X2	b2 =	−1.0093	1.1425	−0.883	.3909	−3.4444	1.4258	−0.0956
X3	b3 =	−2.0470	0.9578	−2.137	.0495	−4.0886	−0.0055	−0.1861
X4	b4 =	18.0256	7.2326	2.492	.0249	2.6097	33.4416	0.2440

ANOVA Table

Source	SS	df	MS	F	p-value
Regression	23,396.9597	4	5,849.2399	31.36	3.99E-07
Residual	2,797.4203	15	186.4947		
Total	26,194.3800	19			

Note how the standardized coefficients for the raw data are the same as the actual coefficients using the z-values for the regression.

Regression Analysis (using standardized data i.e. z-values)

R^2 0.893
Adjusted R^2 0.865   n 20
R 0.945   k 4
Std. Error of Estimate 0.368   Dep. Var. zY

Regression Output   *confidence interval*

variables		coefficients	std. error	t (df=15)	p-value	95% lower	95% upper	std. coeff.
Intercept	a =	0.0000						
zX1	b1 =	0.8775	0.1091	8.045	8.03E-07	0.6450	1.1099	0.877
zX2	b2 =	−0.0956	0.1083	−0.883	.3909	−0.3264	0.1351	−0.096
zX3	b3 =	−0.1861	0.0871	−2.137	.0495	−0.3718	−0.0005	−0.186
zX4	b4 =	0.2440	0.0979	2.492	.0249	0.0353	0.4527	0.244

ANOVA Table

Source	SS	df	MS	F	p-value
Regression	16.9709	4	4.2427	31.36	3.99E-07
Residual	2.0291	15	0.1353		
Total	19.0000	19			

STANDARDIZED COEFFICIENTS   Learning Activity **13.B–1**

- Open **Mregr1.xls!Data.**
- Copy/Paste the data to a new workbook.
- Create the standardized data as shown in Exhibit 13-10.
- Run the multiple regression on the actual data and the standardized data. Compare the two regression outputs.
- *Solution:* See **Mregr1-z.xls!Regression_Output.**

CHAPTER FOURTEEN

Chi-Square Applications

14.1 Nonparametric Methods and Chi-Square Tests (p. 250)

14.2 Contingency Table: Chi-Square Test of Independence (Test #11) (p. 250)

14.3 Goodness of Fit Test (Test #12) (p. 257)

   Summary (p. 260)

   Exercises (p. 260)

Modules for Chapter Fourteen

14.A Using the Chi-Square Distribution (p. 261)

14.B Contingency Table Options (p. 262)

14.C Dice Toss Goodness of Fit Simulation (p. 263)

14.D Normal Curve Goodness of Fit (p. 263)

14.1   Nonparametric Methods and Chi-Square Tests

In earlier chapters we looked at hypothesis tests for means and proportions, ANOVA, and regression analysis. These tests are called parametric methods because they make certain assumptions about population values; for example, they typically assume a normal population. The tests are generally not sensitive to violations of those assumptions, but there could be some lingering doubt about the impact of assumption violation on any specific test. Also, traditional parametric methods mostly work with quantitative (preferably ratio) data.

There is another branch of statistics known as **nonparametric methods** or nonparametric statistics. Nonparametric methods do not rely on assumptions about population distributions and often are based on basic probability methods. Most traditional tests have a nonparametric counterpart. Nonparametric tests are usually slightly less powerful than parametric methods, but they have the advantage of not relying on population assumptions. Also, nonparametric methods often can work with qualitative data.

In the hypothesis testing chapter, we saw how to do a proportion versus hypothesized value test by using the binomial distribution (Module 10.C). That was actually a nonparametric approach since it used a basic probability distribution to perform a test.

There are many nonparametric procedures. If you look at MegaStat's menu, you will see a menu item that lists several nonparametric procedures. The most commonly used nonparametric methods are the family of chi-square tests. They are used so widely that they have their own menu item in MegaStat even though, technically speaking, they should be on the nonparametric menu.

14.2   Contingency Table: Chi-Square Test of Independence (Test #11)

In Chapter 4, we used the following **Contingency Table** example to introduce some basic probability terms and concepts. Take a few minutes to go back and review that chapter, especially the section on statistical independence (Section 4.3). Assume a market research company has a contract with an automobile manufacturer to determine whether marital status is related to the type of automobile that is purchased. A randomly selected sample of 120 people are asked what type of vehicle they own (A = sport vehicle, ~A = nonsport vehicle) and if they are married (B = married, ~B = not married). Assume the company gets the results shown in Exhibit 14-1 (**Prob1.xls**).

As you reviewed Chapter 4, you saw that we showed that marital status and type of car were not independent but that they did not seem to be dramatically different from independence; perhaps they really were independent and this

EXHIBIT 14-1
Contingency table (duplicate of Exhibit 4-1).

Type of Vehicle		Married B	Not Married ~B	
	Sport Vehicle A	14	27	41
	Non Sport Vehicle ~A	43	36	79
		57	63	120

Marital Status

particular sample was off a bit because of sampling error. We said we would examine a more powerful tool for testing independence. That tool is the chi-square test for independence, often called a contingency table test.

The question still is: How much can the frequencies deviate from perfect independence and still be considered statistically independent? First we have to answer the question: How many observations would we expect in each cell with perfect independence?

Recall that the probability for each cell under perfect independence is the product of the corresponding marginal probabilities; that is, the definition of independence (Equation [4.4]):

$$P(A \ and \ B) = P(A) \cdot P(B)$$

To get the *number* expected in each cell, we multiply the probability by the total sample size: $p(A) \cdot p(B) \cdot N$, where N is the total sample size.

For the upper left cell of the table, the calculation would be

$$\frac{57}{120} \cdot \frac{41}{120} \cdot 120 = 19.475$$

The question often arises, How can we have a fractional number for an expected frequency in light of the fact that frequencies have to be integers? The answer is that this is a calculated value and does not have to be an integer. It does show that since our observed frequencies have to be integers, we rarely can have exactly perfect independence unless the expected frequencies turn out to be integers.

Note that since both denominators are 120 and we multiply by 120, one of the denominators always cancels with N, as follows:

$$\frac{57}{120} \cdot \frac{41}{\cancel{120}} \cdot \cancel{120}$$

Generalizing this, we see that the equation for the expected value in each cell is

$$\text{Expected value} = \frac{(\text{row total})(\text{column total})}{\text{grand total}} \qquad \textbf{[14.1]}$$

Applying this equation to the rest of the cells, we get the expected values:

expected	B	~B	
A	19.475	21.525	41
~A	37.525	41.475	79
	57	63	120

Note that the expected values sum to the same row and column totals as the observed values. Because of this you can get by in a 2 by 2 table by calculating just one expected frequency and subtracting to get the others. We talk later about the degrees of freedom for this test; it turns out that the degrees of freedom corresponds to the number of cells you need to calculate before you can subtract to get the remaining values.

Now that we have observed and expected frequencies, how do we compare them? Given the title of this chapter, you should not be surprised to find that we do it with a chi-square test statistic:

$$\chi^2 = \sum_{\text{all cells}} \left[\frac{(O - E)^2}{E} \right] \qquad \textbf{[14.2]}$$

where O is the observed value and E is the corresponding expected value for each cell. Putting this equation into words:

1. Calculate the expected values for each cell.
2. For each cell:
   - Subtract O − E.
   - Square the result.
   - Divide by E.
3. Sum for all the cells.
   - The sum is the **chi-square value.**

Note that with perfect independence, O − E would be zero for every cell and thus chi-square would be zero. How large does chi-square have to be to reject the null hypothesis of independence? The following section shows the seven-step hypothesis test. In step 4 you will see the chi-square table (Module 14.A) and find out how to use it to determine the critical value for the test.

Example of Contingency Table Test of Independence

The contingency table relating marital status to type of vehicle is shown above in Exhibit 14-1 and in **Prob1.xls.**

Hypothesis Testing Steps

1. H_0: The factors are independent (marital status is not related to type of vehicle).

   H_1: The factors are not independent (marital status is related to type of vehicle).

2. $\alpha = .05$ (default).
3. Test: Chi-square Contingency Table—test of independence (Test #11).
4. Decision rule: Reject H_0 if $\chi_1^2 > 3.841$ or if the p-value < 0.5.

   Where df = (number of rows − 1)(number of columns − 1) = (2 − 1)(2 − 1) = 1 See Module 14.A regarding the chi-square table.

5. Calculation: Use a calculator or Excel to verify that the calculated value of the chi-square test statistic is 4.45, as shown in Exhibit 14-2.
6. Decision: Reject the null hypothesis because the calculated chi-square of 4.45 is larger than the critical value of 3.84 and the p-value < 0.5.
7. Interpretation: We can infer that marital status and type of vehicle are not statistically independent. However, we should be careful not to say they are dependent, which would imply that one factor causes the other. As always, correlation does not imply causation.

   Note 1. This example used a 2 by 2 table, but chi-square tables can be larger. There is no fixed limit on the size, but a contingency table with more than five rows or columns is unusual.

EXHIBIT 14-2
MegaStat output for a Contingency Table Test of Independence.

Chi-square Contingency Table Test for Independence

		B	~B	Total
A	Observed	**14**	**27**	41
	Expected	19.48	21.53	41.00
	O − E	−5.48	5.48	0.00
	$(O - E)^2/E$	1.54	1.39	2.93
~A	Observed	**43**	**36**	79
	Expected	37.53	41.48	79.00
	O − E	5.48	−5.48	0.00
	$(O - E)^2/E$	0.80	0.72	1.52
Total	Observed	57	63	120
	Expected	57.00	63.00	120.00
	O − E	0.00	0.00	0.00
	$(O - E)^2/E$	2.34	2.12	4.45

4.45 chi-square
1 df
.0348 p-value

REPLICATE TEXT CONTINGENCY TABLE
Learning Activity **14.2–1**

- Use a calculator to replicate the computations in the text. Use the tables to look up the chi-square values.
- *Solution:* See **Prob3.xls!Chisquare_calculation**.
- Use MegaStat I ChiSquare/CrossTab I Contingency Table to replicate the calculations, using the observed frequencies table displayed in **Prob3.xls!Chisquare_calculation**.
- *Solution:* See **Prob3.xls!Contingency table output**.

EXPLORING CONTINGENCY TABLES
Learning Activity **14.2–2**

- Open **2x2_Table.xls**. This worksheet is a template for a 2 by 2 contingency table.
- Look at the cell formulas to see how they work. The observed table initially has the values from the text example. The values in the shaded cell can be changed. Try entering some values in cell B3. If you change a cell and get a negative value or error condition, you have entered an invalid value. If this occurs, figure out why it happened and change it.
- What would the table look like with perfect independence?
  - *Solution:* Perfect independence exists when the observed frequencies are the same as the expected frequencies. The expected frequency in the upper left cell is 19.475, and so the closest integer number would be 19. When you put this value in cell B3, you see that the chi-square value is small and the p-value is large. If the frequencies were such that the expected values were integers, chi-square would be zero and the p-value would be 1.
    - If you change cell B5 to 60 and cell B3 to 20, you see perfect independence. When you are done, change cell B5 back to 57.
- What would the table look like with maximum nonindependence? This would happen if the value in cell B3 was as large as possible and as small as possible. What would these values be? Determine these values and note the results.
  - *Solution:* The smallest frequency in B3 would be 0; the largest would be 41. With each of these values, the chi-square will be large and the p-value will be small.

Note 2. If any cell has a small expected frequency, be cautious about the resulting chi-square test. How small is small? Certainly less than 1 is small; most books say less than 5. MegaStat shades cells where the expected frequency is less than 5. Why are small expected frequencies a problem? Because the chi-square equation involves dividing by the expected value, and the smaller it is, the larger chi-square becomes. Thus, tiny expected values can inflate the chi-square.

CONTINGENCY TABLE PRACTICE   Learning Activity **14.2–3**

A realtor in the city in **RealEstateData.xls** wants to know if there is a relationship between the first three subdivisions (Burbsville, Englewood, and Briar Hills) and whether a home has a swimming pool.

- Open **2x3_Table.xls!Data,** which contains the contingency table. Do the hypothesis test by using a calculator and the chi-square table. Verify your calculations with MegaStat.
- Here is the solution.

Hypothesis Testing Steps

1. H_0: The factors are independent (subdivision is not related to pool).

   H_1: The factors are not independent (marital status is related to type of vehicle).

2. $\alpha = .05$ (default).

3. Test: chi-square contingency table—test of independence (Test #11).

4. Decision rule: Reject H_0 if $\chi_2^2 > 5.991$.

   Where df $=$ (number of rows $-$ 1)(number of columns $-$ 1) $= (2-1)(3-1) = 2$.
   See Module 14.A regarding the chi-square table.

5. Calculation: Use a calculator or Excel to verify that the calculated value of the chi-square test statistic is 1.735. The MegaStat output is in **2x3_Table.xls!Solution1.**

6. Decision: Fail to reject the null hypothesis because the calculated chi-square of 1.735 is smaller than the critical value of 5.991 and the p-value > 0.5.

Interpretation: There does not appear to be a relationship between pools and subdivisions. Looking at each cell, the observed and expected values are very close.

In the MegaStat output, a couple of the cells are shaded because the expected frequencies are less than 5. However, since the outcome was not significant, there is no cause for concern.

EFFECT OF SAMPLE SIZE   Learning Activity **14.2–4**

How does sample size affect a contingency table.?

- Open **2x3_Table.xls!Big_Data.** This worksheet contains the original contingency table with each frequency multiplied by 10. Do the chi-square calculation with a calculator or MegaStat and comment on the outcome.
  - *Solution:* **2x3_Table.xls!Solution2** shows the result. This table is quite significant whereas the original one was not even though the relative sizes of the cells are the same. Note also that the chi-square value is 10 times larger than the original chi-square. Alternately click the **Solution1** and **Solution2** worksheets to see the similarities and differences.

When the relative size of the frequencies is the same in both tables, how can one be significant and the other one not? Because with the larger sample size we are more certain of the results.

Comparing Multiple Proportions

In Section 10.6 we saw how to compare two proportions. The chi-square test also can be used to compare two proportions, but it has the advantage of being able to compare multiple proportions. For example, a political pollster wants to know if the proportion of people who say they will vote for a candidate is the same in three different precincts. Assume the proportions turn out to be 40.3%, 65.9%, and 51.9% and that the respective sample sizes are 62, 44, and 54. Putting this into table form you would get a 2 by 3 table:

25	29	28	82
37	15	26	78
62	44	54	160
40.3%	65.9%	51.9%	

Note that you need to multiply the proportion by the sample size and round to the nearest integer to get the table values. You then would do a contingency table test on the 2 by 3 table. Any contingency table with two rows could be interpreted as a test for comparing proportions. The full hypothesis test and output for comparing proportions are shown below.

Hypothesis Testing Steps

1. H_0: $\pi_1 = \pi_2 = \pi_3$ (the proportions are equal).

   H_1: $\pi_1 \neq \pi_2 \neq \pi_3$ (the proportions are not equal).
2. $\alpha = .05$ (default).
3. Test: Chi-square Contingency Table—test of independence (Test #11).
4. Decision rule: Reject H_0 if $\chi_2^2 > 5.991$.

   Where df = (number of rows − 1)(number of columns − 1) = (2 − 1)(3 − 1) = 2

   See Module 14.A regarding the chi-square table.
   or
   Reject H_0 if the p-value $< .05$.

5. Calculation of test statistic: Use a calculator or Excel to verify that the chi-square value is 6.76, as shown in Exhibit 14-3.

EXHIBIT 14-3
Comparison of multiple proportions using a contingency table test.

Chi-square Contingency Table Test for Independence

		Col 1	Col 2	Col 3	Total
Row 1	Observed	**25**	**29**	**28**	82
	Expected	31.78	22.55	27.68	82.00
Row 2	Observed	**37**	**15**	**26**	78
	Expected	30.23	21.45	26.33	78.00
Total	Observed	62	44	54	160
	Expected	62.00	44.00	54.00	160.00

6.76 chi-square
2 df
.0341 p-value

COMPARING MULTIPLE PROPORTIONS: REPLICATE TEXT OUTPUT

Learning Activity **14.2–5**

- Use a calculator to replicate the values in the text section.
- Do the calculations with MegaStat.

COMPARING MULTIPLE PROPORTIONS: PRACTICE

Learning Activity **14.2–6**

A sales manager wants to know if the proportion of female salespersons in three regions is the same. Three of the percentages are 39.3%, 64.4%, and 48.9%. The respective sample sizes are 61, 45, and 47.

Here is the solution.

Hypothesis Testing Steps (Short Form)

1. H_0: $\pi_1 = \pi_2 = \pi_3$ (the proportions are equal).
   H_1: $\pi_1 \neq \pi_2 \neq \pi_3$ (the proportions are not equal).
2. $\alpha = .05$ (default).
3. Test: Chi-square Contingency Table—test of independence (Test #11).
4. Decision rule: Reject H_0 if $\chi_2^2 > 5.991$.

   Where df $=$ (number of rows $-$ 1)(number of columns $-$ 1) $= (2-1)(3-1) = 2$.

   See Module 14.A regarding the chi-square table.
   or
   Reject H_0 if the p-value < 0.5.
5. Calculation of test statistic: Use a calculator or Excel to verify that the chi-square value is 6.54 as shown in **MultProp.xls!Data** and **MultProp.xls!Solution.**
6. Decision: Reject the null hypothesis since the calculated value of 6.54 is greater than the critical value of 5.991 and the p-value is less than .05.

Interpretation: The proportions appear to be different.

6. Decision: Reject the null hypothesis since the calculated value of 6.76 is greater than the critical value of 5.991 and the p-value is less than .05.

7. Interpretation: The proportions appear to be different.

Crosstabulation

TUTORIAL 15

The contingency table test for independence assumes that we have frequencies in the form of a table. But where do those frequencies come from? We get them by counting the original data. **Prob3.xls!Raw_data** shows what the raw data looked like after it was collected. The worksheet shows how the data would have been collected in text form and also coded as 1's and 0's. The text version

CROSSTABULATION   Learning Activity **14.2–7**

- Open **Prob3.xls!Raw_data.**
- Use MegaStat | ChiSquare/CrossTab | Crosstabulation to get the frequencies using both the text-coded and the number-coded data.
- Open **RealEstateData.xls!Data.**
- Use MegaStat | ChiSquare/CrossTab | Crosstabulation to get the frequencies for Learning Activity 14.3 to replicate **2x3_Table.xls!Data.**

perhaps is more meaningful to interpret, but in entering the data, it takes more keystrokes and they have to be exactly right, including case sensitivity ("married" is not the same as "Married"). Entering the numbers as 1's and 0's (or any other values) is a lot faster and less error-prone, but unless you are familiar with the codes, you cannot look at the data and know what it represents. Whichever method you use, the MegaStat Crosstabulation option counts the values for the contingency table and also can do the chi-square test.

Other Contingency Table Options

The MegaStat Contingency Table also has options for the Phi coefficient, the Coefficient of Contingency, Cramer's V, and Fisher's Exact Test. Fisher's Exact Test provides an exact p-value for 2 by 2 tables, and the others are measures of association that measure strength of relationship. Module 14.B discusses these options.

14.3   Goodness of Fit Test (Test #12)

Introduction and Uniform Distribution Goodness of Fit Test

The **goodness of fit (GOF) test** is another variation of a chi-square test. As the name implies, it tests whether observed data match some theoretical distribution. The data is always of the following form of observed and expected pairs:

observed	expected

Both columns must sum to the same value. The number of pairs depends on the test you are doing.

Let's start by testing whether observed data fit a discrete uniform distribution in which every outcome is equally likely. For example, let's say you want to test whether a particular die is fair. You would start by tossing it a large number of times and observing the number of occurrences of each number. For example, if you tossed it 600 times, you would expect approximately 100 occurrences of each number of dots. Here is the result of tossing the die 600 times:

observed	expected
87	100
97	100
101	100
96	100
107	100
112	100

The chi-square test statistic is calculated the same way as the contingency table:

$$\chi^2 = \sum_{\text{all cells}} \left[\frac{(O - E)^2}{E} \right]$$

where O and E are the observed and expected values. The following section shows the seven-step hypothesis test, which also addresses ways to determine the degrees of freedom.

Example of a Goodness of Fit Test

The data for the dice toss experiment described in the previous section is found in **GOF1.xls.**

Hypothesis Testing Steps

1. H_0: The observed frequencies could have come from a uniform distribution (appears to be a fair die).

   H_1: The observed frequencies are unlikely to have come from a uniform distribution (appears to be an unfair die).
2. $\alpha = .05$ (default).
3. Test: Goodness of Fit Test (Test #12).
4. Decision rule: Reject H_0 if $\chi_5^2 > 11.07$.

The degrees of freedom is the number of observed/expected pairs $-1 = 6 - 1 = 5$.

See Test Summary #12 and Module 14.D for calculating the degrees of freedom for other distributions.

5. Calculation: Use a calculator or Excel to verify that the calculated value of the chi-square test statistic is 3.88, as shown in Exhibit 14-4.
6. Decision: Fail to reject because $3.88 < 11.07$ and $.5668 > .05$.
7. Interpretation: It turns out that the p-value for this test is .5668. That is not close to being under .05, and so it appears that we easily could have gotten this pattern with a fair die. Notice that the "% of chisq" column indicates how much each row contributes to the chi-square. In this example, even though the result is not significant, we see the pattern one would expect if

EXHIBIT 14-4
Goodness of Fit output.

Goodness of Fit Test

observed	expected	O − E	(O − E)²/E	% of chisq
87	100.000	−13.000	1.690	43.56
97	100.000	−3.000	0.090	2.32
101	100.000	1.000	0.010	0.26
96	100.000	−4.000	0.160	4.12
107	100.000	7.000	0.490	12.63
112	100.000	12.000	1.440	37.11
600	600.000	0.000	3.880	100.00

3.88 chi-square
5 df
.5668 p-value

the "1" side was weighted: It goes down more than expected, which makes the opposite side "6" go up more than expected.

When doing a hypothesis test, we generally want to reject the null hypothesis because that means we have a significant difference or effect; however, when doing a goodness of fit test, you probably do not want a significant result because that would mean that your observed data do not correspond well with the expected data. By the way, you can never prove that a given observed distribution is a perfect fit; you can only present evidence that it may not be a good fit.

Module 14.C describes a dice toss simulation that illustrates the goodness of fit test.

Other Goodness of Fit Tests

Goodness of fit tests for other distributions work the same way. The only difference is in how the expected values are calculated: They could come from a binomial, hypergeometric, Poisson, or any other distribution. If you are doing a goodness of fit on a distribution that has "tails" on one end or both ends, you may need to collapse some of the cells.

One common goodness of fit test is for the normal distribution. When we say "approximately normally distributed," what we usually mean is a nonsignificant goodness of fit test. Since the normal curve is a continuous distribution, we need to break it down into discrete chunks. Module 14.D describes two approaches to doing a normal curve goodness of fit test.

GOODNESS OF FIT: REPLICATE TEXT CALCULATIONS

Learning Activity **14.3–1**

- Use a calculator and a table to replicate the goodness of fit calculations in the text.
- Replicate with MegaStat | ChiSquare/CrossTab | Goodness of Fit Test. The data are in **GOF1.xls!Data**.
- *Solution:* See **GOF1.xls!Solution.**

Summary

Conceptual

- The hypothesis testing and regression analyses discussed in earlier chapters are known as parametric tests because they rely on certain population assumptions. Chi-square tests are examples of nonparametric tests because they do not depend on population assumptions. Parametric tests require quantitative data, whereas chi-square tests analyze the frequencies we get by counting qualitative data.
- Chi-square hypothesis tests are based on the chi-square probability distribution.

Applied

Two important chi-square tests were introduced: the Contingency Table Test for Independence and the goodness of fit test. See Appendix B for a summary and details of these tests. Know when to use each test and be able to do the calculations.

$$\chi^2 = \sum_{\text{all cells}} \left[\frac{(O - E)^2}{E} \right] \qquad \text{Equation [14.2]}$$

- Contingency table test (Test #11):
  - Used for contingency tables at least 2 by 2 in size.
  - Also can be used to compare multiple proportions.
- Goodness of fit test (Test #12):
  - Used to compare observed and expected values.

Exercises

The exercises and data are found in **Ch_14_Chi_Square.xls** in the exercises folder of the CD.

Worksheet	Content
1	Chi-square distribution
2	2 by 2 contingency table
3	2 by 2 contingency table, min/max chisquare
4	3 by 2 contingency table
5	3 by 3 contingency table
6	2 by 2 compare proportions from ch 10
7	2 by 2 compare proportions from ch 10
8	compare proportions three proportions
9	RealEstateData pool by subdivision
10	Regions data
11	Regions data crosstab (what-if)
12	GOF uniform
13	GOF binomial
14	GOF Poisson
15	GOF normal—good fit
16	GOF normal—bad fit

Modules for Chi-Square Applications

14.A   USING THE CHI-SQUARE DISTRIBUTION

The chi-square distribution is a continuous distribution with the significance region always in the upper tail of the distribution.

The shape of the chi-square distribution depends on the degrees of freedom. For df = 1 and df = 2, the distribution has a "ski-slope" shape, as shown in Exhibit 14-5. For df up to 10, it looks similar to the F-distribution in Exhibit 11-9. For larger degrees of freedom, it takes on an almost normal distribution shape. You can explore the shapes with the MegaStat option dis-cussed below.

Chi-Square Table

The degrees of freedom depends on the test. **Tables.xls!Chi-square** has columns for 10%, 5%, 2%, and 1% significance levels.

Exhibit 14-6 shows a portion of the chi-square table from **Tables.xls! Chi-square** with the critical value of 3.841 highlighted for 1 degree of freedom.

Excel Chi-Square Functions

CHIDIST(chi-square, df) is Excel's chi-square distribution function. This function gives the probability of being greater than the specified chi-square value; thus, it gives the p-value.

=CHIDIST(3.841,1) displays .05, which corresponds to Exhibit 14-6.

=CHIDIST(4.454, 1) displays .0348, which is the p-value in Exhibit 14-2.

CHIINV(probability, df) gives the chi-square value corresponding to a probability.

=CHIINV(.05, 1) displays 3.841, which corresponds to the table in Exhibit 14-6.

EXHIBIT 14-5
MegaStat output showing chi-square upper 5% area for df = 1.

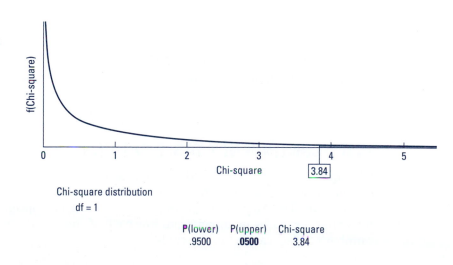

	P(lower)	P(upper)	Chi-square
	.9500	**.0500**	3.84

EXHIBIT 14-6
Portion of chi-square table showing df = 1, significance level = .05.

Critical Values of Chi-square

df	right-tail area			
	0.10	0.05	0.02	0.01
1	2.706	3.841	5.412	6.635
2	4.605	5.991	7.824	9.210
3	6.251	7.815	9.837	11.345
4	7.779	9.488	11.668	13.277
5	9.236	11.070	13.388	15.086
6	10.645	12.592	15.033	16.812
7	12.017	14.067	16.622	18.475
8	13.362	15.507	18.168	20.090
9	14.684	16.919	19.679	21.666
10	15.987	18.307	21.161	23.209
11	17.275	19.675	22.618	24.725
12	18.549	21.026	24.054	26.217
13	19.812	22.362	25.471	27.688
14	21.064	23.685	26.873	29.141
15	22.307	24.996	28.259	30.578
16	23.542	26.296	29.633	32.000

USING THE CHI-SQUARE DISTRIBUTION

Learning Activity **14.A–1**

- Determine the critical value of chi-square at the .05 level for df = 1, using
  - Chi-square table
  - Excel function: CHIINV
  - MegaStat | Probability | Chi-Square Distribution
- If the computer outputs do not quite match the table values, use the rounding options to make them match.
- *Solution:* The chi-square value is 3.84.
- Replicate the other values in Module 14.A.

MegaStat Chi-Square Distribution

MegaStat | Probability | Chi-Square Distribution allows calculation of chi-square probabilities and inverse probabilities and includes a plot of the distribution; see, for example, Exhibit 14-5.

14.B CONTINGENCY TABLE OPTIONS

Chi-square is proportional to the sample size. Thus, if you want to compare the degree of association in different contingency tables, you need a measure of association. The MegaStat contingency table test has options to calculate the following measures of association. For each of the equations below, N = total number of observations in the table.

Phi

$$\Phi = \sqrt{\frac{\chi^2}{N}}$$

[14.3]

This measures the degree of association from 0 (no relationship) to 1 (perfect relationship) if one of the dimensions of the table is 2 (either two rows or two columns).

Cramer's V

This measure of association works for larger tables.

$$\text{Cramer's V} = \sqrt{\frac{\chi^2}{N(L-1)}}$$

[14.4]

where L is the smaller of the number of rows or the number of columns. Note that when L = two rows or two columns, Cramer's V and phi are the same.

Coefficient of Contingency

$$cc = \sqrt{\frac{\chi^2}{\chi^2 + N}}$$

[14.5]

The measure of association ranges from 0 to nearly 1 as N becomes large.

Fisher's Exact Test

For a 2 by 2 contingency table, Fisher's Exact Test gives the exact p-value. Fisher's exact probability will be close to the Contingency Table Test p-value.

The formula for Fisher's Exact Test is

$$p = \frac{(a+b)!(c+d)!(a+c)!(b+d)!}{N!a!b!c!d!}$$

[14.6]

where a, b, c, and d are the frequencies in the four cells of the table.

14.C   DICE TOSS GOODNESS OF FIT SIMULATION

The dice toss simulation (**dice toss sim.xls**) simulates tossing a die 600 times and performs a goodness of fit test for each iteration. Each time you press the F9 function key or click the ReCalc button, you get a new batch of 600 tosses. Exhibit 14-7 shows a portion of the worksheet.

Assuming that Excel's random number generator is truly random, the die is fair. However, if you keep recalculating, you eventually will get a p-value that is under .0500, which would indicate an unfair die. Such an outcome is an example of a Type I error and will occur about 5% of the time.

14.D   NORMAL CURVE GOODNESS OF FIT

One very common statistical assumption is the assumption of a normal distribution. Many hypothesis tests assume a normal distribution, and for normal curve probabilities to be meaningful, the distributions must be at least

EXHIBIT 14-7
Portion of dice toss goodness of fit simulation.

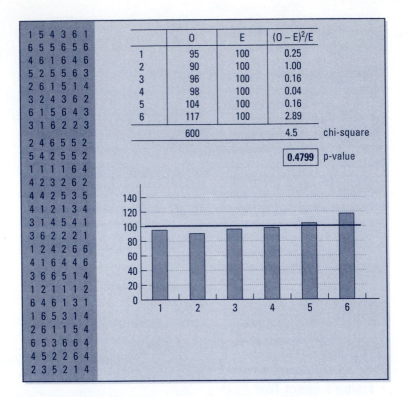

DICE TOSS SIMULATION (GOF)   Learning Activity **14.C–1**

- Open **DiceToss_sim.xls**.
- Click the ReCalc button or press F9 until you get a p-value less than .05 (a Type I error).
- Click the ReCalc button or press F9 until you get a p-value greater than .95 (a very good fit). If you get all 100's, print it. I have never known anyone who got all 100's for the outcome.

approximately normal. But how do you know if a distribution is normal? With a goodness of fit test, of course. Once you have the expected frequencies, the test is run the same way as the uniform GOF test. The trick is to determine the expected frequencies.

Let's see if the GPA data in Exhibit 3-11 (**GPAdata.xls**) could have come from a normal distribution. Since the normal curve is continuous and the frequency distribution has seven discrete intervals, we need to estimate the expected frequencies, that is, estimate how many observations would fall in each interval under the assumption of a normal distribution. This is done by adding four columns to the frequency distribution, as shown in Exhibit 14-8.[1] You should

---

[1] The cumulative frequency columns have been removed because they are not needed for this calculation.

EXHIBIT 14-8
Frequency distribution with columns added to calculate expected values.

GPA						A	B	C	D
						2.58 mean 0.82 stdev calculation of expected values			
Frequency Distribution – Quantitative									
lower	upper	midpoint	width	frequency	percent	z-upper	P(z)	p(z)	Expected
0.50	< 1.00	0.75	0.50	5	3.3	−1.93	0.0268	0.0268	4.07
1.00	< 1.50	1.25	0.50	12	7.9	−1.32	0.0934	0.0666	10.12
1.50	< 2.00	1.75	0.50	19	12.5	−0.71	0.2389	0.1455	22.12
2.00	< 2.50	2.25	0.50	31	20.4	−0.10	0.4602	0.2213	33.64
2.50	< 3.00	2.75	0.50	34	22.4	0.51	0.6950	0.2348	35.69
3.00	< 3.50	3.25	0.50	27	17.8	1.12	0.8686	0.1736	26.39
3.50	≤ 4.00	3.75	0.50	24	15.8	6.00	1.0000	0.1314	19.97
				152	100.0			1.0000	152.00

be able to do the calculations with a calculator and the normal curve table; however, it is more efficient to use Excel functions.

First you must find the mean and the standard deviation by using Excel functions or MegaStat. The mean and the standard deviation are shown at the top. Then you fill in columns A through D.

Column A is the z-value corresponding to the upper limit of each interval. For example, the second z-value would be calculated as follows: $−1.32 = (1.50 − 2.58)/.82$. Since the normal distribution theoretically goes to infinity, a z-value of 6.00 is always placed in the last cell to make the top interval effectively open-ended.

Column B is the corresponding normal curve probabilities from the table or NORMSDIST().

Column C is the probability you would expect in each interval. It is found by taking each probability in column B and subtracting the one right above it. For example, $.1736 = .8686 − .6950$. For the top interval (.0268), use the value from column B since we want the bottom interval to be open-ended to the low side. If the probabilities in column C sum to 1.0000, you probably have done things correctly.

Column D contains the expected frequencies that are calculated by multiplying column C by the sample size, 152 in this example. The expected frequencies should sum to the sample size.

If any expected frequencies are less than 1, you should consider combining those frequencies, as well as the observed frequencies, with the row above or below. This is often necessary with a normal curve GOF since the frequencies get small in the tails of the distribution. Now that we have the observed frequencies and expected frequencies (the shaded columns), we can do the hypothesis test, as shown below.

The test is the same as the uniform distribution except for one detail: the degrees of freedom. The official expression for degrees of freedom for a normal curve test is number of obs/exp pairs $− 1 − m$, where m is the number of parameters estimated from the data. For the uniform distribution, m was zero, and so we ignored it. However, in the normal curve we needed to calculate z-values, and in order to do that we needed a mean and a standard deviation. We got the mean and the standard deviation from the sample. By using the mean and the standard deviation from the sample, we are maximizing the chances that the normal curve will fit the data. The "penalty" we pay for getting the values from the actual data is that we lose 1 degree of freedom for each one that is estimated. Thus, in this case m = 2 : 1 for the mean and 1 for the standard deviation.

If you could specify the mean and the standard deviation a priori, you would not lose the degrees of freedom. For example, if you wanted to know if data fit an IQ distribution, you would use mean = 100 and stdev = 16 no matter what the sample values were, and m would equal zero.

Hypothesis Testing Steps

1. H_0: The observed frequencies could have come from a normal distribution.
   H_1: The observed frequencies are unlikely to have come from a normal distribution.
2. $\alpha = .05$ (default).
3. Test: Goodness of Fit Test (Test #12).
4. Decision rule: Reject H_0 if $\chi^2_4 > 9.488$.

The degrees of freedom is the number of observed/expected pairs $- 1 - m = 7 - 1 - 2 = 4$ (m = 2 because the mean and the standard deviation were estimated from the sample).

5. Calculation: Use a calculator or Excel to verify that the calculated value of the chi-square test statistic is 2.12, as shown in Exhibit 14-9.
6. Decision: Fail to reject because $2.12 < 9.488$ and the p-value of .7144 is much larger than .05.
7. Interpretation: Even though the distribution did not look perfectly normal, it did not come close to rejecting the hypothesis of normality. In practice, almost any distribution that is sort of peaked in the center will pass the normal GOF test. One cell is shaded because the expected frequency is less than 5, but unless the expected frequency is less than 1, there is no reason to collapse the rows unless the "% of chisq" value is quite high.

Note that the number of intervals, the width of the intervals, and the boundaries of the intervals can affect the shape of the distribution and thus affect the

EXHIBIT 14-9
Goodness of fit test for normal distribution.

Goodness of Fit Test				
observed	expected	O − E	(O − E)²/E	% of chisq
5	4.070	0.930	0.213	10.04
12	10.120	1.880	0.349	16.50
19	22.120	−3.120	0.440	20.79
31	33.640	−2.640	0.207	9.79
34	35.690	−1.690	0.080	3.78
27	26.390	0.610	0.014	0.67
24	19.970	4.030	0.813	38.43
152	152.000	0.000	2.116	100.00

2.12 chi-square
4 df
.7144 p-value

EXHIBIT 14-10
Normal curve GOF from MegaStat's descriptive statistics.

Descriptive Statistics	
	GPA
count	152
mean	2.5809
sample standard deviation	0.8182
sample variance	0.6695

Normal Curve GOF	
p-value	.3608
chi-square(df=5)	5.47
E	19.00
O(−1.15)	24
O(−0.67)	12
O(−0.32)	21
O(+0.00)	19
O(+0.32)	15
O(+0.67)	19
O(+1.15)	20
O(inf.)	22

test. However, this should not make a dramatic difference if the values are reasonable.

An Alternative Normal Curve Goodness of Fit Test

MegaStat's descriptive statistics program has an option for doing a normal curve goodness of fit test. The output for the grade point average example is shown in Exhibit 14-10. First the program determines the number of intervals it would use if it were to do a frequency distribution: eight in this case. Then it chooses z-values that divide the range into eight equal probability intervals. If the data are distributed normally, approximately an equal number of observations will fall into each interval. In this example, $19 = 152/8$ observations would fall in each interval with a perfect normal distribution. (Note that 19 is an integer in this example, but it could, and typically would, be a fractional value.)

NORMAL CURVE GOODNESS OF FIT TEST

Learning Activity 14.D–1

- Open **GPAdata.xls.**
- Replicate the frequency distribution and normal curve GOF calculations in Module 14.D.
- Use MegaStat I Random Number Generator to create a sample of approximately 100 exponentially distributed random numbers with mu equal to approximately 4 (fixed values, two decimal places).
- Use MegaStat to do a frequency distribution on the numbers and then do a normal curve goodness of fit test.
  - *Solution:* You should find the distribution skewed and should reject the hypothesis of normality.
- Use MegaStat I Descriptive Statistics with the normal goodness of fit option checked. Compare the results to those of your other GOF test.

The program counts the frequencies and then does a uniform distribution goodness of fit test. We see in Exhibit 14-10 that the chi-square of 5.47 has a p-value of .3608 and thus does not reject the assumption of normality.

So which test is better? Although the two tests will never have the exact same p-value, they generally will give the same conclusion. The Descriptive Statistics version is easier (just check the box), does not lose degrees of freedom from calculating parameters, and gets around the problem of small expected frequencies in the tails of the distribution. However, the traditional version gives you more control and is a good learning and review technique.

CHAPTER FIFTEEN

Time-Series Analysis

15.1 Introduction to Time Series and Forecasting (p. 270)

15.2 Linear Trend (p. 270)

15.3 Polynomial Trend (p. 272)

15.4 Exponential Trend (p. 278)

15.5 Which Trendline Is Best? (p. 283)

15.6 Moving Averages (p. 283)

15.7 Deseasonalization (p. 285)

Summary (p. 290)

Exercises (p. 291)

Module for Chapter Fifteen

15.A Durbin-Watson Statistic (p. 291)

15.1 Introduction to Time Series and Forecasting

A forecast is a prediction of a future value. For example, a company would like to forecast sales so that it can schedule the appropriate level of production. But isn't regression analysis about prediction? Indeed it is, but regression is a cross-sectional approach in which data on dependent and independent variables are collected at the same point in time. The prediction implies that if the same level of the independent variable is observed in the future, we can expect to observe the level of the dependent calculated in the regression equation.

Time-series analysis is based on the assumption that what has been happening over a period of time will continue to happen in the future. Of course, unforeseen economic, political, climatological, and technological events will wreak havoc on any time-series model that, by definition, assumes that the future is related to the past.

There are many forecasting methods and many books and courses devoted to the topic. The techniques discussed in this chapter are particular applications of regression analysis in which the independent variable is time-related. In the simplest case, the independent variable is just a series of numbers that count time periods, usually years but sometimes quarters or months. In Chapter 12, we said that you should not extrapolate; that is, you should not make predictions for values of the independent variable that are not in the range of the original data. However, that is the main concept in time-series analysis: trying to project the past into the future.

Basic Model

In time-series analysis, we are attempting to identify trends in the data that can be extended into the future. If the data are measured quarterly or monthly, the trend can be adjusted upward or downward by a seasonal factor. Anything that is not attributable to trend or season is considered error. The model is

$$Y = T * S * E \qquad \text{[15.1]}$$

where Y is the observed value of the time series, T is the trend component, and S is the seasonal index. A value of 1 for the index would have no effect; values greater or less than 1 would adjust the trend upward or downward for a given season. The E, or error component, would be any irregular part that could not be attributable to trend or season.[1]

In Sections 15.2, 15.3, and 15.4, we will examine some common **trendline** patterns. Here, we will treat the seasonal component, if there is one, as a part of the error component. In Section 15.7 we will discuss a method for identifying seasonal indexes.

15.2 Linear Trend

Exhibit 15-1 shows annual sales data for a company from 1993 through 2004 (**TS01-Linear.xls!Data**). Note that the horizontal axis for the scatterplot is the variable t, which is just the integers 1 through 12 used for numbering the

---

[1]Many forecasting books also include a cyclical index, C, to accommodate recurring patterns not attributable to seasonal factors. However, identifiable cyclical patterns are not common, and isolating them is beyond the scope of this chapter.

EXHIBIT 15-1
Sales data from 1993 through 2004 with a scatterplot.

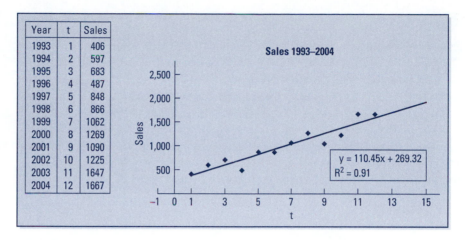

Year	t	Sales
1993	1	406
1994	2	597
1995	3	683
1996	4	487
1997	5	848
1998	6	866
1999	7	1062
2000	8	1269
2001	9	1090
2002	10	1225
2003	11	1647
2004	12	1667

Sales 1993–2004

$y = 110.45x + 269.32$
$R^2 = 0.91$

EXHIBIT 15-2
Regression output showing forecasts.

Regression Analysis

r^2	0.910		n	12
r	0.954		k	1
Std. Error of Estimate	131.119		Dep. Var.	**Sales**

Regression Output

						confidence interval	
variables		coefficients	std. error	t (df=10)	p-value	95% lower	95% upper
Intercept	a =	269.318					
t	b =	110.451	10.965	10.073	1.49E-06	86.020	134.882

ANOVA Table

Source	SS	df	MS	F	p-value
Regression	1,744,519.093	1	1,744,519.093	101.47	1.49E-06
Residual	171,921.157	10	17,192.116		
Total	1,916,440.250	11			

Predicted Values for: Sales

t	Predicted	95% Confidence Intervals		95% Prediction Intervals		Leverage
		lower	upper	lower	upper	
13	1,705.18	1,525.38	1,884.99	1,362.13	2,048.23	0.379
14	1,815.63	1,613.92	2,017.34	1,460.61	2,170.65	0.477
15	1,926.08	1,701.95	2,150.22	1,557.86	2,294.31	0.589

years. The scatterplot and the computations are simpler if we use t rather than the Year variable. Note that the scatterplot uses the "Markers and Lines" option to connect the dots.

If the company wanted to forecast sales for the next 3 years, it would extend the regression line as shown in Exhibit 15-1, and the height of the line for t = 13, 14, and 15 would be the forecasts for the years 2005, 2006, and 2007.

Exhibit 15-2 shows the MegaStat regression output with predictions (i.e., forecasts) for the next 3 years. The slope of 110.451 is the average amount of sales growth calculated for the data, and the linear model forecasts by assuming that rate of growth will continue in each subsequent year.

LINEAR TREND FIT   Learning Activity **15.2–1**

- Open **TS01-Linear.xls.**
- Use MegaStat | Correlation/Regression | Scatterplot to replicate Exhibit 15-1.
- Use MegaStat | Correlation/Regression | Regression to replicate Exhibit 15-2. Make sure to calculate the predicted values for t = 13, 14, and 15.
- Use MegaStat | Time Series | Trendline Curve Fit (specify linear trendline, start value of 1, forecast for 2 periods, starting with period 13; check the scatterplot box).
- Use a calculator and/or Excel to calculate at least one of the predicted values.

LINEAR TREND FIT PRACTICE   Learning Activity **15.2–2**

- Open **TS01-Linear-B.xls.**
- Use MegaStat to do a scatterplot and regression analysis similar to that in Learning Activity 15.1–1. In other words, do the scatterplot, the analysis with the regression option, and an analysis with the time-series option. Make predictions for 2006 and 2007.
  - ○ *Note:* The Time Series | Trendline Curve does not do anything that you cannot do with a scatterplot and regression; it is a more convenient way to do time-series operations.
- Use a calculator and/or Excel to calculate at least one of the predicted values.

Note that the leverage values are shaded, indicating extrapolation, that is, making predictions beyond the range of values of the original dependent variable. We indicated in the regression chapters (Chapters 12 and 13) that you should avoid extrapolation; however, extrapolation is the methodology of forecasting: extending the past into the future. Thus, the leverage values always indicate extrapolation in doing time-series forecasting, and the values always get larger the farther you extend the forecast.

Also note that the confidence intervals and the prediction intervals get wider as the forecast is extended; that makes intuitive sense. If we have had a stable pattern over several years, it would seem reasonable for it to continue for another year or so. However, even without major unforeseen events, the farther we try to extend the line, the less certain we are of our forecasts.

Once the company gets new data for the next year, it should see how the data compare with the forecast and also update the forecast with the new data point. Also, it should not blindly go by its calculated forecast; it always should look for external trends and events that might affect the company.

15.3   Polynomial Trend

Although a linear trend line is the most common, there are situations in which the time series is clearly nonlinear. Exhibit 15-3 shows an example of a nonlinear trend (**TS02-Quad.xls**). Assuming that the dependent variable, Y, is

EXHIBIT 15-3
Nonlinear trend.

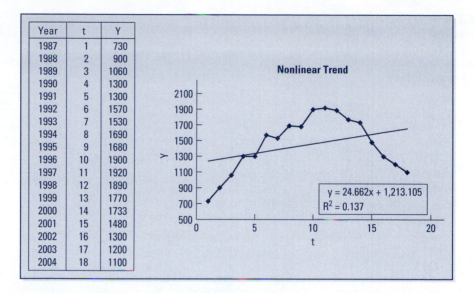

Year	t	Y
1987	1	730
1988	2	900
1989	3	1060
1990	4	1300
1991	5	1300
1992	6	1570
1993	7	1530
1994	8	1690
1995	9	1680
1996	10	1900
1997	11	1920
1998	12	1890
1999	13	1770
2000	14	1733
2001	15	1480
2002	16	1300
2003	17	1200
2004	18	1100

sales, the sales increase for several years, but around 1997 they level off for a few years and then start to decrease. The linear regression line is not a good fit. Not only is the r^2 low, the slope is upward, which would lead to a forecast of increased sales in the future in spite of the fact that the last several years have been trending downward.

Exhibit 15-4 shows the regression output. First of all, note that the sales for 3 years into the future predict increasing sales, as we noted in looking at the scatterplot. Also note that the regression is not statistically significant; this is not surprising when you look at the scatterplot. Obviously, fitting a straight line to curved data does not work, and so we need to fit a curved line. Before we do that, let's look a little more closely at how we can show that a linear function is not a good fit. In this case, it is evident from looking at the scatterplot, but it may not always be so obvious.

The output in Exhibit 15-4 also shows the residuals and a plot of the residuals. Recall that a residual is the difference between Y and Y′, that is, the difference between the actual sales value and the predicted value. In Chapter 12, one of the assumptions of regression was that error values (i.e., residuals) should be independent; in other words, the plot of the residuals should look random. However, the plot of the residuals in Exhibit 15-4 shows a distinct pattern. If the residuals tend to be close to the values on either side of them, the residuals are not independent. The official name for this is autocorrelation.

To see whether there is a statistically significant degree of autocorrelation, a **Durbin-Watson statistic** is calculated. Section 15.A discusses the computation and the interpretation of the Durbin-Watson statistic. In this example, the Durbin-Watson statistic of .21 is clearly significant, meaning that there is still a pattern in the data after the linear effect has been removed.

One nonlinear curve fit is a **polynomial** function. A polynomial function is of the form

$$Y = a + b_1X_1 + b_2X_2^2 + b_3X_3^3 \cdots b_kX^k \qquad \textbf{[15.2]}$$

EXHIBIT 15-4
Regression output showing residuals and plot of residuals.

Regression Analysis

r^2	0.137		n	18
r	0.370		k	1
Std. Error of Estimate	341.174		Dep. Var.	Y

Regression Output *confidence interval*

variables		coefficients	std. error	t (df=16)	p-value	95% lower	95% upper
Intercept	a =	1,213.105					
t	b =	24.662	15.500	1.591	.1312	−8.197	57.520

ANOVA Table

Source	SS	df	MS	F	p-value
Regression	294,668.013	1	294,668.013	2.53	.1312
Residual	1,862,398.265	16	116,399.892		
Total	2,157,066.278	17			

Observation	Y	Predicted	Total	=	Residual	+	Regression
1	730.0	1,237.8	−717.4		−507.8		−209.6
2	900.0	1,262.4	−547.4		−362.4		−185.0
3	1,060.0	1,287.1	−387.4		−227.1		−160.3
4	1,300.0	1,311.8	−147.4		−11.8		−135.6
5	1,300.0	1,336.4	−147.4		−36.4		−111.0
6	1,570.0	1,361.1	122.6		208.9		−86.3
7	1,530.0	1,385.7	82.6		144.3		−61.7
8	1,690.0	1,410.4	242.6		279.6		−37.0
9	1,680.0	1,435.1	232.6		244.9		−12.3
10	1,900.0	1,459.7	452.6		440.3		12.3
11	1,920.0	1,484.4	472.6		435.6		37.0
12	1,890.0	1,509.0	442.6		381.0		61.7
13	1,770.0	1,533.7	322.6		236.3		86.3
14	1,733.0	1,558.4	285.6		174.6		111.0
15	1,480.0	1,583.0	32.6		−103.0		135.6
16	1,300.0	1,607.7	−147.4		−307.7		160.3
17	1,200.0	1,632.4	−247.4		−432.4		185.0
18	1,100.0	1,657.0	−347.4		−557.0		209.6

Durbin-Watson = 0.21			0.0	0.0	0.0	Sum
			2,157,066.3	1,862,398.3	294,668.0	
			SSTotal=	SSE	+ SSR	

Predicted Values for: Y

		95% Confidence Intervals		95% Prediction Intervals		
t	Predicted	lower	upper	lower	upper	Leverage
19	1,681.67	1,326.00	2,037.34	875.69	2,487.65	0.242
20	1,706.33	1,321.50	2,091.17	887.07	2,525.60	0.283
21	1,731.00	1,316.45	2,145.54	897.36	2,564.63	0.329

Residuals

LINEAR TREND FIT ON CURVED DATA   Learning Activity **15.3–1**

- Open **TS02-Quad.xls!Data**.
- Use MegaStat | Correlation/Regression | Scatterplot to replicate Exhibit 15-3.
- Replicate Exhibit 15-4 using MegaStat | Time Series | Trendline Curve Fit (specify linear trendline, start value of 1, forecast for 3 periods, starting with period 19; check the following option boxes: plot residuals and Durbin-Watson).
- Use a calculator and/or Excel to calculate at least one of the predicted values.

Although we will use this function for nonlinear curve fitting, the simplest version of it is when k = 1 is bivariate linear regression: $Y = b_0 + b_1X$, where the intercept is b_0 and the slope is b_1.

As you may recall from algebra courses, every additional power of X adds another bend to the curve. Since our scatterplot appears to have one bend, let's start with a second-degree polynomial, sometimes called a quadratic curve fit:

$$Y = a + b_1X_1 + b_2X^2 \qquad \text{[15.3]}$$

To perform this analysis you would create a new variable, t^2, as shown in Exhibit 15-5.

With these variables you would do a multiple regression using t and t^2 as the independent variables. You also could use the MegaStat | Time Series/Forecasting | Trendline Curve Fit option, which will create the appropriate variables automatically.

Exhibit 15-6 shows the output for quadratic curve fit. First of all, note that the R^2 is up to 94.7% compared with 13.7% for the linear curve fit and that the p-value for the ANOVA is very small, indicating a strong degree of relationship that is confirmed in the scatterplot.

The Durbin-Watson value of 1.42 is in the gray area, indicating that there still may be some autocorrelation in the data. Examining the residuals scatterplot, we see that the residuals do not look entirely random. However, the quadratic curve accounts for nearly 95% of the variance, and so we should not be too concerned about whether there may be a pattern in the remaining 5% even if the Durbin-Watson statistic is small enough to be clearly significant.

Looking at the predicted values for 3 years into the future, we see that, unlike the linear trend, they are decreasing. In fact, if we pushed it a bit further, they would be predicted to become negative, which could not happen since the data represent sales. It is possible that the sales are heading for zero, but it is also possible that the curve is about to turn around and head back up again. Therein lies a problem with polynomial curve fitting: Although we can get a good fit for a given set of data, it is risky to extrapolate the curve very far into the future.

Since a quadratic function improved our curve fit compared with a linear function, would adding even higher powers improve the fit? Every power adds another bend in the curve that can accommodate the data better. Although this will improve the R^2, it probably does not make any logical sense and can lead to bizarre forecasts (see Learning Activity 15.3–3).

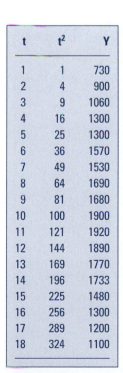

t	t^2	Y
1	1	730
2	4	900
3	9	1060
4	16	1300
5	25	1300
6	36	1570
7	49	1530
8	64	1690
9	81	1680
10	100	1900
11	121	1920
12	144	1890
13	169	1770
14	196	1733
15	225	1480
16	256	1300
17	289	1200
18	324	1100

EXHIBIT 15-5
Data for quadratic curve fit.

**EXHIBIT 15-6
Output for
quadratic
curve fit.**

Regression Analysis

R^2	0.947			
Adjusted R^2	0.940		n	18
R	0.973		k	2
Std. Error of Estimate	87.609		Dep. Var.	Y

Regression Output

						confidence interval	
variables		coefficients	std. error	t (df=15)	p-value	95% lower	95% upper
Intercept	a =	389.657					
t	b1 =	271.696	16.850	16.125	6.97E-11	235.782	307.610
t^2	b2 =	−13.002	0.862	−15.088	1.79E-10	−14.839	−11.165

ANOVA Table

Source	SS	df	MS	F	p-value
Regression	2,041,937.380	2	1,020,968.690	133.02	2.85E-10
Residual	115,128.898	15	7,675.260		
Total	2,157,066.278	17			

Durbin-Watson = 1.42

Predicted Values for: Y

			95% Confidence Intervals		*95% Prediction Intervals*		
t	t^2	Predicted	lower	upper	lower	upper	Leverage
19	361	858.2	710.0	1,006.4	619.8	1,096.6	0.630
20	400	622.9	440.4	805.3	361.8	883.9	0.955
21	441	361.5	140.4	582.6	72.1	650.9	1.402

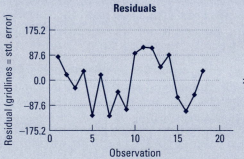

Residuals

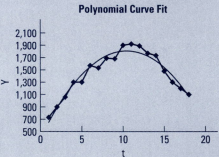

Polynomial Curve Fit

Data:

t	t^2	Y
1	1	730
2	4	900
3	9	1,060
4	16	1,300
5	25	1,300
6	36	1,570
7	49	1,530
8	64	1,690
9	81	1,680
10	100	1,900
11	121	1,920
12	144	1,890
13	169	1,770
14	196	1,733
15	225	1,480
16	256	1,300
17	289	1,200
18	324	1,100

POLYNOMIAL CURVE FIT　　　　Learning Activity **15.3–2**

- Open **TS02-Quad.xls!Data2.**
- Create the values in the t^2 column by squaring the values in Column C; the data should look like those in Exhibit 15-5. Also, create squared values for $t = 18, 19, 20$ to be used for prediction. See **TS02-Quad.xls!Data2_done.**
- Run MegaStat multiple regression, using the t and t^2 variables as the independent variables and Y as the dependent variable.
  - Select "Predictor values from worksheet cells" and select cells B21:D23.
  - Check "Durbin-Watson" and "Plot Residuals by Observation."
- Compare the output with that in Exhibit 15-6.
- Replicate Exhibit 15-6, using MegaStat | Time Series | Trendline Curve Fit (specify 2nd degree polynomial trendline, start value of 1, forecast for 3 periods, starting with period 19; check the following option boxes: scatterplot, plot residuals, and Durbin-Watson). (Your output will not be positioned or sized exactly as in Exhibit 15-6, but the values should be the same.) See **TS02-Quad.xls!Solution.**

EXPERIMENTING WITH HIGHER-DEGREE POLYNOMIALS　　　　Learning Activity **15.3–3**

- Open **TS02-Quad.xls.**
- Run MegaStat | Time Series | Trendline Curve Fit (specify 6th-degree polynomial trendline, start value of 1, forecast for 3 periods, starting with period 19; check the scatterplot box).
- Right-click the box on the scatterplot that shows the equation and R^2 and select "Clear."
- Note that the line has several bends and fits the data points fairly closely; also, the R^2 is .981 versus .947 with the quadratic (second-degree) polynomial.
- It would seem that the higher-degree polynomial is a good fit, and it is; however, look at the predicted values. The prediction for 2007 ($t = 21$) is 3657.2, which is nearly twice as high as the largest input value for the dependent variable.
- To see the predictions graphically, right-click on the trendline and select "Format Trendline." Click the Options tab; in the "Forecast forward" box, type 3 (or use the spinner buttons); click "OK." See **TS02-Quad.xls!6th_degree_polynomial.**
- These data illustrate why it is risky to forecast with higher-degree polynomials. Although the fit is good within the range of the actual data, the forecasts for even a few periods into the future can be extreme. The data appear to trending downward at the end; there is nothing to indicate an extreme turn upward. This happens because of the t^6 term. Even if the coefficient is small, any value raised to the sixth power becomes large. If the coefficient happened to be negative, the forecast would be very small or even negative.

In looking at the data and the scatterplot in Exhibit 15-3, it appears that something happened around 1997 that caused sales to level off and start decreasing. Perhaps new technology and/or new competitors led to a decrease in sales. Although polynomial curve fitting is a sophisticated technique and MegaStat can handle the computations easily, it might make more sense to look at these data as two linear time series, one for the increasing data and the other for the decreasing data.

15.4 Exponential Trend

The equation for the average[2] rate of growth is shown in Equation [15.4]:

$$\text{Average rate of growth} = \left(\frac{\text{FV}}{\text{PV}}\right)^{(1/n)} - 1 \qquad \textbf{[15.4]}$$

However, this formula looks only at the starting and ending values—the PV (present value) and FV (future value)—and ignores the values between them. With regression, we can estimate the average rate of change by fitting a curve that accommodates all the data points.

Exhibit 15-7 illustrates time-series data, showing an **exponential** growth pattern (**TS03-Exp.xls!Data**), that is, a constant percentage growth (compounding) represented by the sales accelerating by the end of the time series. If the linear regression line is extended for forecasting, it appears that it will underestimate the way the sales are trending. Indeed, if you look at the forecast for 2007 (time period 19), you will see that the forecast is barely higher than the actual value for 2004.

Exhibit 15-7 also shows a pattern in the residuals and a significant Durbin-Watson value. Both indicate that there may be a better curve fit even though the linear fit is very significant and has an r^2 of nearly 94%.

We will now see how to fit a compound growth line to these data. Equation [15.5] shows the basic financial equation for compound growth. If we substitute Y' for FV, a for PV, b for $(1 + i)$, and X for n, we get the financial model stated in regression terms, as shown in Equation [15.6], where a represents the intercept and b represents the slope.

$$\text{FV} = \text{PV}(1 + i)^n \qquad \textbf{[15.5]}$$

$$Y = ab^x \qquad \textbf{[15.6]}$$

Equation [15.6] is an exponential equation; that is, the variable, X, is an exponent. To use this model with linear regression, we need to convert it to a linear equation. This is done by taking the logarithm[3] of both sides, as shown

AVERAGE RATE OF CHANGE   Learning Activity **15.4–1**

- Open **TS03-Exp.xls!Data.**
- Calculate the average rate of change by using Equation [15.4].
- Check the solution in **TS03-Exp.xls!Average_rate_solution.** Look at the cell formulas.

[2]In Chapter 2, we said that you should avoid the use of *average* and instead use *mean*; however, *average* is appropriate here because the mean implies summing and dividing by n, and that is not what this formula does. In fact, the mean percent change gives the wrong answer.

[3]It could be either common (base 10) log or natural (base e) log. This example will use common logs.

EXHIBIT 15-7
Exponential sales growth with linear curve fit.

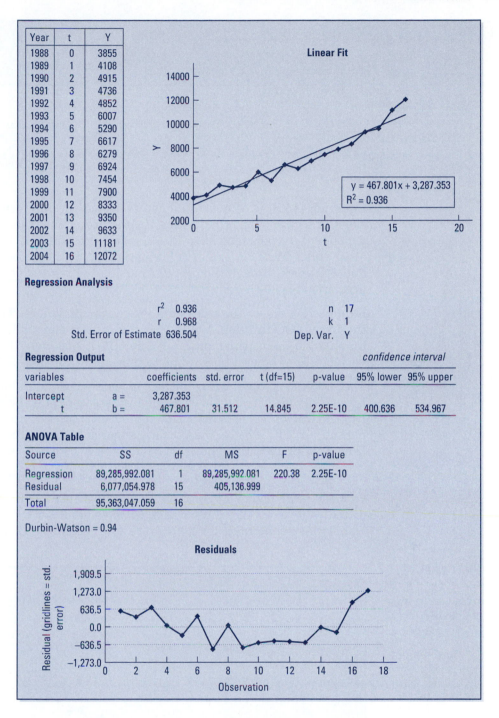

Year	t	Y
1988	0	3855
1989	1	4108
1990	2	4915
1991	3	4736
1992	4	4852
1993	5	6007
1994	6	5290
1995	7	6617
1996	8	6279
1997	9	6924
1998	10	7454
1999	11	7900
2000	12	8333
2001	13	9350
2002	14	9633
2003	15	11181
2004	16	12072

Linear Fit: $y = 467.801x + 3{,}287.353$, $R^2 = 0.936$

Regression Analysis

r^2	0.936		n	17
r	0.968		k	1
Std. Error of Estimate	636.504		Dep. Var.	Y

Regression Output   *confidence interval*

variables		coefficients	std. error	t (df=15)	p-value	95% lower	95% upper
Intercept	a =	3,287.353					
t	b =	467.801	31.512	14.845	2.25E-10	400.636	534.967

ANOVA Table

Source	SS	df	MS	F	p-value
Regression	89,285,992.081	1	89,285,992.081	220.38	2.25E-10
Residual	6,077,054.978	15	405,136.999		
Total	95,363,047.059	16			

Durbin-Watson = 0.94

in Equation [15.7], and applying the rules of logarithms to the right-hand side, as shown in Equation [15.8]:

$$\log(Y) = \log(ab^x) \qquad \textbf{[15.7]}$$

$$\log(Y) = \log(a) + \log(b)X \qquad \textbf{[15.8]}$$

LINEAR CURVE FIT ON EXPONENTIAL DATA

Learning Activity **15.4–2**

- Open **TS03-Exp.xls!Data**.
- Replicate Exhibit 15-7, using MegaStat | Time Series | Trendline Curve Fit (specify linear trendline, start value of 0, forecast for 3 periods, starting with period 17; check the following option boxes: scatterplot, plot residuals, and Durbin-Watson).
- The layout and sizing will not be exactly the same as in Exhibit 15-7, but make sure the values are the same.

Equation [15.8] is a linear function in which the intercept is log(a) and the slope is log(b). What this means in practice is that we take the log of the dependent variable and then fit a linear regression line to the new variable. MegaStat's "Time Series Curve Fit" option can do this procedure automatically, but let's work through the procedure using the regression option and make a prediction for 2007.

Exhibit 15-8 shows the sales data (Y) converted to logs. This was done using the Excel LOG function. Notice that the values seem to fit a straight line better than do the original data in Exhibit 15-7. Also note that the independent variable, X, is labeled t according to time-series convention.

The regression output using the log values is shown in Exhibit 15-9. The result is very significant, and the r^2 is slightly greater than the linear fit. Also, the Durbin-Watson value is no longer significant, and so it appears that the exponential curve fit is better than the linear curve fit. Using the slope and intercept from Exhibit 15-9, the regression equation is shown in Equation [15.9]:

$$Y' = 3.5905 + .0291(t) \qquad \textbf{[15.9]}$$

To make a prediction for 2007, we would substitute $t = 19$ and calculate a predicted value of 4.1425. But how can we have predicted sales of 4.1425 for 2007 when the actual sales for 2004 were over 12,000? The answer is that the

EXHIBIT 15-8
Sales data converted to logs and scatterplot of the log values.

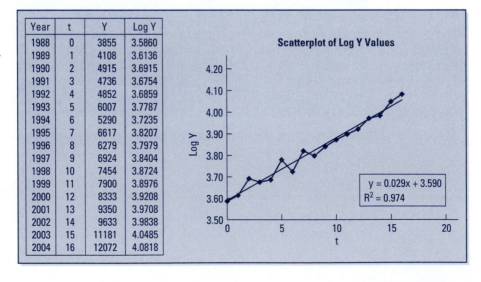

Year	t	Y	Log Y
1988	0	3855	3.5860
1989	1	4108	3.6136
1990	2	4915	3.6915
1991	3	4736	3.6754
1992	4	4852	3.6859
1993	5	6007	3.7787
1994	6	5290	3.7235
1995	7	6617	3.8207
1996	8	6279	3.7979
1997	9	6924	3.8404
1998	10	7454	3.8724
1999	11	7900	3.8976
2000	12	8333	3.9208
2001	13	9350	3.9708
2002	14	9633	3.9838
2003	15	11181	4.0485
2004	16	12072	4.0818

Scatterplot of Log Y Values

y = 0.029x + 3.590
$R^2 = 0.974$

EXHIBIT 15-9
Linear regression on the log Y values.

Regression Analysis

r^2	0.974	n	17
r	0.987	k	1
Std. Error of Estimate	0.025	Dep. Var.	log(Y)

Regression Output

						confidence interval	
variables		coefficients	std. error	t (df=15)	p-value	95% lower	95% upper
Intercept	a =	3.5905					
t	b =	0.0291	0.001	23.557	2.91E-13	0.026	0.032

coefficients in terms of the model: ab^x

3894.518 = a, beginning value
1.069 = b, growth factor
6.92% average rate of change

ANOVA Table

Source	SS	df	MS	F	p-value
Regression	0.3444	1	0.3444	554.95	2.91E-13
Residual	0.0093	15	0.0006		
Total	0.3537	16			

predicted value is a log value. To convert it back to the original units, you calculate the inverse log. To find the inverse log for a common log, use the log value as an exponent for the base 10, as shown in Equation]15.10][4]:

$$10^{4.1425} = 13883.53 \qquad \textbf{[15.10]}$$

The average rate of change is estimated by taking the inverse log of the slope: $10^{.0291} = 1.0692$. Since this is the $(1 + i)$ term in Equation [15.5], we subtract 1 to get the average rate of growth estimated from the regression analysis as 6.92%.

We also can take the inverse log of the intercept to get the PV term in Equation [15.5] and calculate the predicted values by using the financial form shown in Equation [15.11]:

$$Y' = 3894.52(1.0692)^t \qquad \textbf{[15.11]}$$

Calculating the average rate of change using Equation [15.4], we find an average rate of change of 7.4%, as shown in Equation [15.12]:

$$\left(\frac{FV}{PV}\right)^{1/n} - 1 = \left(\frac{12072}{3855}\right)^{1/16} - 1 = 1.0740 - 1 = .0740 \qquad \textbf{[15.12]}$$

So which is best: 6.92% from the regression analysis or 7.40% from Equation [15.4]? If you want a mathematically precise measure of average percent change for a specific set of data, Equation [15.4] is preferable. Since the regression method is based on sample data, it is not as precise, but because the real world usually is not precise, perhaps that is better. In fact, you could take the inverse log of the confidence interval values to get a confidence interval for the estimated average rate of change.

[4]This value is calculated using the numbers shown. If you do the calculation in Excel with no rounding, you will get 13883.45.

EXPONENTIAL CURVE FIT USING MᴇɢᴀSᴛᴀᴛ REGRESSION

Learning Activity **15.4–3**

- Open **TS03-Exp.xls!Data.**
- Create the values in the Log(Y) column by using Excel's LOG function; the data should look like those in Exhibit 15-8 (solution: **TS03-Exp.xls!Log_scatterplot**). Use MegaStat to do the scatterplot for the log values.
- Use MegaStat's regression option to replicate Exhibit 15-9.
- Use Excel or a calculator to calculate the predicted value for 2007 and take the inverse log of the predicted value, as shown in Equations [15.9] and [15.10].

EXPONENTIAL CURVE FIT USING MᴇɢᴀSᴛᴀᴛ TIME SERIES

Learning Activity **15.4–4**

- Open **TS03-Exp.xls!Data.**
- Replicate the values in Exhibit 15-7 and the predicted values in Equations [15.9] and [15.10] using MegaStat | Time Series | Trendline Curve Fit.
  - ◦ Specify the following:
    - ▪ Cells D3:D19 as the data.
    - ▪ Exponential (log) trendline.
    - ▪ Start value of 0.
    - ▪ Forecast for 3 periods, starting with period 17.
    - ▪ Check the following option boxes: scatterplot, plot residuals, and Durbin-Watson.
- Verify that the values are the same as they are in Exhibit 15-7 and Equations [15.9] and [15.10].

PRACTICE WITH EXPONENTIAL CURVE FITTING

Learning Activity **15.4–5**

- Open **TS03-Exp-B.xls!Data.** These are enrollment data from a midwestern college from 1994 to 2005.
- Use MegaStat to do a linear curve fit and make a forecast for 2007.
- Create the log values (see the **Log_data** worksheet) and use MegaStat to do a linear curve fit and make a forecast for 2007. Calculate the average percent change in enrollment.
- Use MegaStat | Time Series | Trendline Curve Fit to verify your linear and exponential curve fit. See the solution in the **Linear_output** and **Exponential_output** worksheets.

15.5   Which Trendline Is Best?

The answer to this question is simple: whatever shape best fits the data. People sometimes think that because polynomial and exponential methods are more complicated, they must be better. However, fitting a curved line to straight data is no better than fitting a straight line to curved data.

Do a scatterplot and look at the data. With MegaStat and/or Excel, it is easy to try different curves; however, avoid "curve shopping" and particularly avoid using higher-power polynomial curves just to improve the fit. If an exponential curve seems to fit best, you should have a rationale for why there would be a constant rate of change.

Even though nonlinear regression can be useful, in most cases a linear function will work about as well and will be simpler to use and explain. Even if there appears to be a nonlinear trend over a longer period of time, often a linear function will work well for the most recent years.

Also, realize that the techniques in this chapter are just a sampling of the forecasting methods available. As way mentioned in Section 15.1, many books, courses, and software programs are devoted to forecasting.

15.6   Moving Averages

A **moving average** is a technique for smoothing time-series data by averaging successive periods of data. (Yes, it should be called a moving mean, but *moving average* is the traditional name.) A moving average can be used as a simple forecasting method when the forecast for the next period is simply the average of the previous few periods; however, moving averages are used more often for smoothing data before fitting one of the trendlines discussed above and also for calculating seasonal indexes as shown in Section 15.7. Equation [15.13] and Exhibit 15-10 illustrate a four-term moving average applied to the data from Section 15.3. The output on the right is from MegaStat's moving average option with the number of periods specified as four. Each term in the moving average is the mean of the previous four values. For example, the first value is calculated as shown in Equation [15.13]:

$$997.5 = \frac{730 + 900 + 1060 + 1300}{4} \qquad \textbf{[15.13]}$$

Note that the moving average is associated with the year at the end of the moving window; for example, the first moving average is associated with year 4. This makes sense because this is the average at that point in time. However, since the moving average is for 4 years, you logically could associate it with the middle of the 4 years: between years 2 and 3. However, Excel cannot put data at row 2½, and so MegaStat uses the former method. One way to get around this problem would be to use an odd number of periods, say, three or five, and this brings up the question of the appropriate number of periods.

As we will see in the next section, if you are smoothing quarterly or monthly data, then 4 or 12 periods make sense. For annual data, use the lowest number

EXHIBIT 15-10
Data smoothed with a four-term moving average.

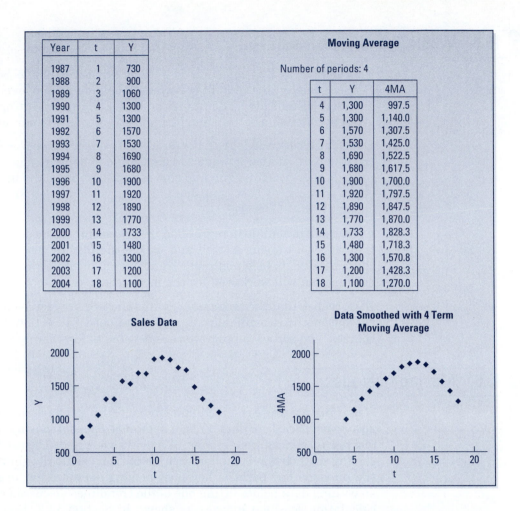

Year	t	Y
1987	1	730
1988	2	900
1989	3	1060
1990	4	1300
1991	5	1300
1992	6	1570
1993	7	1530
1994	8	1690
1995	9	1680
1996	10	1900
1997	11	1920
1998	12	1890
1999	13	1770
2000	14	1733
2001	15	1480
2002	16	1300
2003	17	1200
2004	18	1100

Moving Average

Number of periods: 4

t	Y	4MA
4	1,300	997.5
5	1,300	1,140.0
6	1,570	1,307.5
7	1,530	1,425.0
8	1,690	1,522.5
9	1,680	1,617.5
10	1,900	1,700.0
11	1,920	1,797.5
12	1,890	1,847.5
13	1,770	1,870.0
14	1,733	1,828.3
15	1,480	1,718.3
16	1,300	1,570.8
17	1,200	1,428.3
18	1,100	1,270.0

CALCULATE MOVING AVERAGES WITH EXCEL AND MEGASTAT

Learning Activity 15.6–1

- Open **Moving Average.xls.**
- Calculate the four-term moving average using the Excel AVERAGE() function. (See the **Solution** worksheet.)
- Calculate the four-term moving average using MegaStat | Time Series/Forecasting | Moving Average.
- Do a scatterplot of the original data and the smoothed data. Your output should look similar to that in Exhibit 15-11.

of periods necessary to give a degree of smoothing. If you have k periods in your moving average, you will lose k – 1 data points. In Exhibit 15-10 the four-term moving average reduces the number of data points from 18 to 15. Also, if you use too many terms in the moving average, you may smooth out more than random fluctuations and affect the fitting of the trend curve. As with any technique, look at the results of the smoothing and use common sense.

EXPERIMENTING WITH MOVING AVERAGES

Learning Activity **15.6–2**

- Open **Moving Average.xls**.
- Calculate the 3-, 5-, 7-, and 15-term moving averages and plot the results. You will find in these data that the pattern is so pronounced that it will survive even extreme smoothing.
- Calculate the 1-term and 18-term moving averages. What do they show?
  - *Answer:* A 1-term moving average does not average anything, and an 18-term moving average does not move; it is just the arithmetic mean.

15.7 Deseasonalization

When data are measured within a year (usually quarterly or monthly), we often see recurring patterns called seasonal effects. Seasonal effects can come from seasons in businesses that are affected by weather. They also can come from holidays, school semesters, events such as conventions and trade shows, and factors unique to a particular business or industry. Exhibit 15-11 shows 7 years of quarterly sales data (**TS04-DS.xls!Data**).

EXHIBIT 15-11
Quarterly sales data 1998–2004 illustrating a seasonal pattern.

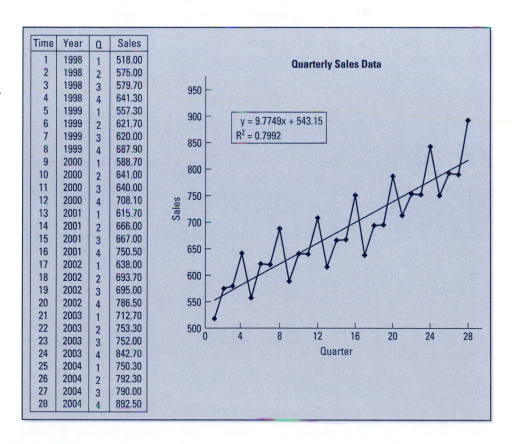

Time	Year	Q	Sales
1	1998	1	518.00
2	1998	2	575.00
3	1998	3	579.70
4	1998	4	641.30
5	1999	1	557.30
6	1999	2	621.70
7	1999	3	620.00
8	1999	4	687.90
9	2000	1	588.70
10	2000	2	641.00
11	2000	3	640.00
12	2000	4	708.10
13	2001	1	615.70
14	2001	2	666.00
15	2001	3	667.00
16	2001	4	750.50
17	2002	1	638.00
18	2002	2	693.70
19	2002	3	695.00
20	2002	4	786.50
21	2003	1	712.70
22	2003	2	753.30
23	2003	3	752.00
24	2003	4	842.70
25	2004	1	750.30
26	2004	2	792.30
27	2004	3	790.00
28	2004	4	892.50

Quarterly Sales Data

$y = 9.7749x + 543.15$
$R^2 = 0.7992$

Looking at the pattern within each year, you see a peak in the fourth quarter and a low in the first quarter. That pattern would be typical of a retail business with large Christmas sales.

Although the r^2 of .7992 is respectable (and statistically significant), the seasonal pattern is just error variation in the linear regression model. If we dampen the seasonal fluctuation, the regression fit should be even better. Also, if we do not adjust for seasonality, forecasts will not be accurate. In particular for these data, the regression line will underestimate for a fourth-quarter prediction and overestimate for a first-quarter prediction.

Also in these data, the first data point is below the regression line and the last data point is well above that line. Those two points "tugging" in opposite directions on each end of the line may act as outliers and make the regression slope steeper than it should be.

How do we get rid of the seasonal effect? Remember that the multiplicative model in Equation [15.1] stated that $Y = T * S * E$. If we divide by a **seasonal index** we will have canceled out the seasonal effect:

$$Y = \frac{T * \cancel{S} * E}{\cancel{S}} = T * E \qquad \textbf{[15.14]}$$

Exhibit 15-12 shows the output from the MegaStat | Time Series | Deseasonalization option. Since there is a large amount of calculation, in practice you undoubtedly would use MegaStat or Excel to do the calculations; however, we will go through the calculations for columns A through D so that you can see how the **deseasonalization** process works.

Column A: Centered Moving Average

Recall that in Section 15.6 we indicated that there was a problem if we wanted to associate a four-term moving average with the center of the four terms: It would involve putting the number between the second and third terms. However, tables (including Excel) are not amenable to putting numbers between two rows. The method for getting around this problem is to use a **centered moving average.** For the first term in Column A, you would combine the sums of the first four quarters with those of the second four quarters and divide by 8 since there would be eight numbers involved. This average would be associated with the third time period. Equation [15.15] shows the calculation of the first centered moving average value.

$$583.413 = \frac{(518.0 + 575.0 + 579.7 + 641.3) + (575.0 + 579.7 + 641.3 + 557.3)}{8}$$

$$\textbf{[15.15]}$$

Not only does this get around the centering problem, it also leads to better smoothing since there are eight terms rather than four. Also note that each of the four quarters is represented twice in each centered moving average. Since all four quarters are involved in the centered moving average, the average should not show any seasonal pattern.

Column B: Ratio to Centered Moving Average

Column B is calculated by dividing the data column (Sales, in this example) by the value in Column A, the centered moving average (CMA). If there is a

**EXHIBIT 15-12:
Deseasonaliza-
tion of quarterly
data.**

Centered Moving Average and Deseasonalization

t	Year	Quarter	Sales	A Centered Moving Average	B Ratio to CMA	C Seasonal Indexes	D Sales Deseasonalized
1	1998	1	518.0			0.935	554.17
2	1998	2	575.0			0.996	577.10
3	1998	3	579.7	583.413	0.994	0.985	588.75
4	1998	4	641.3	594.163	1.079	1.084	591.46
5	1999	1	557.3	605.038	0.921	0.935	596.21
6	1999	2	621.7	615.900	1.009	0.996	623.97
7	1999	3	620.0	625.650	0.991	0.985	629.68
8	1999	4	687.9	631.988	1.088	1.084	634.44
9	2000	1	588.7	636.900	0.924	0.935	629.80
10	2000	2	641.0	641.925	0.999	0.996	643.34
11	2000	3	640.0	647.825	0.988	0.985	649.99
12	2000	4	708.1	654.325	1.082	1.084	653.07
13	2001	1	615.7	660.825	0.932	0.935	658.69
14	2001	2	666.0	669.500	0.995	0.996	668.43
15	2001	3	667.0	677.588	0.984	0.985	677.41
16	2001	4	750.5	683.838	1.097	1.084	692.17
17	2002	1	638.0	690.800	0.924	0.935	682.55
18	2002	2	693.7	698.800	0.993	0.996	696.23
19	2002	3	695.0	712.638	0.975	0.985	705.85
20	2002	4	786.5	729.425	1.078	1.084	725.37
21	2003	1	712.7	744.000	0.958	0.935	762.46
22	2003	2	753.3	758.150	0.994	0.996	756.05
23	2003	3	752.0	769.875	0.977	0.985	763.74
24	2003	4	842.7	779.450	1.081	1.084	777.21
25	2004	1	750.3	789.075	0.951	0.935	802.69
26	2004	2	792.3	800.050	0.990	0.996	795.19
27	2004	3	790.0			0.985	802.33
28	2004	4	892.5			1.084	823.14

Calculation of Seasonal Indexes

	1	2	3	4	
1998			0.994	1.079	
1999	0.921	1.009	0.991	1.088	
2000	0.924	0.999	0.988	1.082	
2001	0.932	0.995	0.984	1.097	
2002	0.924	0.993	0.975	1.078	
2003	0.958	0.994	0.977	1.081	
2004	0.951	0.990			
mean:	0.935	0.997	0.985	1.084	4.001
adjusted:	0.935	0.996	0.985	1.084	4.000

CALCULATE DESEASONALIZATION BY USING EXCEL

Learning Activity **15.7–1**

- Open **TS04-DS!Worksheet.xls.**
- Calculate the seasonal indexes and deseasonalize the data by using basic Excel calculator functions. Your final result should look like Exhibit 15-12. Also see **Moving Average!Worksheet_solution.xls.** Examine the cell formulas.

consistent seasonal pattern, the values for any quarter should be approximately the same. For example, the values for the fourth quarter are all approximately 1.08, meaning 8% above the moving average.

Column C: Seasonal Indexes

In this step, the ratios for each quarter in Column B are collected in the table below the data. The columns represent the four quarters, and there is a row for each year. Look at the table and see how each of the values in Column B is placed in the table. If there is a consistent seasonal pattern, the numbers in each column should be fairly similar, and we see that that is the case in this example.

The mean of each column then is calculated. The sum of the four means should be 4.000. We see that the sum in this example is 4.001. Although that is very close, we can make it exactly 4.000 by multiplying each mean by the adjustment factor shown in Equation [15.16]:

$$\text{adj} = \frac{4}{\text{sum}} = \frac{4}{4.001} = .9998 \qquad \textbf{[15.16]}$$

In this example, the effect of the adjustment cannot be seen even at the third decimal place, but it changes the means enough that the sum is exactly 4.000. In general, the adjustment does not make much difference; if it does, that is probably an indication that the seasonal pattern is not very consistent.

The adjusted means are the seasonal indexes, and they are transferred to Column C for each year. Look at Column C and note how the values for each year are the same as the adjusted means from the table.

Column D: Deseasonalized Data

In this column we apply Equation [15.14] to deseasonalize the data: The data values in the data column (Sales) are divided by the corresponding seasonal index. Note in particular that the data values below the average are divided by a number less than 1, making them larger (the first-quarter values have the most upward adjustment), and the values above the average are divided by a value greater than 1, making them smaller (the fourth quarter); thus, the seasonal effect is canceled out (see Exhibit 15-12).

Exhibit 15-13 shows the MegaStat output from the time-series deseasonalization option. Note how the original data (Sales) has much more variability than the deseasonalized line. In comparing Exhibit 15-13 to Exhibit 15-11, you see that the r^2 for the deseasonalized data is substantially higher (.9750 versus .7992). The slope of the deseasonalized data is somewhat less (9.2080 versus 9.7749), which indicates that the low first quarter at the beginning and the high fourth quarter at the end were acting as outliers to rotate the regression line upward.

Predicting with Deseasonalized Data

Assume the company wants to predict sales for the fourth quarter of 2005. Since the last data point for the fourth quarter of 2004 was t = 28, counting four more quarters to the fourth quarter of 2005, t becomes 32. Substituting

EXHIBIT 15-13
Plot of sales data with deseasonalized values.

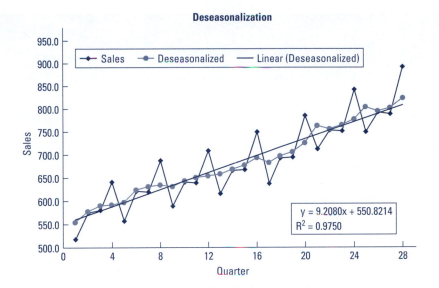

Deseasonalization

$$y = 9.2080x + 550.8214$$
$$R^2 = 0.9750$$

DESEASONALIZATION WITH MEGASTAT   Learning Activity 15.7–2

- Open **TS04-DS!Data.xls.**
- Replicate Exhibit 15-12 and Exhibit 15-13 by using MegaStat I Time Series/Forecasting I Deaseasonalization.

FORECASTING WITH DESEASONALIZED DATA   Learning Activity 15.7–3

- Open **TS04-DS!Deseasonalization output.xls.**
- Use MegaStat to do a regression analysis on the deseasonalized data. Make a forecast for the fourth quarter of 2005 and reseasonalize the data as shown in Section 15.7.

PRACTICE WITH DESEASONALIZATION (QUARTERLY DATA)   Learning Activity 15.7–4

- Open **TS04-DS-B!Data.xls.** The file has 7 years of quarterly sales data.
- Use MegaStat I Time Series/Forecasting I Deaseasonalization to deseasonalize the data. Select quarterly data and specify the first quarter of 1997 as the first data period.
- Use Excel or a calculator to calculate at least one of the values in the CMA, ratio to CMA, and deseasonalization columns.
- Use MegaStat to do a regression analysis on the deseasonalized data, using t as the independent variable. Make a forecast for third quarter of 2004 (t = 31).
- Reseasonalize the forecast. See **TS04-DS-B.xls!Solution.xls cell B99.** Look at the cell formula.

PRACTICE WITH DESEASONALIZATION (MONTHLY DATA)

Learning Activity **15.7–5**

- Open **TS04-DS-B!Data.xls.** The file has 7 years of quarterly sales data.
- Use MegaStat | Time Series/Forecasting | Deseasonalization to deseasonalize the data. Select quarterly data and specify Jan. 1998 as the first data period.
- Use Excel or a calculator to calculate at least one of the values in the CMA, ratio to CMA, and deseasonalization columns.
- Use MegaStat to do a regression analysis on the deseasonalized data, using t as the independent variable. Make a forecast for May 2005 (t = 89).
- Reseasonalize the forecast. See **TS04-DS-C.xls!Solution.xls cell B156.** Look at the cell formula.

t = 32 into the regression equation shown in Exhibit 15-13, we get a predicted value of 845.48, as shown in Equation [15.17]:

$$Y' = 9.2080(32) + 550.8214 = 845.48 \qquad \textbf{[15.17]}$$

However, since the prediction was made using deseasonalized data, we must perform one more step: reseasonalizing the data. Since the data were deseasonalized by *dividing* by a seasonal index, the predicted value is reseasonalized by *multiplying* the corresponding seasonal index. Since we are predicting for the fourth quarter, the seasonal index is 1.084 and the actual predicted value is $845.48 * 1.084 = 916.5$.

Summary

Conceptual

There are many techniques for business forecasting; indeed, many books are devoted to this subject. This chapter focused on techniques related to regression analysis.

The basic idea of time-series forecasting is to project the past into the future. This approach is based on the assumption that whatever has been happening in the past and the present will continue in the same manner into the future.

In many instances a linear trend will suffice, at least for the short term. Polynomial curve fitting can fit very complex curves to data but often gives bizarre forecasts, especially when higher-power terms are used. The exponential curve that models compound growth is often applicable in a business setting in which there is a fairly steady rate of growth.

When data are collected on a quarterly or monthly basis, there can be seasonal patterns. The chapter showed one method for deseasonalizing data.

Applied

- Always look at a scatterplot and visually determine what would be the best trend fit.
- The Durbin-Watson statistic measures patterns in data (autocorrelation). Be able to interpret it.
- Be able to use MegaStat to do a linear, polynomial, or exponential curve fit and interpret the output and make predictions.

- From an exponential curve fit regression output, be able to calculate the estimated average percent change.
- Be able to calculate seasonal indexes, deseasonalize the data, and make a forecast using the deseasonalized data given monthly or quarterly data.

Exercises

The exercises and data are found in **Ch_15_Time_Series.xls** in the exercises folder of the CD.

No.	Content
1	Linear trend
2	Linear trend—low rsq
3	Polynomial trend
4	Polynomial trend
5	Exponential decreasing
6	Exponential increasing
7	Deseasonalization—quarterly
8	Deseasonalization—monthly

Module for Time-Series Analysis

15.A   DURBIN-WATSON STATISTIC

The Durbin-Watson value, d, is calculated from the residuals. In Equation [15.18], residuals are shown as $e_i = Y_i - Y'_i$:

$$d = \frac{\sum_{i=2}^{n} (e_i - e_{i-1})^2}{\sum_{i=1}^{n} e_i^2} \qquad [15.18]$$

The numerator compares each residual with the one immediately preceding it; for example, when i = 3, the difference would be $e_3 - e_2$. If there is a pattern in

---

CALCULATE THE DURBIN-WATSON VALUE BY USING EXCEL

Learning Activity **15.A–1**

- Open **DW_practice!Data.xls.**
- Use MegaStat to do a regression analysis using t and Y as the independent and dependent variables. Check the Durbin-Watson option box.
- Use Excel to calculate the Durbin-Watson value by using Equation [15.18].
- Look at the shaded cells in: **DW_practice!Solution1.xls.** Look at the underlying cell formulas.

EXAMPLE OF A POSITIVE DURBIN-WATSON VALUE

Learning Activity **15.A–2**

- Open **DW_practice!Data2.xls.**
- Use MegaStat | Time Series | Trendline Curve Fit (specify linear trendline, start value of 1; check the following option boxes: Scatterplot, Output Residuals, Durbin-Watson).
- Note the alternating pattern in the scatterplot and the residuals plot.
- Use the Durbin-Watson table to verify that the calculated Durbin-Watson value is significant.

the residuals, the adjacent residuals will be close to each other, and the Durbin-Watson value will be small as the squared differences of the adjacent residuals are squared and summed. The denominator is just the sum of the squared residuals and the SSE value in the ANOVA table.

Durbin-Watson values can range from 0 to 4, with a value of 2 in the center indicating no autocorrelation. Values less than 2 indicate positive autocorrelation, that is, a pattern in the residuals. Exhibit 15-15 shows a table of Durbin-Watson 5% critical values (see also **DW_table.xls**). In other words, how small does the Durbin-Watson value have to be in order to be significant? Find the row corresponding to the sample size, n, and the column corresponding to the number of predictor variables, k. If the calculated Durbin-Watson value is less than dL, we can say that there is a statistically significant degree of autocorrelation; if the Durbin-Watson value is greater than dU, it is not significant. If the calculated Durbin-Watson value is between dL and dU, the answer is "maybe."

For the example in Section 15.3, n = 18 and k = 1. The values from the table are dL = 1.16 and dU = 1.40. The calculated Durbin-Watson value of .21 is well below dL, and so there is a significant degree of positive autocorrelation.

We typically are looking for positive autocorrelation; however, a Durbin-Watson value greater than 2 implies negative autocorrelation. Negative autocorrelation results from a systematic alternating pattern of positive and then negative residuals. The test values for negative autocorrelation are 4 – dU and 4 – dL, respectively.

The interpretation of Durbin-Watson values is summarized in Exhibit 15-14.

EXHIBIT 15-14
Interpretation of Durbin-Watson value.

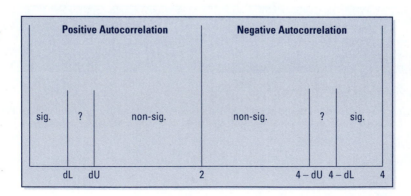

EXHIBIT 15-15   **Table of Durbin-Watson 5% critical values.**

	Durbin-Watson 5% critical values				k = number of independent variables, n = sample size							
	k = 1		k = 2		k = 3		k = 4		k = 5		k = 6	
n	dL	dU	dL	dU	dL	dU	dL	dU	dL	dU	dL	dU
6	0.61	1.40										
7	0.70	1.36	0.47	1.90								
8	0.76	1.33	0.56	1.78	0.37	2.29						
9	0.82	1.32	0.63	1.70	0.45	2.13	0.30	2.59				
10	0.88	1.32	0.70	1.64	0.53	2.02	0.38	2.41	0.24	2.82		
11	0.93	1.32	0.76	1.60	0.59	1.93	0.44	2.28	0.32	2.64	0.20	3.00
12	0.97	1.33	0.81	1.58	0.66	1.86	0.51	2.18	0.38	2.51	0.27	2.83
13	1.01	1.34	0.86	1.56	0.71	1.82	0.57	2.09	0.44	2.39	0.33	2.69
14	1.04	1.35	0.91	1.55	0.77	1.78	0.63	2.03	0.51	2.30	0.39	2.57
15	1.08	1.36	0.95	1.54	0.81	1.75	0.69	1.98	0.56	2.22	0.45	2.47
16	1.11	1.37	0.98	1.54	0.86	1.73	0.73	1.94	0.61	2.16	0.50	2.39
17	1.13	1.38	1.02	1.54	0.90	1.71	0.78	1.90	0.66	2.10	0.55	2.32
18	1.16	1.39	1.05	1.54	0.93	1.70	0.82	1.87	0.71	2.06	0.60	2.26
19	1.18	1.40	1.07	1.54	0.97	1.69	0.86	1.85	0.75	2.02	0.65	2.21
20	1.20	1.41	1.10	1.54	1.00	1.68	0.89	1.83	0.79	1.99	0.69	2.16
21	1.22	1.42	1.12	1.54	1.03	1.67	0.93	1.81	0.83	1.96	0.73	2.12
22	1.24	1.43	1.15	1.54	1.05	1.66	0.96	1.80	0.86	1.94	0.77	2.09
23	1.26	1.44	1.17	1.54	1.08	1.66	0.99	1.79	0.89	1.92	0.80	2.06
24	1.27	1.45	1.19	1.55	1.10	1.66	1.01	1.78	0.92	1.90	0.84	2.04
25	1.29	1.45	1.21	1.55	1.12	1.65	1.04	1.77	0.95	1.89	0.87	2.01
26	1.30	1.46	1.22	1.55	1.14	1.65	1.06	1.76	0.98	1.87	0.90	1.99
27	1.32	1.47	1.24	1.56	1.16	1.65	1.08	1.75	1.00	1.86	0.92	1.97
28	1.33	1.48	1.26	1.56	1.18	1.65	1.10	1.75	1.03	1.85	0.95	1.96
29	1.34	1.48	1.27	1.56	1.20	1.65	1.12	1.74	1.05	1.84	0.97	1.94
30	1.35	1.49	1.28	1.57	1.21	1.65	1.14	1.74	1.07	1.83	1.00	1.93
31	1.36	1.50	1.30	1.57	1.23	1.65	1.16	1.74	1.09	1.83	1.02	1.92
32	1.37	1.50	1.31	1.57	1.24	1.65	1.18	1.73	1.11	1.82	1.04	1.91
33	1.38	1.51	1.32	1.58	1.26	1.65	1.19	1.73	1.13	1.81	1.06	1.90
34	1.39	1.51	1.33	1.58	1.27	1.65	1.21	1.73	1.14	1.81	1.08	1.89
35	1.40	1.52	1.34	1.58	1.28	1.65	1.22	1.73	1.16	1.80	1.10	1.88
36	1.41	1.52	1.35	1.59	1.30	1.65	1.24	1.72	1.18	1.80	1.11	1.88
37	1.42	1.53	1.36	1.59	1.31	1.66	1.25	1.72	1.19	1.79	1.13	1.87
38	1.43	1.53	1.37	1.59	1.32	1.66	1.26	1.72	1.20	1.79	1.15	1.86
39	1.43	1.54	1.38	1.60	1.33	1.66	1.27	1.72	1.22	1.79	1.16	1.86
40	1.44	1.54	1.39	1.60	1.34	1.66	1.28	1.72	1.23	1.79	1.18	1.85
41	1.45	1.55	1.40	1.60	1.35	1.66	1.30	1.72	1.24	1.78	1.19	1.85
42	1.46	1.55	1.41	1.61	1.36	1.66	1.31	1.72	1.25	1.78	1.20	1.85
43	1.46	1.56	1.42	1.61	1.37	1.66	1.32	1.72	1.27	1.78	1.21	1.84
44	1.47	1.56	1.42	1.61	1.37	1.66	1.33	1.72	1.28	1.78	1.23	1.84
45	1.48	1.57	1.43	1.61	1.38	1.67	1.34	1.72	1.29	1.78	1.24	1.83
46	1.48	1.57	1.44	1.62	1.39	1.67	1.34	1.72	1.30	1.77	1.25	1.83
47	1.49	1.57	1.44	1.62	1.40	1.67	1.35	1.72	1.31	1.77	1.26	1.83
48	1.49	1.58	1.45	1.62	1.41	1.67	1.36	1.72	1.32	1.77	1.27	1.83
49	1.50	1.58	1.46	1.63	1.41	1.67	1.37	1.72	1.33	1.77	1.28	1.82
50	1.50	1.58	1.46	1.63	1.42	1.67	1.38	1.72	1.33	1.77	1.29	1.82
60	1.55	1.62	1.51	1.65	1.48	1.69	1.44	1.73	1.41	1.77	1.37	1.81
70	1.58	1.64	1.55	1.67	1.52	1.70	1.49	1.74	1.46	1.77	1.43	1.80
80	1.61	1.66	1.59	1.69	1.56	1.72	1.53	1.74	1.51	1.77	1.48	1.80
90	1.63	1.68	1.61	1.70	1.59	1.73	1.57	1.75	1.54	1.78	1.52	1.80
100	1.65	1.69	1.63	1.72	1.61	1.74	1.59	1.76	1.57	1.78	1.55	1.80
120	1.69	1.72	1.67	1.74	1.65	1.75	1.63	1.77	1.62	1.79	1.60	1.81
140	1.71	1.74	1.70	1.75	1.68	1.77	1.67	1.78	1.65	1.80	1.64	1.81
160	1.73	1.75	1.72	1.77	1.70	1.78	1.69	1.79	1.68	1.81	1.66	1.82
180	1.74	1.77	1.73	1.78	1.72	1.79	1.71	1.80	1.70	1.81	1.69	1.83
200	1.76	1.78	1.75	1.79	1.74	1.80	1.73	1.81	1.72	1.82	1.71	1.83

Summary and Integration

16.1   A Brief Review (p. 296)

16.2   Putting It Together (p. 297)

16.1   A Brief Review

Let's go back and briefly summarize what we have covered and provide a framework for integration.

Chapter 1: Defined statistics and looked at types of data (quantitative and qualitative).

Descriptive Statistics

Chapter 2: Summarized data with descriptive statistics.

- Measures of central tendency (mean) and variation (SSX-variance-stdev).

Chapter 3: Summarized data with frequency distributions.

- Frequency distributions show the shape of data and are an important tool for descriptive statistics.

Probability Chapters

Chapter 4: Introduced basic probability concepts (defined probability as a number between 0 and 1); also discussed probability concepts and independence.

Chapter 5: Discrete probability distributions:

- Introduced the general concept of a discrete distribution.
- Discussed the binomial distribution as the main example of a discrete distribution.

Chapter 6: Normal distribution and how to use it.

Theoretical Foundations of Statistical Inference

Chapter 7: Sampling distribution as the theoretical foundation of statistics; central limit theorem states that sampling distributions of means will be normal.

Chapter 8: Application of sampling distributions: confidence intervals and sample size.

Chapter 9: Introduction to the concept of hypothesis testing:

- Seven steps of hypothesis testing.

Applications of Statistical Inference

Chapter 10: Tests for means and proportions (one- and two-group tests).

Chapter 11: ANOVA for multiple groups:

- Looked at One-Factor ANOVA in detail; showed how and when to use Randomized Blocks; briefly introduced Two-Factor ANOVA.

Chapter 12: Regression analysis:

- The scatterplot is the graphical model for regression.
- Regression analysis tests strength of relationship and makes predictions.

Chapter 13: Multiple regression: prediction with two or more variables.

Chapter 14: Chi-square tests for independence and goodness of fit.

Chapter 15: Time-series and forecasting:

- Looked at some basic models using regression.

TAKING ANOTHER LOOK — Learning Activity **16.1–1**

- Skim through the book, looking at chapter and section headings.
- Read the chapter summaries.
- Read the test summaries in Appendix B.

16.2 Putting It Together

The most challenging thing in a statistics course is knowing what to do with data. In the real world, you will not know that you are supposed to do an ANOVA test simply because you are at the end of the ANOVA chapter.

When faced with a set of data, the first thing you should do is look at it carefully. That seems obvious, but it is a step that often is skipped. Identify whether the variables are qualitative or quantitative, look for outliers, and see if you can determine what would be appropriate further analyses for the data.

It is almost always a good idea to do a frequency distribution and basic descriptive statistics (mean, standard deviation, boxplot, outliers) even if you are planning to do other analyses.

The next big decision is whether you are looking at differences between groups (tests for means) or relationships within groups (regression).

The **Summary.xls** workbook attempts to summarize the book on one page. Going across the columns helps guide you to the appropriate test or procedure. It also is cross-referenced by section numbers and the test summary numbers (Test 1 through Test 12).

PUTTING IT TOGETHER — Learning Activity **16.1–2**

- Open **Procedures.xls.**
- Column B has various descriptions of situations and/or datasets. Your task is to select the appropriate procedure or procedures from the summary of statistical procedures sheet. Column C has the code number from the sheet, and Column D has the name. Columns C and D appear to be blank because white was selected as the font color. To see what is in the cell, you can select the cell and read its contents in the formula bar, or you can select a cell and click on the font color button to select a font color other than white.

  Try to determine the correct procedure before you look at the answer.
  Column E has random numbers (hidden). If you click in Column E and then click the Sort button, it will sort the examples randomly.

Excel Statistical Functions

The values in parentheses are the information that function needs. These values are called *arguments*. In the examples below, the "data" argument means a cell, a block of cells, or a named range that you want to use as input to the function.

All functions below are available from the Function Wizard and have more detailed descriptions in the Excel help system. They are shown in all caps, but that is not required.

AVERAGE(data): calculates the arithmetic mean.

SUMSQ(data): squares and then sums data values.

DEVSQ(data): calculates the sum of squared deviations (SSX) for a set of data.

VAR(data): calculates sample variance.

STDEV(data): calculates the sample standard deviation.

>   *Note:* **VARP**() and **STDEVP**() calculate the population variance and the standard deviation.

AVEDEV(data): calculates the mean absolute deviation.

MEDIAN(data): calculates the midpoint of a set of data.

QUARTILE(data, q): where q = 1, 2, 3 to calculate Q1, Q2, Q3.

PERCENTILE(data, k): where k is a number from 0 to 1 specifying the percentile.

MODE(data): finds the most frequently occurring data value.

MAX(data): finds the largest number in the range.

MIN(data): finds the smallest number in the range.

RAND(): calculates a random number between 0 and 1. Pressing the F9 function key calculates a different value. To get larger random numbers, multiply by a constant; for example, RAND()*100 will give random numbers between 0 and 100.

NORMSDIST(z): calculates the cumulative probability given a z-value. *Note:* Cumulative probability is the probability of being below z.

NORMDIST(x, mean, stdev, 1): calculates the cumulative probability given an input value, x, with a mean and a standard deviation. Make sure to type the "1" at the end.

NORMSINV(p): calculates the z-value corresponding to a cumulative probability.

NORMINV(p, mean, stdev): calculates the data value corresponding to a cumulative probability, given a mean and a standard deviation.

TDIST(t, degrees of freedom, tails): calculates the probability of being above or outside the t-value specified; t must be nonnegative. If you have a negative t-value, use the absolute value in the function.

TINV(probability, degrees of freedom): calculates t-value corresponding to the probability value. The probability is assumed to be two-tailed. If you want the one-tailed t-value, double the input probability value.

CONFIDENCE(1 − confidence level, std. dev., size): calculates the margin of error for the confidence interval using z. If you want a 95% confidence interval, the first argument is $1 - .95 = .05$. To actually construct a confidence interval, you would have to add and subtract the function to and from the sample mean to get the upper and lower limits.

FDIST(F, df1, df2): calculates the probability that an F-ratio will be larger than the given value.

FINV(probability, df1, df2): calculates the F-value associated with an upper-tail probability.

CHIDIST(chi-square, degrees of freedom): calculates the probability that a chi-square value will be larger than the given value.

CHIINV(probability, degrees of freedom): calculates the chi-square value associated with an upper-tail probability.

Hypothesis Test Summaries

B.1   Mean versus Hypothesized Value (Test #1)

B.2   Compare Two Independent Groups (Test #2)

B.3   Paired Observations (Test #3)

B.4   Proportion versus Hypothesized Value (Test #4)

B.5   Compare Two Independent Proportions (Test #5)

B.6   One-Factor ANOVA (Test #6)

B.7   Randomized Blocks ANOVA (Test #7)

B.8   Two-Factor ANOVA (Test #8)

B.9   ANOVA Test for Regression (Test #9)

B.10 t-Test for Regression Slope (Test #10)

B.11 Contingency Table Test for Independence (Test #11)

B.12 Goodness of Fit Test (Test #12)

B.1   Mean versus Hypothesized Value (Test #1)

test statistic: $t = \dfrac{\overline{X} - \mu_0}{s/\sqrt{n}}$ $\overline{X}$ = sample mean

d.f. = n − 1 $\qquad$ s = sample standard deviation

n = sample size

μ_0 = hypothesized value

Data form:

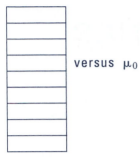

versus μ_0

When to use: To compare the mean of a sample to some hypothesized value.

If the population standard deviation is known (which is rare) or if the sample size is large, the test statistic is calculated the same way but is a z-value.

B.2   Compare Two Independent Groups (Test #2)

test statistic: $t = \dfrac{(\overline{X}_1 - \overline{X}_2) - D_0}{\sqrt{\dfrac{s_p^2}{n_1} + \dfrac{s_p^2}{n_2}}}$

d.f. = $n_1 + n_2 - 2$

where pooled variance: $s_p^2 = \dfrac{SSX_1 + SSX_2}{df_1 + df_2}$

Data form:

X1 $\qquad$ X2

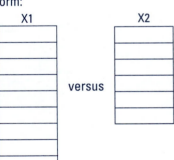

versus

When to use: To compare the means from two independent groups.

There is a large z-test version of this test, but since you never know the population variance, it is always appropriate to do the t-test even if you have large samples.

The groups do not have to be the same size, but it is better if they are approximately the same size.

If the variances are significantly different, do the MegaStat test for unequal variances.

B.3 Paired Observations (Test #3)

Sometimes called paired differences, paired comparisons, or dependent samples

Test statistic: $t = \dfrac{\bar{d} - D_0}{s_d/\sqrt{n}}$

d.f. $= n - 1$ (where n is the number of pairs)

Data form:

X1	X2

subtract

d

> **When to use:** When you have paired data and want to test the mean difference.
>
> Note that when you subtract the pairs to get differences, this test is identical to test 1; only the notation is different.

B.4 Proportion versus Hypothesized Value (Test #4)

Test statistic: $z = \dfrac{p - \pi_0}{\sqrt{\dfrac{\pi_0(1 - \pi_0)}{n}}}$

Data: a sample proportion: $p = \dfrac{X}{n}$

Compared to hypothesized proportion: π_0

> **When to use:** To compare a sample proportion to some hypothesized value.
>
> *Note:* This test can be performed more precisely using the binomial distribution.

B.5 Compare Two Independent Proportions (Test #5)

Data: two sample proportions from independent groups

$p_1 = \dfrac{X_1}{n_1}$ and $p_2 = \dfrac{X_2}{n_2}$

> **When to use:** To compare proportions from two independent groups.

Test statistic: $z = \dfrac{(p_1 - p_2) - D_0}{\sqrt{\dfrac{p_c(1 - p_c)}{n_1} + \dfrac{p_c(1 - p_c)}{n_2}}}$

where p_c is the combined proportion: $p_c = \dfrac{X_1 + X_2}{n_1 + n_2}$ or $p_c = \dfrac{n_1 p_1 + n_2 p_2}{n_1 + n_2}$

B.6   One-Factor ANOVA (Test #6)

Sometimes called one-factor completely randomized ANOVA, independent groups ANOVA, one-way ANOVA, single-factor ANOVA

Data form:

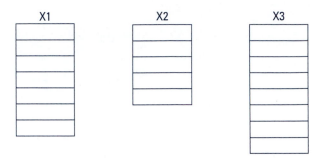

When to use: To test whether independent groups have different means. Usually used for three or more groups but also works for two groups and gives the same results as test 3. The groups do not have to be the same size.

If there is a significant result, post hoc analysis helps identify how the groups are different from each other.

The test statistic is the F-ratio, and the results usually are presented in an ANOVA table:

Source	SS	df	MS	F
Treatment	SST	$k - 1$	$\dfrac{SST}{k-1}$	$\dfrac{MST}{MSE}$
Error	SSE	$N - k$	$\dfrac{SSE}{N-k}$	
Total	SSTotal	$N - 1$		

Where:
  k = number of treatments, i.e., groups
  N = total number of observations in all groups

B.7   Randomized Blocks ANOVA (Test #7)

Sometimes called two-factor ANOVA without replication, repeated measures ANOVA

Data form:

	Treatment A	Treatment B	Treatment C	Treatment D
Block 1				
Block 2				
Block 3				
Block 4				
Block 5				
Block 6				

When to use: To test whether treatment means are different when there are blocks of data. The data in each block have to "go together," usually by being from the same person.

There is an F-test for the treatment and an F-test for the blocks. Although we are most interested in the treatment means, the test for block also can be useful.

If there is a significant result, post hoc analysis helps identify how the groups are different from each other.

The test statistics are two F-ratios, and the results usually are presented in an ANOVA table:

Source	SS	df	MS	F
Treatment	SST	$k-1$	$\dfrac{SST}{k-1}$	$\dfrac{MST}{MSE}$
Blocks	SSB	$b-1$	$\dfrac{SSB}{b-1}$	$\dfrac{MSB}{MSE}$
Error	SSE	$N-k$	$\dfrac{SSE}{N-k}$	
Total	SSTotal	$N-1$		

Where:
k = number of treatments, i.e., groups
b = number of blocks, i.e., rows
N = total number of observations in all groups

B.8   Two-Factor ANOVA (Test #8)

Data form:

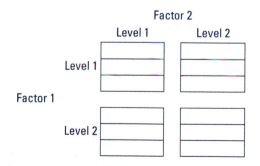

When to use: To test means of independent groups when there are measurements on two factors. The groups must be the same size.

If there is a significant result, post hoc analysis helps identify how the groups are different from each other.

The test statistics are three F-ratios that usually are presented in an ANOVA table:

Source	SS	df	MS	F
Factor 1	SS1	$r - 1$	$\dfrac{SS1}{r - 1}$	$\dfrac{MST}{MSE}$
Factor 2	SS2	$c - 1$	$\dfrac{SS2}{c - 1}$	$\dfrac{MSB}{MSE}$
Interaction	SSI	$(r - 1)(c - 1)$	$\dfrac{SS1}{(r - 1)(c - 1)}$	$\dfrac{MSI}{MSE}$
Error	SSE	$rc(m - 1)$	$\dfrac{SSE}{rc(m - 1)}$	
Total	SSTotal	$rcm - 1$		

Where:
r = number of levels of factor 1
n = number of levels of factor 2
m = number of observations per cell

B.9 ANOVA Test for Regression (Test #9)

Data form:

Simple Regression

X	Y

Multiple Regression

Y	X1	X2

When to use: To test whether there is a statistically significant amount of predictability in a regression model.

The test statistic is an F-ratio that usually is presented in an ANOVA table:

Source	SS	df	MS	F
Regression	SSR	k	$\dfrac{SSR}{k}$	$\dfrac{MSR}{MSE}$
Residual	SSE	$n - k - 1$	$\dfrac{SSE}{n - k - 1}$	
Total	SSTotal	$n - 1$		

Where:
   k = number of predictor, X, variables; k = 1 for simple regression
   n = sample size

B.10   t-Test for Regression Slope (Test #10)

Test statistic:
d.f. = n − k − 1

$$t = \frac{b - 0}{s_b}$$

k = number of predictor, X, variables; k = 1 for simple regression
n = sample size
s_b = standard error of the slope (get this value from the computer output)

Data form: regression data; see test #9

When to use: To test whether a regression slope is significantly different from zero.

For simple regression, this test is the same as the ANOVA test: $t^2 = F$.

B.11   Contingency Table Test for Independence (Test #11)

Data form: a 2 by 2 or larger table containing observed frequencies; the table rarely would have more than five rows or columns.

	Col 1	Col 2
Row 1		
Row 2		

When to use: To test whether the factors representing the rows and columns are statistically independent.

Test statistic:
$$\chi^2 = \sum_{all\ cells} \left[\frac{(O - E)^2}{E} \right]$$

d.f. = (number of rows − 1)(number of columns − 1)

where O and E are the observed and expected values in each cell

1. Calculate expected values for each cell using $\dfrac{(\text{row total})(\text{column total})}{\text{grand total}}$
2. For each cell:
   - Subtract O − E.
   - Square result.
   - Divide by E.
3. Sum for all cells:
   - The sum is the chi-square value.

B.12 Goodness of Fit Test (Test #12)

Sometimes called G.O.F. or GOF

Data form: observed frequencies paired with expected frequencies

observed	expected

> When to use: To test whether observed frequencies match the expected values predicted by some probability distribution.

Test statistic: $\chi^2 = \displaystyle\sum_{\text{all cells}} \left[\dfrac{(O - E)^2}{E} \right]$

d.f. = number of obs/exp pairs $-1 - m$

where m = number of the parameters estimated from the observed data

For example, if you estimated the mean and standard deviation for a normal curve from the sample data, m would equal 2; for a uniform distribution, m = 0.

1. For each obs/exp pair:
   - Subtract O − E.
   - Square result.
   - Divide by E.
2. Sum for all pairs:
   - The sum is the chi-square value.

Glossary and Key Equations

adjusted R^2	Used in multiple regression. A way of adjusting R^2 to compensate for the number of independent variables. The adjusted R^2 is used primarily to compare regression models with different numbers of independent variables.
alpha (α)	Symbol for level of significance.
alternative hypothesis (H_1)	The hypothesis we accept if we reject the null hypothesis.
ANOVA (analysis of variance)	A hypothesis testing technique based on partitioning variance into explained and unexplained (error) components.
arithmetic mean	See *mean*.
autocorrelation	Used in time series. A measure of whether there is still a pattern in data after a particular curve fit.
average	The sum of numbers divided by the number of numbers. Formally called the arithmetic mean. See *mean*.
binomial distribution	A discrete probability distribution that calculates the probability of x occurrences in n trials where the probability of occurrence on any trial is p.
boxplot	A graphical descriptive display sometimes called a box and whisker display. The ends of a box represent the first and third quartiles; a line in the middle of the box represents the median. The maximum and minimum values are represented by lines on each side of the box (whiskers). Refer to the text discussion to see an example and to the discussion of how outliers are shown.
centered moving average	Used in time series. A moving average technique that centers the result on a particular time period. For example, the first value of a centered moving average for quarterly data would sum time periods (1 + 2 + 3 + 4) + (2 + 3 + 4 + 5) divided by 8 and would be associated with time period 3.
central limit theorem	The sampling distribution of sample means will approach a normal distribution as the sample size becomes large no matter what the shape of the population distribution is.
chi-square value	A test statistic based on the chi-square distribution.
classical probability	Probabilities calculated by counting the number of outcomes in a sample space that qualify for a particular event relative to the number of outcomes in the entire sample space.
collectively exhaustive	Comprising the entire sample space. Heads and tails are collectively exhaustive for a coin toss experiment.
combinations	The number of ways one can select r things from n when one does not care about the exact arrangement. It is the

number of permutations divided by r!. In other words, n!/(r!(n − r)!). Sometimes you might see this written as nCr.

complement	All the events in the sample space not included in any particular event. If A represents an event, ~A is the complement.

$$P(A) + P(\sim A) = 1 \qquad P(A \ and \sim A) = 0$$
$$P(\sim A) = 1 - P(A)$$

conditional probability	The probability of one event given that another event has occurred. The vertical bar ($|$) reads "given."

$$P(A|B) = \frac{P(A \ and \ B)}{P(B)} \qquad or \qquad P(B|A) = \frac{P(A \ and \ B)}{P(A)}$$

confidence interval	Sample statistic $\pm$ margin of error. By adding and subtracting the margin of error, we get a lower limit and an upper limit known as a confidence interval. If the confidence level is 95%, there is a 95% chance that any given confidence interval includes the population parameter.

confidence
interval, mean

$$\overline{X} \pm z \frac{\sigma}{\sqrt{n}} \quad \text{when } \sigma \text{ is known (which is rare)}$$

$$\overline{X} \pm z \frac{s}{\sqrt{n}} \quad \text{when } s \text{ is used to estimate } \sigma \text{ (acceptable if the sample is large)}$$

$$\overline{X} \pm t \frac{s}{\sqrt{n}} \quad \text{when } s \text{ is used to estimate } \sigma$$

The last expression is always the proper one to use when one is using the sample standard deviation, s, but it is especially important if the sample size is small.

confidence interval, proportion	$p \pm z\sqrt{\dfrac{p(1 - p)}{n}}$

contingency table	A joint frequency table that shows occurrences of two factors represented by the rows and the columns. For example, if you wanted to know if houses with swimming pools also tended to have basements, you would have a 2 by 2 table where the rows were "Pool-No" and "Pool-Yes" and the columns were "Basement-No" and "Basement-Yes." The cells would have the number of houses in each category.
continuous random variable	See *random variable.*
continuous variable	Refers to an infinite number of points along a scale and could have more and more precise measurement with more precise instrumentation.

correlation coefficient	A measure of the relationship of two variables. A correlation coefficient, r, is the square root of r^2. It can range from -1 to $+1$. The sign is positive or negative depending on the slope of the regression line.
correlation matrix	A table (i.e., matrix) showing all possible pairs of correlations among a set of variables.
critical value	The comparison value in a decision rule.
cross-sectional data	Data that are collected at a point in time or at least with no time sequencing.
cumulative frequencies	The number of occurrences in frequency distribution at and below a given value or interval.
data	Symbols that represent things or events. Data are usually words or numbers. See also *quantitative data* and *qualitative data*
dataset	A general term for a collection of data values; can refer to a sample or a population.
decision rule	Step 4 of the hypothesis testing process, stating the criterion for rejecting the null hypothesis. Always of the form "Reject the null hypothesis if . . ." A decision rule can be stated in terms of a test statistic, for example, "Reject if z > 1.645," or in terms of a p-value, for example, "Reject if the p-value is <.05."
definitional form	Calculation of the mean, SSX, variance, and standard deviation by calculating and listing each deviation, squaring the deviations, summing the squared deviations to get SSX, dividing SSX by $n-1$ to get the variance, and taking the square root of the variance to get the standard deviation. This procedure shows how these measures work and also allows detection of outliers.
degrees of freedom	A value needed to use the t, F, and chi-square distributions. The value depends on the distribution and the context. Do not try to read a literal meaning into the phrase; an explanation of why it is called degrees of freedom is beyond an introductory statistics course.
deseasonalization	Used in time series. The removal of a seasonal effect by dividing by a seasonal index.
deviation	$\text{deviation} = (X_i - \text{mean})$ The distance of any given observation from the mean.
df or d.f.	Abbreviation for degrees of freedom.
discrete random variable	See *random variable*
discrete variable	Refers to specific, countable outcomes or events.

Durbin-Watson statistic (DW)	Used in time series. A measure of autocorrelation. A value of 2 means no autocorrelation; a value near 0 implies autocorrelation. A pattern in the residuals.
empirical rule	Approximately two-thirds of a normal curve is within 1 standard deviation of the mean, 95% is within 2 standard deviations, and almost all is within 3 standard deviations.
error tolerance (E)	In sample size estimation, how close we want the sample value to be to the population value with a given level of confidence. Corresponds to the margin of error in a confidence interval.
event	An outcome or a group of outcomes. For example, if an event is defined as a card suit of diamonds for a randomly drawn card, any card drawn would be a specific outcome, but any of the 13 outcomes with diamonds would qualify for the event called diamonds.
expected value, discrete probability distribution	The mean outcome one would expect in the long run with a discrete probability distribution.$$\mu = E(X) = \sum (X \cdot P(X))$$
experiment	A process that leads to a well-defined outcome. A simple experiment would be noting whether a tossed coin came up heads or tails. In a more general sense, an experiment is any assessment or measurement.
exponential	Used in time series. A function in which the variable is an exponent. Used to model the constant rate of growth in time-series analysis. For example, $Y = 1.06^X$ is an exponential function that represents a 6% rate of compound growth.
extrapolation	Used in regression. Attempting to predict Y by using an X value that is not in the range of the original data.
factorial	The factorial operation is represented by the ! symbol. n! ("n factorial") means the product of all integers from n to 1. For example, $5! = 5 \cdot 4 \cdot 3 \cdot 2 \cdot 1 = 120$.
	Sometimes a factorial is the number of permutations of n things taken n at a time. Always think of this example: If there are five people and five chairs, how many unique arrangements can there be? There are five ways the first chair can be filled, and for each of those ways there are four ways the second chair can be filled, and so on. There would be $5! = 120$ ways the chairs could be filled.
	0! is 1 Many students think 0! should be zero, but permutations are the number of ways things can occur, and there is only one way to have nothing (there is only one way to have no people filling no chairs).

F-ratio | A test statistic based on the F-distribution.

frequency distribution | A way of summarizing data by counting the number of occurrences. *Qualitative frequency distributions* count individual occurrences of words or numbers. *Quantitative frequency distributions* (sometimes called grouped frequency distributions) count the number of occurrences of numbers in intervals.

fundamental rule | The total number of outcomes is the product of the number of outcomes for each trial.

goodness of fit test | A chi-square test that is used to compare observed and expected values. Usually used to test whether an observed distribution fits a particular probability distribution.

histogram | A graphical representation of a frequency distribution in which vertical bars represent the frequency of occurrences in each category.

hypergeometric distribution | A discrete probability distribution that calculates the probability of x occurrences in n trials, where there are S possible occurrences in a finite, countable population of size N and sampling is done without replacement.

hypothesis testing | One of the main tools of statistical inference. The basic procedure is as follows

- Make a statement about something.
- Collect sample data relating to the statement.
- If the sample outcome is unlikely given that the statement is true, the statement probably is not true.

This procedure is formalized in the seven steps introduced in Chapter 9.

hypothesis tests | This book emphasizes 12 major hypothesis tests numbered 1 through 12. These tests are summarized in Appendix B and are not listed in this glossary.

indicator variable | Used in regression. Patterns of 0's and 1's used to identify groups so that group differences can be tested by using regression analysis. Sometimes called a dummy variable or binary variable.

influential value | Used in regression. A data point in a regression that has an undue amount of influence on the analysis; in other words, the slope, intercept, and/or standard error of estimate will change if that value is removed.

interpolated median | A method of estimating the median (and percentiles) from a frequency distribution.

intersection probability	P(A *and* B) The probability of two events occurring simultaneously. In a contingency table it would be the number of observations in any given cell relative to the total. See also *multiplication rule*.
interval	Scale of measurement: constant units but no absolute zero. An example is temperature.
level of significance	The probability of rejecting the null hypothesis by chance alone; also known as the probability of a Type I error. The traditional default value is .05.
leverage	Used in regression. A measure of extrapolation.
margin of error	The quantity that is added and subtracted to and from the sample statistic to calculate a confidence interval. Sometimes called the half-width. The margin of error = (t or z) · (standard error) where t or z is selected to correspond to the confidence level.
marginal probability	Probabilities based on the row or column totals in a contingency table. In a contingency table, P(A) would be the number of observations in any given row relative to the total and P(B) would be the number of observations in any given column relative to the total.
mean	The sum of the numbers in a dataset divided by the number of numbers; informally called the average (Excel AVERAGE function).

$$\overline{X} = \frac{\sum_{i=1}^{n} X_i}{n} = \frac{X_1 + X_2 + X_3 + \cdots X_n}{n}$$

The sample mean is $\overline{X}$; the population mean is μ.

mean absolute deviation (MAD)	A measure of variation calculated by averaging absolute deviations (Excel AVEDEV function). Although the name implies just an average deviation, it uses absolute deviations.
mean deviation	The sum of the deviations divided by n. This value will always equal zero since the positive and negative deviations always cancel.
median	The halfway point in a dataset; the 50th percentile. If there are an odd number of values, the median is the middle value; if there is an even number of values, the median is the average of the middle two numbers (Excel MEDIAN function).
MegaStat	An Excel statistical add-in program.

mode	The most frequently occurring value in a dataset (Excel MODE function).
moving average	Used in time series. A moving window of averaged values used to smooth data.
multicollinearity	Used in regression. The extent to which independent variables are correlated in regression analysis.
multiplication rule	An expression for intersection probability:

$$P(A \ and \ B) = P(A) \cdot (B|A) = P(B) \cdot P(A|B)$$

multivariate extrapolation	Used in multiple regression. Attempting to predict Y by using X values not represented in the original data.
mutually exclusive	Events that cannot occur at the same time. Heads and tails are mutually exclusive.
nominal	A synonym for qualitative data. As a scale of measurement, it can refer to counts associated with qualitative data.
nonparametric methods	Statistical inference tests that do not rely on assumptions about population distributions.
null hypothesis (H_0)	The hypothesis we are testing. It is the condition of no difference or no effect.
odds	A way of stating the concept of probability by referring to the ratio of the number of ways an event can occur to the number of ways it cannot occur. For example, if you toss a die, the odds are 1 to 5 (or 1:5) that the die will show four dots because there is one way that can happen and five ways that it will not.
ogive	A plot of cumulative frequencies.
ordinal	Scale of measurement. Refers to position or rank order. May be stated in words or numbers.
outcome	The result of an experiment.
outlier	A value that is distinctly different from other values in a dataset.

Formal definition:

Let: Q1 = 25th percentile
       Q3 = 75th percentile
        H = Q3 − Q1 (the interquartile range)

An *outlier* is defined as any value less than Q1 − 1.5*H or greater than Q3 + 1.5*H. An *extreme outlier* is defined as any value less than Q1 − 3.0*H or greater than Q3 + 3.0*H.

parameter	A value associated with a population. For example, the true mean weight of every U.S. citizen at any instant in time is unknown, but the number nevertheless exists and is called a parameter. Lowercase Greek letters are used to refer to population parameters.
permutations	The number of arrangements (i.e., permutations) of n things taken r at a time is $n!/(n - r)!$. Sometimes you may see the notation nPr.
Poisson distribution	A discrete probability distribution that calculates the probability of x occurrences per a unit of time (or distance or some other continuous scale) when the mean rate of occurrence is μ.
polynomial	Used in time series. A function based on powers of X. The simplest polynomial function is a linear function; a quadratic function is based on X and X^2.
population	The entire universe of objects we are studying. Since statistics works with data, we really are thinking about data associated with the physical objects.
post hoc analysis	Used in ANOVA. A procedure used with analysis of variance in testing multiple groups. It is used to identify which groups are different and which groups are clusters that are not different.
predicted value	Used in regression. A value calculated by substituting values for X in a regression equation. Notation: Y'.
probability	A number between 0 and 1 that measures the likelihood of occurrence of an event. In a general sense people often think of a probability as the likelihood, but in a statistical context you always should think of a probability as a number between 0 and 1.
probability distribution, continuous	The height of a probability function is plotted for every value along a continuous axis. The total area under the curve equals 1, and probabilities correspond to proportional areas under the curve. The normal distribution is the first continuous distribution we study (t, F, and chi-square are other continuous distributions).
probability distribution, discrete	Probabilities associated with values of a discrete random variable such that the probabilities sum to 1. The binomial, hypergeometric, and Poisson distributions are examples of discrete probability distributions.
proportion	The number of times something occurs relative to the total occurrences. If data are coded 0 = no and 1 = yes, the mean is the same as the proportion of occurrences. In other words, a proportion is a special case of a mean. The symbol for the population proportion is π; the symbol for a sample proportion is p.

p-value	The probability of a hypothesis test result occurring by chance alone.
Q1, Q2, Q3	Notation for quartiles.
qualitative data	Data that identify or classify. Some terms that are associated with qualitative data are *text, words, names, labels, ID, categorical,* and *nominal.*
quantitative data	Numbers that measure something.
quartile	Values that divide a dataset in fourths. Q1 is the 25th percentile, Q2 is the 50th percentile (i.e., the median), and Q3 is the 75th percentile.
R, multiple R	Used in multiple regression. The square root of R^2. R is the correlation between Y and Y'. The multiple R cannot be negative.
random variable	A variable that by chance assumes numeric values based on the outcome of an experiment. Refers to numeric values that are associated with probabilities. *Discrete random variable* refers to numeric values associated with discrete events. *Continuous random variable* refers to a random variable that can assume any of an infinite number of values along a continuous scale.
range	The distance between the largest value and the smallest value in a dataset (Excel MAX – MIN functions).
ratio	Scale of measurement: constant units and absolute zero, for example, time, distance, and weight. Ask yourself, "Does a number twice as big mean twice as much?"
regression analysis	A statistical procedure that studies the relationship between a dependent variable (Y) and one or more independent variables (X), usually with the goal of predicting Y by using a value or values of X.
regression line	A line that is fitted to X,Y pairs of data in regression analysis. The slope and the intercept of the line are chosen to minimize the sum of the squared distances from the points to the line (Excel SLOPE and INTERCEPT functions).
relative frequency probability	Probabilities estimated by observed proportions. Sometimes called empirical probability.
residual	Used in regression. Actual value minus predicted value: Y – Y'. The terms *residual* and *error* are used synonymously in regression.
r-squared, r^2, R^2	Used in regression. A measure of the degree of fit of a regression line. It is the ratio of explained variance to total variance and thus can range from 0 to 1. With an r^2 of 1, the points line up perfectly on the regression line;

with an r^2 of 0, the points are randomly scattered and the regression line is horizontal. The lowercase r^2 is used for bivariate regression, and the uppercase R^2 is used for multiple regression (however, Excel always uses the uppercase R^2) (Excel RSQ function).

sample	A subset of a population.
sample, cluster	A sampling technique used to make sampling more efficient. The population is divided into areas (clusters). A random selection of clusters is selected, and a group of items is selected from within the cluster. For example, to get a random sample of U.S. citizens, you might first randomly select states, then within those states randomly select cities, and then within each city randomly select a few people for the sample.
sample, convenience	Taking whatever group of people is convenient and hoping the sample is more or less random. This is done often, but it is usually not a very good approximation to a simple random sample.
sample, simple random	A sample in which every item in the population has the same probability of being selected. This is the best type of sample but is often difficult to implement.
sample, stratified	A sampling technique in which one makes sure certain elements are represented in a sample.
sample, systematic	A method of trying to ensure randomness by selecting every nth item in a population to be included in a sample.

sample size estimation, mean

$$n = \left(\frac{z\sigma}{E}\right)^2$$

where z corresponds to the confidence level, σ is the population standard deviation (or more likely an estimate), and E is the error tolerance.

sample size estimation, proportion

$$n = \pi(1 - \pi)\left(\frac{z}{E}\right)^2$$

where z corresponds to the confidence level, π is the population proportion (or more likely an estimate), and E is the error tolerance. Since we most likely do not know π, we have to estimate it or be conservative and let $\pi = .5$.

sample space	All possible outcomes for a given experiment; often displayed in the form of a table or list.
sampling distribution	The probability distribution of all possible values of a sample statistic.
scatterplot	A graphical representation of the relationship between two variables by plotting X,Y pairs on coordinate horizontal and vertical axes.

seasonal index	Used in time series. A value indicating whether a given point in a time series is above or below the trend.
SSX	The sum of squared deviations for the variable X. SSX is used as the general expression, but the letter "X" can change. For example, SSY would be the sum of squared deviations for the variable Y (Excel DEVSQ function).

$$SSX = \sum (X_i - \overline{X})^2$$

standard deviation	A measure of variation; the square root of the variance.

$$\text{population standard deviation} = \sigma = \sqrt{\sigma^2} = \sqrt{\frac{\sum (X_i - \mu)^2}{N}} = \sqrt{\frac{SSX}{N}}$$

where N is the population size (Excel STDEVP function).

$$\text{sample standard deviation} = s = \sqrt{s^2} = \sqrt{\frac{\sum (X_i - \overline{X})^2}{n - 1}} = \sqrt{\frac{SSX}{n - 1}}$$

where n is the sample size (Excel STDEV function).

standard error	The standard deviation of a sampling distribution.
standard error of a proportion	The standard deviation of a sampling distribution of proportions:

$$\sigma_p = \sqrt{\frac{\pi(1 - \pi)}{n}}$$

standard error of estimate	A measure of variation around a regression line.
standard error of the mean	The standard deviation of a sampling distribution of sample means:

$$\sigma_{\overline{X}} = \frac{\sigma}{\sqrt{n}}$$

standardized coefficients	Used in regression. Multiple regression coefficients based on standardized data (z-values). This allows the relative importance of the variables to be compared.
statistic	A value calculated from a sample in order to estimate a population parameter.
statistical independence	A special case of the multiplication rule:

$$P(A \text{ } and \text{ } B) = P(A) \cdot P(B)$$

In other words, if A and B are independent, the intersection probability is equal to the product of the corresponding marginal probabilities. In a general sense, if two events are independent, they are unrelated; knowing that one has occurred does not change the probability that the other one will occur.

statistical inference	A general term referring to decision making with statistics.
statistics	1. Tools and concepts that are used to analyze data and make decisions from data
	2. A value calculated from a sample
	3. Data
stdev, sd, s.d.	Abbreviations for *standard deviation*.
Stepwise Selection	Used in regression. A MegaStat tool for regression model building that shows the one best regression model of each possible number of independent variables.
subjective probability	Probability based on experience and knowledge, not calculation or direct observation.
test statistic	A value calculated as part of a hypothesis test to determine whether the sample result is an unlikely outcome.
time-series data	Data that are collected at regular points over time, usually annual, quarterly, or monthly.
trendline	A regression line fitted to time-series data. Excel calls all regression lines trendlines.
t-value	A test statistic based on the t-distribution.
Type I error	Rejecting the null hypothesis when it is true, based on sampling error.
Type II error	Failing to reject the null hypothesis when it is false.
union probability	The probability of either (or both) of two events occurring:

$$P(A \ or \ B) = P(A) + P(B) - P(A \ and \ B)$$

variable	1. "A symbol for an unspecified quantity." For example, the letter "X" is a commonly used mathematical variable.
	2. A reference to the underlying entity that is being represented with data.
	3. A column of numbers (often in an Excel worksheet), usually with a label at the top.
variance	A measure of variation.

$$\text{population variance} = \sigma^2 = \frac{\sum (X_i - \mu)^2}{N} = \frac{SSX}{N}$$

where N is the population size (Excel VARP function).

$$\text{sample variance} = s^2 = \frac{\sum (X_i - \overline{X})^2}{n - 1} = \frac{SSX}{n - 1}$$

where n is the sample size (Excel VAR function).

variance, discrete probability distribution	The expected value of the squared deviations: $$\sigma^2 = E((X - \mu)^2) = \sum ((X - \mu)^2 \cdot P(X))$$ $$\sigma = \sqrt{\sigma^2}$$
VIF (variance inflation factor)	Used in regression. A measure of multicollinearity. A VIF value indicates how much a variable is related to the other independent variables.
z-value	If we have a variable, X, the equation for the corresponding z-value is $$z = \frac{X - \text{mean}}{\text{stdev}}$$ This sometimes is called standardizing a variable. z-values always have a mean of 0 and a standard deviation of 1.

Tables

D.1 Normal Distribution

D.2 t-Distribution

D.3 F-Distribution

D.4 Chi-square Distribution

Normal Curve Table (Positive z-Values)

Excel formula: =NORMSDIST(z)

z	P	z	P	z	P	z	P	z	P	z	P
0.00	0.5000	0.50	0.6915	1.00	0.8413	1.50	0.9332	2.00	0.9772	2.50	0.9938
0.01	0.5040	0.51	0.6950	1.01	0.8438	1.51	0.9345	2.01	0.9778	2.51	0.9940
0.02	0.5080	0.52	0.6985	1.02	0.8461	1.52	0.9357	2.02	0.9783	2.52	0.9941
0.03	0.5120	0.53	0.7019	1.03	0.8485	1.53	0.9370	2.03	0.9788	2.53	0.9943
0.04	0.5160	0.54	0.7054	1.04	0.8508	1.54	0.9382	2.04	0.9793	2.54	0.9945
0.05	0.5199	0.55	0.7088	1.05	0.8531	1.55	0.9394	2.05	0.9798	2.55	0.9946
0.06	0.5239	0.56	0.7123	1.06	0.8554	1.56	0.9406	2.06	0.9803	2.56	0.9948
0.07	0.5279	0.57	0.7157	1.07	0.8577	1.57	0.9418	2.07	0.9808	2.57	0.9949
0.08	0.5319	0.58	0.7190	1.08	0.8599	1.58	0.9429	2.08	0.9812	2.58	0.9951
0.09	0.5359	0.59	0.7224	1.09	0.8621	1.59	0.9441	2.09	0.9817	2.59	0.9952
0.10	0.5398	0.60	0.7257	1.10	0.8643	1.60	0.9452	2.10	0.9821	2.60	0.9953
0.11	0.5438	0.61	0.7291	1.11	0.8665	1.61	0.9463	2.11	0.9826	2.61	0.9955
0.12	0.5478	0.62	0.7324	1.12	0.8686	1.62	0.9474	2.12	0.9830	2.62	0.9956
0.13	0.5517	0.63	0.7357	1.13	0.8708	1.63	0.9484	2.13	0.9834	2.63	0.9957
0.14	0.5557	0.64	0.7389	1.14	0.8729	1.64	0.9495	2.14	0.9838	2.64	0.9959
0.15	0.5596	0.65	0.7422	1.15	0.8749	1.65	0.9505	2.15	0.9842	2.65	0.9960
0.16	0.5636	0.66	0.7454	1.16	0.8770	1.66	0.9515	2.16	0.9846	2.66	0.9961
0.17	0.5675	0.67	0.7486	1.17	0.8790	1.67	0.9525	2.17	0.9850	2.67	0.9962
0.18	0.5714	0.68	0.7517	1.18	0.8810	1.68	0.9535	2.18	0.9854	2.68	0.9963
0.19	0.5753	0.69	0.7549	1.19	0.8830	1.69	0.9545	2.19	0.9857	2.69	0.9964
0.20	0.5793	0.70	0.7580	1.20	0.8849	1.70	0.9554	2.20	0.9861	2.70	0.9965
0.21	0.5832	0.71	0.7611	1.21	0.8869	1.71	0.9564	2.21	0.9864	2.71	0.9966
0.22	0.5871	0.72	0.7642	1.22	0.8888	1.72	0.9573	2.22	0.9868	2.72	0.9967
0.23	0.5910	0.73	0.7673	1.23	0.8907	1.73	0.9582	2.23	0.9871	2.73	0.9968
0.24	0.5948	0.74	0.7704	1.24	0.8925	1.74	0.9591	2.24	0.9875	2.74	0.9969
0.25	0.5987	0.75	0.7734	1.25	0.8944	1.75	0.9599	2.25	0.9878	2.75	0.9970
0.26	0.6026	0.76	0.7764	1.26	0.8962	1.76	0.9608	2.26	0.9881	2.76	0.9971
0.27	0.6064	0.77	0.7794	1.27	0.8980	1.77	0.9616	2.27	0.9884	2.77	0.9972
0.28	0.6103	0.78	0.7823	1.28	0.8997	1.78	0.9625	2.28	0.9887	2.78	0.9973
0.29	0.6141	0.79	0.7852	1.29	0.9015	1.79	0.9633	2.29	0.9890	2.79	0.9974
0.30	0.6179	0.80	0.7881	1.30	0.9032	1.80	0.9641	2.30	0.9893	2.80	0.9974
0.31	0.6217	0.81	0.7910	1.31	0.9049	1.81	0.9649	2.31	0.9896	2.81	0.9975
0.32	0.6255	0.82	0.7939	1.32	0.9066	1.82	0.9656	2.32	0.9898	2.82	0.9976
0.33	0.6293	0.83	0.7967	1.33	0.9082	1.83	0.9664	2.33	0.9901	2.83	0.9977
0.34	0.6331	0.84	0.7995	1.34	0.9099	1.84	0.9671	2.34	0.9904	2.84	0.9977
0.35	0.6368	0.85	0.8023	1.35	0.9115	1.85	0.9678	2.35	0.9906	2.85	0.9978
0.36	0.6406	0.86	0.8051	1.36	0.9131	1.86	0.9686	2.36	0.9909	2.86	0.9979
0.37	0.6443	0.87	0.8078	1.37	0.9147	1.87	0.9693	2.37	0.9911	2.87	0.9979
0.38	0.6480	0.88	0.8106	1.38	0.9162	1.88	0.9699	2.38	0.9913	2.88	0.9980
0.39	0.6517	0.89	0.8133	1.39	0.9177	1.89	0.9706	2.39	0.9916	2.89	0.9981
0.40	0.6554	0.90	0.8159	1.40	0.9192	1.90	0.9713	2.40	0.9918	2.90	0.9981
0.41	0.6591	0.91	0.8186	1.41	0.9207	1.91	0.9719	2.41	0.9920	2.91	0.9982
0.42	0.6628	0.92	0.8212	1.42	0.9222	1.92	0.9726	2.42	0.9922	2.92	0.9982
0.43	0.6664	0.93	0.8238	1.43	0.9236	1.93	0.9732	2.43	0.9925	2.93	0.9983
0.44	0.6700	0.94	0.8264	1.44	0.9251	1.94	0.9738	2.44	0.9927	2.94	0.9984
0.45	0.6736	0.95	0.8289	1.45	0.9265	1.95	0.9744	2.45	0.9929	2.95	0.9984
0.46	0.6772	0.96	0.8315	1.46	0.9279	1.96	0.9750	2.46	0.9931	2.96	0.9985
0.47	0.6808	0.97	0.8340	1.47	0.9292	1.97	0.9756	2.47	0.9932	2.97	0.9985
0.48	0.6844	0.98	0.8365	1.48	0.9306	1.98	0.9761	2.48	0.9934	2.98	0.9986
0.49	0.6879	0.99	0.8389	1.49	0.9319	1.99	0.9767	2.49	0.9936	2.99	0.9986
										3.00	0.9987
										3.25	0.99942
										3.50	0.99977
										3.75	0.99991
										4.00	0.99997

Normal Curve Table (Negative z-Values)

Excel formula: =NORMSDIST(z)

z	P	z	P	z	P	z	P	z	P	z	P
−4.00	0.00003										
−3.75	0.00009										
−3.50	0.00023										
−3.25	0.00058										
−3.00	0.0013	−2.50	0.0062	−2.00	0.0228	−1.50	0.0668	−1.00	0.1587	−0.50	0.3085
−2.99	0.0014	−2.49	0.0064	−1.99	0.0233	−1.49	0.0681	−0.99	0.1611	−0.49	0.3121
−2.98	0.0014	−2.48	0.0066	−1.98	0.0239	−1.48	0.0694	−0.98	0.1635	−0.48	0.3156
−2.97	0.0015	−2.47	0.0068	−1.97	0.0244	−1.47	0.0708	−0.97	0.1660	−0.47	0.3192
−2.96	0.0015	−2.46	0.0069	−1.96	0.0250	−1.46	0.0721	−0.96	0.1685	−0.46	0.3228
−2.95	0.0016	−2.45	0.0071	−1.95	0.0256	−1.45	0.0735	−0.95	0.1711	−0.45	0.3264
−2.94	0.0016	−2.44	0.0073	−1.94	0.0262	−1.44	0.0749	−0.94	0.1736	−0.44	0.3300
−2.93	0.0017	−2.43	0.0075	−1.93	0.0268	−1.43	0.0764	−0.93	0.1762	−0.43	0.3336
−2.92	0.0018	−2.42	0.0078	−1.92	0.0274	−1.42	0.0778	−0.92	0.1788	−0.42	0.3372
−2.91	0.0018	−2.41	0.0080	−1.91	0.0281	−1.41	0.0793	−0.91	0.1814	−0.41	0.3409
−2.90	0.0019	−2.40	0.0082	−1.90	0.0287	−1.40	0.0808	−0.90	0.1841	−0.40	0.3446
−2.89	0.0019	−2.39	0.0084	−1.89	0.0294	−1.39	0.0823	−0.89	0.1867	−0.39	0.3483
−2.88	0.0020	−2.38	0.0087	−1.88	0.0301	−1.38	0.0838	−0.88	0.1894	−0.38	0.3520
−2.87	0.0021	−2.37	0.0089	−1.87	0.0307	−1.37	0.0853	−0.87	0.1922	−0.37	0.3557
−2.86	0.0021	−2.36	0.0091	−1.86	0.0314	−1.36	0.0869	−0.86	0.1949	−0.36	0.3594
−2.85	0.0022	−2.35	0.0094	−1.85	0.0322	−1.35	0.0885	−0.85	0.1977	−0.35	0.3632
−2.84	0.0023	−2.34	0.0096	−1.84	0.0329	−1.34	0.0901	−0.84	0.2005	−0.34	0.3669
−2.83	0.0023	−2.33	0.0099	−1.83	0.0336	−1.33	0.0918	−0.83	0.2033	−0.33	0.3707
−2.82	0.0024	−2.32	0.0102	−1.82	0.0344	−1.32	0.0934	−0.82	0.2061	−0.32	0.3745
−2.81	0.0025	−2.31	0.0104	−1.81	0.0351	−1.31	0.0951	−0.81	0.2090	−0.31	0.3783
−2.80	0.0026	−2.30	0.0107	−1.80	0.0359	−1.30	0.0968	−0.80	0.2119	−0.30	0.3821
−2.79	0.0026	−2.29	0.0110	−1.79	0.0367	−1.29	0.0985	−0.79	0.2148	−0.29	0.3859
−2.78	0.0027	−2.28	0.0113	−1.78	0.0375	−1.28	0.1003	−0.78	0.2177	−0.28	0.3897
−2.77	0.0028	−2.27	0.0116	−1.77	0.0384	−1.27	0.1020	−0.77	0.2206	−0.27	0.3936
−2.76	0.0029	−2.26	0.0119	−1.76	0.0392	−1.26	0.1038	−0.76	0.2236	−0.26	0.3974
−2.75	0.0030	−2.25	0.0122	−1.75	0.0401	−1.25	0.1056	−0.75	0.2266	−0.25	0.4013
−2.74	0.0031	−2.24	0.0125	−1.74	0.0409	−1.24	0.1075	−0.74	0.2296	−0.24	0.4052
−2.73	0.0032	−2.23	0.0129	−1.73	0.0418	−1.23	0.1093	−0.73	0.2327	−0.23	0.4090
−2.72	0.0033	−2.22	0.0132	−1.72	0.0427	−1.22	0.1112	−0.72	0.2358	−0.22	0.4129
−2.71	0.0034	−2.21	0.0136	−1.71	0.0436	−1.21	0.1131	−0.71	0.2389	−0.21	0.4168
−2.70	0.0035	−2.20	0.0139	−1.70	0.0446	−1.20	0.1151	−0.70	0.2420	−0.20	0.4207
−2.69	0.0036	−2.19	0.0143	−1.69	0.0455	−1.19	0.1170	−0.69	0.2451	−0.19	0.4247
−2.68	0.0037	−2.18	0.0146	−1.68	0.0465	−1.18	0.1190	−0.68	0.2483	−0.18	0.4286
−2.67	0.0038	−2.17	0.0150	−1.67	0.0475	−1.17	0.1210	−0.67	0.2514	−0.17	0.4325
−2.66	0.0039	−2.16	0.0154	−1.66	0.0485	−1.16	0.1230	−0.66	0.2546	−0.16	0.4364
−2.65	0.0040	−2.15	0.0158	−1.65	0.0495	−1.15	0.1251	−0.65	0.2578	−0.15	0.4404
−2.64	0.0041	−2.14	0.0162	−1.64	0.0505	−1.14	0.1271	−0.64	0.2611	−0.14	0.4443
−2.63	0.0043	−2.13	0.0166	−1.63	0.0516	−1.13	0.1292	−0.63	0.2643	−0.13	0.4483
−2.62	0.0044	−2.12	0.0170	−1.62	0.0526	−1.12	0.1314	−0.62	0.2676	−0.12	0.4522
−2.61	0.0045	−2.11	0.0174	−1.61	0.0537	−1.11	0.1335	−0.61	0.2709	−0.11	0.4562
−2.60	0.0047	−2.10	0.0179	−1.60	0.0548	−1.10	0.1357	−0.60	0.2743	−0.10	0.4602
−2.59	0.0048	−2.09	0.0183	−1.59	0.0559	−1.09	0.1379	−0.59	0.2776	−0.09	0.4641
−2.58	0.0049	−2.08	0.0188	−1.58	0.0571	−1.08	0.1401	−0.58	0.2810	−0.08	0.4681
−2.57	0.0051	−2.07	0.0192	−1.57	0.0582	−1.07	0.1423	−0.57	0.2843	−0.07	0.4721
−2.56	0.0052	−2.06	0.0197	−1.56	0.0594	−1.06	0.1446	−0.56	0.2877	−0.06	0.4761
−2.55	0.0054	−2.05	0.0202	−1.55	0.0606	−1.05	0.1469	−0.55	0.2912	−0.05	0.4801
−2.54	0.0055	−2.04	0.0207	−1.54	0.0618	−1.04	0.1492	−0.54	0.2946	−0.04	0.4840
−2.53	0.0057	−2.03	0.0212	−1.53	0.0630	−1.03	0.1515	−0.53	0.2981	−0.03	0.4880
−2.52	0.0059	−2.02	0.0217	−1.52	0.0643	−1.02	0.1539	−0.52	0.3015	−0.02	0.4920
−2.51	0.0060	−2.01	0.0222	−1.51	0.0655	−1.01	0.1562	−0.51	0.3050	−0.01	0.4960
										0.00	0.5000

t-Distribution Critical Values

	One-Tailed						=TINV(2 * prob, df)
	0.1	0.05	0.025	0.01	0.005	0.0005	
	Two-Tailed						=TINV(prob, df)
df	0.20	0.10	0.05	0.02	0.01	0.001	
1	3.078	6.314	12.706	31.821	63.656	636.578	
2	1.886	2.920	4.303	6.965	9.925	31.600	
3	1.638	2.353	3.182	4.541	5.841	12.924	
4	1.533	2.132	2.776	3.747	4.604	8.610	
5	1.476	2.015	2.571	3.365	4.032	6.869	
6	1.440	1.943	2.447	3.143	3.707	5.959	
7	1.415	1.895	2.365	2.998	3.499	5.408	
8	1.397	1.860	2.306	2.896	3.355	5.041	
9	1.383	1.833	2.262	2.821	3.250	4.781	
10	1.372	1.812	2.228	2.764	3.169	4.587	
11	1.363	1.796	2.201	2.718	3.106	4.437	
12	1.356	1.782	2.179	2.681	3.055	4.318	
13	1.350	1.771	2.160	2.650	3.012	4.221	
14	1.345	1.761	2.145	2.624	2.977	4.140	
15	1.341	1.753	2.131	2.602	2.947	4.073	
16	1.337	1.746	2.120	2.583	2.921	4.015	
17	1.333	1.740	2.110	2.567	2.898	3.965	
18	1.330	1.734	2.101	2.552	2.878	3.922	
19	1.328	1.729	2.093	2.539	2.861	3.883	
20	1.325	1.725	2.086	2.528	2.845	3.850	
21	1.323	1.721	2.080	2.518	2.831	3.819	
22	1.321	1.717	2.074	2.508	2.819	3.792	
23	1.319	1.714	2.069	2.500	2.807	3.768	
24	1.318	1.711	2.064	2.492	2.797	3.745	
25	1.316	1.708	2.060	2.485	2.787	3.725	
26	1.315	1.706	2.056	2.479	2.779	3.707	
27	1.314	1.703	2.052	2.473	2.771	3.689	
28	1.313	1.701	2.048	2.467	2.763	3.674	
29	1.311	1.699	2.045	2.462	2.756	3.660	
30	1.310	1.697	2.042	2.457	2.750	3.646	
40	1.303	1.684	2.021	2.423	2.704	3.551	
60	1.296	1.671	2.000	2.390	2.660	3.460	
120	1.289	1.658	1.980	2.358	2.617	3.373	
∞	1.282	1.645	1.960	2.326	2.576	3.290	

Note that t-values become z-values as the degrees of freedom becomes large.

F-Distribution Critical Values at the 5% Level of Significance, α = .05

=FINV(.05, df1, df2)

numerator degrees of freedom (df1)

	1	2	3	4	5	6	7	8	9	10	12	15	20	24	30	40	60	120	∞
1	161	199	216	225	230	234	237	239	241	242	244	246	248	249	250	251	252	253	254
2	18.5	19.0	19.2	19.2	19.3	19.3	19.4	19.4	19.4	19.4	19.4	19.4	19.4	19.5	19.5	19.5	19.5	19.5	19.5
3	10.1	9.55	9.28	9.12	9.01	8.94	8.89	8.85	8.81	8.79	8.74	8.70	8.66	8.64	8.62	8.59	8.57	8.55	8.53
4	7.71	6.94	6.59	6.39	6.26	6.16	6.09	6.04	6.00	5.96	5.91	5.86	5.80	5.77	5.75	5.72	5.69	5.66	5.63
5	6.61	5.79	5.41	5.19	5.05	4.95	4.88	4.82	4.77	4.74	4.68	4.62	4.56	4.53	4.50	4.46	4.43	4.40	4.37
6	5.99	5.14	4.76	4.53	4.39	4.28	4.21	4.15	4.10	4.06	4.00	3.94	3.87	3.84	3.81	3.77	3.74	3.70	3.67
7	5.59	4.74	4.35	4.12	3.97	3.87	3.79	3.73	3.68	3.64	3.57	3.51	3.44	3.41	3.38	3.34	3.30	3.27	3.23
8	5.32	4.46	4.07	3.84	3.69	3.58	3.50	3.44	3.39	3.35	3.28	3.22	3.15	3.12	3.08	3.04	3.01	2.97	2.93
9	5.12	4.26	3.86	3.63	3.48	3.37	3.29	3.23	3.18	3.14	3.07	3.01	2.94	2.90	2.86	2.83	2.79	2.75	2.71
10	4.96	4.10	3.71	3.48	3.33	3.22	3.14	3.07	3.02	2.98	2.91	2.85	2.77	2.74	2.70	2.66	2.62	2.58	2.54
11	4.84	3.98	3.59	3.36	3.20	3.09	3.01	2.95	2.90	2.85	2.79	2.72	2.65	2.61	2.57	2.53	2.49	2.45	2.40
12	4.75	3.89	3.49	3.26	3.11	3.00	2.91	2.85	2.80	2.75	2.69	2.62	2.54	2.51	2.47	2.43	2.38	2.34	2.30
13	4.67	3.81	3.41	3.18	3.03	2.92	2.83	2.77	2.71	2.67	2.60	2.53	2.46	2.42	2.38	2.34	2.30	2.25	2.21
14	4.60	3.74	3.34	3.11	2.96	2.85	2.76	2.70	2.65	2.60	2.53	2.46	2.39	2.35	2.31	2.27	2.22	2.18	2.13
15	4.54	3.68	3.29	3.06	2.90	2.79	2.71	2.64	2.59	2.54	2.48	2.40	2.33	2.29	2.25	2.20	2.16	2.11	2.07
16	4.49	3.63	3.24	3.01	2.85	2.74	2.66	2.59	2.54	2.49	2.42	2.35	2.28	2.24	2.19	2.15	2.11	2.06	2.01
17	4.45	3.59	3.20	2.96	2.81	2.70	2.61	2.55	2.49	2.45	2.38	2.31	2.23	2.19	2.15	2.10	2.06	2.01	1.96
18	4.41	3.55	3.16	2.93	2.77	2.66	2.58	2.51	2.46	2.41	2.34	2.27	2.19	2.15	2.11	2.06	2.02	1.97	1.92
19	4.38	3.52	3.13	2.90	2.74	2.63	2.54	2.48	2.42	2.38	2.31	2.23	2.16	2.11	2.07	2.03	1.98	1.93	1.88
20	4.35	3.49	3.10	2.87	2.71	2.60	2.51	2.45	2.39	2.35	2.28	2.20	2.12	2.08	2.04	1.99	1.95	1.90	1.84
21	4.32	3.47	3.07	2.84	2.68	2.57	2.49	2.42	2.37	2.32	2.25	2.18	2.10	2.05	2.01	1.96	1.92	1.87	1.81
22	4.30	3.44	3.05	2.82	2.66	2.55	2.46	2.40	2.34	2.30	2.23	2.15	2.07	2.03	1.98	1.94	1.89	1.84	1.78
23	4.28	3.42	3.03	2.80	2.64	2.53	2.44	2.37	2.32	2.27	2.20	2.13	2.05	2.01	1.96	1.91	1.86	1.81	1.76
24	4.26	3.40	3.01	2.78	2.62	2.51	2.42	2.36	2.30	2.25	2.18	2.11	2.03	1.98	1.94	1.89	1.84	1.79	1.73
25	4.24	3.39	2.99	2.76	2.60	2.49	2.40	2.34	2.28	2.24	2.16	2.09	2.01	1.96	1.92	1.87	1.82	1.77	1.71
30	4.17	3.32	2.92	2.69	2.53	2.42	2.33	2.27	2.21	2.16	2.09	2.01	1.93	1.89	1.84	1.79	1.74	1.68	1.62
40	4.08	3.23	2.84	2.61	2.45	2.34	2.25	2.18	2.12	2.08	2.00	1.92	1.84	1.79	1.74	1.69	1.64	1.58	1.51
60	4.00	3.15	2.76	2.53	2.37	2.25	2.17	2.10	2.04	1.99	1.92	1.84	1.75	1.70	1.65	1.59	1.53	1.47	1.39
120	3.92	3.07	2.68	2.45	2.29	2.18	2.09	2.02	1.96	1.91	1.83	1.75	1.66	1.61	1.55	1.50	1.43	1.35	1.25
∞	3.84	3.00	2.60	2.37	2.21	2.10	2.01	1.94	1.88	1.83	1.75	1.67	1.57	1.52	1.46	1.39	1.32	1.22	1.00

denominator degrees of freedom (df2)

F- Distribution Critical Values at the 1% Level of Significance, α = .01

=FINV(.01, df1, df2)

numerator degrees of freedom (df1)

	1	2	3	4	5	6	7	8	9	10	12	15	20	24	30	40	60	120	∞
1	4052	4999	5404	5624	5764	5859	5928	5981	6022	6056	6107	6157	6209	6234	6260	6286	6313	6340	6366
2	98.5	99.0	99.2	99.3	99.3	99.3	99.4	99.4	99.4	99.4	99.4	99.4	99.4	99.5	99.5	99.5	99.5	99.5	99.5
3	34.1	30.8	29.5	28.7	28.2	27.9	27.7	27.5	27.3	27.2	27.1	26.9	26.7	26.6	26.5	26.4	26.3	26.2	26.1
4	21.2	18.0	16.7	16.0	15.5	15.2	15.0	14.8	14.7	14.5	14.4	14.2	14.0	13.9	13.8	13.7	13.7	13.6	13.5
5	16.3	13.3	12.1	11.4	11.0	10.7	10.5	10.3	10.2	10.1	9.89	9.72	9.55	9.47	9.38	9.29	9.20	9.11	9.02
6	13.7	10.9	9.78	9.15	8.75	8.47	8.26	8.10	7.98	7.87	7.72	7.56	7.40	7.31	7.23	7.14	7.06	6.97	6.88
7	12.2	9.55	8.45	7.85	7.46	7.19	6.99	6.84	6.72	6.62	6.47	6.31	6.16	6.07	5.99	5.91	5.82	5.74	5.65
8	11.3	8.65	7.59	7.01	6.63	6.37	6.18	6.03	5.91	5.81	5.67	5.52	5.36	5.28	5.20	5.12	5.03	4.95	4.86
9	10.6	8.02	6.99	6.42	6.06	5.80	5.61	5.47	5.35	5.26	5.11	4.96	4.81	4.73	4.65	4.57	4.48	4.40	4.31
10	10.0	7.56	6.55	5.99	5.64	5.39	5.20	5.06	4.94	4.85	4.71	4.56	4.41	4.33	4.25	4.17	4.08	4.00	3.91
11	9.65	7.21	6.22	5.67	5.32	5.07	4.89	4.74	4.63	4.54	4.40	4.25	4.10	4.02	3.94	3.86	3.78	3.69	3.60
12	9.33	6.93	5.95	5.41	5.06	4.82	4.64	4.50	4.39	4.30	4.16	4.01	3.86	3.78	3.70	3.62	3.54	3.45	3.36
13	9.07	6.70	5.74	5.21	4.86	4.62	4.44	4.30	4.19	4.10	3.96	3.82	3.66	3.59	3.51	3.43	3.34	3.25	3.17
14	8.86	6.51	5.56	5.04	4.69	4.46	4.28	4.14	4.03	3.94	3.80	3.66	3.51	3.43	3.35	3.27	3.18	3.09	3.00
15	8.68	6.36	5.42	4.89	4.56	4.32	4.14	4.00	3.89	3.80	3.67	3.52	3.37	3.29	3.21	3.13	3.05	2.96	2.87
16	8.53	6.23	5.29	4.77	4.44	4.20	4.03	3.89	3.78	3.69	3.55	3.41	3.26	3.18	3.10	3.02	2.93	2.84	2.75
17	8.40	6.11	5.19	4.67	4.34	4.10	3.93	3.79	3.68	3.59	3.46	3.31	3.16	3.08	3.00	2.92	2.83	2.75	2.65
18	8.29	6.01	5.09	4.58	4.25	4.01	3.84	3.71	3.60	3.51	3.37	3.23	3.08	3.00	2.92	2.84	2.75	2.66	2.57
19	8.18	5.93	5.01	4.50	4.17	3.94	3.77	3.63	3.52	3.43	3.30	3.15	3.00	2.92	2.84	2.76	2.67	2.58	2.49
20	8.10	5.85	4.94	4.43	4.10	3.87	3.70	3.56	3.46	3.37	3.23	3.09	2.94	2.86	2.78	2.69	2.61	2.52	2.42
21	8.02	5.78	4.87	4.37	4.04	3.81	3.64	3.51	3.40	3.31	3.17	3.03	2.88	2.80	2.72	2.64	2.55	2.46	2.36
22	7.95	5.72	4.82	4.31	3.99	3.76	3.59	3.45	3.35	3.26	3.12	2.98	2.83	2.75	2.67	2.58	2.50	2.40	2.31
23	7.88	5.66	4.76	4.26	3.94	3.71	3.54	3.41	3.30	3.21	3.07	2.93	2.78	2.70	2.62	2.54	2.45	2.35	2.26
24	7.82	5.61	4.72	4.22	3.90	3.67	3.50	3.36	3.26	3.17	3.03	2.89	2.74	2.66	2.58	2.49	2.40	2.31	2.21
25	7.77	5.57	4.68	4.18	3.85	3.63	3.46	3.32	3.22	3.13	2.99	2.85	2.70	2.62	2.54	2.45	2.36	2.27	2.17
30	7.56	5.39	4.51	4.02	3.70	3.47	3.30	3.17	3.07	2.98	2.84	2.70	2.55	2.47	2.39	2.30	2.21	2.11	2.01
40	7.31	5.18	4.31	3.83	3.51	3.29	3.12	2.99	2.89	2.80	2.66	2.52	2.37	2.29	2.20	2.11	2.02	1.92	1.80
60	7.08	4.98	4.13	3.65	3.34	3.12	2.95	2.82	2.72	2.63	2.50	2.35	2.20	2.12	2.03	1.94	1.84	1.73	1.60
120	6.85	4.79	3.95	3.48	3.17	2.96	2.79	2.66	2.56	2.47	2.34	2.19	2.03	1.95	1.86	1.76	1.66	1.53	1.38
∞	6.63	4.61	3.78	3.32	3.02	2.80	2.64	2.51	2.41	2.32	2.18	2.04	1.88	1.79	1.70	1.59	1.47	1.32	1.00

denominator degrees of freedom (df2)

Chi-Square Critical Values   =CHIINV(prob, df)

Right-Tail Area

df	0.10	0.05	0.02	0.01
1	2.706	3.841	5.412	6.635
2	4.605	5.991	7.824	9.210
3	6.251	7.815	9.837	11.345
4	7.779	9.488	11.668	13.277
5	9.236	11.070	13.388	15.086
6	10.645	12.592	15.033	16.812
7	12.017	14.067	16.622	18.475
8	13.362	15.507	18.168	20.090
9	14.684	16.919	19.679	21.666
10	15.987	18.307	21.161	23.209
11	17.275	19.675	22.618	24.725
12	18.549	21.026	24.054	26.217
13	19.812	22.362	25.471	27.688
14	21.064	23.685	26.873	29.141
15	22.307	24.996	28.259	30.578
16	23.542	26.296	29.633	32.000
17	24.769	27.587	30.995	33.409
18	25.989	28.869	32.346	34.805
19	27.204	30.144	33.687	36.191
20	28.412	31.410	35.020	37.566
21	29.615	32.671	36.343	38.932
22	30.813	33.924	37.659	40.289
23	32.007	35.172	38.968	41.638
24	33.196	36.415	40.270	42.980
25	34.382	37.652	41.566	44.314
26	35.563	38.885	42.856	45.642
27	36.741	40.113	44.140	46.963
28	37.916	41.337	45.419	48.278
29	39.087	42.557	46.693	49.588
30	40.256	43.773	47.962	50.892

Tutorial List

The tutorials are Excel and MegaStat applications with voice-over commentary by Professor Orris. They are in the tutorials folder of the textbook CD.

To use the tutorials, do the following:

- Click on the filename to run.
- Click the toolbar buttons to stop/pause.
- Space bar pauses and restarts.
- When it is paused, you can click the toolbar buttons to move forward and backward 1 second per click. The right and left arrow keys move forward and backward one frame at a time (15 fps), or hold the key down for continuous movement.
- Alt-Enter toggles a full-screen view.

Number	Name	Time (min:sec)
	Excel Basics 1	22:31
	Excel Basics 2	14:52
	MegaStat Setup	2:33
1	MegaStat introduction	11:30
2	Mean and standard deviation	17:37
3	Qualitative frequency distribution	5:07
4	Quantitative frequency distribution	14:07
5	Probability concepts	15:14
6	Discrete probability distributions	6:28
7	Normal distribution	14:52
8	Central limit theorem simulation	6:21
9	Confidence interval simulation	5:50
10	Random numbers	9:24
11	Hypothesis testing—two groups	8:17
12	ANOVA—one factor	4:47
13	Regression—bivariate	10:54
14	Multiple regression	12:03
15	Chi-square crosstabulation	11:52

Index

A

Absolute differences, 149
Accuracy
  in binomial distributions, 168
  of calculations, 8–9, 143
  in Excel, 8, 143
  in exponential trend analysis, 281
  in MegaStat, 8
  in proportion calculations, 101, 168
Adjusted R^2, 236–237, 241, 242, 312
"All Possible Regressions" option, 241–243
Alpha (α) symbol, 127, 312
Alternative hypothesis (H_1), 312
  in comparing two independent groups test,
    142–143, 145
  in comparing two independent proportions test,
    155, 157
  decision rules for different, 128
  in mean vs. hypothesized value test, 137, 139
  in One-Factor ANOVA test, 172, 174
  in paired observations test, 148, 150, 166
  in proportion vs. hypothesized value test,
    151–153
  in Randomized Blocks ANOVA test, 177, 179
  specifying, as step 1 of hypothesis testing,
    124, 125
  in Two-Factor ANOVA test, 201
Analysis of variance (ANOVA), 170–203, 312
  definition of, 170
  and linear regression, 220–222, 230, 308–309
  and multiple regression, 237
  One-Factor, 170–177, 181, 188–190, 198–201, 306
  partitioning the sum of squares in, 182–186
  post hoc analysis, 190–194
  Randomized Blocks, 176–181, 194, 196–201,
    306–307
  simulation for, 175, 188–190
  table for regression for, 211–212
  t-tests vs., 181, 190–197
  Two-Factor, 181–182, 201–202, 307–308
  using the F-distribution, 186–188
  worksheet for partitioning, 184–186
"Approximately normally distributed," 259
Area under a curve, 82
Arithmetic mean, 15–17, 312
Autocorrelation, 312
AVEDEV( ) function, 300

Average
  arithmetic mean and, 15
  definition of, 312
  as example of calculated statistic, 2
  of samples, 6
AVERAGE( ) function, 16, 18, 79, 83, 113, 300
Average rate of change, 278, 281

B

Balance point, 16–17
Bell curve, 82 (*See also* Normal distribution(s))
Best fitting regression line, 206, 207
Betas, 238 (*See also* Standardized coefficients)
Bin range, 44–46
Binary variable, 217, 228
Binomial distribution(s), 68–70, 312
  assumptions of the, 70
  comparing to hypergeometric/Poisson
    distributions, 76
  computer output for the, 71–73
  normal distributions and, 89–90
  proportion vs. hypothesized value using the,
    167–168
Bivariate regression, 230, 232, 241, 243
Boxplot, 14, 19, 26–28, 297, 312

C

Calculations, accuracy of, 8–9, 143
Calculator, 7–9, 143
Causation, correlation vs., 215–216
Cells
  counting, 13
  shaded, 192, 193
Centered moving average, 286–288, 312
Central limit theorem, 98, 100, 106–107, 312
Central tendency, 12–18
  arithmetic mean, 15–17
  boxplot, 14
  median, 14
  mode, 12–14
  and outliers, 17–18
  quartiles, 14, 15
Centroid, 239
CHIDIST( ) function, 261, 262, 301

CHIINV( ) function, 262, 301
Chi-square tests
    contingency table test of independence, 250–257
    goodness of fit, 257–259, 263–268, 310, 315
    nonparametric methods and, 250
    table of critical values for, 330
    and using the chi-square distribution, 261–262
Chi-square value, 252, 312
Chi-Square Variance Test, 158
Classical probability, 55, 312
Cluster sampling, 97, 320
Coefficient(s)
    of contingency, 263
    correlation, 211, 234, 313
    of determination, 209 (*See also* r-squared (r^2))
    standardized, 237–238, 247–248, 322
Coins, 69, 70, 124, 125
Collectively exhaustive, 54, 312
COMBIN( ) function, 64
Combinations, 63, 312
Commonsense, in hypothesis testing, 130
Complement, 55, 313
Complementary events, 57
Completely randomized ANOVA, 306 (*See also* One-Factor ANOVA)
Conditional distributions, 215
Conditional probability, 57, 58, 313
CONFIDENCE( ) function, 300–301
Confidence interval(s), 110–114
    definition of, 313
    equations for, 119–120, 222
    in hypothesis testing, 158–160
    for intercept, 212
    mean, 110–113, 313
    for prediction, 213–214, 222–223
    and proportion, 113–114, 313
    sample size estimation and, 116–117
    simulation for, 120–121
    for slope, 212
    in time-series analysis, 272
Contiguous columns, 170
Contingency table(s), 56, 313
    and independent probabilities, 58, 59
    measures of association for, 263
    test for independence, 250–257, 309
Continuous probability distribution
    definition of, 319
    normal distribution as a, 82
    t-distribution as a, 161
Continuous random variable, 66, 313
Continuous variables, 3–4, 66, 313
Convenience sampling, 97, 320
Cook's D value, 225–228, 241
Correlation, causation vs., 215–216

Correlation analysis, 204
Correlation coefficient, 211, 234, 313
Correlation matrix, 211, 233–235, 244–247, 313
COUNT( ) function, 16
Counting rules, 62–64
Cramer's V, 263
Critical values, 127, 130, 314, 328, 330
Cross-sectional data, 3, 314
Crosstabulation, 256–257
Cumulative frequencies, 39, 314
Cumulative percents, 39
Cumulative probability, 72
Curve fit
    exponential, 279–280, 282
    linear, 279–280
    polynomial, 276–277
    quadratic, 275, 276
Curved line, 273
Custom intervals, 44–46

D

Data, 2–6, 314
    accuracy of, 143
    challenge of using, 297
    continuous, 4
    cross-sectional vs. time-series, 3
    descriptive measures to summarize, 26–30
    deseasonalized, 288–290
    identifying, 4–5
    information vs., 2
    measurement of, 4
    qualitative, 2–4, 230, 297, 319
    quantitative, 2–4, 230, 297, 319
    randomizing, 104, 105 (*See also* Random number generation)
    reseasonalizing, 290
    smoothing, 283–285
Dataset, 2, 314
Decision, interpreting the
    in comparing two independent groups test, 144, 145–146
    in comparing two independent proportions test, 156, 157
    in mean vs. hypothesized value test, 138–140
    in One-Factor ANOVA test, 172, 174
    in paired observations test, 148–149, 151
    in proportion vs. hypothesized value test, 153, 154
    in Randomized Blocks ANOVA test, 178, 179
    as step 7 of hypothesis testing, 124, 130
    in Two-Factor ANOVA test, 202
Decision rule
    for alternative hypothesis, 128
    comparing to test statistic, 129

in comparing two independent groups test, 143, 145

in comparing two independent proportions test, 155, 157

definition of, 314

in mean vs. hypothesized value test, 137–139

in One-Factor ANOVA test, 172, 174

in paired observations test, 148, 150

in proportion vs. hypothesized value test, 152, 154

in Randomized Blocks ANOVA test, 178

as step 4 of hypothesis testing, 124, 127–128, 130

in Two-Factor ANOVA test, 201

Definitional form, 20–21, 314

and outliers, 18

for variance/standard deviation, 21–23

Degree of association (in contingency tables), 263

Degrees of freedom (df), 21

and chi-square distribution, 261

in comparing two independent groups test, 141

and confidence intervals, 158

definition of, 314

and the F-distribution, 187

and goodness of fit test, 258

in mean vs. hypothesized value test, 136, 137

in paired observations test, 147

and t-distribution, 161, 163

Deleted residuals, 224, 225

Dependent variable, 204

Descriptive statistics, 12–31

boxplot, 26–28

central tendency, 12–18

measures of variation, 18–24

scatterplot, 28–29

stem and leaf plot, 29–30

Descriptive Statistics option (in MegaStat), 26–30

definitional form box on, 21, 22

finding range with, 38

sample output from, 24–26

Deseasonalization, 285–290, 314

Destructive sampling, 96

Deviation(s)

definition of, 19, 314

error, 208

mean, 19, 317

mean absolute deviation, 19–20, 317

total, 208, 209

(*See also* Standard deviation)

"Devil's advocate," 130

DEVSQ( ) function, 23, 300

df (*see* Degrees of freedom)

Dice, 258, 263–264

"Diminishing returns" pattern, 242

Discrete outcome, 66, 67

Discrete probability distribution(s)

binomial distributions, 68–73, 76, 89–90, 167–168, 312

computer output for, 71–73

definition of, 319

and expected value, 66–68, 315

hypergeometric distribution, 68, 69, 73–76, 316

Poisson distribution, 68, 69, 75–77, 318

simulation for, 78–79

variance, 323

Discrete random variable, 66, 314

Discrete variables, continuous vs., 3–4

Dummy variable, 217, 228, 230, 237

Durbin-Watson (DW) statistic, 273, 275, 278–280, 291–293, 314

E

Empirical rule, 88–89, 314

Equation numbers, 8

Error deviation, 208

Error tolerance, 114, 120, 314

Error variance, 175

Estimated mean (*see* Interpolated mean)

Event(s)

complementary, 57

in contingency tables, 56

definition of, 54, 315

Excel

accuracy of, 8, 143

AVEDEV( ) function of, 300

AVERAGE( ) function of, 16, 18, 79, 83, 113, 300

CHIDIST( ) function of, 261, 262, 301

CHIINV( ) function of, 262, 301

chi-square functions in, 261, 262

COMBIN( ) function of, 64

CONFIDENCE( ) function of, 300–301

COUNT( ) function of, 16

counting cells in, 13

definitional form in, 23

deseasonalization using, 287

determining best trendline with, 283

DEVSQ( ) function of, 23, 300

discrete probability distributions in, 78–79

Durbin-Watson value in, 291

effect of outlier in, 18

FACT( ) function of, 63, 64

factorials in, 63, 73

FDIST( ) function of, 187, 301

F-functions in, 187

finding inverse values in, 85

finding range with, 38

Excel (*continued*)
  FINV( ) function of, 187, 301
  FREQUENCY( ) function of, 107
  hypothesis testing in, 133–134
  IF( ) statement, 78, 120, 121
  INT( ) function of, 103
  INTERCEPT( ) function of, 206, 207
  LOG( ) function of, 280
  MAX( ) function of, 19, 38, 300
  mean absolute deviation in, 20
  mean in, 16
  MEDIAN( ) function of, 14, 49, 300
  MIN( ) function of, 19, 38, 300
  MODE( ) function of, 12, 13, 300
  moving averages in, 283, 284
  and multiple regression, 233
  normal distributions with, 92
  NORMDIST( ) function of, 265, 300
  NORMINV( ) function of, 92, 105, 300
  NORMSDIST( ) function of, 92, 300
  NORMSINV( ) function of, 92, 300
  option to force intercept to equal zero, 207
  PERCENTILE( ) function of, 300
  PERMUT( ) function of, 64
  preparing calculations with, 7–9
  quantitative frequency distribution output in, 39
  QUARTILE( ) function of, 15, 300
  RAND( ) function of, 78, 103–106, 300
  random number generation in, 78–79, 97,
      103, 263
  Recalc button, 134
  regression partitioning with, 220
  ROUND( ) function of, 105, 106
  R-squared (R^2) in, 211
  scientific notation in, 9
  simulation using, 78–79
  SLOPE( ) function of, 206, 207
  Sort Ascending button, 104, 105, 117
  Sort Descending button, 105, 117
  spreadsheets, 9
  statistical functions for, 300–301
  STDEV( ) function of, 23, 83, 113, 300
  STDEVP( ) function of, 300
  SUM( ) function of, 16
  SUMSQ( ) function of, 300
  TDIST( ) function of, 138, 163, 300
  t-functions in, 163
  TINV( ) function of, 163, 300
  toggling formula view in, 83
  trendline in, 211
  tutorial instructions for, 332
  VAR( ) function of, 23, 300
  variation in, 23
  VARP( ) function of, 300
    workbooks in, 7–9
    worksheets in, 9, 184–186
Expected frequency, 253, 254, 264, 265
Expected value
    in chi-squares tests of independence, 251
    definition of, 67, 315
    discrete probability distributions and, 66–68, 79
    of hypergeometric distributions, 73
    of Poisson distributions, 75
    probability for, 72
Experiential probability, 56
Experiment(s)
    and contingency table, 56
    definition of, 54, 315
Explained variance, 170, 171, 207, 208
Exponential, 315
Exponential trend, 278–282
Extrapolation
    definition of, 315
    in linear regression analysis, 216, 223
    multivariate, 239, 317
    in time-series analysis, 271, 272, 275
Extreme outlier, 18

F

FACT( ) function, 63, 64
Factorial, 63, 73, 315
Factors (in contingency tables), 56
Fair coin, 124, 125
Fair dice, 258, 263
FDIST( ) function, 187, 301
F-distribution
    table for, critical values at 1% level of
        significance, 329
    table for, critical values at 5% level of
        significance, 329
    using the, 186–188
FINV( ) function, 187, 301
Fisher's Exact Test, 263
Forecasting
    with deseasonalized data, 289
    moving averages and, 283
    in time-series analysis, 270, 272
    (*See also* Time-series analysis)
Formula view (toggling), 83
F-ratio
    in ANOVA test for regression, 221
    definition of, 315
    for Randomized Blocks ANOVA, 177
    significant, 173
    test statistic as, 171, 172, 174, 221
    in Two-Factor ANOVA, 182
FREQUENCY( ) function, 107

Frequency distribution(s), 34–51
  as basic analysis, 297
  capping the top interval for, 46–48
  custom intervals in, 44–46
  definition of, 315
  estimating the median and quartiles from a, 48–51
  of the means, 98
  normal curves and, 86
  qualitative, and histogram, 34–37
  quantitative, and histogram, 38–43
Frequency polygon, output for, 41–43
Frequency(-ies)
  cumulative, 39
  observed vs. expected, 253
  as quantitative data, 3
Functions (Excel)
  notation/convention for, 8
  (*See also specific functions, e.g.:* FDIST( ) function)
Fundamental rule (of multiplication), 62–63, 315

G

GOF test (*see* Goodness of fit test)
Goodness of fit (GOF) test, 257–259, 315
  alternative normal curve, 267, 268
  hypothesis test for, 310
  for normal distributions, 259, 264–268
  for other distributions, 259
  simulation for, 263–264
Gravity, center of, 21, 22 (*See also* Balance point)
Greater than, probability for, 72
Greek letters
  alpha (α) symbol, 127
  for population values, 16
  for proportion values, 100, 101
Group means, 141, 217, 229
Groups
  comparing two, in linear regression, 228–230
  comparing two independent, 140–146, 181, 304
  hypothesis test for comparing two independent, 304
  independence and, 141
  relationships between, 297
  two, set with indicator variables, 228
  upper limit of, in ANOVA, 170
Growth pattern (exponential), 278

H

Half-width, 111
Held constant, 240
Higher-degree polynomials, 277

Histogram(s)
  definition of, 34, 316
  qualitative frequency distributions and, 34–37
  quantitative frequency distribution and, 38–43
  and scaling, 36–37
Hypergeometric distributions, 68, 69, 73–76, 316
Hyperspace, 233
Hypothesis test, definition of, 124, 316
Hypothesis testing
  for ANOVA, 172–174, 177–178, 201, 220–221, 306–309
  applications of, 136–168
  for comparing two independent groups, 140–146, 304
  for comparing two independent proportions, 154–157, 305
  concepts of, 124–134
  confidence intervals in, 158–160
  for contingency table test of independence, 252–256, 309
  definition of, 124, 316
  for goodness of fit test, 258, 259, 266, 267, 310
  for linear regression, 220–222
  long form of, 137–138
  for mean vs. hypothesized value, 136–140, 147, 304
  for One-Factor ANOVA, 172–174, 306
  for paired observations, 146–151, 164–166, 305
  playing "devil's advocate" in, 130
  for proportion vs. hypothesized value, 151–154, 167–168, 305
  for Randomized Blocks ANOVA, 177–178, 181, 194–198, 306–307
  as a sampling process, 132
  seven steps of, 137–138, 172–174
  short form of, 172–174
  simulation for, 133–134
  summaries for, 304–310
  t-distributions in, 161–164
  tests for variance in, 158
  for t-test for slope, 221–222, 309
  for Two-Factor ANOVA, 201, 307–308
Hypothesized value
  in comparing two independent groups, 141
  mean vs., 136–140, 147, 304
  proportion vs., 151–154, 167–168, 305

I

IF( ) statement, 78, 120, 121
Independence
  and binomial distributions, 70
  chi-squares tests of, 250–257

Independence (*continued*)
contingency table test for, 250–257, 309
groups and, 141
perfect, 253
and Poisson distributions, 77
statistical, 58–60, 322
Independent groups
ANOVA for comparing two, 181
comparing two, 140–146, 181, 304
One-Factor ANOVA compared to t-tests for, 194, 195, 197
test of paired observations, 165, 166
Independent groups ANOVA, 306 (*See also* One-Factor ANOVA)
Independent proportions, comparing two, 154–157, 305
Independent variable(s)
in linear regression, 204, 217
and multiple regression, 232
for prediction, 239
in time-series analysis, 270
Indicator variable, 217, 228–230, 237, 239, 316
Influential values, 225–228, 316
Information, data vs., 2
INT( ) function, 103
Interaction test, 202
Intercept
confidence interval for, 212
forced to equal zero, 207
in linear regression, 206–208, 210, 212, 213
t-test for, 212
Interpolated mean, 48–50, 316
Intersection probabilities, 57, 58, 316, 317
Interval (data), 4, 316
Interval widths, 38–40
Intervals
capping the top, 46–48
custom, 44–46
setup, 38–40
Inverse probability calculations, 85, 86, 88
IQ scores, 83–86, 91, 125, 127–129

L

Least-squares regression, 208, 210
Least-squares regression line, 206
Less than, probability for, 72
Level of Significance (*see* Significance level)
Levels of measurement, 4
Leverage, 216, 222, 223, 227–228, 271, 272, 316
Linear curve fit, 279–280
Linear regression, 204–230
ANOVA and, 220–222, 230, 308–309
assumptions of, 215

comparing two groups in, 228–230
confidence intervals for prediction in, 222–223
correlation vs. causation in, 215–216
diagnostics in, 223–228
extrapolation in, 216, 223
indicator variables in, 228–230
influential values in, 225–228
intercept in, 206–208, 210, 212, 213
of log values, 281
measuring the strength of a relationship in, 207–210
outliers in, 216–217, 224
output for, 210–212
partitioning the sum of squares in, 219–220
predictions with, 212–214
and regression line, 206–208, 211, 223, 320
and scatterplots, 205–206
slope in, 206–208, 210, 212, 221–222
testing group means in, 217
and t-test for slope, 221–222
(*See also* Multiple regression)
Linear trends, 270–272, 275
LOG( ) function, 280
Log values (in exponential trends), 279–282
Logical condition, 78

M

MAD (*see* Mean absolute deviation)
Margin of error, 111, 112, 115, 116, 121, 158, 316
Marginal probability, 57, 317
Matrix algebra model, 233
MAX( ) function, 19, 38, 300
Mean absolute deviation (MAD), 19–20, 317
Mean deviation, 19, 317
Mean outcome, 79
Mean rate of occurrence, 75
Mean sample size estimation, 114–115, 320
Mean square error, 194
Mean vs. hypothesized value test
hypothesis test for, 136–140, 147, 181, 304
using Randomized Blocks ANOVA to perform, 181, 194–198
Mean(s)
arithmetic, 15–17, 312
average vs., 15
as basic analysis, 297
confidence interval, 110–113, 313
definition of, 317
deviation, 19, 317
graphical representation of the, 16–17
group, 141, 217, 229
hypothesized value vs., 181
interpolated, 48–50, 316

outliers' affect on the, 18
population, 82, 98, 110
proportion as a, 100, 101, 107–108
sample, 114–115, 141
of the sampling distributions, 98–99
standard error of the, 99, 108, 112, 119, 321
Measurement, levels of, 4
Median
    definition of, 14, 317
    estimating from a frequency distribution, 48–51
    estimating from an ogive, 50–51
    outliers' affect on the, 18
MEDIAN( ) function, 14, 49, 300
MegaStat, 7–8, 317
    accuracy of, 8
    "All Possible Regressions" option in, 241–243
    ANOVA output from, 191
    best trendline with, 283
    binomial distributions in, 71–73
    boxplot in, 26–28
    capping the top interval in, 46–48
    chi-square distribution in, 261, 262
    comparing two independent groups in, 144, 146
    comparing two independent proportions in, 156
    contiguous columns in, 170
    contingency table test in, 253, 254, 263
    Cook's D value in, 225–228
    custom intervals in, 44–46
    decision rule for, 131
    definitional form in, 21–23
    deseasonalization using, 289
    Durbin-Watson value in, 292, 293
    estimating median from an ogive with, 51
    expected frequencies in, 254
    exponential curve fit in, 282
    factorials in, 63, 73, 74
    F-distribution in, 188
    force intercept to equal zero in, 207
    formatting charts in, 34, 35
    frequency polygon and ogive in, 41–43
    hypothesis testing in, 129
    interpolated median with, 49
    interval width in, 38–40
    inverse values in, 85
    linear regression in, 210–212
    mean in, 16, 18
    median in, 14, 18, 49, 51
    moving averages in, 283, 284
    multiple regression in, 233, 236, 238–241
    normal distributions in, 92, 93
    for One-Factor ANOVA, 189–190
    outliers in, 18
    paired observations in, 149, 150, 164
    post hoc analysis in, 194
    proportion vs. hypothesized value test in, 152
    p-values in, 131, 138, 149, 156
    quantitative frequency distribution and
        histogram in, 38–39
    quartiles in, 15
    random number generation in, 97, 103–105
    Randomized Blocks ANOVA test in, 178–180
    range in, 19, 38
    residual diagnostics in, 216, 224–228
    sample output from, 24–26
    scaling in, 36–37
    scatterplots in, 28–29
    scientific notation in, 9
    "specification range" in, 34
    SSX output in, 24–26
    stem and leaf plot in, 29–30
    Stepwise Selection in, 242–244
    t-distributions in, 164
    "Time Series Curve Fit" option in, 280
    time-series analysis in, 282
    Tukey simultaneous comparison test in, 190–194
    tutorial instructions for, 332
    Two-Factor ANOVA in, 201
    variance in, 158
    variance inflation factors in, 238–239
    variation in, 23
MIN( ) function, 19, 38, 300
"Minus zero," 142
Mode, 12–14, 317
MODE( ) function, 12, 300
Model building (in multiple regression), 240–244
Mortality table, 66–67
Moving average, 283–285, 317
Moving average, centered, 286–288
Multicollinearity, 234, 317
Multiple correlation, 235, 236
Multiple R (multiple correlation R), 235–236,
    245–247, 319
Multiple regression, 232–248
    adjusted R^2 in, 236–237, 241, 242, 312
    ANOVA for, 237
    correlation matrix and, 233–234
    equations for, 233
    graphical representation of, 233
    and group analysis, 229, 230
    interpreting output for, 235–244
    as matrix algebra model, 233
    model building in, 240–244
    multiple R in, 245–247
    outliers in, 239–241
    prediction in, 239, 240
    residuals in, 239–241, 246
    R-squared (R^2) and multiple R in, 235–238,
        240–244, 246

Multiple regression (*continued*)
standardized coefficients in, 237–238, 247–248
Stepwise Selection in, 242–244, 322
variance inflation factors in, 238–239
(*See also* Linear regression)
Multiplication
fundamental rule for, 62–63, 315
rule for intersection probabilities, 58, 317
Multivariate extrapolation, 239, 317
Mutually exclusive, 54, 317

N

Nominal, 4, 317
Nonindependence (maximum), 253
Nonlinear trend, 273, 275
Nonnumeric probability, 55–56
Nonparametric methods, 250, 317
Normal curve, 82
assumptions of, 85, 86
and binomial distribution, 89–90, 168
determining probabilities for, 91–92
goodness of fit test for, 264–265, 267, 268
importance of, 88, 89
plotting a, 82
tables for (z-values), 326, 327
Normal distribution(s), 82–93
assumptions of, 85, 86
binomial distributions and, 89–90
determining probabilities for, 91–92
and determining values corresponding to a given probability, 84–85
goodness of fit test for, 259, 264–268
and importance of normal curve, 88, 89
inverse, 86–88, 92
t-distribution and, 161–163
z-values and, 83, 85–87, 92, 93, 110
NORMDIST( ) function, 265, 300
NORMINV( ) function, 92, 105, 300
NORMSDIST( ) function, 92, 300
NORMSINV( ) function, 92, 300
Null hypothesis (H_0)
in comparing two independent groups test, 142–143, 145
in comparing two independent proportions test, 155, 157
definition of, 317
failing to reject, 126, 153
falsely rejecting, 125–126
in mean vs. hypothesized value test, 137, 139
in One-Factor ANOVA test, 172, 174
in paired observations test, 148, 150

in proportion vs. hypothesized value test, 151–153
proving a, 153
in Randomized Blocks ANOVA test, 177, 179
rejecting a, 125–131, 134, 153, 159, 167, 259
as step 1 of hypothesis testing, 124, 125
in Two-Factor ANOVA test, 201
Numerical integration, 82

O

Odds, 54, 61–62, 318
Ogive, 39, 318
estimating the median from an, 50–51
example output for, 41–43
One-Factor ANOVA, 170–176
for comparing two independent groups, 181
hypothesis test for, 306
Randomized Blocks ANOVA vs., 177, 198–201
simulation for, 188–190
One-way ANOVA, 306 (*See also* One-Factor ANOVA)
Ordinal, 4, 318
Outcome
definition of, 54, 318
discrete, 66, 67
good vs. bad, 130
in hypothesis testing, 130
mean, 79
Outlier(s), 17–18, 318
in analysis of data, 293
as basic analysis, 297
and boxplots, 27
influential values and, 225
in linear regression, 216–217, 224
in multiple regression, 239–241

P

Page, fitting output on a, 42
Paired observations, 146–151
hypothesis test for, 181, 305
issues related to, 164–166
Randomized Blocks ANOVA vs., 194, 196, 197
Pairing, 146–147
Pairwise comparisons, 190
Parameter, 5–6, 318
Parameters, population, 16
Partitioning
regression, 209–210
the sum of squares, 182–186, 219–220
Percentages, 3
PERCENTILE( ) function, 300
Perfect independence, 253
Perfect negative relationship, 211

Perfect positive relationship, 211
PERMUT( ) function, 64
Permutations, 63, 318
Phi, 263
Pi (π) symbol, 100, 101
"Plug and chug," 48
Poisson distributions, 68, 69, 75–77, 318
Polynomial, 318
Polynomial curve fit, 276–277
Polynomial function, 273, 275
Polynomial trend, 272–277
Pooled variance, 141–143, 146
Population
    definition of, 96, 318
    Greek letters for values of, 16
    parameters, 16
    sample vs., 5–6
    variance, 20
Population mean, 82, 98, 110
Population proportion, 113
Population standard deviation, 111, 114,
    136, 141
Post hoc analysis, 175, 190–194, 318
Predicted value, 206, 230, 246, 318
Prediction analysis, 204, 212, 213, 216, 222–223
    (*See also* Linear regression)
Prediction interval, 213, 214, 222–223, 272
Prediction(s)
    confidence intervals for, 213–214, 222–223
    with deseasonalized data, 288–290
    independent variables for, 239
    in linear regression, 212–214, 222–223
    in multiple regression, 239, 240
    in time-series analysis, 270, 272, 275, 280, 281
Predictor variables, 204, 235, 237
Probability, 54–64
    assessing, 55–56
    concepts of, 56–60
    counting rules for, 62–64
    definition of, 319
    odds vs., 54, 61–62
    terms/definitions for, 54–55
Probability distribution, continuous (*see* Continuous
    probability distribution)
Probability distributions, discrete (*see* Discrete
    probability distribution(s))
Probability for greater than, 72
Probability for less than, 72
Probability for range of values, 72
Proportion vs. hypothesized value test, 151–154,
    167–168, 305
Proportion(s), 100–101
    comparing multiple, 255–256
    comparing two independent, 154–157, 305

    confidence intervals and, 113–114
    as a mean, 100, 101, 107–108
p-value(s), 130–131, 319
    in ANOVA, 175–176, 190–193, 194, 202
    in comparing two independent groups, 144
    in comparing two independent proportions, 156
    in hypothesis testing, 130–132
    in mean vs. hypothesized value test, 138
    in multiple regression, 240, 241
    in paired observations, 149
    in proportion vs. hypothesized value test, 153,
        167, 168
    with Randomized Blocks ANOVA, 197
    test statistic vs., 131, 132
    in t-tests vs. ANOVA, 194
    in Two-Factor ANOVA, 202

Q

Q1, Q2, Q3, 14, 319
Quadratic curve fit, 275, 276
Qualitative data, 2–3, 319
    and analysis of data, 297
    discrete variables and, 3
    in multiple regression, 230
    nominal, 4
Qualitative frequency distribution and histogram,
    34–37
Quantitative data, 2–3, 319
    and analysis of data, 297
    discrete variables and, 3–4
    in multiple regression, 230
Quantitative frequency distributions and histogram,
    38–43
QUARTILE( ) function, 15, 300
Quartiles
    definition of, 14, 15, 319
    estimating, from a frequency distribution,
        48–51
    interpolated, 15

R

R, multiple R (multiple correlation) (*see* Multiple R)
R^2 (*see* R-squared)
RAND( ) function, 78, 103–106, 300
Random number generation, 103–105
    for discrete probability distributions, 78–79
    in Excel, 78–79, 97, 103, 263
    and fair dice, 263
    in MegaStat, 97, 103–105
Random sampling, 74
Random variable, 66, 314, 319

Randomized Blocks ANOVA
    hypothesis testing for, 177–178, 181, 194–198,
       306–307
    mean vs. hypothesized test using, 181, 194–198
    One-Factor ANOVA vs., 177, 198–201
    paired observations tests vs., 194, 196, 197
Randomized plots ANOVA (*see* Randomized Blocks
    ANOVA)
Randomness of sample, 139
Range, 19, 38, 72, 319
Ratio, 4, 319
Recalc button, 134
Regression analysis, 297
    definition of, 204, 320
    time-series analysis and, 270
    as two-phase process, 204
    (*See also* Linear regression; Multiple regression)
Regression line, 206–208, 320
    best fitting, 206, 207
    least squares, 206
    as trendline in Excel, 211
    variance around the, 223
    variance of the, 223
Relationship analysis, 204, 297 (*See also* Linear
    regression)
Relative frequency method, 66
Relative frequency probabilities, 55, 56, 320
Repeated measures ANOVA, 306 (*See also*
    Randomized Blocks ANOVA)
Replications (in Two-Factor ANOVA), 182
Reseasonalizing data, 290
Residual(s)
    definition of, 208, 320
    deleted, 224, 225
    diagnostics for, 224–225
    diagnostics in MegaStat, 216, 224–228
    in multiple regression, 239–241, 246
    in regression assumptions, 215
    scatterplot of, 209
    in time-series analysis, 273, 274, 278, 279
Response variables, 204
ROUND( ) function, 105, 106
Rounding, 101, 105
R-squared (R^2)
    adjusted, 236–237, 241, 242, 312
    definition of, 320
    in multiple regression, 235–238, 240–244, 246
    variance inflation factors and, 238
r-squared (r^2), 209, 211, 320

S

Sample mean, 114–115, 141
Sample proportion, 113

Sample size, 111
    confidence intervals and estimation of, 116–117
    effect on contingency tables of, 254
    equation for, 120
    estimation, 114–117, 320, 321
    and the mean, 114–115, 320
    and proportions, 115–116, 321
    rule of thumb for, 98
Sample size estimation for proportions, 115–116, 321
Sample size estimation for the mean, 114–115, 320
Sample space, 54, 321
Sample standard deviation, 99, 111, 136
Sample variance, 20, 141
Sample(s)
    cluster, 320
    definition of, 5, 320
    and hypothesis testing, 125
    population vs., 5–6
    in prediction analysis, 213
    randomness of, 139
    and relative frequency probabilities, 55
Sampling
    cluster, 97, 320
    concepts of, 96–97
    convenience, 97, 320
    destructive, 96
    error, 59
    and generating random numbers, 103–104
    hypothesis testing as a process of, 132
    random, 74, 96, 97, 320
    simple random, 96, 97, 320
    stratified, 97, 320
    a subset of a population, 96
    systematic, 97
Sampling distributions, 98–101, 321
Sampling error, 59
SAT scores, 164
Scaling, 36–37
Scattercloud, 233
Scatterplot(s), 27–28, 321
    best trendline with, 283
    in linear regression analysis, 205–206
    of log values, 280
    for nonlinear trend, 273, 275
    of outliers, 217
    of residuals, 209
    three-dimensional, 233
    for time-series analysis, 271
Scientific notation, 9
sd (s.d.) (*see* Standard deviation)
Seasonal index, 286, 288, 321
Setup intervals, 38–40
Shaded cells, 192, 193
Shuffling data, 104, 105, 117, 165
Sigma notation, 15, 16

Significance
    in hypothesis testing, 130, 138–139
    in paired observations, 165
    p-value approach and, 131
Significance level
    in comparing two independent groups, 143, 145
    in comparing two independent proportions, 155, 157
    definition of, 316
    in hypothesis testing, 127–128
    in mean vs. hypothesized value test, 137, 139
    in One-Factor ANOVA test, 172, 174
    in paired observations test, 148
    in proportion vs. hypothesized value test, 152, 153
    in Randomized Blocks ANOVA test, 177, 179
    as step 2 of hypothesis testing, 124, 125–127
    in Two-Factor ANOVA test, 201
Simple random sampling, 96, 97, 320
Simulations
    for ANOVA, 175, 188–190
    for confidence intervals, 120–121
    for discrete probability distributions, 78–79
    for goodness of fit, 263–264
    for hypothesis testing, 133–134
    for One-Factor ANOVA, 188–190
    using Excel, 78–79
Single-factor ANOVA, 306 (*See also* One-Factor ANOVA)
Slope
    in bivariate regression, 230
    confidence interval for, 212
    in linear regression, 206–208, 210, 212, 221–222
    in multiple regression, 232, 237
    t-test for, 212, 221–222, 309
SLOPE( ) function, 206, 207
Smoothing, 283–285
Sort Ascending button, 104, 105, 117
Sort Descending button, 105, 117
"Specification range," 34
Spreadsheets (Excel), 9
SS Error (SSE), 171, 183, 200, 207, 209, 219
SS Treatment (SST), 171
SSRegression (SSR), 207, 209, 219
SST (*see* SS Treatment)
SSTotal, 171, 182–183
    in linear regression, 207, 209
    partitioning, 182–186, 219–220
    for Randomized Blocks ANOVA, 176
SSX (*see* Sum of squared deviations)
Standard deviation
    as basic analysis, 297
    definition of, 21, 321
    definitional form for, 21–23
    graphical interpretation of the, 24

    and normal curve, 83, 110
    normal distributions and, 88, 93
    population, 111, 114, 136, 141
    sample, 99, 111, 136
Standard error, 321
    in comparing two independent groups, 141
    in comparing two independent proportions test, 155
    of estimate, 211, 321
    of the mean, 99, 108, 112, 119, 321
    of paired observations, 164
    of the proportion, 100, 101, 108, 113, 119, 321
Standardized coefficients, 237–238, 247–248, 322
Standardizing a variable, 83 (*See also* z-value(s))
Statistical independence, 58–60, 322
Statistical inference, 98
Statistical interference, 322
Statistic(s) (as calculated value)
    definition of, 2, 322
    and samples, 6
Statistics (discipline of)
    challenge of, 297
    definitions of, 2, 322
Statistics (for summarizing data)
    definition of, 2, 322
    descriptive, 12 (*See also* Descriptive statistics)
    how to lie with, 36–37
stdev (*see* Standard deviation)
STDEV( ) function, 23, 83, 113, 300
STDEVP( ) function, 300
Stem and leaf plot, 29–30
Stepwise Selection, 242–244, 322
Stratified sampling, 97, 320
Subjective probability, 55–56, 322
Sum, 15, 16
SUM( ) function, 16
Sum of squared deviations (SSX), 21–24, 321
    in ANOVA (as SSTotal), 170–171, 176, 182–186, 207, 209, 219–220
    and outliers, 18
    for two independent groups, 141
SUMSQ( ) function, 300
Systematic sampling, 97

T

Tables
    ANOVA, 186, 211–212
    chi-square, 261, 262, 330
    F-distribution critical values at 1% level of significance, 329
    F-distribution critical values at 5% level of significance, 329
    F-table, 186–187, 329

Tables (*continued*)
  normal curve, 92, 326, 327
  of random numbers, 97
  t-distribution critical values, 328
  using to find inverse values, 85
Tail (of the distribution), 86, 87
TDIST( ) function, 138, 163, 300
t-distribution
  confidence intervals using the, 160
  in hypothesis testing, 138, 161–164
  normal distributions vs., 163
  tables for, 328
Test statistic, calculating using sample data
  in comparing two independent groups, 143, 145
  in comparing two independent proportions test, 155, 157
  in mean vs. hypothesized value test, 138, 140
  in One-Factor ANOVA test, 173, 174
  in paired observations test, 148, 150
  in proportion vs. hypothesized value test, 152, 154
  in Randomized Blocks ANOVA test, 178, 179
  as step 5 of hypothesis testing, 124, 129
  in Two-Factor ANOVA test, 201
Test statistic, determining which test and
  in comparing two independent groups test, 143, 145
  in comparing two independent proportions test, 155, 157
  in mean vs. hypothesized value test, 137, 139
  in One-Factor ANOVA test, 172, 174
  in paired observations test, 148, 150
  in proportion vs. hypothesized value test, 152, 153
  in Randomized Blocks ANOVA test, 177, 179
  as step 3 of hypothesis testing, 124, 127
  in Two-Factor ANOVA test, 201
Test statistic, using to make a decision
  in comparing two independent groups, 144, 145
  in comparing two independent proportions test, 156, 157
  in mean vs. hypothesized value test, 138, 140
  in One-Factor ANOVA test, 173, 174
  in paired observations test, 148, 151
  in proportion vs. hypothesized value test, 153, 154
  in Randomized Blocks ANOVA test, 179
  as step 6 of hypothesis testing, 124, 129–130
  in Two-Factor ANOVA test, 202
Test statistic (general)
  for comparing two independent groups, 141–142
  definition of, 127, 322
  as F-ratio, 171, 172, 174, 221
  p-value vs., 131, 132
Tests, two-tailed (*see* Two-tailed tests)

"Time Series Curve Fit" option, 280
Time-series analysis, 270–293
  basic model in, 270
  best trendline in, 283
  deseasonalization in, 285–290
  Durbin-Watson statistic in, 291–293
  exponential trends in, 278–282
  and linear trends, 270–272
  and moving averages, 283–285
  polynomial trends in, 272–277
Time-series data, cross-sectional data vs., 3
TINV( ) function, 163, 300
Title, adding a descriptive, 35
Top interval, capping the, 46–48
Total deviations, 208, 209
Total variation, 208, 209
Treatment effect, 171, 199, 200
Treatments, 176, 177
Trendline, 211, 270, 277, 283, 322
t-table, 161–162
t-test(s)
  ANOVA and, 181, 190–197
  for intercept, 212
  for slope, 212, 221–222, 309
Tukey simultaneous comparison test, 190–194
Tutorials, 332
t-value, 136–137, 322
  confidence intervals and, 158, 159
  and degrees of freedom, 163
  in paired observations, 149
  Tukey, 194
Two independent groups, comparing, 140–146, 181, 304
Two-Factor ANOVA, 181–182, 201–202, 307–308
Two-Factor ANOVA with Replication, 306 (*See also* Randomized Blocks ANOVA)
Two-Factor ANOVA without Replication, 176 (*See also* Randomized Blocks ANOVA)
Two-tailed tests
  ANOVA tests as, 172
  confidence intervals and, 159–160
  hypothesis testing of a, 128, 142–143
  in paired observations, 148
  p-values and, 131
  using Randomized Blocks ANOVA, 197
Type I error, 126, 127, 134, 148, 322
Type II error, 126, 127, 134, 148, 322

U

Unexplained variance, 170, 171, 207
Union probability, 57, 322
Unlikely (sample result), 125, 126
Upper boundary, 44

V

Values, influential (*see* Influential values)
VAR( ) function, 23, 300
Variable(s)
    binary, 217, 228
    continuous, 3–4, 313
    continuous random, 66, 313
    definition of, 3, 322
    dependent, 204
    discrete random, 66, 314
    discrete vs. continuous, 3–4
    dummy, 217, 228, 230, 237
    independent, 204, 217, 232, 239, 270
    indicator, 217, 228–230, 237, 239, 316
    predictor, 204, 235, 237
    random, 66, 314, 319
    response, 204
    standardizing a, 83
Variance
    around the regression line, 223
    of binomial distributions, 69
    definition of, 20, 323
    definitional form for, 21–23
    discrete probability distribution, 323
    error, 175
    explained, 170, 171, 207, 208
    of hypergeometric distributions, 73
    in hypothesis testing, 158
    and normal curve table, 83
    of Poisson distributions, 75
    pooled, 141–143, 146
    population, 20
    of probability distributions, 67, 323
    of the regression line, 223
    sample, 20, 141
    tests for, 158
    unexplained, 170, 171, 207

Variance inflation factors (VIF), 238–239, 323
Variation
    around the regression line, 211
    calculating, 23
    measures of, 18–24, 170
    range, 19
    regression, 208
    total, 208, 209
VARP( ) function, 300
VIF (*see* Variance inflation factors)

W

"Washes out" (of predictor variables), 237
Workbooks (Excel), 7–9
Worksheets (Excel), 9, 184–186

Y

Ya-buts (in hypothesis testing), 130, 139, 166

Z

Zero, 142, 149
z-test, 167, 168
z-value(s)
    benchmark, 86–87
    in comparing proportions, 156
    in comparing two independent groups, 141–142
    confidence intervals and, 110–112, 114, 159
    definition of, 323
    in hypothesis testing, 128
    normal distribution and, 83, 85–87, 92, 93, 110
    and population standard deviation, 136
    for a sampling distribution, 120, 127
    and t-distribution, 163